OXFORD PRIVATE INTERNATIONAL LAW SERIES

Series Editors:

ANDREW DICKINSON

Fellow and Tutor, St Catherine's College and Professor of Law, University of Oxford

JONATHAN HARRIS QC

Barrister, Serle Court
Professor of International Commercial Law, Kings College, London

International Negotiable Instruments

OXFORD PRIVATE INTERNATIONAL LAW SERIES

Series Editors

Andrew Dickinson & Jonathan Harris QC

The aim of this series is to publish works of quality and originality in a number of important areas of private international law. The series is intended for both scholarly and practitioner readers.

ALSO IN THIS SERIES

The Anti-Suit Injunction (Second Editon)
Thomas Raphael QC

Sovereign Defaults before Domestic Courts
Hayk Kupelyants

Civil Jurisdiction and Judgments in Europe: The Brussels I Regulation, the Lugano Convention, and the Hague Choice of Court Convention
Trevor C Hartley

Conflict of Laws and Arbitral Discretion: The Closest Connection Test
Benjamin Hayward

Human Rights and Private International Law
James J. Fawcett, Máire Ní Shúilleabháin, Sangeeta Shah

Choice-of-Court Agreements under the European and International Instruments
Trevor C Hartley

Freedom of Establishment and Private International Law for Corporations
Paschalis Paschalidis

Substance and Procedure in Private International Law
Richard Garnett

Employment Contracts in Private International Law
Louise Merrett

The Arrest of Ships in Private International Law
VeróNica Ruiz Abou-Nigm

Intellectual Property and Private International Law (Second Edition)
James J. Fawcett, Paul Torremans

Cross-Border Divorce Law: Brussels II *bis*
Máire Ní Shúilleabháin

The Rome II Regulation: The Law Applicable to Non-Contractual Obligations
Andrew Dickinson

Cross-Border Consumer Contracts
Jonathan Hill

Agreements on Jurisdiction and Choice of Law
Adrian Briggs

Civil Jurisdiction Rules of the EU and their Impact on Third States
Thalia Kruger

Conflict of Laws within the UK
Kirsty J Hood

Insolvency in Private International Law (Second Edition)
Ian F. Fletcher

The Transfer of Property in the Conflict of Laws
Janeen M. Carruthers

International Sale of Goods in the Conflict of Laws
James Fawcett, Jonathan Harris, and Michael Bridge

Choice of Law for Equitable Doctrines
T M Yeo

Procedural Law in International Arbitration
Georgios Petrochilos

Foreign Law in English Courts: Pleading, Proof and Choice of Law
Richard Fentiman

Declining Jurisdiction in Private International Law
J. J. Fawcett

OXFORD
UNIVERSITY PRESS

Great Clarendon Street, Oxford, OX2 6DP,
United Kingdom

Oxford University Press is a department of the University of Oxford.
It furthers the University's objective of excellence in research, scholarship,
and education by publishing worldwide. Oxford is a registered trade mark of
Oxford University Press in the UK and in certain other countries

First Edition published in 2020

Published in the United States of America by Oxford University Press
198 Madison Avenue, New York, NY 10016, United States of America

British Library Cataloguing in Publication Data

Data available

Library of Congress Control Number: 2020934590

ISBN 978–0–19–882868–6

International Negotiable Instruments

BENJAMIN GEVA
Osgoode Hall Law School, York University

SAGI PEARI
UWA Law School, University of Western Australia

OXFORD
UNIVERSITY PRESS

General Editors' Foreword

The Bills of Exchange Act 1882 is, in many ways, a remarkable piece of legislation. As its principal draftsman, Sir Mackenzie Chalmers proudly observed, it was, at the time, 'the only enactment codifying any branch of the Common Law, which has found its way into the Statute Book' (Chalmers, *A Digest of the Law of Bills of Exchange, Promissory Notes & Cheques* (3rd edn, 1887), xxxv). That the Act reached the statute book at all was not only due to Chalmers' academic enterprise—inspired by Sir Fitz-James Stephen's work on the law of evidence and Frederick Pollock's on the law of partnership, and manifested in the first edition of Chalmers' work (published in 1878)—but also a result of the commercial vision of the Institute of Bankers and Associated Chambers of Commerce, which instructed him to prepare a Parliamentary Bill and undertook further preparatory work to encourage its passage (Chalmers, ibid, xxxvi-vii).

Within the 1882 Act, the conflict of laws plays a small, but nonetheless significant, role. Section 72, containing the partial codification of choice of law rules, was well ahead of its time, predating the Geneva Convention for the Settlement of Certain Conflict of Laws in Connection with Bills of Exchange (1930) by almost fifty years and the Rome Convention on the law applicable to contractual obligations (1980) by almost a century.

However, as explained in the introduction to this monograph, the conflict of laws rules that govern bills of exchange and other negotiable instruments are ripe for review. The commercial and technological conditions today are radically different from those prevailing in the periods of the 1882 Act and Geneva Convention, and the Rome Convention is, in this respect, notable only for its disinclination to bring the subject matter within the sphere of EU private international law (Art 1(2)(c); also Regulation (EC) No 593/2008 on the law applicable to contractual obligations (Rome I), Art 1(2)(d)). The most recent edition of *Dicey, Morris & Collins on the Conflict of Laws* (15th edn, 2012) expresses the view that 'the rules contained in the 1882 Act are neither comprehensive nor easy to understand and apply' and urges '[a] radical overhaul of the law in this area, whether by legislation or international convention'.

It is against this background that Professor Benjamin Geva and Dr Sagi Peari have prepared this work on the subject that Chalmers first addressed nearly one hundred and fifty years ago. Their central thesis challenges the isolation of bills of exchange and other negotiable instruments within the domain of the conflict of laws, and encourages their assimilation with (or at least alongside) mainstream choice of law theory governing contractual obligations and tangible property. Having laid the groundwork in Chapters I to IV, later chapters unfold the authors' vision of 'a new global harmonized framework of the choice-of-law rules relating to negotiable instruments'. This suggested framework, summarised in Appendix A, advocates the repeal of section 72 of the 1882 Act, to be replaced with a new set of rules giving much greater prominence to the principle of party autonomy.

Although the authors' academic enterprise is in many ways different from their predecessor's, they have a common desire to promote the use of negotiable instruments in cross-border commercial and financial transactions by ensuring a stable and transparent legal framework. It remains to be seen where this enterprise will lead. In the meantime, as editors of the *Oxford Private International Law Series*, we congratulate the authors on the publication of their thought-provoking monograph.

Professor Andrew Dickinson
Oxford
Professor Jonathan Harris QC
London
25 September 2020

Preface

Frustration from the language of the Bills of Exchange Act provisions relating to international instruments prompted the more senior co-author, a negotiable instruments specialist, to try to get to the bottom of the matter. Remaining dissatisfied from the yield of statutory interpretation and comparative study, he sought the cooperation of the other co-author. The latter, specializing in conflict of laws, became very excited to approach the matter from a broader perspective of choice of law scholarship. The present book is the product of this fruitful collaboration. The study covers international negotiable instruments, with a particular focus on conflict of laws principles and rules relating to them.

Benjamin Geva wishes to acknowledge the support he received from Osgoode Hall Law School, particularly in the form of Research Fellowship, secretarial assistance provided by Mary Rosati, law library reference assistance provided by Sharon Wang, and research assistance provided by Alexander Davis and Simona Ristic, respectively, of the 2019 and the 2021 graduating Osgoode classes. Financial support, acknowledged with gratitude, was provided by the Foundation for Legal Research and standard Osgoode faculty research grants. Indispensable moral support and inspiration were provided by wife Esther, daughters Anat and Dorit, sons-in-law Joshua and Aaron, and grandchildren Avital, Toren, Sarel, and Nuria.

Sagi Peari wishes to warmly thank Benjamin Geva for the unique opportunity to work with him during the formative years of this project. The University of Western Australia has provided a welcoming and supportive intellectual home over the two years of intensive writing. The audience at the Obligations Group workshop (December 2018) and Business Partners seminar (September 2018) provided valuable feedback. Sagi Peari would like to especially acknowledge the advice and support of the following colleagues: Robyn Carol, Penny Carruthers, Ian Murray, Nolan Sharkey, Peter Sinden, and Natalie Skead. Caroline Kazdan and Emma Woodley provided valuable editing assistance. Last, but not least, the immensurable support and unconditional love of his wife Mali, and daughters Donna and Michelle, must be noted. Thanks guys, you mean everything to me.

Last but not least, we both acknowledge with gratitude the editorial support provided in the course of the production process by Catherine Rogers and Zoe Tustin of OUP, Afrose Syed, Arokia Anthuvan Rani, and their teams.

Benjamin Geva
Toronto, Canada
Winter (Toronto) 2020

Sagi Peari
Perth, Australia
Summer (Perth) 2020

Table of Contents

Table of Cases

AUSTRALIA

CANADA

SINGAPORE

SOUTH AFRICA

UNITED KINGDOM

UNITED STATES OF AMERICA

Table of Legislation

UNITED KINGDOM STATUTES

UNITED KINGDOM STATUTORY INSTRUMENTS

OTHER LEGISLATION AND RELATED MATERIAL

Australia

Canada

China

France

Germany

India

Israel

EUROPEAN REGULATIONS

INTERNATIONAL INSTRUMENTS

List of Abbreviations

ABEA	Australia Bills of Exchange Act
BEA	Bills of Exchange Act
BNCC	The Convention for the Settlement of Certain Conflicts of Laws in Connection with Bills of Exchange and Promissory Notes
CBEA	Canada Bills of Exchange Act
CCC	Convention for the Settlement of Certain Conflicts of Laws in Connection with Cheques
CDS	Central depository of securities
COGSA	Carriage of Goods by Sea Act
DPC	Deferred payment credit
ECCHO	Electronic check clearinghouse organization
EFT	Electronic funds transfers
EPO	Electronic payment order
GCC	Geneva Conflicts Conventions
HDC	Holder in Due Course
IACC	Inter-American Convention on Conflict of Laws
IBEO	Bills of Exchange Ordinance [New Version] 1957, Laws of the State of Israel
LEC	Law on Electronic Commerce
LETR	Law on Electronic Transferable Records
MSR	Most significant relationship
OCTA	Ontario Securities Transfers Act
PRIMA	Primary Intermediary Approach
SGA	Sale of Goods Act
UBL	Convention Providing a Uniform Law for Bills of Exchange and Promissory Notes
UCC	Uniform Commercial Code
UCL	Convention Providing a Uniform Law for Cheques
UDIDROIT	Geneva Convention on Substantive Rules for Intermediated Securities
UNIBNC	United Nations Convention on International Bills of Exchange and International Promissory Notes

Introduction

This book marries two fields of law: negotiable instruments and choice-of-law. Bills of exchange, cheques, and promissory notes are the main classical negotiable instruments. For centuries, these instruments have played a vital role in the smooth operation of domestic and international commerce, including in transactions between distantly located parties. Through their evolution, fusion, and sophistication, they have remained one of the primary tools for everyday commercial activity, serving as one of the principal methods of payment and credit and one of the cornerstones of the contemporary bank-centred system. The rapid technological progress of payment mechanisms has embraced the traditional institution of negotiable instruments leading to their further adaptation and sophistication in order to meet the challenges of the contemporary reality of frequent mobility of people, goods, and high daily volumes of cross-border transactions and international commerce. **0.01**

While the principal fundamentals governing negotiable instruments tend to be based on a common set of organizing ideas, detailed rules vary from place to place, which requires the identification and knowledge of the national law that should govern an international negotiable instrument. Take, for example, a bill of exchange payable in Italy, signed in England by a New York resident, delivered in France to an Australian resident, who has transferred it to a Dutch person in Belgium. Which law will apply to the instrument? Will one law apply to all aspects of it? Here the question of choice-of-law enters the picture. **0.02**

The cross-disciplinary partnership between us, the authors, one specializing in negotiable instruments and the other in choice-of-law, purports to offer a comprehensive and thorough analysis of the choice-of-law rules applicable to negotiable instruments. The internal structure of negotiable instruments law is complex, which has given rise to a popular view favouring the mythological 'law merchant',[1] the exclusion of negotiable instruments from the scope of general contract and property law doctrines, and their subsequent exclusion from ordinary choice-of-law analysis. **0.03**

The central thesis of this book is to challenge this common view. Indeed, the complex structure of negotiable instruments creates a significant challenge for traditional contract and property doctrine and the choice-of-law analysis applicable to them. Yet, in contrast to the common view, we argue that the complex case of international negotiable instruments should be analysed through the lens of traditional contract and property choice-of-law doctrines rather than by crafting new specially designed rules for negotiable instruments. **0.04**

In order to illustrate this point, consider the well-known in choice-of-law literature *Giuliano & Lagarde* Report ['Report'],[2] which has served as a basis for contemporary **0.05**

[1] See Chapter II section F(1).

[2] Report on the Convention on the law applicable to contractual obligations by Mario Giuliano, Professor, University of Milan, and Paul Lagarde, Professor, University of Paris I, Official Journal C 282, 31/

European Rome I Regulations[3] on the question of applicable law. The Report excludes negotiable instruments law from the scope of ordinary choice-of-law analysis.[4] However, one can reassess the three rationales mentioned in the Report to justify negotiable instruments' law exclusion. First, it makes a point that a negotiable instrument is not a contract.[5] In this book we argue the opposite—from their very origin to their present-day doctrinal analysis, negotiable instruments are very much contracts and carefully follow the essentials of contract law doctrine, alongside the basic elements of tangible property law.[6]

0.06 Second, the Report characterizes a negotiable instrument as a 'complex contract'.[7] Indeed, in our book we provide a precise demarcation of the special nature of the negotiable instrument as a 'special' contract to delineate its divergence from the 'ordinary' contract; its relation to basic elements of tangible property transfer; and how this divergence affects (if at all) the choice- of- law rules of negotiable instruments, comparatively to choice-of-law rules of 'ordinary' contracts and tangible property. While throughout our book we show that negotiable instruments present 'complicated special rules' that should be analysed, modified, and distinguished from 'ordinary' contract law/property law rules, they are very much based on them.

0.07 Finally, the Report makes a reference to the existing harmonization processes.[8] In this book we provide a detailed comparative analysis of the various rules in diverse legal systems and we show that they are far from uniform.[9] We discuss the various harmonization processes of negotiable instruments,[10] and make some suggestions for possible reforms within the process of international harmonization of the choice-of-law rules,[11] which would capture the challenges of the digital age.[12] In contrast to the Report, we argue that the traditional choice-of-law rules in the areas of contract law and tangible property can serve as a model for such reform of choice-of-law rules of negotiable instruments.

0.08 The book is structured, as follows. Chapter I introduces the reader to the basic concept of 'negotiability' as the transferability of an instrument embodying monetary claims by its physical delivery—possibly free of adverse claims and contract defences

10/1980 P. 0001–0050 < http://eur-lex.europa.eu/LexUriServ/LexUriServ.do?uri=CELEX:31980Y1031(01):EN:HTML>, accessed 20 December 2019 (hereafter Report)

[3] Commission Regulation (EC) 593/2008 of the European Parliament and of the Council of 17 June 2008 on the Law Applicable to Contractual Obligations (Rome I), 2008 OJ (L 177) 6 (EU); Commission Regulation 864/2007, on the Law Applicable to Non-Contractual Obligations (Rome II), 2007 OJ (L 199) 40 (EC)

[4] Report 10, s 4.

[5] ibid.

[6] See Chapters I and II.

[7] Report 10, s 4.

[8] ibid.

[9] See Chapter I.

[10] See Chapter I section A and Chapter III section C.

[11] See Chapters V–VII.

[12] See Chapter VIII.

to liability under it. Accordingly, one of the typical features of a negotiable instrument is that it may be divorced from the underlying causes and has to be judged on its own merits, independent from the bargain from which the instrument originated and the underlying contract. The chapter then sets out the principal instruments that, subsequent to their emergence and earlier development, were accorded with the quality of negotiability. These instruments are bills of exchange, promissory notes, and cheques. Having then discussed the rules governing liability under and transfer of such instruments as a crystallization of the general rules of contract and tangible property (as shared by all major legal systems), the chapter describes their contemporary uses. This chapter also outlines early national codification, major difference among the global systems, and considerable international (unsuccessful) efforts to unify and substantively harmonize this area of law.

Chapter II delves into the evolution of negotiable instruments as a cross-border migration of ideas, challenges of innovation and progress, sophistication of legal doctrines, principles, and concepts. It further demonstrates the key role that negotiable instruments have played in the evolution of payment and banking systems. An important theme of the chapter is the application of private law's general principles of contract and property to these instruments and hence the rejection of a special mythological 'law merchant' governing them. **0.09**

Chapter III introduces the reader to the question of choice-of-law and delineates its common thread within contemporary private law choice-of-law rules. In particular, the chapter demonstrates that despite the variety of various names and titles, one can point to the following three cornerstone developments within the contemporary choice-of-law doctrine, which can all be traced to different degrees of divergence within the various systems: (1) a relaxation within the classical classification of the subject according to the presence of the so-called 'foreign element' in the factual matrix of the case; (2) the advances of the so-called 'party autonomy' principle according to which the parties can agree on the identity of the applied law; (3) the advances of the so-called 'most significant relationship' (MSR) principle. According to this principle courts are required to assess the factual situation of a case as a whole and to evaluate the significance of the various factors relative to the degree of their connectedness to the particular liability event and the litigating parties. Given the failure of the systems to agree on unification of the substantive law this chapter makes some observations about the need of harmonization of choice-of-law relating to negotiable instruments. **0.10**

Chapter IV provides a comprehensive examination of the existing choice-of-law frameworks set in the statutory provisions under the UK Bills of Exchange Act,[13] Geneva Conflicts Conventions,[14] the Second Restatement,[15] and the Inter-American **0.11**

[13] 1882, Chapters 61, 45, and 46 Vict.

[14] Convention for the Settlement of Certain Conflicts of Laws in Connection with Bills of Exchange and Promissory Notes, signed at Geneva 7 June, 1930 143 LNTS 319; Convention for the Settlement of Certain Conflicts of Laws in Connection with Cheques, signed at Geneva 19 March, 1931143 LNTS 407.

[15] American Law Institute).

Convention.[16] The examination is descriptive and yet analytical in its nature. The discussion is comparative and critical only to the extent of the application and interpretation of the existing rules. It does not question existing rules but endeavours to enhance their understanding.

0.12 Chapters V–VIII call for a dramatic reassessment of the existing rules outlined in Chapter IV. The chapters offer an alternative set of rules to serve as a basis for a global harmonized framework of the choice-of-law rules relating to negotiable instruments, summarized in the Appendix. Specifically, Chapter V supports the incorporation of the party autonomy principle as a governing principle of choice-of-law rules relating to negotiable instruments law. It also argues that this area of law should not remain immune from the relaxation in the 'foreign element' requirement—a development that has taken place within ordinary choice-of-law doctrine. Chapter VI favours the incorporation of the MSR principle to negotiable instruments law. It calls for a re-examination of the choice-of-law rules in cases where the parties have not specified the identity of the applicable law. It carefully re-examines the very underpinnings of the traditional rules and argues that these reflect an outdated conception of the subject. It argues that the very nature of negotiable instruments' law—its historical developments and the trends that have taken place within choice-of-law doctrine—all support a reconsideration of the traditional rules. Furthermore, it argues that a careful review of the case law in this area of law suggests the existence of support for the alternative framework that we offer.

0.13 Chapter VII defends the broad application of the suggested proposition and addresses a possible objection that could be raised against it. Further, we demonstrate the relevance of our argument to other types of commercial instruments: securities and documents of title to goods. Despite the different nature of these instruments compared to classical negotiable instruments (ie bills, notes, and cheques), we show how our insights on the application of traditional contract and property doctrine enables us to make some important observations on the identity of choice-of-law rules in the area of securities and documents of title. Finally, we elaborate on the possible limits to the suggested argument. Specifically, we draw attention to some exceptions to the choice-of-law process which appear within different systems under various names and titles, such as 'public policy' or 'international human rights', which effectively set a limit to the operational dynamics of the ordinary (and subsequently negotiable instruments') choice-of-law analysis.

0.14 The last chapter, Chapter VIII, makes suggestions with respect to the application of the proposition to the advancing era of digitalization, when negotiable instruments will take an electronic form. It outlines the various 'electronification' moves that have taken place within the traditional versions of negotiable instruments and contemplates the various international legislative frameworks that might be relevant to the digital version of negotiable instruments. We argue that the suggested framework of

[16] Inter-American Convention on Conflict of Laws Concerning Bills of Exchange, Promissory Notes, and Invoices, 1975 1438 UNTS 211.

choice-of-law rules should be attractive to the digital era of the instruments. As we will show, the expected loss of the physical aspect of the instrument does not challenge the validity of our argument and, in fact, enhances it.

In effect, our call for a redesign of the present choice-of-law rules relating to negotiable instruments finds traces in contemporary literature. The commentators of one of the leading textbooks in the field have framed the need for a reconsideration of the choice-of-law rules of negotiable instruments in the following terms: **0.15**

> it must be noted that the Bills of Exchange Act 1882 and much of the case referred to in the following paragraphs is now more than a century old. In that time, the role and significance of bills of exchange in commercial intercourse and the approach of the conflict of laws to freely incurred obligations such as these has changed radically. As the following commentary makes clear, the rules contained in the 1882 Act are neither comprehensive nor easy to understand and apply. A radical overhaul of the law in this area, whether by legislation or international convention, seems long overdue.[17]

In this book we are indeed willing to take up the challenge of a 'radical overhaul'. In line with the above-stated quotation, we suggest a radical reorientation of choice-of-law rules, which would not be limited to the choice-of-law provisions of the UK Bills of Exchange Act 1882 (BEA), but would also extend to three other choice-of-law frameworks: the negotiable instruments' provisions in the Second Restatement, the Geneva Conflict Conventions, and the Inter-American Convention. **0.16**

We argue that choice-of-law rules in the area of international negotiable instruments need to be dramatically amended and harmonized. The contemporary choice-of-law rules within this area of law have originated from flawed premises about the nature of the subject. Further, contemporary rules have left behind the modern development of choice-of-law doctrine. Relying on the foundation of negotiable instruments' law within the traditional ordinary doctrines of contract and movable property and invoking developments within modern choice-of-law thought, we endeavour to challenge the traditional orthodoxy and offer a complete re-examination of the choice-of-law rules of negotiable instruments. **0.17**

[17] LCollins, Harris (eds) *Dicey, Morris and Collins on the Conflict of Laws* (15th edn, Sweet & Maxwell 2012) 2077.

I

Negotiability, Negotiable Instruments, and the Law of Bills, Notes, and Cheques

A. The Nature of the Negotiable Instrument

1.01 A negotiable instrument is a piece of paper (or in theory any tangible item of property) containing one or more obligations to pay money. Transfer of the paper passes with it the right to enforce the obligation(s) and may confer on the transferee a better right than that of the transferor.

1.02 Not every document containing obligation(s) to pay money is endowed with the attributes of negotiability. At present, in each country, there may be a statute defining with precision the features of instruments that are negotiable. Such statutes typically provide for parties' liability on such instruments, enforcement of the liability, and the transferability of the instrument. Certainty is an important objective of such statutes; hence, they contain simple and yet strict requirements as to the form, as well as procedures, required for both enforcement and transfer.

1.03 With the view of accommodating commerce and finance, both the types of instruments that have become negotiable and the law that governs them have evolved throughout the centuries, in various places, and under diverse legal systems. The numerous instruments and laws that have emerged bear similarities to each other, but are not identical. In each time and place, the law that governs negotiable instruments is anchored and applied in the context of a governing domestic legal system. Inevitably, negotiable instruments used in international payments give rise to questions concerning applicability of law, which are discussed in length later in this book.

1.04 With respect to instruments endowed with it, 'negotiability' addresses *first* the reciprocal relationship between the right to enforce an obligation, an abstract chose in action, and the right to the document that expresses it, a tangible chose in possession.

Second, negotiability addresses the transferability of the document and the right to enforce the obligation thereon free from adverse claims and defences. Stated otherwise, with a negotiable instrument, the right to the paper and the right to enforce the obligation expressed in it are intertwined; their transfer involves physical delivery of the paper, and may confer on the transferee a better title than that of the transferor.

Possession of a document expressing any obligation may be used as a piece of evidence supporting the possessor's entitlement to enforce the obligation. The evidentiary value of the presentation of the document, or even of the lawful possession of the document to confer the transferee the right to enforce the obligation, depends on the terms of the obligation and may vary. Furthermore, in the absence of suspicious circumstances, and again, depending on the terms of the obligation, performance of an obligation to the person presenting the document may give a discharge to the debtor. This, however, is not conclusive as to whether the document is negotiable. Rather, to satisfy the first point of reciprocity, the right *to* the document must be inseparable from the right to sue and give discharge *on* the obligation. Accordingly, an attempted transfer of a negotiable instrument to one person, and the rights on it to another, will lead to a dispute between the two transferees as to who is entitled to both the paper and the rights thereon, but not to a split between the right to the paper and the right to enforce the obligation. Indeed, by agreement, the possessor may not be the owner; but otherwise, the right to possess and own the paper is inseparable from the right to sue and receive discharge on the debt embodied therein. **1.05**

For example, when receiving clothes from a customer, a laundry service will typically issue a ticket to be presented at pickup. The service provider is likely to be discharged upon the return of the clothes in good faith to whoever will pick them up while presenting the ticket. However, a transfer of a laundry ticket from one person to another is not a usual way for transferring rights thereon and the laundry service may insist on verifying the pickup entitlement according to its own books. Stated otherwise, the laundry ticket is not a negotiable instrument. **1.06**

Effectively speaking of the first point, that of the relationship between the right to and on the document, Goode defines an 'instrument' as 'a document of title to money'.[1] The term thus corresponds to the Germanic *Wertpapier*[2] defined in art 965 of the Swiss Code of Obligations as 'any document in which a right is incorporated in such a way that it cannot be claimed nor transferred to others ... without the document'.[3] An **1.07**

[1] E McKendrick (ed), *Goode on Commercial Law* (5th edn, Penguin 2016) (hereafter McKendrick, *Commercial Law*) 517.

[2] According to D V Cowen and L Gering, *Cowen The Law of Negotiable Instruments in South Africa Vol. One: General Principles* (5th edn, Juta 1985) (hereafter Cowen and Gering, *Negotiable Instruments*) 94, the word 'Wertpapier' cannot be well translated to English, so that words such as 'security' or 'commercial paper' do not convey its accurate meaning.

[3] Swiss Code of Obligations: English Translation of the Official Text (Swiss–American Chamber of Commerce 2003). On the German *Wertpapier* see in general L Dabin, *Fondements du droit cambiaire Allemand* (Faculté de droit de Université de Liège 1959) (hereafter Dabin, *Fondements*). For a comprehensive discussion on the German conceptual framework, and as to whether it sheds additional light on the nature of a negotiable instrument, see Cowen and Gering, *Negotiable Instruments* 79–98 (where a slightly different translation, albeit to the same effect, of the Swiss provision is reproduced at 82). Their negative conclusion as to whether the *Wertpapier* sheds additional light on the nature of a negotiable instrument at 110, is criticized by JT Pretorius' book review in 1986, 103 SALJ 151 at 154–56. On the negotiable instrument

instrument differs from a documentary piece of evidence in 'locking' the debt obligation into the paper on which it is written so that the entitlement to the debt becomes co-extensive with the entitlement to the document. It is in this sense that the claim to the debt, otherwise a chose in action, is said to become allegorically 'reified', so as to be 'merged' or 'locked' into the document.[4] The claim then acquires features of a 'chose in possession', even as it survives the destruction and sometimes the loss of the document,[5] and 'splits' into 'parts' of a 'set', each capable of circulating on its own, and yet altogether forming 'one bill'.[6]

1.08 This is, however, only one facet of 'negotiability' that may exist on its own for some types of 'instruments'[7] that are nevertheless not 'negotiable', at least in the full sense. Rather, to enhance circulation of at least some 'documents of titles to payment in money', the law may confer on a transferee, under prescribed circumstances, a better title than that of the transferor. This is the second point addressed by 'negotiability', which distinguishes negotiable instruments from ordinary chattels with respect to the general rule that a transferee may not acquire more rights than those of the transferor.[8] At the heart of full 'negotiability' are thus the ideas of 'easy transferability' involving the physical transfer of the paper (sometimes called 'procedural' or 'formal' negotiability) and of 'transferability free from claims and defences' (sometimes called 'substantive' negotiability).

1.09 However, according to Cowen and Gering, it is the nexus between the right to the document and the right to enforce the promises embodied in it, an idea first articulated by Savigny, which 'provides the key to the analytical and systematic understanding of the nature of a negotiable instrument'.[9] Relating both to 'a chattel, a tangible scrap of paper' and 'a bundle of contracts', a claim to a negotiable instrument thus involves not only 'the right to possess a thing but [also] the right to sue several persons [liable to it]'.[10] The right to the document is intertwined with the right to enforce the contracts thereon and it is procedural negotiability that allows substantive negotiability to exist. The rights to and on an instrument are inseparable so that,

> A negotiable instrument is a document of title embodying rights to payment of money ... which, ... is (a) transferable by delivery (or by indorsement and delivery)

as *Wertpapier* see also FR Malan, JT Pretorius, and SF Du Toit, *Malan on Bills of Exchange, Cheques and Promissory Notes in South African Law* (5th edn, LexisNexis 2009) 4, 7.

[4] See eg G Gilmore, 'The Commercial Doctrine of Good Faith Purchase' (1954) 63 Yale LJ 1057, 1067, 1074.

[5] J Marius, *Advice Concerning Bills of Exchange* (Horne 1684) 19, qualified (for lost instruments) in *Pierson v Hutchinson* (1899) 2 Camp 211, 170 ER 1132; *Crowe v Clay* (1854) 9 Exch 605, 156 ER 258.

[6] See eg Bills of Exchange Act 1882 (UK), 45 and 46 Vict, c 61, s 71, as amended (hereafter BEA).

[7] See eg Ontario Personal Property Security Act, RSO 1990, c P.10, defining 'instrument' in s 1 to include 'any ... writing that evidences a right to the payment of money and is of a type that in the ordinary course of business is transferred by delivery with any necessary endorsement or assignment'. See also the dispute in Germany as to whether only a negotiable instrument may be *Wertpapier*: Dabin, *Fondements* 243–44, in the context of his general discussion on the *Wertpapier* at 236–84.

[8] See eg Sale of Goods Act 1979, c 54, s 21.

[9] Cowen and Gering, *Negotiable Instruments* 23.

[10] Z Chaffee Jr, 'Rights in Overdue paper' (1918) 31 Harv L Rev 1104, 1109.

in such a way that the holder *pro tempore* may sue on it in his own name and in his own right, and (b) a *bona fide* transferee [for value][11] may acquire a good and complete title to the document and the rights embodied therein, notwithstanding that his predecessor has a defective title or no title at all.[12]

A 'holder' who 'may sue on it in his own name and in his own right' under (a), is one in possession of the document and to whom the promises run by its terms. Such is the case for a bearer of an instrument payable to the bearer, as well as for the payee or indorsee ('endorsee'[13] in Canada) in possession of an instrument payable to order. To acquire 'a good and complete title to the document and the rights embodied therein' under (b), in addition to complying with the taking in good faith and other requirements, the 'transferee' must be such a 'holder'. This describes the central role of the holder in the law of negotiable instruments. **1.10**

In contrast to the negotiable instrument, an ordinary debt cannot be transferred under the common law.[14] Courts of equity viewed this state of law as 'too absurd ... to adopt.'.[15] Having admitted the assignee's title, they nevertheless required the assignee to sue in the assignor's name. [16] Thus, when Cowen and Gering speak of the holder's right to sue 'in his own name and in his own right' they ought to be taken as distinguishing such a right from that of the equitable assignee who must sue in the original creditor/assignor's name. They ought not to be taken to identify holding with ownership. Indeed, while in a given case, ownership and holding may converge[17] so as to confer on the holder the right to sue not only 'in his own name' but also 'in his own right', the holder is not necessarily the legal owner. For example, a 'holder' may be an agent for collection for the owner of an instrument that the owner had transferred and made payable to him or her; such a holder may sue in his or her own name albeit in the owner's right.[18] By the same token, a non-holder owner may be in possession of an instrument not payable to him or her, in which case there is no holder,[19] and the owner may sue in his or her right even if not necessarily in his or her own name. Furthermore, possession may be either lawful or unlawful—a distinction that does not impact on the holder's standing to bring an action, but may impact his or her right to successfully recover. In the final analysis, regardless of the lawfulness of the possession, while **1.11**

[11] But see sections D and E of this chapter as to the lack of this requirement under the Geneva Conventions.

[12] Cowen and Gering, *Negotiable Instruments* 52.

[13] According to JM Holden, *The History of Negotiable Instruments in English Law* (first published 1955, WM W Gaunt & Sons 1993) 44, , '[t]he spelling "endorse", is more common than "indorse" in commercial practice'. At the same time, he goes on to say, '[t]he Bills of Exchange Act, 1882, adopted the spelling "indorse"'. I should add that on that point, UCC Article 3 follows suit and uses 'indorse'. In contrast, the Canadian spelling, reflected in the Bills of Exchange Act, RSC 1985, c B-4 (hereafter CBEA), is 'endorse'.

[14] *Master v Miller* (1791) 4 TR 320, 100 ER 1042; affd (1793) 2 Hy Bl 141, 126 ER 474.

[15] A statutory form of assignment was ultimately introduced in England by s 25(6) of the Judicature Act 1873, 36 and 37 Vic 66.

[16] *Crouch v The Credit Foncier of England* (1873) LR 8 QB 374 [380], 29 LT 259; see also eg *Di Giulio v Boland* [1958] OR 384, 13 DLR (2d) 510 [515] (Ont CA).

[17] As in *Milnes v Dawson* (1855) 5 Ex 948, 155 ER 413 (hereafter, *Milnes v Dawson*) where the holder got the instrument by way of gift. See Cowen and Gering, *Negotiable Instruments* 36.

[18] In such a case the owner's right to give a discharge was recognized (albeit as obiter) in *Milnes v Dawson*.

[19] As in *Mason v Morgan* (1834) 2 Ad & El 30, 111 ER 12 and *Stone v Rawlinson* (1745) Willes 559, 125 ER 1320.

every holder must be in possession, not everyone in possession is a holder. Similarly, not every holder is an owner and not every owner is a holder.[20] While it is true that s/he 'may not be the legal owner of [the instrument]', it is unhelpful to characterize the holder as 'the mercantile owner of [it]'[21] as this characterization does not inform us as to his or her powers and rights.[22]

1.12 Locking the right therein, the negotiable instrument is said to be a 'documentary intangible'.[23] It is a chattel, chose in possession, carrying obligations for which the entitlement is a chose in action. As a chattel and intangible, it is governed by the law of property. The various contracts it carries are governed by the law of contract. Indeed, it is general law that determines the application of insolvency and inheritance law to negotiable instruments. As well as an ordinary chattel, a negotiable instrument may be transferred by mere delivery. Similarly, as a chose in action, it may be assigned without the transfer of possession,[24] even while either giving the assignee the right to demand possession or appointing the possessor as an agent. Likewise, as under a contract, liability hinges on an offer and acceptance[25] and requires consideration in common law[26] and *causa* in civil law.[27]

1.13 As will be discussed, the three common types of negotiable instruments are bills of exchange ('bills'), promissory notes ('notes'), and cheques. Bills are also known as drafts and cheque is spelled in the USA as 'check'. While bills and cheques are unconditional orders, the note is an unconditional promise, in each case, to pay a sum certain in money. The cheque is an order to a 'bank', payable on demand. Bills and notes may be payable either on demand or at a determinable future time. With some variation, they may all be either payable to the bearer or to the order of a specified person.

1.14 Each legal system adopted a specialized distinct body of law dealing with specific proprietary and obligatory characteristics of such instruments, such as matters relating to the form, issue, aspects of liability, negotiation and negotiability, and discharge. A document governed by this body of law is said to be not only an obligation (or obligations) contained in a chattel but also a 'negotiable instrument'—namely, 'a document

[20] To confuse matters further—even an owner may have an unlawful possession as eg where he or she has unlawfully took the instrument from a pledgee.

[21] As proposed by Chalmers in AG Gleeson, *Chalmers and Guest on Bills of Exchange, Cheques and Promissory Notes* (18th edn, Sweet & Maxwell, Thomson Reuters 2017) 1-022 (hereafter Gleeson, *Chalmers and Guest*).

[22] An extensive study is A Barak, *The Nature of a Negotiable Instrument* (Jerusalem Academic Press 1983) [in Hebrew] 23–139.

[23] McKendrick, *Commercial Law* 517.

[24] Gleeson, *Chalmers and Guest* 5-067.

[25] On this point, we agree with Cowen and Gering, *Negotiable Instruments* 105 that in this sense the contract is not unilateral.

[26] That is, all 'contracts in writing . . . [which are] merely written and not specialties, . . . are parol' and require consideration. *Rann v Hughes* (1778) 7 TR 350n, 2 ER 18.

[27] P Ellinger, 'Negotiable Instruments' in U Drobnig and K Zweigert (eds), *International Encyclopedia of Comparative Law*, vol IX of U (JCB Mohr 2000) 18, 88–89 (hereafter Ellinger, 'Negotiable Instruments'). In civil law, in the footsteps of Roman law, in the absence of the (common law) consideration requirement, an informal contract is based on some 'cause' other than the adherence to a formula, such as the delivery of an object or the actual agreement of the parties; hence, informal contracts are also called 'causal'. RW Lee, *The Elements of Roman Law with a Translation of the Institutes of Justinian* (4th edn, Sweet & Maxwell 1956) 287, who goes on to discuss how 'In the course of time abstract contracts tend to become causal.'

governed by the specific legal principles applying to negotiable instruments'.[28] These specific principles have been formed by the adaptation of general principles of law to the unique mixture of rights to, and obligations on, a negotiable instrument.

Aspects of general law governing negotiable instruments form 'the law of bills and notes in the wide sense'. At the same time, the set of laws providing for the specific elements of the bills, notes, and cheques is characterized as 'the law of bills and notes in the strict sense'.[29] **1.15**

As will be discussed in Chapter II, the negotiable bill, note, and cheque each has its own distinctive features and history so that the law governing it has evolved in a process of the adaptation of the general law to accommodate it. Furthermore, categories share common elements that are not necessarily directly linked to their common denominator of negotiability. Accordingly, the distinctive nature of a document of debt as a 'negotiable instrument' does not convey the full scope of what falls into 'strict sense' matters. For example, in England, the focus of the evolution had been the liability on a bill or note in 'an action upon the case' on the basis of 'the custom of merchants'.[30] Regardless, negotiable instruments legislation even provides for a non-negotiable instrument.[31] Hence, 'negotiability' is too narrow a component of the 'strict sense' law—the evolution of which had been well underway irrespective of whether, and before, specific documents of debt acquired negotiability. As a subject of a specific set of laws, a bill, note, or cheque is thus a 'negotiable instrument' in the sense of being governed by a body of law addressing matters pertaining specifically to instruments that are negotiable but include, although nonetheless is not restricted to, negotiability. To that end, Falconbridge described this area to include 'the form, issue, negotiation, and discharge of bills or notes, but not including all the consequences of, or the all the rights or liabilities resulting from contracts entered into by parties to bills or notes'.[32] **1.16**

B. Brief History of Codification: Domestic Statutes and International Conventions

As will be seen in Chapter II, the bill, note, and cheque each has its own distinct history that arose in response to the needs of commerce as they have developed. As they evolved, and notwithstanding the myth of 'law merchant', further discussed in Chapter II, as a unifying source of law governing all such instruments everywhere, they were initially governed by principles of Roman law in the Continent and principles of common law in England. At present, the unifying element for these types **1.17**

[28] A Barak, 'The Nature of the Negotiable Instrument' (1983) 18 IsLR 49, 75.

[29] See in general A Barak, 'The Requirement of Consideration for Bills or Notes in Israel' (1967) 2 IsLR 499, 500–05. See also B Crawford, *The Law of Banking and Payment in Canada*, vol 3 (Canada Law Book, Looseleaf, 2014 edition) ss 20:30.20(2) and 21:40.80(3).

[30] See eg *Chat and Edgar Case* (1663) 1 Keble 636, 83 ER 1156.

[31] See CBEA, governing 'a bill [containing] words prohibiting transfer, or indicating an intention that it should not be transferable'.

[32] A W Rogers, *Falconbridge on Banking and Bills of Exchange* (7th edn, Canada Law Book 1969) 456 (hereafter Rogers, *Falconbridge on Banking*). Most certainly, he used 'bills' to include 'cheques'.

of instruments is negotiability and the principal sources of law governing them throughout the world are statutory. However, this does not preclude courts from recognizing new types of negotiable instruments once they are so treated by participants in financial markets.[33] Nor are Legislatures precluded from applying negotiability to other type of 'documentary intangible[s]'[34] such as investment securities[35] or documents of title to goods.[36] 'Negotiability', albeit not necessarily to the full extent,[37] is said to be established by estoppel[38] or contract.[39] At the same time, when speaking in the strict sense, negotiable instruments legislation is limited to bills, notes, and cheques.

1.18 Codification relating to bills of exchange is traced to the seventeenth century in Continental Europe. In France, the *Ordonnance de Commerce* of 1673[40] is considered to be 'influential',[41] though it is said to be superseded by the *Code de Commerce* of 1807.[42] Another 'influential enactment'[43] is said to be the German *Wechselordnung* of 1848.[44] However, the first comprehensive codifying statute is the UK Bills of Exchange Act 1882 (BEA),[45] which was characterized in *Bank of Baroda v Punjab National Bank* as a 'codifying Act'.[46] Indeed, the BEA was acknowledged to have been 'intended to be a code of the law relating to negotiable instruments'. However, it was held that in its interpretation, 'the proper course is in the first instance to examine [its] language . . . and to ask what is its natural meaning uninfluenced by any considerations derived from the previous state of law'.[47]

1.19 The BEA is a comprehensive codifying statute in two major ways. First, it covers bills, notes, and cheques. It addresses both commonalities and differences among such instruments. Second, the BEA is not limited in its coverage to the negotiability of such instruments, but rather covers all of their aspects as instruments. At the same time, it

[33] See eg *Goodwin v Robarts* (1875) LR 10 Exch 337, affd. (1876) 1 1 App Cas 476, [1874-80] All ER Rep 628 (HL); *Bechuanaland Exploration Co. v London Trading Bank Ltd* [1898] 2 QB 658; and *Edelstein v Schuler &Co.* [1902] 2 KB 144, [1900-3] All ER 884. See scholarly discussion by EP Ellinger, 'Legal Problems of Modern Commercial Paper' (1990–91) 6 BFLR 65, 69–71.

[34] McKendrick, *Commercial Law* 517.

[35] Uniform Commercial Code (US) (hereafter UCC): While UCC Article 8—Investment Securities (1994) does not mention the term, the Prefatory Note specifically stresses (in (II)(B)) the application 'to investment securities [of] the principles of negotiable instruments law' as a 'principal' or 'primary' purpose of the enactment. See eg UCC § 8-303, providing for the acquisition of a security by a 'protected purchaser' free of 'any adverse claim'.

[36] For a negotiable document of title, see eg UCC § 7-104.

[37] That is, it could be either material or procedural, or even if material, could be limited to freedom from either contract defences or adverse claims.

[38] *The Colonial Bank v Cady* and Williams (1890) 15 App Cas 267, 60 LJ Ch 131.

[39] *Re Ex Parte Asiatic Banking Corporation* (1867) LR 2 Ch App 391 [397]; *Re Goy & Co. Ltd.* [1900] 2 Ch 149 [154].

[40] https://babel.hathitrust.org/cgi/pt?id=mdp.39015063718178;view=1up;seq=8, accessed 20 December 2019.

[41] Cowen and Gering, *Negotiable Instruments* 117.

[42] ibid. <https://archive.org/details/commentaireducod01alau/page/n8>, accessed 20 December 2019.

[43] Cowen and Gering, *Negotiable Instruments* 118.

[44] The *Allgemeine Deutsche Wechselordnung* of 1848 https://archive.org/details/protocollederzur00mannuoft/page/n9, accessed 20 December 2019.

[45] BEA.

[46] [1944] AC 176, [1944] 2 All ER Rep 83 [86].

[47] *Bank of England v Vagliano Bros* [1891] AC 107, [1891-4] All ER Rep 93 [44] (Lord Herschell).

does not purport to cover all of their aspects that extend beyond those they have as instruments. Thus, under BEA s 97,

(1) The rules in bankruptcy relating to bills of exchange, promissory notes, and cheques, shall continue to apply thereto notwithstanding anything in this Act contained.
(2) The rules of common law including the law merchant, save in so far as they are inconsistent with the express provisions of this Act, shall continue to apply to bills of exchange, promissory notes, and cheques.

The BEA 'furnished the model for the law of negotiable instruments of most members of the commonwealth and of some other countries which, at one time or another, came under the influence of English law'.[48] These are mostly common law jurisdictions,[49] but the list also includes non-common law countries such as South Africa,[50] Israel,[51] and Sri Lanka.[52] The BEA also applies in the Province of Quebec in Canada, where the Canadian BEA[53] applies as a federal statute and where it was held that the counterpart of BEA s 97(2)[54] is limited to 'strict sense' matters.[55] Accordingly, any other matter affecting negotiable instruments and not governed by the BEA is to be dealt with under the civil law of the province and not the rules of common law.[56] **1.20**

Ellinger divides BEA countries into those with minor variations, and those with major departures,[57] with Canada and Australia[58] belonging to the latter category.[59] Within the common law systems, Ellinger then enumerates the Roman–Dutch Group that adopted the BEA, as well as the Indian Act Group and the Uniform Commercial Code (UCC) Group. **1.21**

The Indian Act[60] is a pre-BEA statute and 'mainly ... codification of English common law'.[61] For its part, Article 3 of the UCC,[62] is the successor in the USA of the Uniform Negotiable Instruments Law (NIL),[63] of which concepts, but not structure, bore a clear influence of the BEA. In turn, the UCC revised the law substantially, even though in relation to some basic concepts English heritage can still be traced. However, uniformity among the various American jurisdictions is not full. Only **1.22**

48 Ellinger, 'Negotiable Instruments' 18.
49 Jurisdictions with the year of adoption by each are listed by Rogers, *Falconbridge on Banking* 431–32.
50 No 364 of 1964 (proclaimed 1 March 2001) (hereafter SABEA).
51 The Bills of Exchange Ordinance [New Version] 1957, Laws of the State of Israel, p 12 (hereafter IBEO).
52 Bills of Exchange Ordinance, Cap. 92.
53 CBEA.
54 ibid, s 9.
55 Civil Code of Québec, CQLR c CCQ-1991.
56 This rule goes back to a case decided on the pre-BEA law in Quebec: *Guy v Paré* (1892) 1 Que SC 443.
57 Ellinger, 'Negotiable Instruments' 46–51.
58 Bills of Exchange Act 1909 (last amended by Act No 46 of 2011).
59 Ellinger, 'Negotiable Instruments' 50–51.
60 Act No 26 of 1881.
61 MS Parthasarathy, *JS Khergamvala on the Negotiable Instruments Act* (17th edn, Tripathi 1990) 1. The quote does not appear in the 20th edn of 2018.
62 UCC Article 3—Negotiable Instruments (2002).
63 Completed in 1896 and adopted by all states by 1924. See Cowen and Gering, *Negotiable Instruments* 121.

eleven states and the District of Columbia have adopted, and one has introduced, the 2002 amendments.[64] Thus, choice-of-law rules remain relevant in the US domestic context as well.

1.23 For their parts, civilians in Europe and elsewhere produced uniform laws first in the Hague Conventions of 1910 and 1912[65] and subsequently in the Geneva Conventions of the early 1930s, or more specifically, the Convention Providing a Uniform Law for Bills of Exchange and Promissory Notes (UBL)[66] and the Convention Providing a Uniform Law for Cheques (UCL).[67] Most civil law countries introduced laws either adopting or influenced by these two Conventions.[68] Ellinger accordingly divides such countries according to their respective level of adherence: strict, intermediate, and strongly influenced,[69] with Germany[70] falling into the strict category[71] and France[72] into the intermediate one.[73]

1.24 Finally, a few countries stand on their own with 'sui generis systems' that may reflect aspects of the BEA, the Geneva Conventions systems, or both, but are nevertheless 'subject to many departures from any conventional system and often include numerous archaic or uncommon provisions' so as to accordingly be 'outside the ambit of the mainstream systems'.[74] China falls into this category.[75]

1.25 The 'great divide' is thus between common and civil law jurisdictions, respectively represented by the BEA (and UCC) and the Geneva Conventions. Nevertheless, on the whole, the variations do not reflect differences between common and civil laws' fundamentals. As will be seen in Chapter II, in recognizing the distinct categories, particularly those of the bill and cheque, each major system had to adapt its own legal principles in order to accommodate the instruments. However, in covering bills, notes, and cheques by statute, each system could either overlook or depart from its own doctrinal underpinning and address each subject matter pragmatically. Thus, there is a great deal of similarity between the BEA and Geneva Conventions and any differences that do exist are mostly a matter of either drafting or, occasionally, policy, which do not necessarily reflect the

[64] Adopting jurisdictions are listed at <https://www.uniformlaws.org/committees/community-home?CommunityKey=d6a2022c-ae5d-4fda-baf5-c1628a68168e >, accessed 20 December 2019.

[65] See Ellinger, 'Negotiable Instruments' 35–36.

[66] 143 LNTS 257 (7 June 1930), Annex I (hereafter UBL).

[67] 143 LNTS 355 (19 March 1931), Annex I (hereafter UCL).

[68] Ellinger, 'Negotiable Instruments' 19.

[69] ibid, 56–80.

[70] Vgl Bekanntmachung, 30 November 1933, RGBl II 974.

[71] Ellinger, 'Negotiable Instruments' 60–61.

[72] Décret.- L. 30 October 1935 introduced (with modifications) into the Code de Commerce both the UBL (CC arts 110 et seq—Bills and Notes Provisions) and the UCL (hereafter French Cheques Law). The former are now New CC arts L. 511-1 à L. 511-81 and the latter has been integrated by an ordinance of 14 December 2000 (JO 16 December 2000) into a new *Code monétaire et financier*, as arts L. 131-1 to L.131-87.

[73] Ellinger, 'Negotiable Instruments' 67–70.

[74] ibid, 57, and for details see 80–84.

[75] Negotiable Instruments Law of the Peoples Republic of China (as amended 28 August 2004). For further discussion on the unification efforts and the 'great divide' between common and civil law jurisdictions, see Chapter III section C.

difference between common or civil law but rather the prevailing view at a given time or place.

Against this background, the United Nations Convention on International Bills of Exchange and International Promissory Notes (UNIBNC)[76] was designed to provide parties engaged in international trade the option to use bills and notes (but not cheques) subject to a uniform reformed legal regime.[77] Implementation efforts have been unsuccessful.[78] **1.26**

Both the BEA and UBL deal in detail with bills and provide for the application of the provisions that govern bills with necessary modifications to notes.[79] The BEA treats cheques as a sub-category of bills.[80] There are, however, a few specific provisions applicable only to notes in both the BEA and UBL and to cheques in the BEA. UCC Article 3 deals with the negotiable instrument as one category and provides separately for rules applicable only to one or some types of instruments. UCC Article 4, to which there is no comparable statute in any other major jurisdictions, covers the collection and payment of cheques and other payment items through the banking system. **1.27**

C. Bills, Notes, and Cheques and Their Respective Uses: Negotiable Instruments Covered by Legislation

Subject to some variations, all statutory sources, namely, the BEA, UCC Article 3, the Geneva Conventions, and the UNIBNC govern the same types of principal instruments and general subjects, including parties to, and liability on, the instruments, and the mode and result of their transfer. **1.28**

Under these sources, the bill (or draft) is an unconditional written and signed order, addressed by one person ('drawer') to another ('drawee'), requiring the latter to pay a sum certain in money.[81] For its part, the promissory note ('note') is an unconditional written and signed promise (by a 'maker') to pay a sum certain in money.[82] The cheque is a bill payable on demand drawn on a bank.[83] Specific categories added by **1.29**

[76] UN Doc A/RES/43/165, 42 Yearbook of the United Nations 1988 (UN 1988) 834 (hereafter UNIBNC).

[77] Cowen and Gering, *Negotiable Instruments* 131–32. Comprehensive commentary can be found in (1979) 27 Am J Comp L 507–63. This includes an overview of the legislative process by WC Vis, discussion on the formal requisites of bills and notes by N Penney, review on instruments denominated in a foreign currency by AG Guest, analysis on forged endorsements by WC Vis, and a selected bibliography.

[78] Only Canada, Russia, and the USA signed and five other countries accessioned to it. This fell short of the '10 actions ... required for entry into force'. See UNCITRAL, 'Status: United Nations Convention on International Bills of Exchange and International Promissory Notes' (New York, 1988) (5 February 2019) http://www.uncitral.org/uncitral/en/uncitral_texts/payments/1988Convention_bills_status.html, accessed 20 December 2019.

[79] BEA s 89 and UBL art 77.

[80] BEA s 73.

[81] BEA s 3; UBL art 1: UCC § 3-104(b)(e) in conjunction with 104(a); UNIBNC art 3(1) (for the international dimension see art 2(1)).

[82] BEA s 83; UBL art 75: UCC § 3-104(b)(e) in conjunction with § 3-104(a); UNIBNC art 3(2) (for the international dimension see art 2(2))

[83] BEA s 73; UCC § 3-104(b)(f); effectively UCL art 1.

UCC Article 3 are certificate of deposit,[84] traveller's cheque,[85] cashier's cheque[86] and teller's cheque.[87]

1.30 A negotiable instrument may be payable to, or to the order of, a designated payee or to the bearer,[88] on demand (or at sight) or (other than with a cheque) at a fixed or determinable future time.[89] A negotiable instrument may be transferred from one person to another by 'negotiation', consisting of either a mere delivery in the case of an instrument payable to the bearer, or of delivery plus the transferor's signed 'indorsement' in the case of an instrument payable to the order.[90] Under certain conditions,[91] it may be enforceable by its holder for its entire sum, free of a third party's adverse claims, as well as of any prior party's contract defences.[92] The holder is the bearer of an instrument payable to bearer or the payee or indorsee in possession of an instrument payable to order.[93]

1.31 The general rule is that a signature is a necessary requirement for liability on an instrument.[94] One exception is under French law, which allows the holder of a bill and cheque to recover from the drawee, on the basis of *la provision*, that is, what the drawee owes the drawer, even without an acceptance.[95] A similar exception applies in Scotland, where a bill is stated to operate as an assignment of funds 'from the time when the bill is presented to the drawee'.[96] However, the broad principle, overwhelmingly applicable

[84] Defined in UCC § 3-104 (j) as 'an instrument containing an acknowledgment by a bank that a sum of money has been received by the bank and a promise by the bank to repay the sum of money', which as such 'is a note of the bank'.

[85] Defined in UCC § 3-104(i) as 'an instrument that (i) is payable on demand, (ii) is drawn on or payable at or through a bank, (iii) is designated by the term "traveler's check" or by a substantially similar term, and (iv) requires, as a condition to payment, a countersignature by a person whose specimen signature appears on the instrument'.

[86] Defined in UCC § 3-104(g) to mean 'a draft with respect to which the drawer and drawee are the same bank or branches of the same bank'.

[87] Defined in UCC § 3-104 (h) to mean 'a draft drawn by a bank (i) on another bank, or (ii) payable at or through a bank'.

[88] BEA s 3; UBL arts 1 and 75 (no 'bearer' option other than by indorsement under art 12); UCL art 5; UCC § 3-104(a); there is no bearer option under then UNIBNC.

[89] BEA s 3; UBL arts 1 and 2; UCL art 28; UCC § 3-104(a); UNIBNC arts 3(1)(b) and 3(2)(b).

[90] BEA s 31; UBL art 11; UCL art 14; UCC § 3-201; UNIBNC art 13. The term 'negotiation' appears only in the BEA, UCL and in UCC Article 3 (but not in the UBL). An indorsement that does not designate the transferee is an 'indorsement in blank', which effectively 'converts' the bill into one payable to the bearer. This is true even where instruments originally issued payable to the bearer are not recognized for the 'conversion' by blank indorsement of the bill payable to order see eg BEA s 34(1); UBL arts 12–13; UCL arts 15–16; UCC § 3-205; UNIBNC arts 13–16.

[91] Fundamentally, these conditions refer to the taking of the instrument by the holder in good faith, without knowledge, and for value. See eg BEA s 29(1); UBL arts 16–17; UCL arts 19 and 21–22; UCC § 3-302; UNIBNC art 29.

[92] BEA s 38(2); UBL arts 16–17; UCL arts 19 and 22; UCC (n 35) §§ 3-305 and 3-306; UNIBNC art 30. For example, a bona fide purchaser from a thief of a note payable to the bearer will defeat both the adverse claim of the person from whom the instrument was stolen and contract defences available to the maker against the party to whom the maker issued the note.

[93] BEA s 2; UNIBNC art 5(f) in conjunction with art 15.

[94] BEA s 23; UBL arts 7–8; UCC § 3-401; UNIBNC art 33.

[95] UCL art 17 (1935); art 20 (2000); Bills and Notes Provisions art 116 (1935); at present L511-7. For *la provision* in French law, see eg J Stoufflet, *Instruments de paiement et de credit* (8th edn, LexisNexis 2012) 115–25; and for a summary, Ellinger, 'Negotiable Instruments' 110–13. See also G Ripert and R Roblot, *Traité de droit commercial* (13th edn, Librairie gènèrale de droit et de jurisprudence 1992) 181–86. For a more extensive analysis, see P Lescot and R Roblot, *Les effets de commerce*, vol 1 (Rousseau 1953) 389–465.

[96] BEA s 53(2).

elsewhere,[97] is that '[a] check or other draft does not of itself operate as an assignment of funds in the hands of the drawee available for its payment';[98] a drawee incurs liability on a bill only by signing as an acceptor.[99] It is against this background that, as long as it has not been paid, the cheque is, in principle, revocable.[100]

The acceptor of a bill, being the drawee who indicated his or her consent to comply with the drawer's order,[101] and the maker of a note, being the promisor thereunder,[102] are primary parties; for each, liability on the engagement is according to its tenor. The drawer, being the order giver,[103] and each indorser, being the transferor of an instrument payable to him or her,[104] are secondary parties. Each is liable only upon the dishonour of the instrument, and usually upon the holder's compliance with presentment and notice requirements, which may be required to be formalized. Generally speaking, while presentment is made to the payer, being either the drawee or a primary party, notice of dishonour is to be sent to parties liable upon the dishonour by the payer. The 'avalist' signs as a guarantor to a party liable on the instrument.[105] There is no 'avalist' under the BEA and the UCC; thereunder, a signer who is not a party to the underlying transaction is an accommodation party.[106] Under the BEA he or she could also be taken to be an anomalous indorser.[107] **1.32**

Cheques are payment instruments. An international foreign currency payment can be made by means of a cheque drawn by a local bank on its correspondent in the country of the currency. For example, banks in Ruritania may provide chequing accounts in the currency of Penguina. Such a cheque may be 'internationalized' by being issued and/or circulated in Penguina and at least paid (and possibly collected even if in part) in Ruritania. Notes are credit instruments used domestically and internationally in connection with sales transactions, loans, and guarantees. Bills are both payment and credit instruments. In international trade, the seller may draw a bill on either the buyer or (particularly in conjunction with a letter of credit) on the buyer's bank. Such a bill may be made payable to the seller and negotiated by him at its present value and with recourse to the seller's bank for transmission or presentment to the buyer or the buyer's bank.[108] The general presumption is that an obligation on a negotiable **1.33**

[97] Though not necessarily in French-based systems, for which see in general Ellinger, 'Negotiable Instruments' 70–72.

[98] UCC § 3-408. See also BEA s 53(1) (almost verbatim).

[99] ibid. See also UNIBNC arts 37 and 40. cf UBL arts 21, 25, and 28.

[100] See eg BEA s 75 ('The duty and authority of a banker to pay a cheque drawn on him by his customer are determined by—(1) Countermand of payment: (2) Notice of the customer's death'); UCC § 4-403; and cf UCL art 32.

[101] BEA s 54(1): UBL art 28; UNIBNC art 40.

[102] BEA s 88(1): UBL art 78; UNIBNC art 39.

[103] BEA s 53(1); UBL art 9 (in conjunction with arts 43–45); UCL art 12 (in conjunction with art 40); UNIBNC art 38.

[104] BEA s 53(2); UBL art 15 (in conjunction with arts 43–45); UCL art 18 (in conjunction with art 40); UNIBNC art 44.

[105] UBL arts 32 and 39; UCL art 27; UNIBNC arts 46–47.

[106] BEA s 28; UCC § 3-419. For further discussion on the point of 'avalist', see Chapter V, the text accompanying nn 30–38.

[107] BEA s 56. In Canada where the corresponding provision (CBEA s 130) contains a variation, the aval contract was read into the statute. *Gallagher v Murphy* [1929] SCR 288.

[108] For a more detailed discussion on the practical uses of negotiable instruments see Ellinger, 'Negotiable Instruments' 19–21.

instrument suspends, that is, conditionally discharges, the debt for which it is given; the debt is, however, revived upon the dishonour of the instrument, at which point the holder may opt to sue either on the instrument or the underlying debt.[109] UCC Article 3 specifically excepts instruments drawn by regulated financial instruments, which are deemed to absolutely discharge the debt for which the instrument is given.[110]

1.34 A specific practice involving bills used in international trade is that of bills in a set. This practice is carried out when bills are mailed with the view of avoiding delay. With the decline of the use of mail in international trade, the use of the practice has been significantly reduced. It is governed by BEA s 71, UBL arts 64–66 and UCL arts 49–50. Thereunder, the instrument is drawn in a set of two identical parts, to be numbered and to refer to each other, and yet to constitute one bill. To minimize risks of delay, misdelivery, and loss in transit, each part is mailed separately and may operate as a separate bill, so that a signer is liable on each part he or she accepted or indorsed. Only the drawer is to sign on each part and is liable on the whole bill; however, the drawer is discharged when he or she pays any part duly presented to him or her. The holder in due course (or lawful holder) whose title accrues first is the true owner entitled to part with acceptance. The owner is the holder in due course (or lawful holder) whose title accrues first; but discharge is upon payment or acceptance of the part first presented. An acceptor who pays on an unaccepted part is not discharged. Otherwise, discharge of any part is discharge of bill.

D. Laws of Bills and Notes: Major Substantive Differences

1.35 Negotiable instruments law represents a delicate balance between the holder's expectation to recover and the reasonable expectations of the signatories. To that end, the law emphasizes form, as well as text, uniformity, and brevity in order to secure predictability. At the same time, for reasons based on local conditions, the impact of local general law, and even accident, variations are rampant.

1.36 Even on its own, Anglo-American law of bills, notes, and cheques is far from uniform. Particularly, American law, having derived from English law and tradition, nevertheless settled down in its own unique course,[111] and is not completely uniform. The Canadian Act, though closely modelled on its English counterpart, is nonetheless not identical to it. For example, it contains provisions undermining the power to acquire rights free from prior parties' defences in instruments issued for patent[112] and consumer[113] transactions. Additionally, the various Geneva Conventions national

[109] *Re Charge Card Services Ltd.* [1989] Ch 497, [1988] 3 All ER 702 [707] (CA).
[110] UCC § 3-310.
[111] A scholarly detailed discussion is by A Barak, 'The Uniform Commercial Code—Commercial Paper: An Outsider's View' (1968) 3 Isr LR, Part I 7; Part II 184.
[112] CBEA ss 13–15.
[113] CBEA Part V.

statutes may not be identical. Accordingly, in connection with an international instrument, the application of a particular law is not a matter of indifference.

Among the Anglo-American systems, only American law effectively equates the position of the holder not in due course to that of an assignee of a debt.[114] Furthermore, under UCC § 3-602, other than in connection with a stolen instrument and wrongful possession, knowledge by a payer of a third party's adverse claim does not preclude discharge. This is contrary to the less protective BEA s 59(1), under which a discharging payment to the holder must be made 'in good faith and without notice that his title to the bill is defective'. The UCC is unique[115] in imposing on a signer,[116] as well as a bank customer,[117] duties of care, and in addressing detailed scenarios in which fraud losses are allocated to parties who are presumed to be able to prevent them.[118] On the other hand, both American and Canadian laws do not provide for particular defences for non-negligent and bona fide banks handling instruments,[119] particularly cheques.[120] **1.37**

Several fundamental dissimilarities exist between an Anglo-American and a Geneva Convention derived statute. Following Cowen and Gering, there are ten major differences:[121] **1.38**

1. In continental Europe, a bill is primarily a payment mechanism, while in the Anglo-American system bills and cheques have developed into a paper currency.
2. In the Anglo-American system, unlike the Continental one, commercial law (including the law of bills and notes) is part of the general law binding all persons and administered by the ordinary courts.
3. A fundamental principle of the Anglo-American system is that no person may acquire a good title to a bill or note, and in fact be a 'holder',[122] under or through a forged (including unauthorized) indorsement.[123] Furthermore, a discharging

[114] UCC § 3-305. The position of a holder not in due course under the BEA is better: *Lamont (James) & Co. v Hyland Ltd* [1950] 1 KB 585, [1950] 1 All ER 341 (CA).

[115] A notable BEA exception following the UCC at least in part is SABEA s 72B requiring a limited category of bank customers to 'exercise reasonable care in the custody of cheque forms and in the reconciliation of its bank statements'.

[116] UCC § 3-406.

[117] UCC § 4-406.

[118] See UCC § 3-404 (impostors; fictitious payees); § 3-405 (employer's responsibility for fraudulent indorsement by employee).

[119] BEA s 60.

[120] For example, s 4 in the UK Cheques Act 1992, c 32 (as amended by the Cheques Act 1992) (hereafter UK Cheques Act).

[121] Cowen and Gering, *Negotiable Instruments* 124–31. In more detail see Ellinger, 'Negotiable Instruments' 86–159. See also WG Crauford, 'Differences between the English and the German Law Relating to Negotiable Instruments' (1957) 6 ILCQ 418. For earlier discussions see eg EG Lorenzen, *The Conflict of Laws Relating to Bills and Notes* (Yale University Press 1919) 17–58; M Hudson and AH Feller, 'The International Unification of Laws Concerning Bills of Exchange' (1930) 44 Harv L Rev 333, 346–70; HC Gutteridge, 'The Unification of the Rules of Conflict Relating to Negotiable Instruments' (1934) 16 J Comp Legis & Int'l L 53.

[122] Other than the payee, a holder must take by 'negotiation', which in turn, for a bill payable to order, must be made by a previous holder (BEA s 31(3); UCC § 3-201(b)), which the taker under a forged indorsement, not himself taking from a holder, is not.

[123] BEA s 24; UCC § 3-403.

payment must be to the 'holder'[124] and hence not to a taker under or through a forged indorsement. In contrast, under UBL art. 16 '[t]he possessor of a bill ... is deemed to be the lawful holder if he establishes his title to the bill through an uninterrupted series of endorsements'. As long as such a possessor 'has [not] acquired it in bad faith, or ... been guilty of gross negligence', he 'is not bound to give up the bill' to a person who had been dispossessed of it. Under UBL art. 40, upon receiving payment, such a possessor gives discharge to a payer who 'has [not] been guilty of fraud or gross negligence', while not being required to be without knowledge of the adverse claim. To obtain the discharge, the payer 'is bound to verify the regularity of the series of endorsements, but not the signature of the endorsers'.

4. Unlike the Anglo-American holder in due course,[125] the Continental counterpart, the lawful holder,[126] needs not take the instrument for value in order to qualify for the elevated status. Furthermore, the latter's freedom from claims of ownership is not related to his or her freedom from equities of defences, and vice-versa. Each freedom is unrelated to the other. While freedom from adverse claims hinges under UBL art. 16 on lack of bad faith and gross negligence, freedom from contract defences is given under UBL art. 17 to a holder who 'has [not] knowingly acted to the detriment of the debtor'. The holder's elevated position is then not an 'all or nothing' situation as is that of the Anglo-American holder in due course.[127] As well, the 'good faith' concept, specifically required by the BEA[128] and UCC[129] for the acquisition of holding in due course status, may not be identical in the Anglo-American and UBL systems.[130]
4. Formal requirements as to the definitions of various instruments are more detailed, specific, and rigid in the UBL[131] than in the Anglo-American statutes.[132] For example, in the former but not the latter, the instrument must actually be described on its face as being a bill of exchange or promissory note. Also, unlike the Anglo-American system, the Geneva Convention requires a bill and note to include statements as to the designated place for payment, and the date and place of issue.[133] Grisoli goes as far as to argue that 'English law and the Uniform Law appear irreconcilably divided on formal requirements'.[134]
5. The adherence of English law to the doctrine of consideration required the inclusion in Anglo-American statutes of provisions and presumptions as to value.[135] In

[124] BEA s 59(1); UCC § 3-602(e).
[125] BEA s 29(1)(b): UCC § 3-302(a)(2).
[126] UBL art 16.
[127] BEA s 38(2); UCC § 3-305(b).
[128] BEA s 29(1)(b).
[129] UCC § 3-302(a)(2).
[130] A point addressed by Cowen and Gering, *Negotiable Instruments* 127–28 and n 89. In fact, 'good faith' is defined differently under the BEA s 90 and the UCC § 1-201(b)(20)).
[131] UBL arts 1 and 75.
[132] BEA ss 3(1) and 83(1): UCC § 3-104.
[133] For a detailed discussion see Ellinger, 'Negotiable Instruments' 89–103.
[134] A Grisoli, 'Uniform Law of Bills of Exchange from the Standpoint of Anglo-American Law' (1958–59) 33 Tul L Rev 289, 291. He also argues (in my view unpersuasively) to a fundamental difference in the theory of liability at 293–96.
[135] Such as BEA ss 27 and 30; UCC § 3-303.

contrast, the Continental adherence to 'causa'[136] did not require corresponding provisions in the Geneva Conventions.

6. The Anglo-American system is more flexible than its Geneva Conventions counterpart. An example of this 'elasticity' or 'flexibility' is the widespread use of the word 'reasonable' in the governing statute, as in connection with the time to present a bill payable 'at sight' under BEA s 40.[137] In contrast, the word does not appear in the UBL.
8. The UBL requires a bill,[138] as well as a note,[139] to be payable either to a named payee or to the order of a named payee. In contrast to both the BEA[140] and the UCC,[141] and interestingly, even to the UCL with respect to cheques,[142] the UBL does not allow a valid bill or note to be made out *initially*, as opposed to being subsequently indorsed,[143] payable to bearer.
9. The Geneva regime treats cheques in a separate convention and not as part of the general statute governing bills and notes as in the Anglo-American system.
10. Under the UBL, upon the dishonour of an instrument, formal authentication in the form of 'protest', is required.[144] Under the BEA, protest is required for a foreign instrument and is optional otherwise.[145] Protest procedure exists under the UCC[146] but is entirely optional.[147] It should be added that the unexcused failure to give a notice of dishonour or default to a secondary party discharges that party under the BEA[148] and the UCC[149] but not under the UBL, under which the failure may nevertheless result in liability for loss.[150]

An additional major difference concerns the 'avalist', who is a party to an instrument under the UBL[151] with no direct parallel in the BEA,[152] other than in South Africa.[153] A much less significant difference is that both the UBL[154] and the BEA[155] (but not the **1.39**

[136] For 'causa', or cause, as reason or grounds for the binding effect of an informal contract in Roman and civil law see in general A Berger, *Encyclopedic Dictionary of Roman Law* (American Philosophical Society, 1953) 382.

[137] See also 'reasonable certainty' in BEA ss 6 and 7; 'reasonable time' in s 20, 'reasonable hour' and 'reasonable diligence' in s 41. The word is also used in BEA ss 45, 46, 49, 50, 51, 74, and 86.

[138] UBL art 1(6).

[139] ibid, art 75(5).

[140] BEA s 3(1).

[141] UCC § 3–104(1).

[142] UCL art 5.

[143] UBL art 12.

[144] ibid, art 44.

[145] BEA s 51.

[146] UCC § 3-505(b).

[147] See Official Comment 2 to UCC § 3-414; Official Comment to § 3-505. In Chapter V of this book, we will say much more on the 'protest' requirement, its origins and relevancy in nowadays reality. See Chapter V section A(2).

[148] BEA ss 48 and 50.

[149] UCC §§ 3-503 and 3-504.

[150] UBL art 45(6).

[151] ibid, arts 30–32.

[152] Cf BEA s 56, stranger signing bill is liable as indorser.

[153] SABEA s 54A.

[154] BEA s 71.

[155] UBL arts 64–66.

UCC) contain rules on instruments issued in a set of two or more identical parts. Only the UBL[156] provides for a case in which a copy supersedes an original.

1.40 Among all these, the two principal areas of difference are those relating to formal requisites and the effect of forged indorsements.

E. Laws of Cheques: Major Substantive Differences[157]

1.41 A cheque is a written unconditional order, addressed to a bank, to pay on demand a sum certain in money. In practice, a bank customer draws it on funds (or against a line of credit) available to the drawer/customer with the drawee bank. As a rule, the cheque is a negotiable instrument, transferable by delivery, with indorsement where it is not payable to the bearer. The holder presents a cheque for payment to the drawee bank either directly or through a collecting bank acting as the holder's agent. The cheque collection machinery is a debit–transfer payment system. Having originated as a paper-based, manually handled mechanism, the cheque collection machinery has become, to some degree or another, automated, with the cheque itself being gradually more and more 'electronified'.

1.42 The current form of the cheque as an instruction or mandate, and the contemporary interbank cheque collection machinery, have their origins in the seventeenth-century goldsmith system in England.[158]

1.43 In civil law countries, cheques are governed by statutes modelled on the 1931 Geneva UCL. This is currently so in France, Germany, Italy, Japan, and Switzerland. The various national statues are nonetheless not identical. In common law jurisdictions, including others that have been under strong British influence, the model statute is the 1882 English BEA, which treats the cheque as a specie of a bill. In the UK, a specific statute concerning cheques supplements the BEA. In Canada, the BEA is federal, so as to be applicable also in the civil law province of Quebec. Other non-common law jurisdictions that passed the BEA include South Africa, Sri Lanka, and Israel. Australia has a specific statute governing cheques, which is nonetheless drawn on the English BEA model. National statutes in all such jurisdictions, particularly in Canada,[159] contain local variations. In the various jurisdictions of the USA, cheques, as negotiable instruments, are governed by Article 3 of the UCC. Cheque deposits and collections are further governed by Article 4 of the UCC, as pre-empted or supplemented by federal law, particularly in dealing with the availability of funds.

156 ibid, arts 67–68.

157 For a detailed discussion, see B Geva, *Bank Collections and Payment Transactions* (Oxford University Press 2011) 131–85.

158 See eg M Vasseur and X Marin, *Le Cheque* (Sibey 1969) 9–11. For the origins and early development of cheques in England, see eg JM Holden, *The History of Negotiable Instruments in English Law* (The Athlone Press 1955; reprinted by Wm W Gaunt & Sons Inc 1993) 204–43.

159 N Wolfe, 'Cheques and Cheque Legislation in the UK and Canada: Separate Paths in the Past, Converging Paths in the Future?' (2012) 28 BFLR 47.

Much of cheques law is concerned with the instruments themselves.[160] However, both the drawer and the depositor of a cheque are bank customers and both their respective banks participate in the cheque collection and payment process. Not surprisingly, the law of cheques as instruments is not always easily separable from the law governing the banking relationship as it applies to cheques. For example, vis-à-vis its customer, the drawee bank will not be discharged unless it pays the cheque to the one entitled to obtain payment, as determined under the law governing cheques as instruments. **1.44**

Fundamental differences between the UCL and the BEA/UCC systems follow those between the UBL and the BEA/UCC systems discussed in section D for bills and notes. They thus concern the effect of a forged indorsement,[161] formal requirements,[162] and aspects relating to acquisition[163] and scope of a superior title defeating adverse claims and prior parties' defences. [164] Other significant differences between the two major cheque systems concern the avalist,[165] and consideration versus causa.[166] At the same time, protest under the UCL is optional.[167] **1.45**

The following is a concise overview of specific distinguishing features of cheques under the various national laws, dovetailed by a discussion on the varied treatment of cheque electronification: **1.46**

1. A cheque is universally defined as an unconditional order in writing, of a drawer, directed to a drawee bank, to pay on demand (or 'at sight') a sum certain in money.[168] The most important local variation is the requirement under the UCL that the term 'cheque' be included. Also under the UCL, a cheque must be drawn on a banker holding funds at the drawer's disposal, but is nonetheless a 'cheque' notwithstanding the violation of this requirement.[169] There is no uniformity among the various jurisdictions as to the definition of 'banker' or 'bank'. [170] In departure from other statutes, UCC § 3-414(b) treats the liability of the drawer of a cheque as primary, which upon dishonour eases the procedural requirements fastened on a holder.
2. UCC Article 3 in the USA and the BEA in the UK, as well as statutes modelled on the BEA, such as in Canada,[171] Israel,[172] and South Africa,[173] but not in Australia,

[160] For a comparative study, as part of the law of bills and notes in general, particularly see Ellinger, 'Negotiable Instruments' 160–75.
[161] UCL arts 19 and 21. However, in the UCL there is no parallel to UBL art 40(2), protecting a payer, as long as he or she 'has [not] been guilty of fraud or gross negligence'.
[162] UCL art 1.
[163] ibid, art 19. Neither a forged indorsement nor lack of value will preclude a superior title.
[164] ibid, arts 19 and 22.
[165] ibid, arts 25–27.
[166] At the same time none of the three statutes address a copied cheque.
[167] UCL art 40.
[168] See eg BEA ss 3(1) and 73 in the UK; UCC § 3-104(f) in the USA and art 1 in the UCL.
[169] UCL arts 1 and 3.
[170] See review by Ellinger, 'Negotiable Instruments' 161–62.
[171] CBEA.
[172] IBEO.
[173] SABEA.

govern cheques, side by side with bills (or drafts) and notes. Australia has a separate statute dedicated to cheques,[174] while selected cheque aspects are dealt with in the UK under a specific statute.[175] Statutes in civil law countries such as Germany,[176] Italy,[177] Japan,[178] Switzerland,[179] and France[180] follow the UCL.

3. Specific legislation dealing with the collection and payment of cheques exists only in the USA.[181]
4. Short periods within which a cheque must be presented for payment are prescribed in civil law countries.[182] Under the BEA, presentment must be made within reasonable time after the issue of the cheque, though under some circumstances delay may be excused.[183] Under UCC § 4-404, a bank is 'under no obligation ... to pay [an uncertified] check ... which is presented more than six months after its date'.
5. Certification of cheques resulting in the liability of the drawee bank to the holder is recognized in the USA,[184] Canada,[185] France,[186] Italy,[187] Japan,[188] and South Africa.[189] Certification is precluded in Germany[190] other than for cheques drawn on the central bank. [191] In Canada, the practice is not backed by any specific statutory provision. In both Canada and the USA, cheque certification is analysed as a form of acceptance of the cheque. In line with the provisions of the UCL,[192] this mode of analysis is precluded in France, Italy, Japan, and Germany. In Canada and the USA certification involves the actual withdrawal of funds from the drawer's account and their placement in a suspense account, pending presentment for payment. Elsewhere, certification may involve the holding or blocking of funds by the drawee bank in the drawer's account for the short period within which a cheque must be presented. In fact, cheque certification is not practised in Japan and Italy. Under the UCC, a certified cheque is part of a broader category of cheques

[174] Cheques Act 1986 (last amended by Act No 61, 2016) (hereafter Australia Cheques Act).

[175] UK Cheques Act.

[176] Cheques Act (Scheckgesetz) of 14 Aug 1933, RGBI. I 597, last amended by ordinance of 31 Aug 2015 BGBI. I p 1474 (hereafter Germany Cheques Act).

[177] RD 21 December 1933, n 1736, as supplemented by L. 15 December 1990, n 386 (hereafter Italy Cheques Law).

[178] Law on Cheques 1933, Law No 57 of 29 July 1933 (as amended by Law No 61 of 1991) (hereafter Japan Cheques Law).

[179] CC 220 Federal Act of 30 March 1911 on the Amendment of the Swiss Civil Code (Part V: The Code of Obligations) arts 1100–44 (hereafter Swiss Cheques Law).

[180] French Cheques Law.

[181] UCC Article 4.

[182] UCL art 29.

[183] BEA s 46(1).

[184] UCC § 3-409.

[185] See eg *Maubach v Bank of Nova Scotia* (1987) 60 OR (2d) 189 (HCJ), affd (1987) 62 OR (2d) 220; and *A.E. Le Page Real Estate Services Ltd. v Rattray Publications* (1991) 5 OR (3d) 216 (Gen Div), affd. (1995), 21 OR (3d) 164 (CA). See in general B Geva, 'Irrevocability of Bank Drafts, Certified Cheques and Money Orders' (1986) 65 Can Bar Rev 107, 123.

[186] French Cheques Law art 4 (1935) art L 131-5 (2000).

[187] Italy Cheques Law art 4(2).

[188] Japan Cheques Law arts 53–58.

[189] SABEA s 72A.

[190] The prohibition to certify cheques is considered as derived from art 4 of the Germany Cheques Act, modelled on art 4 of the UCL, precluding the acceptance of a cheque.

[191] See s 23 of the Deutsche Bundesbank Act of 26 July 1957, BGBI. I 745.

[192] UCL art 4.

on which a bank is obligated,[193] such as cashier's cheques (on which the drawer and drawee are the same banks) and teller's cheques (on which the drawer and the drawee are two separate banks).[194] Italian Cheque Law provides in arts 82–83 for circular cheques issued by banks, each carrying with it the issuing bank's 'unconditional promise' to pay. UCC Article 3 also covers the '[t]raveller's check'.[195]

6. Cheques are payable 'on demand'[196] or 'at sight'[197] all of which are pretty much interchangebale terms designed so show that cheques are not credit instruments to be made payable at a future time. Under UCL art 28, '[a]ny contrary stipulation is not recgonized'. Post-dating, namely dating a cheque later than its date of issue with the intent that it will not be presented for payment until the date the cheque bears, is accordingly ignored in civil law countries, except for determining the end of the statutory mandated period within which cheques must be presented.[198] Post-dating is not recognized in the USA, but could be given effect by temporary stop-payment orders.[199] Case law recognized cheque post-dating under the BEA[200] so that payment by the drawee bank prior to the ostensible date of the cheque is wrongful.
7. Countermand of payment (namely, ordering stop payment) of cheques is recognized under the BEA[201] as well as in the USA.[202] Under UCL art 32, a cheque countermand is effective only after 'the expiration of the limit of time for presentment'. In France, inasmuch as it transfers the cover to the payee, the cheque is irrevocable and hence uncountermandable. In Australia, the statute invalidates any agreement purporting to negate the right to countermand payment altogether.[203]
8. Notice of the customer's death revokes the drawee bank's duty and authority to pay cheques under the BEA,[204] as well as in the USA.[205] In both Australia[206] and the USA,[207] revocation does not become fully effective until ten days after the receipt of the notice of death by the bank. The drawee bank's duty and authority to pay a cheque drawn by its customer also comes to an end upon receiving notice of the customer's bankruptcy in Israel;[208] mental incapacity in Australia;[209] and the adjudication of incompetence in the USA.[210] Similar events terminate the bank's

[193] UCC § 3-411.
[194] See definitions in UCC § 3-104.
[195] For a definition see UCC § 3-104(b)(e) in conjunction with § 3-104(a).
[196] BEA s 73 and UCC § 3-104(f). The US spelling is 'check'.
[197] UCL art 28.
[198] ibid, art 29.
[199] UCC § 4-401(c).
[200] See eg *Shapiro et al v Greenstein* (1969) 10 DLR (3d) 746 (Que CA). Under ACSS Rule A1 s 10 '[n]o Item that is post-dated shall be Exchanged, for the purpose of Clearing and Settlement'.
[201] BEA s 75. The effect of s 75A is to extend the right to Scotland, notwithstanding the effect of BEA s 53(2), discussed in the text accompanying n 96.
[202] UCC § 4-403.
[203] Australia Cheques Act s 6(2).
[204] BEA s 75.
[205] UCC § 4-405.
[206] Australia Cheques Act s 90(2).
[207] UCC § 4-405.
[208] IBEO s 75.
[209] Australia Cheques Act s 90(2).
[210] UCC § 4-405.

authority to pay in South Africa.[211] In contrast, under UCL art 33, neither the death of the drawer nor his or her incapacity, occurring after the issue of the cheque, have any effect with regards to the cheque.

9. The wrongful dishonour of a cheque by the drawee bank, notwithstanding the availability of cover in the customer's account (either in the form of credit balance or due to an overdraft facility), is actionable by the customer in all jurisdictions. In the UK, substantial damages for injury to credit may be awarded to the customer without proof of actual damage.[212] Conversely, under the UCC, a drawee bank 'is liable to its customer for damages proximately caused by the wrongful dishonor of an item'. However, in principle, '[l]iability is limited to actual damages proved'.[213] In France, a wrongfully dishonouring drawee bank becomes liable to the drawer for any resulting damages.[214]
10. As a negotiable instrument, the cheque is payable to order or, in contrast to a bill or note under the UBL, also to bearer.[215] It is transferable by 'negotiation',[216] namely delivery, and, other than a cheque payable to bearer, with the transferor's indorsement.[217] Upon compliance with specified conditions[218] a transferee by negotiation may take the cheque free from adverse claims and prior parties' defences.[219] There is no consensus as to the transferability of a cheque other than by negotiation and in some jurisdictions, the question may be unsettled. Thus, under BEA s 8(1), a bill containing words prohibiting transfer, or indicating an intention that it should not be transferable, 'is valid as between the parties thereto' but 'is not negotiable'. While under the BEA, a cheque is a type of bill,[220] it was doubted in *National Bank v Silke*[221] whether BEA s 8(1) applies to cheques. A hundred years later, in 1992, the UK amended the BEA by passing s 81A, stating that a crossed cheque bearing across its face the words 'account payee', or 'a/c payee', with or without the word 'only', 'shall not be transferable, but shall only be valid as between the parties thereto'. South Africa followed suit albeit with some modifications.[222] No other BEA jurisdiction passed a similar amendment. Conversely, under s 39 of the Australian Cheques Act, until it is discharged, and 'notwithstanding anything written or placed on the cheque', '[e]very cheque is transferable by negotiation'. Arguably, restrictions on the transferability or negotiability of cheques are to be disregarded in the USA.[223] For its part, UCL art 14(2) covers

211 SABEA s 73.

212 *Kpohraror v Woolwich Building Society* [1996] 2 LRC 526, [1996] 4 All ER 119 (CA).

213 UCC § 4-402(b).

214 French Cheques Law s 65(2) (1935); art 131-70(2) (2000).

215 BEA s 8(2); UCL art 5; UCC § 3-104(a). There is no consensus as to a cheque payable to a name payee rather than to that person's order.

216 BEA s 31; UCL art 14(1) (with respect to cheques not payable to the bearer); UCC § 3-201. Surprisingly, the term does not appear at the UBL.

217 BEA s 2; UCL art 16; UCC § 3-204.

218 BEA s 29(1); UCL arts 21–22; UCC § 3-302.

219 BEA (s 38(2); UCL arts 19 and 22; UCC § 3-305.

220 BEA s 73.

221 [1891] 1 QB 435.

222 SABEA s 75A.

223 In fact, UCC Article 3 is silent as to restrictions on transferability other than by the omission of the word 'order', which is to be disregarded. Arguably, however, the combined effect of § 3-104(c) and (d), at least by implication, is that in connection with cheques, any restriction on transferability, and not only on

a cheque 'made payable to a specified person, in which the words "not to order" or any equivalent expression have been inserted' and provides that such a cheque 'can only be transferred according to the form and with the effects of an ordinary assignment'. In Italy, the statute provides for cheques marked 'non-transferable' to be payable only to the payee.[224]

11. In principle, cheques are payable to the holder by the drawee bank either in cash over the counter, or to the holder's bank account. Restrictions on payment, either in cash or to non-customers, can be imposed by using either 'payable in account' or crossed cheques. Both forms are recognized in the UCL.[225] Only cheque crossing is provided under the BEA.[226] Neither payable in account cheques nor cheque crossing exist in the USA. Crossed cheques are recognized[227] but not used in Canada. With regards to civil law countries, crossed cheques are not recognized in Germany,[228] while cheques payable in account are not provided for in Japan[229] and France.[230] Both forms exist in Switzerland.[231]
12. A short six-month limitation period, running from the expiration of the time limit prescribed for presentment, is provided for by UCL art 52. In the USA, an action to enforce liability on a cheque is barred three years after the dishonour of the cheque or ten years after its date, whichever comes first.[232] No limitation period is prescribed under cheque or negotiable instrument legislation in common law jurisdictions, and the matter may be governed in each place by general law. In Canada[233] and the USA,[234] until presentment for payment, the holder's action against the drawee of a certified cheque is not barred by any limitation period. After presentment, the holder's action is barred in the USA after three years. In Japan,[235] an action on a certified cheque is barred one year after the expiration of the ten-day presentment period.

negotiability (in the sense of passability free of any defence or adverse claim into the hands of a holder in due course), is ineffective.

[224] Italy Cheques Law art 43.
[225] UCL arts 37–39.
[226] BEA ss 76–82.
[227] CBEA ss 168–175.
[228] While the provisions relating to crossed cheques are included in the Cheques Act, they are not in force. According to art 1 sentence 2 of the Introductory Act on the Cheques Act of 14 Aug 1933, RGBI. I 605, 'articles 37, 38 [of the Germany Cheques Act] on the crossed cheque enter into force only at a later point of time which will be determined by the Imperial Minister of Justice'. So far, the provisions have not been proclaimed in force. Nor is such proclamation expected to take place in the foreseeable future. A crossed cheque issued outside Germany is treated as a cheque payable in account. Whether a domestic crossed cheque is to be treated either similarly, or like an ordinary cheque, payable in cash, has not been settled.
[229] Where crossed cheques are recognized in Japan Cheques Law arts 37–38.
[230] Foreign cheques payable in account are treated as crossed cheques. Japan Cheques Law arts 37–39.
[231] Swiss Cheques Law arts 1123–27.
[232] See UCC §§ 3-401(a), 3-414(b) (together with Official Comment 2, characterizing the drawer's liability, in departure of former law, as primary), and 3-118(c) (together with Official Comment 3).
[233] This is so with respect to Canadian funds cheques, of $500 or more, certified by chartered banks. See Bank Act, SC 1991, c 46, s 438 and Bank of Canada Act, RSC 1985, c B-2, s 22(1) as amended by SC 1991, c 46, ss 582 and 583; SC 1991, c 48, s 494; SC 1997, c 15, s 100; SC 1999, c 28, s 97; SC 2001, c 9, s 196; SC 2007 c 6, s 394; SC 2012, c 5, s 183. See B Geva, 'Lost Cheques, Certification and Countermand—Is the Law Satisfactory?' (1987–8), 2 BFLR 357.
[234] UCC § 3-118(d).
[235] Japan Cheques Law arts 53–58 in conjunction with art 29.

13. The collection and payment of cheques into a bank account held at a bank other than the drawee bank is universally governed by interbank clearing rules. Such rules constitute an interbank agreement, binding and benefiting subscribing participating banks. The degree to which clearing rules indirectly bind or benefit bank customers, namely, the drawer and depositor of a cheque, is not uniform. In the USA, clearing rules are stated by statute to bind and inure to the benefit of parties not specifically assenting to them, such as bank customers.[236]
14. In the USA only, there are statutory rules dealing with the time a cheque is 'paid', in the context of the failure to timely return it dishonoured.[237]

F. Conclusion

1.47 'Negotiability' has been the glue uniting three different types of financial instruments used domestically and internationally into one branch of law. Expediencies of commerce militate in favour of similar solutions to the diverse issues that have arisen in connection with the use of these instruments. At the same time, concrete solutions have strongly been flavoured with, if not anchored in, the various legal systems within which instruments have evolved. Thus, there exists a need for choice-of-law rules to ensure the smooth operation of international trade. Before moving to the analysis of these rules, the ensuing chapter will establish the basic thesis as to the variations amongst laws as premised on the diverse roots of these instruments in different localities, under various legal systems, and by references to different uses.

236 UCC § 4-103(b).
237 ibid, §§ 4-215 and 4-302.

II
General Law and Negotiable Instruments
A Brief Historical Perspective

A. Introductory Note[1]

Together with orders for withdrawals, payment orders addressed and issued by payers directly to depositaries and instructing them to pay identified payees go back to Mesopotamia,[2] Ancient Greece,[3] and Ancient Rome.[4] Unique payment orders issued by payers to payees and payable by the depositaries upon their presentment by respective holders, or non-transferable cheques, came later. They are traced to Ptolemaic Egypt,[5] but their use was eclipsed in Egypt in the course of the Roman **2.01**

[1] A detailed discussion is available in B Geva, *The Payment Order of Antiquity and the Middle Ages: A Legal History* (Hart Publishing 2011).

[2]. R Bogaert, *Les Origines antiques de la banque de dépôt* (AW Sijthoff 1966) (hereafter Bogaert, *Les Origines*). Roughly speaking, at 41–129, Bogaert surveys a period extending over 1,500 years commencing at the end of the twenty-first century BCE.

[3] R Bogaert, *Banques et banquiers dans les cités grecques* (AW Sijthoff 1968) 50–60, 331–45; ibid, 130–58; EE Cohen, *Athean Economy and Society: A Banking Perspective* (Princeton University Press 1992) 8–11, 14–18, 62–66, 111–21.

[4] See J Andreau, *Banking and Business in the Roman World* (trans by J Lloyd, Cambridge University Press 1999) 561–83.

[5] RS Bagnall and R Bogaert, 'Orders for Payment from A Banker's Archive: Papyri in the Collection of Florida State University' (1975) in R Bogaert (ed), *Trapezitica Aegyptiaca, Recueil de recherches sur la banque en Égypte Gréco-Romaine* (Edizioni Gonelli 1994) 129 (hereafter Bogaert, *Trapezitica*); and R Bogaert, 'Note sur l'emploi du chèque dans l'Égypte ptolémaïque' (1983) in *Trapezitica*; ibid 245.

period.[6] As will be discussed, legal doctrine underlying the cheque goes back to the Talmud and the Islamic *hawale*. The Islamic *suftaj* may have heralded the Continental bill of exchange.

2.02 In terms of continuity, both the cheque and bill, as we know them, started as Continental Medieval instruments governed by legal principles adapted from Roman law. Cheques originated in domestic transactions; bills originated in international payments. Notes may have been inspired by earlier instruments; however, as we know them, together with cheques, notes go back to the post-Medieval English banking system.

2.03 There are common themes to the evolution of the various instruments in different eras in diverse places. They point to a common denominator in issues and solutions, rather than to the existence of 'foreign' or 'imported' legal principles and concepts into each legal system to shape the law of these instruments.

2.04 *First*, needs of commerce and available technology, rather than interests of rulers and states, have continuously shaped this evolution in each era and locality and under each legal system. *Second*, each of the three instruments, the bill, cheque, and note, evolved on its own, within its own domestic legal system. Similar questions relating to liability and transferability that dominated the discussion were resolved in each system on its own terms—even if given solutions were, to one degree or another, influenced by those reached in other systems. But there has not been a universal 'law merchant' under which governing principles evolved and moved from one system to another. *Third*, autonomy of parties has been an underlying factor in each legal system in facilitating the development of obligations under each instrument and the law applicable. General principles of contract and property have been the building materials in the construction of this law. *Fourth*, in the development of the instruments and the law governing them, the emergence of 'negotiability', and its evolution into a unifying factor in a body of law governing them, is quite late.

B. Nascent Cheque Law Without Cheques Under the Talmud

2.05 The *Talmud* quotes Rav Huna to say in Rav's name that if a payer-debtor instructs his or her own debtor (drawee) to give the money owed (by the drawee to the instruction giver) to the instruction giver's creditor, the latter thereby acquires the right to that money.[7] This is, however, true only as long as all three of them are present together at the time the instruction is given. The payer-debtor thus pays his or her debt to the payee-creditor by conferring on him or her the right to the money owed by the

[6] For a cheque from Roman Egypt from 125 BCE, giving rise to a dispute involving the unavailability of funds to cover payment, see R Bogaert, 'Recherches sur la banque en Égypte Gréco-Romaine' (1987) in *Trapezitica* 6, 23.

[7] Talmud, *Gitin* 13A. Unless specifically indicated otherwise, all Jewish law sources cited and discussed in this book are in Hebrew (or Hebrew-Aramaic).

drawee. This mode of acquisition by the creditor of the right to the money owed by the drawee is known in Talmudic law as '*ma-amad shloshtam*'—'in the presence of all three', or 'presence-of-all-three', declaration.

2.06 One post-Talmudic disputation is concerned with the discharge accorded to the payer-debtor towards the payee-creditor by the presence-of-all-three declaration. On the basis of an extract from the *Jerusalem Talmud*,[8] one view supports an absolute discharge so that upon the default of the drawee, no recourse is available to the payee-creditor against the payer-debtor.[9] The other supports a conditional discharge,[10] so that, upon the default of the drawee, recourse from the payer-debtor is available to the payee-creditor.[11]

2.07 Involving a situation in which all three are present, the case demonstrates the importance of consent in leading to its legal implications. However, in the facts of the case, it remains unclear whether the drawee is required to act on the basis of the payer-debtor's instruction communicated to him or her by the payer-debtor (albeit in the presence of the payee-creditor) or whether the drawee is required to act on the basis of that instruction as it is communicated to him or her by the payee-creditor (albeit in the presence of the payer-debtor). Only in the latter case do we have a cheque.

2.08 A case closer to a cheque transaction is in *Bava Metzia*. The *Mishna* discusses a scenario in which an employer ('debtor'), having owed his or her worker ('creditor') wages, directs the worker to receive payment from a storekeeper or money-changer ('drawee').[12] The *Gemara* asks whether the worker has recourse against the employer or not. Rav Shesheth does not allow the recourse, while Rabbah permits it.[13]

2.09 *Tosafot* lays down two alternative scenarios in which, in the absence of either a formal act of acquisition[14] or express absolute renunciation[15] by the creditor, the recourse controversy could arise.[16] The first scenario is that of the worker's *absolute* renunciation,

[8] Jerusalem Talmud, *Kiddushin*, Section 3, Rule 4.

[9] Nimukei Yoseph, D'H 'Yerushalmi' commenting on the Rif on Talmud, *Bava Metzia* 68B (of Rif's page numbering).

[10] Baal Ha-Itur, Section 5, 'Hamcha-a', as expanded by the Tur, *Chosen Mishpat* Section 126.

[11] See Shulchan Aruch, *Choshen Mishpat*, Section 126, Rule 9.

[12] Talmud, *Bava Metzia* 111A.

[13] ibid 112A.

[14] Such acts include pulling, transferring, controlling, lifting, or exchanging an article. See, in general, A Steinsaltz, *The Talmud-The Steinsaltz Edition—A Reference Guide* (Random House 1989) 254. According to Tosafot, even Rabbah would agree that renunciation accompanied by such an act is effective to generate a discharge so that recourse has been lost.

[15] An express absolute renunciation affects an absolute discharge and eliminates any recourse. Talmud, *Kiddushin* 16A, cited by Tosafot in Talmud, *Bava Metzia* 112A D'H 'Hozer'. According to Tosafot, where an express release of the employer by the worker is stated to be conditional on the drawee's default, even Rav Shesheth agrees that recourse against the employer becomes available to the worker at least as of the default of the drawee.

[16] A third sub-scenario, under which the recourse does not relate to the underlying debt owed to the worker but rather to the remedy for the violation of the prohibition against delaying payment, is not relevant to the present discussion and is thus not elaborated on here.

implied from his or her reliance on the drawee. The alternative scenario is that of the worker's *express* renunciation, *conditional* on payment made by the drawee.

2.10 In *Tosafot*'s view, an absolute release of the employer-debtor by the worker is possible in the context of the *first scenario* when the drawee assumes, towards the worker, an implied, albeit binding and irrevocable, obligation guaranteeing that of the employer. *Nimukei Yoseph*[17] explains the binding effect or irrevocability of the drawee's implied guarantee as premised on the nature of the storekeeper's or moneychanger's calling. In invalidating the renunciation and allowing recourse under the alternative scenario, that of the worker's express renunciation that is *conditional* on payment made by the drawee, Rabbah is taken to hold that renunciation is mistaken since it is based on contingent and hence unknown facts as to whether the drawee will honour his or her undertaking to pay.[18]

2.11 The final ruling in Jewish law treats the *Bava Metzia* text as relating to the *second scenario*—that of an *express conditional* discharge pending default by the drawee. Rav Shehsheth's position represents the minority view,[19] so that the law is according to Rabbah, who considers the worker-creditor's renunciation to be ineffective, and permits recourse against the employer even prior to the drawee's default.[20]

2.12 Unfortunately, a third scenario, that of an *implied* renunciation *conditional* on payment made by the drawee, and not depending at all on an undertaking given by the drawee, which is effective under modern law,[21] has not been considered. Moreover, as discussed, the Rabbis preferred the second scenario, that of the worker's *express* renunciation, *conditional* on payment made by the drawee. They rejected Rav Shesheth's position, upholding such a renunciation, albeit in connection with an undertaking by the drawee, which is closer to modern law than that of Rabbah who must be taken to consider such renunciation as mistaken.

2.13 It has been resolved in Jewish law that in the case dealt with in the *Bava Metzia* text, all three (employer/payer-debtor, worker/payee-creditor, and moneychanger-storekeeper/drawee) are present together.[22] The scenario dealt with is nevertheless close to that of the issuance of a cheque, since the text speaks of the employer directing the worker to the drawee so that the drawee may be seen as acting on the basis of the payee-creditor's demand advising of the payer-debtor's payment order.[23]

2.14 However, this system ultimately does not qualify as a cheque system. First, the employer/payer-debtor's instruction is said to be oral. Second, the prevailing view[24] is that the text deals with a situation under which the drawee is extending credit to the

[17] Nimukei Yoseph, D'H 'Hozer' commenting on Talmud, *Bava Metzia* 68A (of Rif's page numbering).

[18] See Rosh, D'H 'Ibaei lehu' commenting on Talmud, *Bava Metzia* 112A as well as the Mordechai, D'H 'Himchah' commenting on Talmud, *Bava Metzia* 112A.

[19] Albeit the one adopted by the Jerusalem Talmud, *Shevuot* 36B–37A.

[20] Mareh Hapanim to the Jerusalem Talmud, *Shevuot* 36B–37A

[21] *Re Charge Card Services Ltd* [1989] Ch 497, [1988] 3 All ER 702 [707].

[22] Kessef Mishna, Rambam, *Kinyan: Hilchot Mechira*, Section 6, Rule 8.

[23] Unlike the case discussed in Talmud, *Shevuot* 45A, and Jerusalem Talmud, *Shevuot* 36B.

[24] Notwithstanding S Albeck, 'The Assignment of Debt in the Talmud' (1957) 26 Tarbiz 262 [in Hebrew].

payer-debtor, rather than charging an asset account in which the payer-debtor deposited funds.[25] Both points do not exclude the possibility of a cheque equivalent drawing on credit extended by the drawee to the payer-debtor but militate against a cheque system. However, in the final analysis, the *Bava Metzia* text and ensuing commentary reflects a most sophisticated and advanced discussion on issues that in hindsight underlie liability on a cheque, its scope and autonomy.

C. Bill Forerunner: Islamic *Hawale* in the Early Middle Ages

Islamic law developed the *hawale* as a mechanism under which a debtor was able to transfer or shift his or her own obligation to pay his or her debt to another person. *Hawale* literally means 'removal'[26] or 'turn'. It denotes the transference of an obligation from one person to another, constituted by 'an agreement by which a debtor is freed from a debt by another becoming responsible for it'.[27] What is transferred from the debtor to another person (usually his or her own debt) is an obligation to pay the debt. In connection with a payment instruction given by a debtor ('transferor') to a drawee ('transferee'), the latter substitutes the former, and takes over the debt owed by the former to the creditor. **2.15**

Legal theory underlying the *hawale* as to who are the parites to a *hawale* agreement is contested among the four principal Islamic legal traditions.[28] Among them, the Hanafi school has been prominent in the East, particularly in Iraq and Syria, while the Maliki school has been prominent in the West, particularly in Egypt and North Africa.[29] The controversy is ample with practical implications.[30] **2.16**

A bilateral contract exists between the creditor and either the drawee-transferee under Hanafi law, or the debtor-transferor according to the other schools.[31] Thereunder, the transferee-drawee becomes indebted to the creditor. Under Hanafi law the debtor's **2.17**

[25] Rashi to Talmud, *Bava Metzia* 111A; Rosh, D'H 'Ibaei lehu' commenting on Talmud, *Bava Metzia* 112A; Rif on Talmud, *Bava Metzia* 68B (of Rif's page numbering). For a comprehensive discussion, see Y Francus, 'The Rif's Methodology in the Law Concerning Presence of All Three' (5748/1988) 102 Sinai 196 [in Hebrew]. See also Mareh Hapanim and the Ridvaz to the Jerusalem Talmud, *Shevuot* 36B–37A.

[26] This is the preferred word used by *The Hedya or Guide: Commentary on the Mussulman Laws*, trans by order of the Governor-General and Council of Bengal. By C Hamilton with preface and index, by SG Grady (2nd edn, New Book House 1957) 330.

[27] For this definition see HAR Gibb and JH Kramers, *Shorter Encyclopaedia of Islam* (EJ Brill, Luzac 1953) 137.

[28] These are the Hanafi, Maliki, Shafi'i, and Hanbali discussed by J Schacht, *An Introduction to Islamic Law* (Clarendon Press 1964, reprinted 1998) 57–68 (hereafter Schacht, *Islamic Law*).

[29] ibid, 65.

[30] For the controversy underlying the *hawale* rules and its implications see ND Ray, 'The Medieval Islamic System of Credit and Banking: Legal and Historical Considerations' (1997) 12 Arab LQ 43, 60–65. For a comprehensive discussion see A Chéron and MS Fahmy Bey, 'Le transport de dette dans les législations européennes et en droit musulman' IIe partie, 'Le transport de dette (*hewala*) en droit musulman' (1931) 22 L'Égypte contemporaine 137.

[31] Notwithstanding SE Rayner, *The Theory of Contracts in Islamic Law* (Graham and Trotman 1991) who asserts at 307 that the *hawale* is a unilateral contract.

agreement is dispensed with, inasmuch as it is up to the creditor to agree to have the drawee replacing the original debtor. For its part, the drawee's agreement is dispensed with under non-Hanafi law inasmuch as he or she is anyway a debtor albiet to the transferor-debtor. The creditor is a party to the bilateral *hawale* agreement under all Islamic schools.

2.18 The *hawale* may be initiated by the payer-debtor's instruction to the payee-creditor to collect from the drawee. To entitle the payee-creditor upon presentment of the instruction to the drawee, the latter's consent is required under Hanafi rules, but is dispensed with under the other schools. However, either way, the *hawale* can be conceptualized on the creditor's powers to demand payment from the transferee-drawee. In this way, the *hawale* can be treated as a precursor for a legal doctrine underlying the bill as well as the cheque.

2.19 Conceptualized by Hanafi law as the drawee-transferee's guarantee, the *hawale* ought to have accommodated a continuous original debtor-transferor's liability to the creditor.[32] Ultimately, however, the notion that prevailed in Hanafi law is that due to the *hawale*'s effect to 'remove' or transfer the debt from the original debtor-transferor to the drawee-transferee,[33] the original debtor-transferor is to be discharged, except for when collection from the drawee-transferee becomes impossible.[34] Consistent with their treatment of the *hawale* as a transfer or sale of a debt, and subject to narrow exceptions,[35] other schools also deny the creditor recourse against the original debtor-transferor who thus does not reincur liability to the creditor upon the drawee-transferee's default.

2.20 According to the Hanafi school, there is no requirement for a pre-existing debt owed by the drawee-transferee to the original debtor-transferor. Conversely, under all non-Hanafi schools, the drawee-transferee must have been liable for the money owed, albeit to the original debtor-transferor. An attempted *hawale* by a drawee-transferee who does not owe to the transferor is treated in Maliki law as an undertaking to pay

[32] According to this logic, the drawee-transferee's liability should have been contingent upon the original debtor-transferor's default. But see eg LWC van den Berg, *Principes du droit musulman selon les rites d' Abou Hanîfah et de Châfi'î* (trans by R de France de Tersant, Typographie Adolphe Jourdan 1896) 101, speaking of the effect of the *hawale* under Hanafi law to confer a conditional discharge upon the original debtor, pending a default by the drawee-transferee (which is obviously the reverse of an ordinary suretyship or guarantee). In Islamic law (at least as long as the guarantee was given at the request of the principal debtor) a suretyship does not discharge the liability of the principal debtor to the guaranteed debt. See eg Schacht, *Islamic Law* 158–9.

[33] For this conceptualization of the creditor's recourse against the original debtor-transferor see E Tyan, 'Le transport de dettes en droit Ottoman' (1925) 1 Gazette des Tribunaux Libano-Syriens 2, 25, 29.

[34] Once a *hawale* has been made, the original debtor-transferor becomes liable to the creditor upon the drawee-transferee's death in poverty. Hedya 332–33; Chéron and Fahmy Bey 140, 162–67; and Tyan, ibid 28–29.

[35] For example, in Maliki law, recourse against the original debtor-transferor is available to the creditor when the debtor is guilty of misrepresentation as well as where the drawee-transferee is shown to have been insolvent already at the time of the *hawale*. According to K Ish'âq, *Abrégé de la loi musulmane selon le rite de'l Imâm Mâlek*: Le patrimoine (trans by GH Bousquet, vol 3, La maison des livres 1961) 69, this is so only where the original debtor-transferor was aware of the drawee-transferee's insolvency.

the debt of another (namely, that of the original debtor). Such drawee's undertaking constitutes an 'indemnity' contract.[36]

Documentation of Islamic payment instruments is quite rich;[37] this is particularly true for the period of the Fatimid Caliphate, during which plenty of documents[38] originated from the Jewish *Geniza* of Cairo.[39] **2.21**

Islamic payment instruments have not always acquired distinct names.[40] Thus, the withdrawal out of an account with a *sarraf* (private moneychanger), in the execution of a non-cash payment made by a small retailer to his or her wholesaler, may be treated simply as a *hawale*. For its part, the *sakk*, from which, linguistically, the modern word 'cheque' may be derived,[41] overlapped with one meaning of the *ruq'a* (ie, a payment order issued to the payee instructing the drawee to make payment against its presentment by the person entitled to obtain payment).[42] Typically, a *ruq'a* or *sakk* does not designate a named payee and is payable to the bearer. **2.22**

A mechanism facilitating payment between distant parties premised on the Islamic *hawale* is the *suftaj*. The latter could be used, for example, by a debtor in a point of origin who wished to pay to a creditor in a point of destination without risking the physical delivery of the money. In such a case, the underlying operation of the *suftaj* was as follows: the debtor 'lent' money to a remitter at the point of origin. A *suftaj* document issued by the remitter contained the remitter's obligation, as well as a grant of authority to a correspondent, to pay the creditor at the point of destination. The *suftaj document* was typically payable to a named payee and (unlike other Islamic payment **2.23**

[36] An indemnity contract is created by express words of the indemnifier and is treated as an undertaking by him or her to substitute the original debtor who is thereby released. No recourse against the original debtor is available to the creditor who accepted the indemnity, M Talbi, 'Opérations bancaires en Ifrīqiya à l'époque d'al-Māzarī (453–536/1061–1141)—crédit et paiement par chèque' in *Études d'Histoire Ifriqiyenne et de Civilisation Musulmane Médiévale* (Publications de l'Université de Tunis 1982) 433 refers to such a contract as *hamāla*. However, according to Foster, the *hamala*, which is a synonym of *kafla*, is an ordinary guarantee, so that the indemnity contract which 'should not be confused with the *hamala*' is the *haml*. See NHD Foster, 'The Islamic Law of Guarantees' (2001) 6 Arab LQ 133, 152.

[37] See eg SK Bakhsh and DS Margoliouth, *The Renaissance of Islam* (trans from the German of Adam Mez) (Jubilee 1937) 476–77; and E Ashtor, 'Banking Instruments Between the Muslim East and the Christian West' (1972) 1 Journal of European Economic History 553; reprinted (with same pagination) in E Ashtor, *East-West Trade in the Medieval Mediterranean* (BZ Kedar ed, Variorum Reprints 1986). For summary and sources see eg Ray, 'Medieval Islamic System' 66–79.

[38] A comprehensive definite study analysing the various Geniza payment instruments is by A Shivtiel, 'Orders of Payment, Order of Supply, Instructions for Payment, and Statement of Credit in the Genizah and other Collections at Cambridge University' in B Outhwaite and S Bhayro (eds) *From a Sacred Source—Genizah Studies in Honour of Porfessor Stefan C. Rief.* (Brill 2011) 331 who builds on earlier work, on the 'monumental book' of SD Goitein, *A Mediterranean Society*, vol I: Economic Foundations (University of California Press 1967) 240–50 (hereafter Goitein, *Mediterranean Society*).

[39] For the Cairo *Geniza* in general, see SC Reif, *A Jewish Archive from Old Cairo, The History of Cambridge University's Genizah Collection* (Curzon 2000).

[40] For the *sakk* and *suftaj* see eg CE Bosworth, 'Abū Abdallāh Al-Khwārazmī on the Technical Terms of the Secretary's Art: A Contribution to the Administrative History of Mediaeval Islam' (1969) 12 Journal of the Economic and Social History of the Orient 8, respectively, 125 and 140.

[41] Goitein, *Mediterranean* Society 245.

[42] But for a *sakk*, from Western Sudan, in effect, as an 'IOU' (acknowledgement of debt) document, see eg N Levtzion, 'Ibn-Hawqal, the Cheque, and Awdaghost' (1968) 9 Journal of African History 223 who nevertheless (not having in mind precise legal terminology) speaks of the document as a 'cheque'.

instruments) not to the bearer and was not transferable.[43] As a rule, a *suftaj* was issued by a drawee of high repute;[44] it entailed a high commission[45] and was hard to get.[46]

2.24 A *suftaj* was usually drafted to be payable on demand, properly authenticated so as to be easily provable,[47] and drafted to impose heavy penalties for any delay in payment.[48] Payment on a *suftaj*, namely, repayment of the loan that gave rise to it, was typically made against its proper presentment by the payee at the place designated for payment.[49] The debtor would send the document to the creditor, who would then present it for payment to the remitter's correspondent at the point of destination. The correspondent may have effectively been same as the remitter, or someone in an ongoing relationship with the remitter who would settle with him or her periodically on a balance resulting from payment activities in both directions.

2.25 The *suftaj* operation can be explained as two *hawales*. Participants in the first *hawale* are the debtor, creditor, and remitter. The debtor drops out in the second *hawale*, in which the participants are the remitter, correspondent, and creditor.

2.26 Under the Hanafi School, parties to a *hawale* agreement are the transferee and the creditor. The agreement between the remitter and creditor (respectively, transferee and the creditor under the first *hawale*) discharges the debtor (transferor under the first *hawale*). This agreement is created by the acceptance by the creditor of the *suftaj* document (issued by the remitter). Parties to the second *hawale* are the correspondent and creditor. The correspondent (transferee under the second *hawale*) becomes indebted to the creditor (so as to discharge the remitter) under the second *hawale* only subsequently, upon the correspondent's agreement (with the creditor) to honour the remitter's order. This agreement materializes upon the presentation of the *suftaj* document by the creditor to the correspondent.

2.27 At the same time, under the Maliki School, the parties to a *hawale* agreement are the transferor and the creditor. The acceptance by the creditor of the *suftaj* document thus operates as (1) an agreement between the creditor and debtor (being the transferor under the first *hawale*) to have the debtor replaced by the remitter as the one owing to him or her, as well as (2) an agreement between the creditor

[43] See eg Goitein, *Mediterranean Society* 245 and AL Udovitch, 'Reflections on the Institutions of Credits and Banking in the Medieval Islamic Neat East' (1975) 41 Studia Islamica 5, 17.

[44] The point is highlighted by Goitein, *Mediterranean Society* 242–43.

[45] For questioning the conformity of the practice with the prohibition to take interest see Ray, 'Medieval Islamic System' 77. Regardless, presumably, the commission was waived for small amounts sent for charity. See Goitein, *Mediterranean Society* 244.

[46] A fact that contributed to the continued parallel practice of sending purses of money from place to place. See eg Goitein, *Mediterranean Society* 244.

[47] For the *suftaj* as instrument, see R Grasshoff, *Das Wechsel Recht der Araber* (Verlag von Otto Liebman 1899) 30–34 [In German—I relied on an unofficial translation].

[48] See eg Udovitch 16. Goitein, *Mediterranean Society* 243 is to the same effect; at 245 he even mentions the possibility of a paymaster making advances on a forthcoming *suftaj* prior to its arrival. For questioning the validity of the penalty clauses as possible violation of the prohibition to take interest, see Ray, 'Medieval Islamic System' 77.

[49] According to SM Imamuddin, 'Bayt Al-Mal and Banks in the Medieval Muslim World' (1960) 34 Islamic Culture 22, 29, 'Each *suftajah* had its own time limit which was generally forty days'; it must thus be presented prior to expiry date.

and remitter, the *suftaj* issuer and the transferor in the second *hawale*, to have the remitter replaced by the correspondent as the one owing to him or her. Stated otherwise, in contrast to the Hanafi School, under the Maliki School, the correspondent's agreement is dispensed with; the correspondent, as the transferee under the second *hawale*, becomes automatically liable to the creditor upon the creditor's acceptance of the *suftaj* document, already prior to the presentation of the *suftaj* document to him. Thus, under Maliki law, a debtor owed by a transferee in one place and who wishes to pay a creditor located in another place, 'can transmit [the transferee's] recognisance of debt to [the creditor]', thereby causing the transferee to become liable to the creditor. This, however, does not work under Hanafi law that requires the presence of the transferee-drawee.[50]

In the final analysis, the *hawale* doctrine is premised on contractual principles that produce a viable financial instrument, rather than only fragmental aspects governing it. **2.28**

D. Continental Medieval Cheques and Bills of Exchange and Roman Law

1. The Payment Order and its Execution Under Roman Law

Under Roman law, the *delegation* is an order given by one person ('delegant') to another ('person to be delegated') to pay to, or assume an obligation towards, a third person ('delegatee').[51] It may be an order by the delegant (a payer/debtor) issued to the person delegated, the drawee, to pay to the delegate (a payee/creditor) a debt owed by the payer to the payee.[52] **2.29**

As to the impact of drawee's undertaking, the choice in Roman law has been between the continued existence of the debt owed by the payer to the payee in an *imperfect execution* of the delegation and the extinction or discharge of this debt in the *perfect execution* of the delegation. No middle ground for suspension or conditional discharge of **2.30**

[50] Ray, 'Medieval Islamic System' 62.

[51] For the definition of *delegatio* see eg A Berger, *Encyclopedic Dictionary of Roman Law* (American Philosophical Society 1953) 429 (hereafter Berger, *Dictionary of Roman Law*). For an analysis of delegation, see eg HJ Roby, *Roman Private Law in the Times of Cicero and the Antonines*, vol 2 (Cambridge University Press 1902) (also reprinted by Scientia Verlag Alen, 1975) 42–45 (hereafter Roby, *Roman Private Law*). See also WA Hunter, *A Systematic and Historical Exposition of Roman Law in the Order of a Code* (3rd edn, Sweet & Maxwell 1897) 631–32 (hereafter Hunter, *Roman Law*); R Dannenbring (trans) *Roman Private Law* (trans of M Kaser, 'Römische Privatrecht' 10th rev edn, 3rd edn, University of South Africa 1980) 269–70 (hereafter Dannenbring, *Roman Private Law*) and P Gide, *Études sur la Novation et le Transport des Créances en Droit Romain* (L LaRose 1879) 379–480 (hereafter Gide, *Droit Romain*). For a comprehensive discussion see S Maxwell, *De la délégation en droit romain* (Imprimerie Ve Cadoret 1895) (hereafter Maxwell, *Droit Romain*) and P Rutsaert, *Étude sur la Délégation en droit privé Romain* (Émile Bruylant ed, Recueil Sirey 1929). See also R Lanata, *Thése pour le doctorat: Droit Romain: de la délégation; droit français: de la competence des tribunaux français a l'égard des étrangers* (Imprimerie de Charles Noblet 1882).

[52] It is the benefit to the order-giver from the execution of the order that turns an order into a delegation order. See eg A Badareu 'Tomsa', *De la Délégation Imparfaite* (M Giard & Brière 1914) 6.

the debtor, until default or performance by the drawee, appears to exist or even to have been considered.

2.31 Up to the time of Justinian, two distinct avenues[53] existed for carrying out an execution of the delegation, each being imperfect: *receptum argentarii* and *constitutum debiti alieni.*[54] The former is limited to a promise given by a banker (*argentarius*), acting under the instruction of his or her client to perform towards a third party on a fixed date. The promise is not limited to the payment of a monetary debt; its potential scope is thus unlimited.[55] The *constitutum debiti alieni* is a specie of *constitutum.*[56] The *constitutum* is not limited to a banker (*argentarius*) and may be given by any person. At its inception, it was limited to an obligation to pay a certain sum of money, and subsequently expanded to cover an obligation to deliver a quantified amount of fungible items, namely items that can be measured, counted, or weighed.

2.32 Each promise does not lead to the novation of the pre-existing debt, and does not supersede it; it gives the creditor the option of an alternative remedy. Contrary to the stipulation discussed later, the *constitutum* promise is given on the initiative of the party to become liable on it, and not in response to a creditor's question. Unlike the *receptum argentarii*, the *constitutum* promise is not presumed to be autonomous and free of defences arising from the pre-existing debt.

2.33 A most frequently used route for a perfect execution of the delegation is *stipulatio.*[57] It is an oral solemn contract concluded in the form of a face-to-face exchange of a question and an answer between two persons who, on the basis of the successful completion of the exchange, become parties to a contract. It is a formal, verbal, unilateral, and *stricti juris* contract.[58] The two parties must be in each other's presence and the question and answer must be spoken; furthermore, 'there should be precise correspondence between question and answer'.[59] A stipulation to pay a sum certain in money is a *stipulatio certa.*[60] Derived from a verbal and formal contract, and not purporting

[53] But see E Guillard, *Les Banquiers Athéniens et Romaines—trapézites & argentarri-suivis du Pacte de Constitut en Droit Romain* (Guillaumin, H Georg 1875), who (contrary to all) appears to challenge the distinct nature of each avenue by maintaining (at 114) that the *receptum* is a *constitut* emanating from a banker.

[54] See Berger, *Dictionary of Roman Law* 668, 410, and RW Lee, *The Elements of Roman Law with a Translation of the Institutes of Justinian* (4th edn, Sweet & Maxwell 1956) 343, 367 (hereafter Lee, *Elements of Roman Law*). For a concise review covering both see JAC Thomas, *The Institutes of Justinian: Text, Translation and Commentary* (Amsterdam/Oxford 1975) 246 (Commentary on Institutes Book III, Title XXVI) 248–49.

[55] G Platon, *Les Banquiers dans la législation de Justinien* (Premiére Partie) (Librairie Recuil Sirey 1912) 46. See also 48.

[56] See Berger, *Dictionary of Roman Law* 410; H Coulon, *Droit romain: Du constitut debiti alieni* (Typographie Oudin 1889); A Philippin, *Le pacte de constitute—actio de pecunia constituta* (Duchemin 1929); and J Déjardin, *L'action pecuniae constitutae* (Rousseau 1914). See also Platon, ibid 164, Chapitre V bis, 'Histoire et Rôle du Constitut'; and Guillard, *Les Banquiers* 104–30.

[57] See definition in Berger, *Dictionary of Roman Law* 716 and an analysis eg in Lee, *Elements of Roman Law* 298–304 and B Nicholas, *An Introduction to Roman Law* (Clarendon Press 1962) 193–96 (hereafter Nicholas, *Roman Law*).

[58] For classification contract obligations under Roman law, see Lee, *Elements of Roman Law* 285–89.

[59] Lee, *Elements of Roman Law* 298. See also, Nicholas, *Roman Law* 193; Berger, *Dictionary of Roman Law* 716, v. 'Stipulatio'. But see Lee, *Elements of Roman Law* 416; Roby, *Roman Private Law* 39; and Maxwell, *Droit Romain* 57 as to the effect of a condition added to the stipulatory answer.

[60] Defined by Berger, *Dictionary of Roman Law* 717 as a 'stipulation in which the thing promised ... its quality ... and quantity were precisely fixed'.

to incorporate any pre-existing obligation, drawee's new obligation to the creditor is *stricti juris* and hence unilateral; it is abstract and self-contained, namely, confined to the contours of the formula and not subject to any outside event. Both original obligations, of the debtor to the creditor and of the drawee to the debtor, are transformed into a novated obligation owed by drawee to the creditor.

To bypass drawee's consent required in the execution of a delegation,[61] under 'a variant of procedural representation',[62] a debtor either appointed a creditor to act as his or her representative or gave the creditor a mandate in the creditor's own interest (*mandatum in rem suam* or *procuratio in rem suam*) to sue and recover from the drawee. Acting on the authorization, the creditor could sue the drawee in the debtor's name, seeking a remedy under which the drawee was to be 'condemned' to pay the creditor.[63] Authorization further permitted the creditor to keep, and not account to the debtor, whatever proceeds the creditor collected from the drawee. The authorization was called '*mandatum ad agentum*'; strictly speaking, however, it was not a mandate, since a mandate cannot be concluded wholly in the interest of the mandatary.[64] **2.34**

By the time of Justinian, the creditor had not been required to sue the drawee as a *cognitor* or *procurator* for the debtor; rather, the creditor was allowed to maintain an *actio utilis*[65] in his or her own name, and even when the 'mandate' had been determined by the debtor's death or revocation.[66] By either giving the drawee a formal notice, called *denuntiatio*,[67] or receiving from him or her part payment, the creditor assumed full control of the debtor's claim against drawee, which precluded the debtor from accepting a settlement from the drawee or otherwise giving him or her a discharge.[68] It is only at this point that Roman law is said, at least in hindsight, to 'eventually ... have arrived at an effective system of assignment [of debts]',[69] or *cessio*, under which the transfer to the creditor of the debtor's claim against the drawee is fully recognized and protected. Nevertheless, in civilian legal systems drawn on the Romanist tradition, doubts persisted until the middle of the nineteenth century when 'the tide was turning'[70] and *cessio* became fully established. Hence, as under the 'competing' **2.35**

[61] For the indispensability drawee's 'voluntary act' for delegation see eg Maxwell, *Droit Romain* 63.

[62] Nicholas, *Roman Law* 200. See also Dannenbring, *Roman Private Law* 271–72 and R Zimmermann, *The Law of Obligations-Roman Foundations of the Civilian Tradition* (Juta 1990) 61 (hereafter Zimmerman, *Obligations*).

[63] See Gaius' Institutes Book IV §§ 83–84 and 86; WM Gordon and OF Robinson, *The Institutes of Gaius* (Cornell 1988) 469–73. Unlike a *procurator*, a *cognitor* was appointed in court in the presence of the other litigant (ibid).

[64] See eg Zimmermann, *Obligations* 422, as well as Gide, *Droit Romain* 467.

[65] As 'an adaptation or extension of an existing action' an *actio utilis* is a praetorian action that usually denotes 'a modification of a civil law formula ... or to the application of a civil law formula to a new state of facts or to persons not entitled to make use of it'. Lee, *Elements of Roman Law* 435.

[66] For creditor's *actio utilis* as contrasted with, and being more advantageous than, creditor's 'direct' action as *procurator* for the debtor, see J Duponchel, *De la cession d'actions en droit romain. Du titre à ordre et des conséquences qui s'y rattachent en droit français* (Impremerie de Beau Jeune 1870) 29–32.

[67] According to Berger, *Dictionary of Roman Law* 431, *Denuntiare* means to give notice, to intimate, or announce. Duponchel ibid discusses at 5–7 issues relevant to the notice.

[68] Having received such notice, the drawee could 'possibly' raise a defence against the debtor's action based on the debtor's fraud (*exceptio doli*). See Zimmermann, *Obligations* 62.

[69] Nicholas, *Roman Law* 201. Yet the transferability of a debt has remained subject to public policy restrictions: Hunter, *Roman Law* 628.

[70] Zimmermann, *Obligations* 63–64.

doctrines in Islamic law, at Roman law, the tripartite payment mechanism has been premised on a bilateral contract, except that it was between the drawer and either the drawee or payee, rather than between the payee and either the drawee or the drawer. But under both legal systems, the payment instrument has been governed by general contract principles.

2. The Medieval Cheque

2.36 A local banking system existed in major cities in Continental Europe throughout the fourteenth and fifteenth centuries. Each such system typically provided a mechanism for book transfer payments out of which cheques may have evolved.

2.37 According to Huvelin, upon a book transfer, the banker's promise to the payee could be explained under Roman law as *receptum argentarii*.[71] One advantage of this explanation is that under the *receptum argentarii*, the banker's undertaking is independent, namely, entirely autonomous and free of defences that may have been available to the client against the third party. At the same time, the banker's undertaking to the third party under *receptum argentarii* does not impact the client's own original obligation to the third party, so as not to be tantamount to be its full discharge.

2.38 An alternative analysis is provided by De Roover, who speaks of the method of payment by book transfer as an 'assignment in bank' that '[a]ccording to the medieval jurists … discharged the debtor from any further obligation'.[72] Relying particularly on a fourteenth-century Italian jurist named Bartolo Da Sassiferrato, he refers to the book transfer as an 'assignation', requiring the consent of the debtor, banker, and creditor. [73] Upon the occurrence in a bank of that transaction, the debtor is irrevocably discharged, so that the transfer is equal to payment in current coins. This is so 'on condition that the banker or moneychanger promises the creditor to hold the sum transferred at the creditor's disposition'. This rule effectively treats the book entry on the banker's books as an absolute discharge of the original debt, upon which the creditor forfeits his or her recourse against the original debtor. This is contrary to an 'assignation' on a third party other than a banker, under which the creditor keeps his or her recourse right against the debtor in case the non-bank third party declines to honour his or her undertaking.[74] Provisions in modern German and Swiss codes addressing payment orders may be traced to this Medieval non-bank 'assignation'. Initiating

[71] P Huvelin, 'Travaux recents sur l'histoire de la lettre de change' (1901) 15(1) Annales de droit français, étranger et international 1, 20–21 (hereafter Huvelin, 'Travaux').

[72] R De Roover, 'New Interpretations of the History of Banking' in J Kirshner (ed) *Business, Banking, and Economic Thought in Late Medieval and Early Modern Europe:* Selected Studies of Raymond de Roover (University of Chicago Press 1974, Phoenix Edition 1976) 200, 215, 216 (respectively) (hereafter De Roover, 'New Interpretations').

[73] This is not the only or even the usual meaning of the term. See eg (from Scots law perspective) R Gilbert Anderson, *Assignation* (Edinburgh Legal Publication 2008), addressing terminology at 78–80.

[74] R De Roover, *L'Evolution de la Lettre de Change* XIVe–XVIIIe siècles (Librairie Armand Colin 1953) 208 and 212–13, summarizing the views of Bartolo Da Sassofferato (1314–1357); Baldo Degli Ubaldi (1327–1400); and Giasone Del Maino (1435–1519) (hereafter De Roover, *Lettre de Change*). De Roover acknowledges Bartolo's text to be 'obscure' (ibid 208) but claims to follow its usual interpretation including by the two other jurists (ibid, 5–87).

the execution of an imperfect, albeit novatory, absolute delegation order,[75] an order generates a defence-free transfer with recourse of a debt on the basis of the tripartite agreement of the payer, payee, and drawee.[76]

De Roover specifically mentions a requirement as to the consent of *all* three, namely the payer, banker, and payee, and not only that of the payer and the payee, as would have been the case under *cessio*. The payer's discharge upon the bank book transfer appears to be premised on the banker's autonomous obligation towards the payee. Unlike under *cessio,* the latter can be enforced by the payee free of the banker's defences against the payer. Nor was it a delegation, generating an autonomous obligation but being satisfied with the creditor–drawee's bilateral agreement and dispensing with that of the debtor. **2.39**

The presence-of-all-three requirement, and hence the lack of reliance on a written instruction, was bound to eliminate fraud. The practice was not a source of inconvenience, because usually all three were situated in the same vicinity and the banker tended to keep his or her books available on his or her desk.[77] However, on occasion, a sick debtor was inhibited from coming to the banker. It is on such rare occasions, as well as for administrative reasons, that written payment orders started to be used. Gradually, already throughout the fourteenth and fifteenth centuries, written payment orders spread and became common, first in Italy, outside Venice, particularly in Tuscany, including Florence, and then elsewhere outside Italy.[78] Initially, '[w]ritten instruments could be used ... only as supplementary memoranda or as instruments appointing an agent'.[79] When they became payment orders, whose presentment to the banker by one party dispensed with the presence of the other, their function was to generate either a cash payment or a book transfer. **2.40**

Such payment orders were in effect cheques, each issued by the payer/debtor to the payee/creditor, instructing the banker to pay to the payee/creditor, as well as authorizing the payee/creditor to collect from the banker. It is in this process that a medieval cheque mechanism was born. Cheques were not negotiable, usually even non-transferable;[80] possibly other than in specific times and places they were not widely used.[81] They initiated either a payment in cash or a book transfer; **2.41**

[75] For the assignation as derived from the delegation, see in general P Sorbier, *L'ancien contrat d'assignation de créance; ou, Délégation commerciale à titre de nantissement: son emploi dans les banques pour garantir un compte courant* (Imprimerie de France 1937).

[76] See arts 466–71 of Swiss *Code of Obligations* (CO) English Translation of the Official Text, Volume I Contract Law (Swiss–American Chamber of Commerce 2008) and § 783–92 of The German *Civil Code* (BGB) revised edition trans with an Introduction by SL Goren (Fred B Rothman & Co 1994) § 783.

[77] AP Usher, *The Early History of Deposit Banking in Mediterranean Europe*, vol I (Harvard University Press 1943) 90 (hereafter Usher, *Deposit Banking*); RC Mueller, 'The Role of Bank Money in Venice, 1300–1500' in Fondazione Giorgio Cini et al (eds) *Studi veneziani* (NS), vol III (Giardini 1979) 47, 50.

[78] For Barcelona, see eg Usher, *Deposit Banking* 283–88.

[79] Usher, *Deposit Banking* 283.

[80] See (in Italian; I relied on an informal partial translation)F Melis, *Note di Storia della Banca Pisana nel Trecento* (Società Storica Pisana 1955) who identifies cheques transferable by the instruction of the payee placed on the back (*recto*) of the cheque (ibid 112, by reference to 98, n 244) but in situations in which the transferee was identified in the original cheque.

[81] See in general, De Roover, 'New Interpretations' 216–17 as well as Usher, *Deposit Banking* 90–94. For an extensive discussion, see M Spallanzani, 'A Note on Florentine Banking in the Renaissance: Orders of Payment and Cheques' (1978) 7(1) Journal of European Economic History 145.

either way the cheque accomplished 'the transfer of the [depositor-drawer]'s right against the banker to a third party[/payee]'[82] on the basis of a tripartite agreement among the payer, payee, and drawee. The common ancestry of the Continental code order and the cheque dispels two myths. First, that of a historical link between bills and cheques and second, that of a distinct 'law merchant' governing cheques. Rather, it was the application of general contract principles that generated the cheque.

3. The Medieval Bill of Exchange

2.42 From its inception in Medieval Continental Europe, the bill or letter of payment was a credit instrument facilitating the transportation of money from place to place, particularly in the execution of the payment obligation by the obligor under an exchange contract. It 'was not only a loan instrument but also a remittance contract that "transferred funds", or more accurately, effected payments between distant cities without any movement of precious metals between them'.[83]

2.43 Typically, the drawer was an exporter of goods who financed their procurement by obtaining a loan from a local exchange banker. The loan was to be repaid in the foreign market out of the proceeds of the sale of the goods there.[84] Drawer-seller signed and delivered the exchange banker a letter of payment, where he or she instructed the drawee (the drawer's agent, partner, or correspondent in the foreign market) to pay the payee (an agent, principal, partner, or correspondent of the lender in the foreign market). For his or her part, the exchange banker/lender acted as a remitter; having delivered the money to the drawer-borrower, he or she sent the letter of payment issued to him or her by the drawer to the payee. Upon receiving the letter, the payee would present it to the drawee for acceptance, and in due course, upon maturity, for payment. The exchange banker and payee would have mutual dealings in such contracts and would settle in a fair mechanism. That mode of settlement would herald organized interbank clearing and settlement systems in a multilateral setting.[85]

2.44 While the letter was addressed from the drawer to the drawee, it was given to the remitter, who was to send it to the payee for presentment to the drawee. According to Huvelin,[86] this circuitous route to the final destination shows a voluntary undertaking, an assumption of liability, by the remitter to the drawee as well as the drawer to

[82] Usher, *Deposit Banking* 91.

[83] JH Munro, 'The Medieval Origins of the Financial Revolution: Usury, *Rentes*, and Negotiability' (2003) 25 International History Review 505, 543 (hereafter Munro, 'Medieval Origins').

[84] See eg De Roover, *Lettre de Change* 29–31 and 43–45.

[85] MT Boyer-Xambeu, G Deleplace, and L Gillard, *Private Money & Public Currencies: The 16th Century Challenge* (trans by A Azodi, ME Sharpe 1994) 70–91. See also De Roover, *Lettre de Change* 74–82; Usher, *Deposit Banking* 110–33; and P Huvelin, *Essai historique sur le droit des Marchés & des Foires* (Arthur Rousseau 1897) 534–93.

[86] Huvelin, 'Travaux' 4, 9–21.

the payee. The bill was originally not transferable; hence, the only party corresponding to the modern 'holder' was the payee.

Two alternative approaches exist with regard to the drawee-acceptor's liability to the payee, each derived from Roman law. The view that ultimately prevailed in Germany is that the basis of this liability is that of a literal contract, namely, a contract created on the basis of a special kind of writing. It is a formal contract, by definition *stricti juris*, namely, binding the promissor to the very thing he or she has promised, and hence unilateral; it may be referred to as abstract. This contract could be either a variant of or inspired by the *stipulatio*. **2.45**

The alternative, and according to Huvelin the earlier, view that prevailed in France is premised on the theory of *la provision*.[87] As codified in 1673,[88] it is constituted by the sum of money either held by the drawee for the drawer or provided to the drawee by the drawer, with which the drawee is obligated to pay the bill.[89] Its passage to the payee is either a matter of *cessio* or 'sale of money'. To that end, the drawee's acceptance is viewed not as a new obligation but rather, in the footsteps of the *constitutum*, as an acknowledgement, or confirmation, of an existing one, based on the receipt of 'the provision'.[90] **2.46**

Huvelin does not discuss the drawer's recourse against the drawee. Nor does he discuss the drawee-acceptor's liability to the remitter as well as the relationship between the remitter and payee. Presumably, being in privity, relationships between the drawer and the drawee as well as between the remitter and payee were governed by respective underlying contracts. **2.47**

Indorsed bills can be traced to the early sixteenth century,[91] but were not a widespread practice until second quarter of the seventeenth century.[92] It is not mentioned **2.48**

[87] See also AE Sayous, 'Les méthodes commerciales de Barcelone au XVe siècle, d'après des documents inédits de ses archives' (1936) 15 (Ser.4) Revue historique de droit français et étranger 255, 281.

[88] For the statutory reference in 1673, see eg JV Tardon, *La provision de la lettre de change* (droit compare—loi uniforme) (Pichon, Roth 1939) 6.

[89] For *la provision* in French law, see eg Jean Stoufflet, *Instruments de paiement et de crédit* (8th edn, LexisNexis 2012) 115–25; and for a summary, P. Ellinger, 'Negotiable Instruments' in JS Ziegel, U Drobnig, and K Zweight (eds), Commercial Transactions and Institutions, vol IX of *International Encyclopedia of Comparative Law* (JCB Mohr 2000) 110–13. See also G Ripert and R Roblot, *Traité de droit commercial* (13th edn, Librairie Gènèrale de droit et de jurisprudence 1992) 181–86. For a more extensive analysis see P Lescot and R Roblot, *Les effets de commerce* (vol I, Rousseau 1953) 389–465. For the meanings of '*la provision*', 'value', and 'cover', see ibid, 390, 411–12. For the transfer of la provision as a 'sale' which defeats the drawer's creditors see eg H Levy-Bruhl, *Histoire de la lettre de change au France aux xviie et xviiie siècles* (Recueil Sirey 1933) 91–95.

[90] For explaining the acceptor's liability as a confirmation of liability, and the procedural advantage accorded to his or her plaintiff suing on the acceptance in the Low Countries, see WDH Asser, 'Bills of Exchange and Agency in the 18th Century Law of Holland and Zeeland—Decisions of the Supreme Court of Holland and Zeeland' in V Piergiovanni (ed), *The Courts and the Developments of Commercial Law* (Duncker & Humblot 1987) 103, 112 (hereafter Asser, 'Bills of Exchange').

[91] De Roover, *Lettre de Change* 83, 143, 151. De Roover reproduces a bill from 1519, discovered in archives in Florence, which at 100 he identifies as possibly bearing the earliest endorsement.

[92] But cf reference to the rise of 'the practice of . . . transferring [bills] by indorsement' 'at the close of the sixteenth or the commencement of the seventeenth century' by CJ Cockburn in *Goodwin v Robarts* (1875) LR 10 Exch 337 [347], 33 LT 272.

by Malynes, who wrote in 1622,[93] but is discussed by Marius, who wrote in 1651[94] and 1684.[95] A full-fledged banking practice premised on discounting indorsed bills of exchange has its origin in the course of the seventeenth century in England; it then spread to the Continent towards the end of the eighteenth century.[96] As it is nowadays, the indorsement has been a mechanism under which the payee, in possession of the bill, instructs the drawee to pay a transferee, such as the payee's creditor, by signing on the bill itself and delivering the signed instrument to the transferee, who has thus become to be known as indorsee. The mechanism came to correspond to the posting of entries under a merchant book transfer; and it made the drawee liable directly to the indorsee, who by analogy to the transferee on a merchant book transfer, remained entitled to recourse from his or her own original debtor *viz.* the payee on the bill. In this sense, the indorsement turned out to become more than a mere transfer of the claim against the drawee; rather, it evolved to be the equivalent of a domestic bill of payment standing on its own.[97]

2.49 By way of concluding observations, the bill of exchange evolved to meet the needs and demands of commerce, irrespective of state interests and boundaries. Its contractual framework, whether under the German or French approach, was rooted in general principles of Roman law. It is also noteworthy that once evolved to meet such needs and demands, each indorsement has been treated as a standalone contract. Arguably, this treatment bears the seeds of the 'several independent contracts' vision of the negotiable instrument, to be addressed in subsequent chapters.

E. Forerunners of the Promissory Note

1. Introductory Note

2.50 Neither Roman nor common law recognized a transferable documentary abstract obligation; hence, the promissory note has no direct ancestor in Antiquity and the Middle Ages. Rather, as set out in section F (2), it derived from the post-Medieval banknote in England. At the same time, oral abstract obligations were known to Roman Law. For their part, non-transferable written abstract obligations were known in Antiquity and much later in Medieval common law. In turn, a transferable documentary debt was recognized in Jewish law. The chance is that the promissory note may have been inspired by such doctrines and documents, further discussed below. As

93 G Malynes, *Consuetudo, vel Lex Mercantoria or The Ancient Law-Merchant* (Printed by Adam Islip 1622) [Electronic Resource].

94 J Marius, *Advice Concerning Bills of Exchange* (1651) 53 (bill indorsed in blank).

95 J Marius, *Advice Concerning Bills of Exchange* (Robert Horne 1684) 6–9 (Payee 'assigns', in effect, special endorsement), 30 (bill endorsed in blank). The Preface advises that this is a longer version of the book published in 1651 (hereafter Marius, *Concerning Bills*).

96 De Roover, *Lettre de Change* 143, with full discussion at 119–42.

97 See in general, De Roover, *Lettre de Change* 116–18. The action against the drawee was premised either on his or her acceptance or the transfer of *la provision*.

in the case of its brother by subsequent adoption, the bill, inspiration for the note came from general principles of contract and property.

2. Tablets, Chirographs, and Syngraphs Outside Roman Law

A 'bearer clause' on a debt obligation on a tablet existed in Ancient Mesopotamia.[98] **2.51**
The original purpose of a bearer clause may have been to facilitate collection by a representative of temple or palace authorities to whom the obligor incurs his or her debt.[99] Even so, it was not within the power of the obligor to object to a demand made by whoever presented a document under which the obligor agreed to pay to the bearer.

Later, under Roman law, a *stricti juris* contract bound the promissor to the very **2.52**
thing he or she had promised, neither less nor more. Being self-contained, namely, confined to the contours of the formula and not to any outside event, a formal contract was by definition *stricti juris* and hence unilateral; it may be referred to as abstract. The *stipulatio*, as a formal, unilateral, and *stricti juris* contract, was the most important verbal contract, consisting essentially of a formal question and answer.[100] It diametrically varied from an informal contract, based on some 'cause' other than the adherence to a formula, such as the delivery of an object or the actual agreement of the parties.[101]

Having provided for a written 'literal contract', [102] Roman law did not recognize an ab- **2.53**
stract literal contract. However, speaking of an obligation special to foreigners arising outside Roman law, Gaius was familiar with 'a literal obligation',[103] arising through the documents called in Greek 'chirographs' and 'syngraphs'. The chirograph was a letter written by the debtor addressed to the creditor. In turn, the syngraph was a witnessed document sealed by both parties and deposited with an official.[104] The chirograph was signed by the debtor alone and the syngraph was signed by both parties.[105] Possibly, 'documents in either form could be abstract contracts, though purporting to be evidence of a debt from some (fictitious) *causa*, the commonest fiction being that of a

[98] Bogaert, *Les Origines* 100. For the use of such clauses in obligations payable to temple authorities, palace authorities, and individuals see 55, 66, 73–74, and 102. Tablets containing such a clause (and arguably complying with negotiability requirements under modern legislation) are compiled by AH Pruessner, 'The Earliest Traces of Negotiable Instruments' (1928) 44(2) The American Journal of Semitic Languages and Literatures 88.

[99] Bogaert, *Les Origines* 55, 127–28.

[100] Lee, *Elements of Roman Law* 298–304.

[101] ibid, 287, who goes on to discuss how 'In the course of time abstract contracts tend to become causal'. For 'causa' or cause as reason or grounds, see in general Berger, *Dictionary of Roman Law* 382.

[102] In general, on contract obligations under Roman law, see Lee, *Elements of Roman Law* 285–89.

[103] F De Zulueta, *The Institutes of Gaius, Part I: Text with Critical Notes and Translation* (Clarendon Press 1946) 195 (hereafter De Zulueta, *Part I*).

[104] F De Zulueta, *The Institutes of Gaius, Part II: Commentary* (first published 1953, Clarendon Press 1963) (hereafter De Zulueta, *Part II*) 166, 195.

[105] See Berger, *Dictionary of Roman Law* 388 (v. Chirographum) and 727 (v. Syngraphe).

loan'.[106] On such documents, without making a stipulation, 'a person writes that he owes or that he will give something'.[107] Both chirographs and syngraphs appear to be non-transferable.

3. The Documentary Debt Under the Talmud

2.54 Under the Talmud, a documentary note of indebtedness issued to a creditor is a *shetar*. As such it is 'a formal document [requiring] the signatures of witnesses';[108] it is effective on the basis of the witnesses' signatures,[109] without the debtor's own signature. The document does not fasten on the debtor a *stricti juris* literal obligation; rather, the debtor's obligation may be subject to oral conditions.[110]

2.55 The Talmud recognized that unlike an ordinary chattel, a loan document had no intrinsic value.[111] At the same time, effectiveness was given to the delivery of the document from the lender to another person with the intention to transfer—almost[112] as if the document were an ordinary chattel. It was, however, disputed whether by itself the delivery of the documentary note was adequate to transfer the right to collect the debt[113] or whether an accompanying properly executed bill of sale was also required from the transferor-lender.[114] In the post-Talmudic era, the bill of sale requirement

[106] De Zulueta, *Part II* 166. Cf JW Jones, *The Law and Legal Theory of the Greeks: An Introduction* (Clarendon Press 1956) 220–22. But cf eg Berger, *Dictionary of Roman Law* 727, according to whom 'It is doubtful whether a *syngraphe* was valid if the obligation assumed therein by a party was not based on a real transaction.'

[107] *The Institutes of Gaius*, Book III § 134. See eg translation by Gordon and Robinson 341. See also De Zulueta, *Part I* 195

[108] AM Fuss, 'Shetar', *The Principles of Jewish Law* (reprinted from M Elon (ed), 1st edn, *Encyclopedia Judaica*, Keter 1975) (column 184).

[109] See Tosafot Rid, Talmud, *Gittin* 18A.

[110] See eg Talmud, *Gittin*, at 29A and 84B (a bill of divorce subject to external conditions) and *Ketuvot* at 19B (validity of testimony as to a condition).

[111] See eg Talmud, *Bava Kamma*, at 62B (dealing with a thief's exemption to pay the double payment for which a thief of an ordinary chattel is liable) and 98A (dealing with loss incurred when a loan document is burnt). Lack of intrinsic value in a loan document is also alluded to eg in Talmud, *Kiddushin* at 9A, 26A, and 48A.

[112] However, while *mesira* (delivery) is available for the transfer of a loan document, not all methods for transferring a chattel, such as *hagbaha* (lifting) and *meshicha* (drawing near or pulling), as well as *chalifin* (barter, namely, the exchange of two chattels) are available for acquiring ownership in a loan document. See in general Talmud, *Kiddushin* at 25B (as well as 22B) and *Bava Batra* at 84B, as well as *Bava Metzia* at 46A. See also Talmud, *Bava Batra* at 76A, commentary by both Rashi D'H 'Ve-otiyot bimsira', and Tosafot, D'H 'Iy', and *Bava Batra* at 77A, commentary by Tosafot, D'H 'Amar Ameimar'.

[113] Those satisfied with mere delivery of the document as a transfer of the right to collect the debt nevertheless disagree as to whether a transferee, or in fact any person in possession of a documentary note payable to another person, is required to prove title (namely, receipt by way of transfer or by way of gift from the named payee or someone deriving title from the named payee) or suffice it for the transferee/possessor to rely on his or her possession. See Talmud, *Bava Batra* 173A.

[114] For the Talmudic discussions, see Talmud, *Kiddushin* at 47B–48A where it is further disputed as to whether, to effect a transfer, the bill of sale (if needed) is required to contain prescribed language. See also Talmud, *Bava Batra* 75B–77B (with Tosafot at 77A D'H 'Amar Ameimar'), Talmud, *Sanhedrin* 31A, and Talmud, *Yevamot* 115B.

appeared to have prevailed.[115] It was further determined that the power of the lender to release the borrower survives the transfer.[116]

4. The English Bond: Debt on an 'Obligation'

Medieval common law recognized the bond, deed, or bill obligatory, as a 'specialty', that was a formal writing under seal on which the debtor was liable in Debt on an Obligation.[117] It was settled that 'in Debt on a contract the plaintiff shows in his count for what cause the defendant has become his debtor: otherwise in Debt on an Obligation [ie specialty], for the obligation is a contract in itself'.[118] Being of 'high nature', the undertaking under a specialty contract was divorced from the consideration thereto and could not be varied or contradicted by any extrinsic evidence.[119] 'The defendant was bound by the deed, the whole deed and nothing but the deed.'[120] As early as 1422, it was determined that 'if I am your debtor ... by a simple contract and I make an obligation to you for the same [amount] on the same contract ... I am discharged of the contract by obligation'.[121] **2.56**

A bond could be conditional so that an action thereon could be met by the debtor's plea of breach of conditions set out or referred to therein,[122] but not outside it.[123] **2.57**

[115] For the shift of position in that direction shortly after the conclusion of the Talmud see E Westreich, 'Elements of Negotiability in Talmudic and Geonic Times' in J Cohen (ed) *Jewish Commercial Law: Essays in Memory of George Weber*, XIX Jewish Association Studies (JALS) 247 (Deborah Charles Publications 2008) 259–66. For a ruling see Rambam, *Kinyan: Hilchot Mechira*, Section 6, Rules 10–11; Choshen Mishpat in both *Tur* and *Shulchan Aruch* Section 66, Rule 1. Cf Rambam, *Mishpatim: Hilchot Malveh ve-Loveh*, Section 16, Rule 7 (in conjunction with the Magid Mishna on the point) discussing evidentiary requirements in circumstances in which the bill of sale has been lost (as well as a plea by the debtor that he or she has paid to the original creditor). The Rambam appears to dispense with the transferee's need to produce evidence for the transfer when sued by the transferor, but not in suing the debtor who contests the transfer.

[116] Rambam, *Kinyan: Hilchot Mechira*, Section 6, Rule 12. See also Choshen Mishpat Section 66, Rules 23–24 (also stressing that the power to release may not be effectively contracted out). For the dispute on the point see Talmud, *Bava Metzia* 20A and *Ketuvot* 85B–86A.

[117] For Debt on an Obligation, namely, on a document deed under seal, see eg JH Baker, *An Introduction to English Legal History* (5th edn, Oxford University Press 2019) 338–49. See also MM Postan, 'Private Financial Instruments in Medieval England' (1930), reprinted in MM Postan, *Medieval Trade and Finance* (Cambridge University Press 1973) 28 (hereafter Postan, 'Medieval Trade'), and AWB Simpson, 'The Penal Bond with Conditional Defeasance' in *Legal Theory and Legal History: Essays on the Common Law* (Hambledon Press 1987) 143 (hereafter Simpson, 'Penal Bond').

[118] *Anon* (1385) Bellewe 111, 72 ER 47, the English translation, according to CHS Fifoot, *History and Sources of the Common Law: Tort and Contract* (Stevens & Sons 1949) 225 (hereafter Fifoot, *History*).

[119] For a specialty obligation that owes its validity only to its formal execution independently of any consideration see eg JB Ames, 'Specialty Contracts and Equitable Defenses' in *Lectures in Legal History and Miscellaneous Legal Essays* (Harvard University Press 1913) 104 (hereafter Ames, *Legal History*).

[120] Fifoot, *History* 231.

[121] *Salman v Barkyng* (1422) YB 1 Hen VI (reprinted 1933, 50 Selden Society 114), 115 per Babington J. Note the medieval terminology: a 'contract' is not a 'promise' but the benefit conferred on the defendant under the transaction. 'Obligation' is the specialty contract. See Fifoot, *History* 225.

[122] JH Baker, 'The Law Merchant and the Common Law Before 1700' (1979) 38 Cambridge LJ 295, 324 (hereafter Baker, 'Law Merchant').

[123] See eg *Esthalle v Esthalle* (1613) YB 6 and 7 Ed 2 Eyre of Kent vol II (27 Selden Society 21), and in Fifoot, *History* 244, 246.

Accordingly, failure of consideration and other defences under the transaction for which an unconditional bond was taken did not constitute at common law a valid defence to an action on the bond.[124] Similarly, upon the production of a bond, the debtor could not raise the defence of payment.[125] According to the same logic, loss of the deed precluded the creditor from suing the debtor altogether.[126]

2.58 'At common law, ... a debt was looked upon as a strictly personal obligation'[127] and its assignment was prohibited.[128] In turn, the autonomy of the bond resembled the abstract nature of the Roman law *stipulatio*. Being self-contained, namely, confined to the contours of the formula and not to any outside event, the *stipulatio* was a formal, unilateral, and *stricti juris* contract. However, the *stipulatio* is a verbal contract, solemnly concluded in a face-to-face exchange of a question and an answer between two persons—it was not a literal, namely, written, contract. Indeed, it is possible for the origins of the English specialty to be traced to formal notarized documents appearing around the time of Justinian,[129] the latter being 'the sole basis of the engagement' agreed upon;[130] at the same time, the underlying legal theory of the specialty is that of a Roman unilateral *stricti juris* formal contract. However, contrary to the verbal *stipulatio*, the English specialty or deed was a literal contract.

2.59 Ultimately, the abstract nature of the obligation on a deed under common law was seriously compromised in England by the Chancellor. In Courts of Equity, defences founded on the conduct of the obligee on a specialty could successfully be raised. Thus, 'whenever it was plainly unjust for [the obligee] to insist upon his strict legal right' the Chancellor would 'furnish the obligor with a defence by enjoining the action'.[131] Equitable jurisdiction encompassed the defence of failure of consideration under the underlying contract.[132] Effectively then, the absolute discharge conferred by law for a simple debt paid by deed did not prevent the Court of Equity from allowing the party liable to meet the action on the deed with defences arising from the contract that gave rise to the debt. In hindsight, this development heralded rules as to the availability of personal defences between immediate parties to a bill or note.

[124] Ames, *Legal History* 108.
[125] ibid, 109.
[126] ibid, 104–05.
[127] *Fitzroy v Cave* [1905] 2 KB 364 [372], [1904-7] All ER Rep 194.
[128] Objections to assignability of choses in action in the common law are summarized by WR Warren, *The Law Relating to Choses in Action* (Sweet & Maxwell 1899) 31–32. They include maintenance, the duty of a debtor to seek out his or her creditor, and the need to complete transfer of ownership by means of physical delivery.
[129] For formal notarized documents under Justinian (and shortly before him), see Usher, *Deposit Banking* 41–44.
[130] Usher, *Deposit Banking* 42.
[131] Ames, *Legal History* 106.
[132] ibid, 108–09. Other defences were fraud, illegality, payment, accord and satisfaction, discharge of surety, accommodation, duress, agreement not to sue, and acquiescence.

F. Bills, Notes, and Cheques in Post-Medieval England: The Origins of the Modern Law of Negotiable Instruments

1. The 'Reception' of the Bill of Exchange in England—The Myth of the 'Law Merchant'

The letter of payment, being the predecessor of the bill of exchange, 'with an English drawer or an English [drawee]', appeared in England at the close of the fourteenth century; its use increased in the course of the fifteenth and sixteenth centuries.[133] As elsewhere in Europe, it originally functioned as a mechanism for the execution of the exchange transaction.[134] Being a latecomer to the European theatre of international trade, England appears to pioneer the employment of the inland bill, used as a payment and credit device for domestic transactions, as of the of the seventeenth century.[135] **2.60**

An early detailed English bill of exchange report on record is *Burton v Davy* (1437).[136] This was an action brought by a bearer of a bill against its drawee. Beutel treats the case as reflecting 'the complete development of the negotiable bill of exchange'.[137] This 'conventional interpretation of *Burton v Davy*' is, however, effectively challenged by Rogers[138] who explains the judgment as enforcing a debt liability on an international exchange transaction in Bruges, rather than on a bill of exchange issued with respect to it. In this case, the drawer bought goods in Flanders for his principal, the drawee in England. He borrowed in Flanders from the remitter, acting as an agent for the payee (the actual lender) in England. The drawee's liability was thus not on the bill, so as not to require acceptance;[139] rather, it was on a simple debt.[140] **2.61**

Towards the end of the seventeenth century, the bill had come to facilitate the remittance of funds between two places, including domestically, and in situations unrelated to an exchange transaction. In the process, the remitter and payee became unrelated; instead of a principal and agent, they became a debtor and creditor. Hence, the **2.62**

133 Postan, 'Medieval Trade' 58.

134 ibid, 54–64 and Munro, 'Medieval Origins' 542–46.

135 Marius, *Concerning Bills* 3, JS Rogers, *The Early History of the Law of Bills and Notes: A Study of the Origins of Anglo-American Commercial Law* (Cambridge University Press 1995) 100–16 (hereafter Rogers, *Early History*).

136 49 SS 117. Seldon Society, *Select Cases Concerning the Law Merchant* (ed by H Hall) vol 3, vol 49 (Selden Society, Bernard Quaritch 1932) 117 (hereafter Selden Society, *Law Merchant*).

137 FK Beutel, 'The Development of Negotiable Instruments in Early English Law' (1938) 51 Harv L Rev 813, 831.

138 Rogers, *Early History* 44–51. See also SE Sachs, 'Burying Burton: Burton v. Davy and the Law of Negotiable Instruments' (*Medieval Studies 117: Constitutional and Legal History of Medieval England, Prof. Charles Donahue, Jr.*, 21 May 2002) http://www.stevesachs.com/papers/paper_burton.html, accessed 25 January 2019. Also, De Roover disagrees with Beutel's interpretation: De Roover, *Lettre de Change* 111.

139 The report does not mention anything re possible acceptance by Davy. Munro's speculation as to the existence of 'acceptance', Munro, 'Medieval Origins' 552, does not appear to us to be supportable.

140 Under Medieval law, the credit purchase of goods by one person to the use of another charged, the latter is debt. See eg *Randolph v Abbot of Hailes* (1313–14) Eyre of Kent, 6 and 7 Edw II (1912) 27 Selden

procedural accommodation to a new action, as just discussed, did not suffice to underpin liability in a new emerging setting.

2.63 Thus, in *Chat and Edgar Case* (1663)[141] a plaintiff-seller, payee of a bill, sued the drawer who lent money to the buyer. In holding for payee/plaintiff-seller, the Court theorized the drawer's liability to the payee in 'an action upon the case' on the basis of 'the custom of merchants'. Unlike under an exchange transaction, the drawer was a lender to the remitter-buyer who promised the remitter-buyer to pay the payee-seller. The latter, in suing the drawer, did not exercise the remitter's right against the drawer, but rather, his (plaintiff-seller)'s own right. Hence, legal doctrine that developed to accommodate the exchange transaction was ill fit to cover the newly emerging remittance facility. This forced a new thinking on the matter of the drawer's liability to the payee.[142]

2.64 Indeed, in a transaction in which the drawer dealt directly with the payee, 'an implicit but real undertaking' made by the drawer to the payee 'could reasonably be said' to exist, so as to be actionable in assumpsit.[143] However, in the facts of *Chat and Edgar Case*, the drawer-lender's bill reflected his promise given to the buyer and there was neither privity between drawer-lender and payee-seller, nor the former's intent to benefit the latter.[144]

2.65 To fasten liability on the payee to the drawer, the Court bypassed the tormented route of adaptation of Roman law principles, as carried out by Continental scholars and discussed in section D (3); rather, the Court purported to rely on 'the custom of merchants'. Echoing the basis for the successful action in *Burton v Davy* (1437), *viz.*, 'the law merchant and custom of the city of London . . . from a time of which no memory survives',[145] the Court avoided the need for a painful, doctrinal, soul-searching exercise. It also linked the decision to an old rationale already used to fasten liability on a bill, albeit on the drawee and not the drawer. Almost in passing, a major innovation came about: a drawer was held liable to a payee even in the absence of privity and actual intention to benefit him or her, and notwithstanding the failure of consideration between the drawer and the remitter.

2.66 *Burton v Davy* (1437)[146] may further be responsible for an emerging interchangeability between 'law merchant' and 'custom'. The conventional wisdom is that in recognizing bills, common law 'received' along with them 'the law which had grown up around them on the Continent'. This occurred in a process of 'reception

Society 32 (purchase by a monk for the use of the Abbot of the House); *Anon* (1379) Bellewe 59, 72 ER 25 (purchase by a servant to the use of his or her master); and *Anon* (1379) Bellewe 110, 72 ER 47 (purchase by 'my bailiff . . . to my use').

141 1 Keble 636, 83 ER 1156.
142 To that effect, see also Rogers, *Early History* 125–26.
143 Baker, 'Law Merchant' 311.
144 While in the course of the seventeenth-century privity requirements were not rigid, a party not in privity, namely, a party other than the promisee, could not sue on a promise, unless he or she was intended by the promissor to benefit from it. See Simpson, 'Penal Bond' 475–85.
145 49 SS 117. Selden Society, *Law Merchant* 117.
146 ibid..

[that] took place under cover of the recognition of mercantile custom'. Ultimately, this body of imported 'mercantile custom' was adapted to be accommodated in the framework of common law vocabulary and legal doctrine.[147] Indeed, reliance on the custom of merchants in pleadings for actions on bills of exchange in common law courts is traced by Rogers back to the early part of the seventeenth century. Towards the middle of that century, reference to the delivery of money in exchange transactions is omitted and adaptation is made to the transformation of the use of the bill of exchange. In the late seventeenth century a detailed recital of mercantile custom disappears. Along the way, any reference to a particular local usage that requires proof is superseded by general custom of the realm that is alleged to exist from time immemorial, so as to become part of the common law of England.[148] Holden speaks in general of an 'action on the case upon the custom of merchants'.[149]

Reliance on custom as a source of innovation in the common law, expanding the frontiers of liability, is nonetheless not unique to bills; rather, it goes back to the early development of action on the case, as the instrument for expanding civil liability in general. This is true for innkeepers' duty to 'keep (*garde*) the goods and chattels which their guests had in their rooms within the inn while they were lodged there';[150] the duty of 'a man [to] answer for his fire, which by misfortune burns another's goods';[151] the duty of 'masters and governors of ships which go from London beyond sea . . . to keep safely day and night' goods which they carry 'without loss or subtraction . . .';[152] or even more generally the duty of every man to 'use his own as not to injure another' as a matter of '[t]he law [in] general'.[153] **2.67**

The reports of these cases do not contain any record of evidence put forward as to the existence of the alleged custom. Nor do they contain any hint as to a factual dispute about its existence. Accordingly, in saying that 'the common custom of the realm is the common law of the realm',[154] judges took upon themselves the power to expand common law liability as they saw fit. **2.68**

Thus, as a manifestation of 'the common custom of the realm', 'law merchant' was not an imported body of substantive law, governing rights and liabilities of parties to a transaction or instrument. Nor was it a self-contained autonomous set of mercantile usages.[155] Rather, 'the custom of the realm', deemed to be universal, general, and **2.69**

[147] W Holdsworth, *A History of English Law*, vol VIII (2nd edn, Methuen, Sweet & Maxwell 1937, reprinted 1966) 151 (hereafter Holdsworth, *English Law*).

[148] See detailed analysis by Rogers, *Early History* 137–50.

[149] JM Holden, *The History of Negotiable Instruments in English Law* (first published 1955, WM W Gaunt & Sons 1993) 33 (hereafter Holden, *Negotiable Instruments*).

[150] *The Innkeeper's Case* (1369) YB Easter 42 Ed 3, f.11, pl 13, as reproduced in Fifoot, *History* 80.

[151] *Beaulieu v Finglam* (1401) YB 2 Hen 4, f.18, pl 6, as reproduced in Fifoot, *History* 166.

[152] *Morse v Slue* (1671) 1 Ventris 190, 86 ER 129; Fifoot, *History* 171.

[153] *Turberville v Stamp* (1697) 12 Mod 152, 88 ER 1228, Fifoot, *History* 167, 168.

[154] *Beaulieu v Finglam* (1401) YB 2 Hen 4, f.18, pl 6, as reproduced in Fifoot, *History* 166.

[155] Baker was prepared to 'settle' on its existence as 'an expeditious procedure especially adapted for the needs of men who could not tarry for the common law'. Baker, 'Law Merchant' 301.

ancient, was just another avenue for action on the case to take over and expand liability in the common law.

2.70 Three judgments involving Lord Holt are of particular interest. First, *Anon* (1694)[156] was 'an action upon the case' on a bill of exchange 'brought by the last indorsee against the first indorsee'. In the view of Lord Holt, '[t]he action well lies; for the indorsement is quasi a new bill, and a warranty by the indorser, that the bill shall be paid'.[157] Neither custom nor law merchant was mentioned. Second, in *Anon* (1696)[158] defendant's liability was established under the law of bill of exchange, in the context of Indebitatus Assumpsit. Third, *Starke v Cheeseman* (1700)[159] was 'an action upon the case upon a bill of exchange' in which the drawer was held liable in assumpsit on a promise implied in the drawing of the bill.[160] 'Custom' as a basis for the action was only mentioned by the plaintiff in argument.[161] It had become apparent that the alleged 'reception' 'was in reality nothing other than a refinement of the common law which had always governed mercantile affairs'[162] so that by the end of the seventeenth century, the utility of 'law merchant' and 'custom' as facades to the actual development of common law principles of liability faded.

2. The Emergence of Notes and Cheques in England

2.71 The use in England of cheques and banknotes, the latter being the forerunners of promissory notes, goes back to the goldsmiths.[163] During the Civil War, they commenced to receive money for safekeeping.[164] During the Cromwellian period, at the beginning of the second half of the seventeenth century, by accepting deposits with full authority to lend out of them, the goldsmith turned into a banker.[165]

2.72 Goldsmiths issued receipts with respect to moneys deposited with them.[166] Some receipts were payable to the order of a payee and others to the bearer. Either way, the instrument contained the goldsmith's undertaking to pay on demand when presented with the receipt. It came to be known as a goldsmith's or banker's note and evolved into an early form of the promissory note.[167] Alternatively, rather than taking goldsmiths'

[156] *Anon* (1694) Holt KB 115, 90 ER 962.
[157] ibid. At present, indorser's liability to the holder upon the dishonour of the bill is set out in s 55(2)(a) of the Bills of Exchange Act, 1882 (UK) 45 and 46 Vict, c 61, as amended (hereafter BEA) (which nonetheless departs from the case in not making the indorser liable *only* 'upon the drawer's default of payment'.
[158] Holt KB 296, 90 ER 1063.
[159] 1 Ld Raym 538, 91 ER 1259.
[160] At present, the drawer's liability to the holder upon the dishonour of the bill is set out in s 55(1)(a) of the BEA.
[161] *Starke v Cheeseman* 1 Ld Raym 538, 91 ER 1259.
[162] Baker, 'Law Merchant' 322.
[163] But cf JK Horsefield, *British Monetary Experiments, 1650–1710* (Harvard University Press 1960) 93–217, canvassing earlier and parallel experimentation in note issuing and other forms of paper money.
[164] Rogers, *Early History* 119.
[165] RD Richards, *The Early History of Banking in England* (first published 1929, AM Kelley 1965) 37.
[166] ibid, 40–43.
[167] Holden, *Negotiable Instruments* 70–73. For the evolution of the form of the goldsmiths' note, see also A Feavearyear, *The Pound Sterling—A History of English Money* (ed by EV Morgan, 2nd edn, Clarendon Press 1963) 107–08.

notes, a depositor was allowed to draw upon the goldsmith various amounts up to the amount of the deposit. Such drafts, payable on demand and made out to a payee or bearer, were cheques.[168]

Originally, the banknote was a deposit certificate on which the running account and its balance were marked.[169] Subsequently, the gross deposit was subdivided into several receipts in various denominations; instead of one note containing a single promise to pay the entire sum, the goldsmith gave a series of promises to pay a number of smaller sums making up the total of the deposit.[170] Finally, such notes might be issued by a goldsmith, as proceeds of a loan,[171] against the negotiation, and hence discount, of bills of exchange and promissory notes.[172] Goldsmith notes could pass freely from hand to hand in payment of debts between each transferor and transferee so as to substitute money. **2.73**

Shortly after its establishment,[173] the Bank of England began to issue to depositors, 'probably to a very considerable extent',[174] notes payable to the bearer, similar to those of the goldsmith.[175] They competed successfully with goldsmith notes and finally superseded them as paper money to further enhance accommodation to the needs of commerce.[176] **2.74**

3. Bills, Notes, and Cheques Acquire Negotiability

(a) Introduction

Bills, notes, and cheques have been distinct types of instruments. By acquiring 'negotiability' on its own, each became governed by the same branch of law. As discussed in Chapter I section A, negotiability addresses two features. The first feature is that of transferability by 'negotiation', that is, the physical delivery, accompanied by the transferor's indorsement when so required; this characteristic is called formal or procedural negotiability. The other feature of negotiability is that of the ability of an acquirer by negotiation to have a better title from that of the transferor. This is material negotiability. **2.75**

(b) Negotiation of Bills Payable to Order

At its inception, the indorsement of a bill of exchange payable to order was not conceptualized as a transfer of the bill. Rather, in the footsteps of the Continental explanation **2.76**

[168] For this development, see Holden, *Negotiable Instruments* 206–10.

[169] For this practice, see eg *Cooksey v Boverie* (1693) 2 Show KB 296, 89 ER 949 [296–97].

[170] JB Martin, *'The Grasshopper' in Lombard Street* (first published 1892, Burt Franklin 1968) 127.

[171] For this development, see Holdsworth, *English Law* 190–91.

[172] A Smith, *The Wealth of Nations*, vol 1 (prefaced by GJ Stigler, ed by E Cannan, first published 1776, University of Chicago Press 1976) 316; G Tucker, *The Theory of Money & Banks Investigated* (first published 1839, AM Kelly 1964) 161, 164.

[173] The Ways and Means Act, 1694 (UK), 5 & 6 Will & Mar, c 20, s XIX.

[174] *Bank of England v Anderson* (1837) 3 Bing NC 589 [654], 132 ER 538 [562], per Tindal CJ (CP).

[175] Holden, *Negotiable Instruments* 89–90. For their evolution see RD Richards, *The Early History of Banking in England* (first published 1929, AM Kelley 1965) 153.

[176] Holden, *Negotiable Instruments* 92.

set out in section D (3), by indorsing a bill, the indorser incurred liability on it. It was the impact as well as the desired effect of that liability to create both the appearance and actual results of a transfer.

2.77 Thus, in *Anon* (1694) Lord Holt theorized the indorsement as 'quasi a new bill, and a warranty by the indorser, that the bill shall be paid'.[177] This was also the theory of *Williams v Field* (1694) where it was held that since 'every indorsement is a new bill', 'the last indorsee may bring an action against any of the indorsers',[178] including those with whom he was not in privity.

2.78 Discounting of bills, first domestic and subsequently foreign bills, originated from London goldsmiths during the seventeenth and eighteenth centuries.[179] Under that practice, a payee of a term bill, drawn on the drawer's factor or buyer, could obtain finance by indorsing the bill and obtaining its present value. In the case of a sale of goods, the bill could have been made payable by the drawer-seller to him or herself, to allow the drawer-seller to obtain its present value shortly after the shipment of the goods before their resale by the buyer. Value could have been obtained against such 'trade bills', even prior to acceptance, against the indorsement of the payee, or after acceptance, also against the credit of the accepting drawee.[180] This method of financing the sale of goods between distant parties proliferated in the nineteenth century[181] and has survived to the present day.[182]

(c) Negotiation of Notes Payable to Order

2.79 Goldsmith notes and, later, Bank of England notes, as well as credit obligations by merchants[183] and repayment obligations of borrowers to their goldsmith lenders, were promissory notes. To accommodate their use as a source of liquidity, merchants required transferability. For notes payable to a named creditor, it was therefore tempting to attempt to transfer them by means of an indorsement, so that the indorsement on a note would have been a bill, instructing the maker to pay the indorsee.

2.80 After some confusion on the matter,[184] and having in fact stated in *Tassell and Lee v Lewis* (1695) that '[a] goldsmith's note indorsed is as a bill of exchange to the

[177] Holt KB 115, 90 ER 962.

[178] 3 Salk 68, 91 ER 696. For an earlier obiter to that effect see *Hodges v Steward* (1691) 1 Salk 125, 91 ER 117 (second point). On the last point see also the earlier case of *Claxton v Swift* (1685) 3 Mod Rep 86, 87 ER 55. In fact this is the rationale for the 'several laws' doctrine discussed at length in Chapter IV (see text accompanying notes 20–72).

[179] R De Roover, 'What is Dry Exchange?' in 'New Interpretations' 184–85, 230–31.

[180] For a detailed analysis see Rogers, *Early History* 100–24. See also P Temin, 'Financial Intermediation in the Early Roman Empire' (2004) 64 Journal of Economic History 705, 713–14.

[181] A point noted by N Ferguson, *The Ascent of Money* (Penguin Press 2008) 53.

[182] See eg W Baker and JF Dolan, *User's Handbook for Documentary Credits under UCP 600* (ICC 2008), describing at 37–42 step by step the documentary draft transaction. See also A Mugasha, *The Law of Letters of Credit and Bank Guarantees* (Federation Press 2003) 6–9.

[183] Whose Continental origins and practice as 'bills obligatory' are discussed by G Malynes, *Consuetudo, vel, Lex Mercatoria* (first published 1685, Professional Books 1981) 72–76.

[184] See eg *Hill v Lewis* (1693) 1 Salk 132, 91 ER 124, where Lord Holt stated that 'goldsmiths [*sic*] bills were governed by the same laws and customs as other bills of exchange'. Alternatively, Lord Holt may have been prepared to set aside goldsmith notes from other promissory notes so to as to be governed by rules applicable to bills of exchange. See also *Williams v Williams* (1693) Carth 269, 90 ER 759.

indorser',[185] Lord Holt ruled decisively against this position in *Clerke v Martin* (1702).[186] This was an action by a payee-lender against his borrower, maker of a promissory note. One count was 'upon the custom of merchants, as upon a bill of exchange'. Having stated that 'this note could not be a bill of exchange', Lord Holt held that the theory underlying that cause of action 'amounted to the setting up a new sort of specialty, unknown to the common law, and invented in Lombard-Street, which attempted ... to give laws to Westminster-Hall'.[187] Around the same time he also consistently ruled elsewhere, on behalf of an entire Court, that 'a declaration upon the *custom of merchants* upon a note ... was void; for it tended to make *a note* ... to *a specialty*'.[188]

Lord Holt's decision in *Clerke v Martin* (1702) was not received well[189] and, shortly thereafter, it was overruled by the Promissory Notes Act 1704. This Act provided that notes payable to order[190] are 'assignable or indorsible over within the Custom of Merchants' and 'in the same Manner as Inland Bills of Exchange'.[191] Thereafter, the characterization of an indorsement of a note as a new bill was specifically confirmed.[192] **2.81**

(d) Negotiation of Instruments Payable to the Bearer

Having originated in Ancient Mesopotamia,[193] and reappearing in Medieval Europe,[194] a bearer clause may have authorized or even required the debtor to pay the bearer, and yet without determining, as between the original creditor and the bearer, to whom the proceeds belong.[195] While a bearer clause appears in *Burton v Davy* (1437),[196] the power of the bearer of an instrument having such a clause to bring an action against a drawer in the bearer's own name was settled in England only as late as in *Grant v Vaughan* (1764).[197] In support of his decision, Lord Mansfield cited *Hinton's Case* (1682),[198] where in order to recover from the drawer, a bearer was required to be a taker in good faith and for value. In fact, Lord Mansfield recognized earlier in *Miller v Race* (1758)[199] the title of a bona fide purchaser for value of a lost or stolen note payable to bearer. He was thus bound in *Grant v Vaughan* (1764) to allow the bearer to **2.82**

185 *Tassell and Lee v Lewis* (1695) 1 Ld Raym 743, 91 ER 1397 [744].

186 *Clerke v Martin* (1702) 2 Ld Raym 757, 92 ER 6.

187 ibid, 758 (Ld Raym), 6 (ER).

188 *Cutting v Williams* (1702) 7 Mod 154 [155], 87 ER 1160 [1161] (emphasis in original).

189 The 'deluge' of criticism is summarized by Holden, *Negotiable Instruments* 80–84. For a forceful (and in my view convincing) defence of Lord Holt, see Rogers, *Early History* 177–86.

190 Or more specifically, 'Notes in Writing signed by the Party who makes the same whereby such Party promises to pay unto any other Person or his Order any Sum of Money therein mentioned.' However, the marginal note refers to 'Promissory Notes'.

191 Promissory Notes Act 1704, 3 and 4 Ann c 8 (Chapter IX in the Common Printed Editions) s 1 (Preamble). The first three sections of the Act (albeit lumped as s 1) are reproduced in Holden, *Negotiable Instruments* 327 (Appendix C).

192 *Harry v Perrit* (1710) 1 Salk 133, 91 ER 126.

193 Bogaert, *Les Origins*.

194 See in general Holdsworth, *English Law* 113–26, as well as by R De Roover, *Lettre de Change* 87–94. For detailed discussions see H Brunner, 'Les Titres au porteur Français du Moyen-Age' (1886) 10 Nouvelle revue historique de droit Français et étranger 11 (Parts I–III) and 139 (Parts IV–V).

195 ibid.

196 49 SS 117. Selden Society, *Law Merchant* 117.

197 3 Burr 1516, 97 ER 957.

198 2 Show KB 235, 89 ER 911.

199 1 Burr 452 [457], 97 ER 398 [401] (KB).

recover; it would have been incongruous to protect the bearer's property right in conversion[200] and yet not allow him to sue for the sum payable on the instrument.

(e) Negotiation of Cheques

2.83 In England, judicial recognition in the transfer by negotiation of cheques came late, and not without hesitation.[201] This disproves the view under which 'cheques ... were simply bills of exchange drawn upon a person carrying on a particular profession and payable on demand'.[202] Rather, historically, the cheque was a distinct type of instrument; only in hindsight did it come to be viewed as a sub-category of the bill.

2.84 Judicial recognition in the transfer by negotiation of cheques goes back to *Grant v Vaughan* (1764).[203] It was held that a 'cash-note' drawn upon a banker, namely a cheque, payable to a named payee or bearer, is 'by law, negotiable'.[204] As well, *Boehm v Sterling* (1797)[205] was an action brought 'upon a bill of exchange'[206] to enforce payment on a cheque payable to the bearer. It was argued there that the cheque was not considered negotiable, so that 'whoever receives it in payment takes it on the credit of the person giving it and not on the intrinsic credit of the instrument itself'.[207] To Lord Kenyon, this proposition 'appear[ed] most extraordinary',[208] and he dismissed it outright. Similarly, *Serle v Norton* (1841)[209] did not question the right of a non-payee holder of a cheque payable to the order to sue the drawer.[210]

2.85 Transferability by negotiation of a cheque was finally confirmed in *Keene v Beard* (1860).[211] Byles J pointed out two unique features of a cheque that distinguish it from an ordinary bill. First, a cheque appropriates drawer's funds held by the drawee.[212] On this point he was subsequently overruled by case law[213] and later by statute.[214] Second, a cheque 'is not discharged by delay in the presentment, unless ... he has been prejudiced thereby'.[215] On this point, his ruling was subsequently codified.[216] Otherwise,

[200] For the action on the case for *Trover and Conversion*, from which the tort of conversion, as misappropriation of property, is derived, and for its effective 'takeover' of Detinue, see Fifoot, *History* 102–25.
[201] For a review of the process, see Holden, *Negotiable Instruments* 215–19.
[202] ibid, 208. See also Holdsworth, *English Law*) 190.
[203] 3 Burr 1516, 97 ER 957.
[204] ibid, 1523 (Burr), 961 (ER).
[205] *Boehm v Sterling* (1797) 7 TR 423, 101 ER 1055.
[206] ibid, 423 (TR), 1056 (ER).
[207] ibid, 428 (TR), 1058 (ER).
[208] ibid, 430 (TR), 1059 (R).
[209] 2 Mood & R 401, 174 ER 331.
[210] Unfortunately, the Report contains a 'somewhat irrelevant and certainly inaccurate footnote' to the contrary. See Holden, *Negotiable Instruments* 218.
[211] 8 CBNS 372, 141 ER 1210 (CCP) (hereafter *Keene*).
[212] ibid, 381.
[213] *Hopkinson v Forster* (1874) LR 19 Eq 74 [76] (Jessel MR).
[214] BEA s 53(1), providing, other than for Scotland, that '[a] bill, of itself, does not operate as an assignment of funds in the hands of the drawee available for the payment thereof, and the drawee of a bill who does not accept as required by this Act is not liable on the instrument'.
[215] *Keene* 381.
[216] BEA s 74.

Byles J was of the view that a cheque 'has ... all the incidents of an ordinary bill of exchange';[217] as such it 'falls within the class of ordinary bills of exchange'.[218]

(f) Material Negotiability

Material negotiability addresses the transferor's power to confer on the transferee a better title than that of the transferor.[219] An early case is *Anon* (1699),[220] in which a purchaser for value from a finder of a 'bank bill' payable to a payee or bearer prevailed over the original payee who lost it.[221] **2.86**

The leading case is *Miller v Race* (1758).[222] This was an action in *Trover and Conversion*[223] by a bona fide purchaser for value of a stolen Bank of England note payable to bearer. Lord Mansfield ruled in the plaintiff's favour, thereby recognizing the effect of his good faith purchase for value to extinguish the dispossessed original owner's property right.[224] **2.87**

The extension of 'negotiability', in the sense of freedom from adverse claims, to instruments was with the view of enhancing liquidity by paper circulation,[225] upon which the expansion of banking became partly dependent.[226] For example, suppose the owner-holder of a bill of exchange payable to order indorsed it and delivered it to an intermediary, either as a pledge for a loan or for safekeeping. The intermediary, however, betrayed the owner (the previous holder); he discounted the bill of exchange with a bank and misappropriated the proceeds. In such a case, as long as the discounting bank (being a purchaser for value) acted in good faith, the effect of negotiability was to protect it from the adverse claim of the defrauded owner.[227] However, so far as protection from adverse claims are concerned, Anglo-American law went its own way in not extending it to one who derives title directly or indirectly through a forged or unauthorized indorsement.[228] **2.88**

Hussey v Jacob (1696)[229] and *Anon* (1697)[230] may be the earliest cases to say that a party liable on an instrument may not raise against a bona fide purchaser of the instrument defences available to the former against the payee. The position was later confirmed in *Haly v Lane* (1741)[231] and *Morris v Lee* (1786).[232] In *Lickbarrow v Mason* (1787), the Court observed with respect to a bill of exchange that 'as between the drawer and the **2.89**

[217] *Keene* 381.
[218] ibid.
[219] See DV Cowen and L Gering, *Cowen on the Law of Negotiable Instruments in South Africa*, vol I General Principles (5th edn, Juta 1985) 31–36.
[220] *Anon* (1699) 3 Salk 71, 91 ER 698.
[221] ibid.
[222] 1 Burr 452 [457], 97 ER 398 [401] (KB).
[223] For *Trover and Conversion*, see reference in Fifoot, *History* 225.
[224] Miller v Race (1758)1 Burr 452 [457–478], 97 ER 398 [401].
[225] See eg Holden, *Negotiable Instruments* 294–98.
[226] See sub-section 1.
[227] See eg *London Joint Stock Bank v Simmons* [1892] AC 201, [1891-4] All ER Rep 415.
[228] *Mead v Young* (1790) 4 TR 28, 100 ER 876.
[229] 1 Comyns 4, 92 ER 929.
[230] 1 Comyns 43, 92 ER 950.
[231] 2 Atk 181, 26 ER 513.
[232] 1 Comyns 43, 92 ER 950.

payee the consideration may be gone into, yet it cannot between the drawer and an indorsee'.[233]

2.90 The inability of an obligor on an instrument to meet an action on it by defences arising from the underlying transaction makes the obligation autonomous or abstract. However, the doctrinal basis of this autonomy or abstraction is not easily traceable.

2.91 In terminology borrowed from Roman law, a written obligation is autonomous or abstract when it is under a literal, unilateral, *stricti juris*, and formal contract.[234] Ames was of the view that '[i]n Scotland, and in Europe generally, a bill or note is recognized to be a *literarum obligatio*'.[235] In fact, this characterization is correct for Germany, but not for France. However, the Continental approach does not prove to be helpful. In both Germany and France, pragmatic considerations prevailed,[236] so that the issue of a bill or note does not novate the obligation for which the instrument was given. As a result, defences arising from the underlying transaction are not forfeited and remain available to the obligor against the payee, and in fact against any transferee other than in good faith.[237]

2.92 It was held in England that a bill 'is itself a contract separate from the [underlying] contract of sale', operating 'as a contract in its own right'.[238] This, however, should not necessarily result in the insulation of a holder of the bill from the defences arising from the underlying sale—the so-called 'personal' defences'.[239] Indeed, in English law, a holder not in due course takes the instrument subject to the defence of total failure of consideration,[240] while under the Uniform Commercial Code, such holder takes it subject to all contract defences.[241] Thus, it was said that '[t]he laws distinguishing negotiable from non-negotiable instruments are not based upon any inherent distinctions between the obligations assumed in the one class or the other of such contracts'.[242] Rather, the unconditionality of the engagement on a negotiable instrument

[233] *Lickbarrow v Mason* (1787) 2 TR 63, 100 ER 35 [71]. According to this decision, '[t]he rule is founded purely on principles of law, and not on the custom of merchants. The custom of merchants only establishes that such an instrument may be indorsed; but the effect of that indorsement is a question of law'. ibid. See also *Trueman v Hurst* (1785) 1 TR 40, 99 ER 960 (ER). Subsequent cases are *Brown v Davies* (1789) 3 TR 80, 100 ER 466; *Puget de Bras v Forbes* (1792) 1 Esp 117, 170 ER 298; *Boehm v Sterling* (1797) 2 Esp 575, 170 ER 460, further proceedings 7 TR 423, 101 ER 1055.

[234] See sections D (1) and E (2); Berger, *Dictionary of Roman Law*).

[235] Ames, *Legal History* 115.

[236] Albeit compared to France, in Germany, where the bill or note is truly a *literarum obligatio*, both the reasoning leading to that result—and the procedural mechanisms to achieve it—are much more torturous. See cites in the ensuing note.

[237] See eg L Dabin, *Fondement du droit cambiaire allemand* (Faculté de droit de l'Université de Liège 1959) 204–13, 261–66, 334–43, 422–27 (for Germany); Stoufflet, *Instruments de paiement et de crédit* 66–67, 84–85 (for France); and Ripert and Roblot, *Traité de droit commercial* 144, 156–60, 216–20 (for France, with a comparison to Germany). For an extensive discussion see Lescot and Roblot, *Les Effets de Commerce* 98–120.

[238] *Nova (Jersey) Knit Ltd. v Kammgarn Spinnerei GmbH* [1977] 1 WLR 713 [733], [1977] 2 All ER 463 (HL) (Lord Russell of Killowen). See also *Anglo-Italian Bank v Wells* (1878) 38 LT 197 [199] (C.A.)

[239] For 'personal defences' as 'defect of title' so as to be distinguished under BEA s 38(2) from 'mere personal defences' see B Geva, 'Equities as to Liability on Bills and Notes: Rights of a Holder Not in Due Course' (1980) 5 Can Bus LJ 53, 66.

[240] For a critical analysis see ibid, *passim*.

[241] Uniform Commercial Code § 3-305(a)(2) and (3) (hereafter UCC).

[242] *Pitman v Walker* (1922) 187 Cal. 667 [672](SC), cited with approval by RW Aigler, 'Conditions in Bills and Notes' (1928) 26 Mich L Rev 471, 479 (hereafter Aigler, 'Conditions')

goes to form only and is not a matter of substance. The right to meet an action on the instrument with defences based on the underlying transaction is thus not to be barred by the unconditional language of the engagement. 'The content of a promise [or order] is one thing, the development and recognition of a defense quite another.'[243]

The view that prevailed in all legal systems is that the defence-free position of a holder is based on the good faith purchase for value of the instrument by the holder. It is not premised on the unconditional language of the engagement of the party liable. This left a few gaps, particularly as to the position of the payee versus the acceptor. American law resolved this difficulty by effectively providing any holder who took the instrument in good faith and for value, and not necessarily by negotiation, with a defence-free position against a party with whom the holder has not dealt.[244] **2.93**

G. Final Observations

The historical development of the negotiable instruments law, both as it governs each instrument and the concept of negotiability, is complex, non-linear, and heavily influenced by domestic and cross-border commerce. Doctrinally, it is grounded in general principles of contract and property. Crucially, a universal 'law merchant' does not exist. This is of course not to deny that the historical evolution of negotiable instruments law has been driven by the need to address risk, cost and inconvenience involved in the physical transfer of money; the enhancement of the flow of commerce; the reasonable expectations of the parties; and the value of predictability. It is interesting to note that the process is an ongoing one. While in the ancient times the physical transportation of money was cumbersome, today, in the digital era, this is the case with respect to the physical nature of negotiable instruments, a point to be addressed in Chapter V. **2.94**

After presenting the essentials of the negotiable instruments law (Chapter I) and its historical development (Chapter II), Chapter III moves to the other fundamental aspect of this book—the question of applicable law. The birth of negotiable instruments law within international commerce (at least with respect to bills of exchange), the present divergence in the substance provisions of this area law amongst legal systems and the complex web of contemporary commerce makes the significance of the question of applicable law evident. **2.95**

[243] Aigler, 'Conditions' 480.
[244] UCC § 3-302.

III

Choice-of-Law Question, Three Major Developments, and the Need for Harmonization

3.01 The chapter considers the choice-of-law question and sets the scene for an analysis of the choice-of-law rules of negotiable instruments in the chapters that follow.

3.02 As we have seen earlier in this book, we contend it is not the mythical *lex mercatoria* that underpins the birth, development, and nature of negotiable instruments law. Rather, those are the categories of private law, contract law, and movable property law, which are central to the internal structure and operational mode of negotiable instruments law.[1] We disagree with the 'exclusion thesis', suggested in the Giuliano and Lagarde Report, under which negotiable instruments law presents a unique category of law, separated from the laws of contract and property.[2] As we elaborate in detail in Chapters V–VIII, there is no reason to exclude negotiable instruments law from the choice-of-law rules applicable to the categories of contract and property. Above all, there is no reason to exclude negotiable instruments law from the significant changes that occurred within those categories. This explains why the present chapter elaborates on the dynamics of the ordinary choice-of-law process applicable to contract and movable property categories. In particular, it focuses on the dramatic changes that have occurred within the ordinary choice-of-law doctrine over the last decades. As we will argue in Chapters V–VIII, these changes should be extended to negotiable instruments law. The argument about the 'unique' nature of this area of law and the thesis about its exclusion must be rejected.

3.03 Accordingly, this chapter proceeds through the following three steps. First, it introduces the reader to the choice-of-law question and its key features. Second, it discusses

[1] See Chapter II.

[2] See Introduction, the text accompanying nn 2–12.

what appears to be three major developments within the subject in recent decades, namely the advances of the party autonomy and the most significant relationship principles and the challenge that the era of technology and international commerce poses for the very classification of the subject. Finally, some observations are made on the need for harmonizing the choice-of-law rules relating to negotiable instruments.

A. What Choice-of-Law is: 'Foreign Element', Rejection of *Lex-Fori*, and Connecting Factors Approach

The choice-of-law question deals with situations involving a foreign element in the factual matrix of the case.[3] Consider a contract signed in Japan between residents of English and Germany respectively with respect to delivery of goods in Brazil. Which law shall govern a dispute in this situation: Japanese, English, German, Brazilian, or even another? This scenario includes a range of 'foreign elements' in their factual bases: the place of residence of the parties, the place of the tort, the place of contract formation, and the place of contract performance. These elements involve different territories, which in turn are governed by a different positive law. Simply stated, the choice-of-law question tackles the identity of the framework[4] to adjudicate litigation when one of the elements within the factual matrix of the case is foreign to the forum that adjudicates it. **3.04**

In the contemporary rapidly changing world, the presence of a 'foreign element' seems to be fairly common. With the complex web of international business and commerce, and growing cross-border tourism, it would be safe to say that soon almost every case in the world will have a foreign element within its factual basis. Often the litigating parties do not reside in the same place, goods are manufactured in different places, and the degree of cross-border activity is rapidly increasing. Furthermore, in the era of the Internet, online contracts and online defamation, the presence of at least a single 'foreign element' appears to be an inherent part of the litigating parties' interaction. **3.05**

Despite its clearly growing significance, the question of the applicable law to govern litigation with a 'foreign element' is still unsettled and the subject of a great deal of debate **3.06**

[3] See eg L Collins, Harris (eds) *Dicey, Morris and Collins on the Conflict of Laws* (15th edn, Sweet & Maxwell 2012) 3 (referring to 'foreign element; as 'simply a contact with some system of law other than English law') (hereafter *Dicey and Morris*); EF Scoles et al *Conflict of Laws* (4th edn, Gale Centage 2004) 1 (referring to a case that 'is connected with more than one country'); J Hill and MN Shúilleabháin (eds) *Clarkson & Hill's Conflict of Laws* (5th edn, Oxford University Press 2016) 1 ('In short, any case involving a foreign element raises potential conflict of laws issues') (hereafter *Clarkson & Hill*); J Fawcett and JM Carruthers (eds) *Cheshire, North & Fawcett: Private International Law* (15th edn, Oxford University Press 2017) 1 ('Private International law is that part of English law which comes into operation whenever the court is faced with a claim that contains a foreign element. It is only when this element is present that private international law has a function to perform') (hereafter *Cheshire & North*). This is at least the predominant position of classical and modern choice-of-law literature. Section B of this chapter delves into some more detail on the classification aspect of the subject.

[4] We use here the word 'framework', rather than 'state' in order to incorporate within the definition of the subject the possibility of the application of non-state law. For a discussion of this point, see the text accompanying nn 49–50.

among classical and contemporary academic scholarship.[5] The easiest solution would probably be to say that the domestic courts should always just apply their own law—the so-called *lex-fori*,[6] whereby the English courts apply English law and the Brazilian courts apply Brazilian law. This solution would probably be the most convenient solution for the court and the litigating parties. Thus, the application of the domestic law means that the litigating parties would not need to bear the burden of proving the content of the foreign law through an expert witness (at least in common law jurisdictions)[7] and it means that the court would not be required to adjudicate cases based on an unfamiliar foreign law.[8] Furthermore, *lex-fori* seems to perfectly reflect the long-standing 'sovereignty' principle of international law, which views domestic judges as long-arm representatives of the domestic sovereign. Under this vision of judicial authority, judges must always apply their own law, as a reflection and execution of the sovereign they represent.[9]

3.07 Yet, the application of *lex-fori* raises questions of fairness to the parties and can lead to outcomes that are contrary to their reasonable expectations.[10] Is it fair, for example, that the plaintiff may acquire jurisdiction over the defendant merely based on the defendant's current residence,[11] which can be entirely irrelevant to the place of the parties' interaction, the place of the parties' business, and the place of their residence at the time of their interaction? How can a defendant's residence in Brazil be relevant to the factual situation in which the parties have signed a contract in Germany with respect to delivery of goods in Germany? Why should a Brazilian court apply Brazilian law to circumstances that seem completely unrelated to Brazil? Precisely on these grounds, one of the foundational fathers of the modern choice-of-law thought, Friedrich Carl von Savigny, described the *lex-fori* solution as no less than 'very dangerous'.[12]

[5] Among the foundational works on the nature of the discipline, the following accounts can be mentioned: FC von Savigny, *A Treatise on the Conflict of Laws, and the Limits of Their Operation in Respect of Place and Time* (trans by W Guthrie, T& T Clark 1880); JH Beale, *A Treatise on the Conflict of Laws* (Baker, Voorhis & Co 1935) (hereafter Beale, *Conflict of Laws*); B Currie, *Selected Essays on the Conflict of Laws* (Duke University Press 1963); and more recently A Mills, *The Confluence of Public and Private International Law* (Cambridge University Press 2009) (hereafter Mills, *The Confluence*); SC Symeonides, *Choice of Law* (Oxford University Press 2016) (hereafter Symeonides, *Choice of Law*); S Peari, *The Foundation of Choice-of-Law: Choice & Equality* (Oxford University Press 2018) (hereafter Peari, *The Foundation*).

[6] For *lex-fori* based approaches within choice-of-law thought see eg G Kegel, 'Story and Savigny' (1989) 37 Am J Comp L 39, 52–54 (hereafter Kegel, 'Story and Savigny'); AA Ehrenzweig, *Private International Law* (Oceana Publications Inc 1967).

[7] See eg A Briggs, *The Conflict of Laws* (3rd edn Oxford University Press 2013) 9–13 (mentioning the practical difficulty involved in ascertaining and applying foreign law); *Clarkson & Hill* 2. As the authors put it with respect to *lex-fori*: 'this solution would be simpler, cheaper and more certain than courts trying to apply foreign laws' (ibid, 8).

[8] ibid, 19 (mentioning the domestic judges who are 'untrained in foreign laws').

[9] Indeed, the defence of the *lex-fori* solution through the lens of the state sovereignty principle can be traced within choice-of-law literature. See eg R de Nova, 'General Course [1966]' 118 Recueil Des Cours 435, 452–56; Currie 152–56, 58990; P Dane, 'The Natural Law Challenge to Choice of Law' in DE Childress (ed), *The Role of Ethics in International Law* (Oxford University Press 2012) 142.

[10] For a comprehensive objection to *lex-fori* along these lines, see Peari, *The Foundation* 192–205.

[11] Indeed, the various contemporary and traditional rules of jurisdiction acquisition provide the plaintiff with an option to acquire jurisdiction over the defendant based on the defendant's present residence. See eg R Michaels, 'Jurisdiction, Foundations' in J Basedow et al (eds) *Encyclopedia of Private International Law* (Edgar Publishing 2017); Ehrenzweig 77 (referring to the principle of state sovereignty as a reflection of the traditional rule of jurisdiction that focuses on the defendant's present location).

[12] FC von Savigny, *A Treatise on the Conflict of Laws, and the Limits of Their Operation in Respect of Place and Time* (trans by W Guthrie, T& T Clark 1880) 145.

Given that *lex-fori* does not provide a panacea to the choice-of-law question, the classical and modern choice-of-law doctrine has predominantly adopted various versions of the so-called 'connecting factors' approach. Under this approach, the adjudicative tribunal shall follow certain pre-determined connecting factors to determine the identity of the applied law, for example, the traditional common law connecting factor to determine the question of the formal validity of a marriage (ie various local procedural requirements, such as the number of witnesses) has been the place where the marriage took place.[13] This means, for example, that if one of the parties challenges the formal validity of a marriage, the court will follow this connecting factor, irrespective of what would be the formal requirements of the marriage under the law of the parties' residence at the time of the marriage. In a similar vein, the general rule of the European Rome II Regulation is that in tort law cases, the court shall apply the law of the place of the plaintiff's injury.[14] The traditional common law approach applying the law of the residence of each of the parties to determine their capacity to engage in a marriage contract[15] is another example. Or, take the example of intestate succession cases, which have been traditionally governed by the connecting factor of the deceased's residence at the time of his or her death.[16] **3.08**

Potentially, the list of the connecting factors could be unlimited: it might refer to such places as the place of residence of each of the parties; the place of each party's business; the place of injury or wrong in tort law cases; or the place of contract formation or performance in contract law cases.[17] Some scholars have suggested the following division of the various potential connecting factors: connecting factors related to the event (ie place of wrong, place of contract formation) can be described as 'territorial connecting factors', to be distinguished from 'personal connecting factors' that refer to the parties themselves (ie place of the parties' residence or the place of their business).[18] **3.09**

[13] See eg *Clarkson & Hill* 21; *Cheshire & North* 893. For further discussions on the choice-of-law rule with respect to capacity to engage in marriage, see Chapter VII, the text accompanying n 30.

[14] Commission Regulation 864/2007, on the Law Applicable to Non-Contractual Obligations (Rome II), 2007 OJ (L 199) 40 (EC), art 4(1) (hereafter Rome II).

[15] See eg *Cheshire & North* 909–10.

[16] See eg *Clarkson & Hill* 11; Briggs, *Conflict of Laws* 21.

[17] For an illuminative list of potential connecting factors, see A Briggs, *Private International Law in English Courts* (Oxford University Press 2014) 123–24 (hereafter Briggs, *PIL*).

[18] See eg L Brilmayer, *Conflict of Laws* (2nd edn, Little Brown 1995) 19–20 (hereafter Brilmayer, *Conflict of Laws*); Briggs, *Conflict of Laws* 29 'Connecting factors fall into two broad categories: those which define a law in terms of a personal connection, and those which define the law in terms of a state of affairs.' Against this classification, it has been argued that both 'personal' and 'territorial' factors are in fact 'territorial', as they both refer to a certain territory which is governed by certain positive law. For instance, consider the following connecting factors: the place of the wrong and the place of the plaintiff's residence. While the former connecting factor (the place of the wrong) seems to be clearly territorial, the same point applies with respect to the latter (the place of the plaintiff's residence). From this perspective the distinction between 'territorial' and 'personal' connecting factors seems to be somewhat artificial. For a discussion of this point, see R Michaels, 'Globalizing Savigny? The State in Savigny's Private International Law, and the Challenge of Europeanization and Globalization' in M Stolleis and W Streeck (eds) *Aktuelle Fragen zu politischer und rechtlicher Steuerung im Kontext der Globalisierung* (Nomos 2007) 119, 134; M Reimann, 'Savigny's Triumph? Choice of Law in Contracts Cases at the Close of the Twentieth Century' (1999) 39 Va J Int'l L 571, 590.

3.10 The traditional, almost exclusive focus of the choice-of-law doctrine on territorial connecting factors has been criticized[19] and arguments made in favour of a more balanced approach under which 'personal' connecting factors play a central role within the choice-of-law process as well.[20] Consider a case of two Ontario friends travelling through several US states. After their vehicle was involved in a car accident in the state of Ohio, one of the friends sues the other for negligent driving.[21] Had the exclusive focus in this case been on the sole territorial connecting factor of the place of the accident, Ohio, this would seem to some as fortuitous. It can be argued that exclusively focusing on the place of the accident would disregard a fairly central element to the parties' relationship—the personal connecting factor of the parties' common residence—Ontario.

3.11 The more balanced approach is illustrated by the American Second Restatement that incorporates such personal connecting factors as the place of the parties' residence[22] and the place of their business.[23] Similarly, the Rome I Regulation[24] incorporates the connecting factors of the place of the seller's residence as a primary rule for contract law cases where the parties have not explicitly determined the choice of the applicable law.[25]

3.12 Naturally, the application of the various connecting factors is an exercise of balance, in the sense that this technique does not disregard the content and quality of the applied laws. Over the years various systems have developed a wide range of exceptions to the operational mechanics of the connecting factors approach. Among these, one can mention such considerations as the 'public policy' doctrine,[26] 'human rights',[27] 'constitutional constraints',[28] 'international due process',[29] and 'minimum international standards of justice'.[30]

3.13 Take, for example, a tort law case between an Ontario resident and a New York resident that took place in Mexico. Given the Ontario court has the jurisdiction

[19] See eg Currie. See also L Brilmayer and R Anglin, 'Choice of Law Theory and the Metaphysics of the Stand-Alone Trigger' (2010) Iowa L Rev 1125, 1138.

[20] See eg P Dane, 'Conflict of Laws' in D Patterson (ed) *A Companion to Philosophy of Law and Legal Theory* (2nd edn, Wiley-Blackwell 2010) 197, 203 (structuring the innovation of modern choice-of-law approaches in terms of the priority of personal connecting factors over territorial).

[21] Cf *Babcock v Jackson* (1963) 12 NY 2d473

[22] Restatement of Conflict of Laws, Second (1971; revised 1986 and 1988, American Law Institute) §§ 145 (2) (c), 188 (2) (e) (hereafter Second Restatement).

[23] ibid.

[24] Regulation (EC) 593/2008 of the European Parliament and of the Council of 17 June 2008 on the Law Applicable to Contractual Obligations (Rome I), 2008 OJ (L 177) 6 (EU) (hereafter Rome I).

[25] ibid, art 4(1)(a).

[26] *Louckas v Standard Oil* 120 NE 198 (NY 1918) (heareafter *Louckas v Standard Oil*); *Oppenheimer v Cattermole* [1976] 72 ILR 446; *Kuwait Airways v Iraq Airways* (Nos 4 and 5) [2002] UKHL 19.

[27] JJ Fawcett, MN Shúilleabháin, and S Shah, *Human Rights and Private International Law* (Oxford University Press 2016); *Cheshire & North* 143–45.

[28] J Paulsson, 'Unlawful Laws and the Authority of International Tribunals (2008) 23 ICSID Rev 215, 218–21; K Roosevelt III, 'The Myth of Choice of Law: Rethinking Conflicts' (1999) 97 Mich L Rev 2448, 2507.

[29] *Society of Lloyd's v Ashenden*, 233 F 3d 473, 477 (7th Cir 2000) (Posner J).

[30] CT Kotuby and LA Sobota, *General Principles of Law and International Due Process* (Oxford University Press 2017) 207–08.

to adjudicate the case and the connecting factor of tort law directs the application of the place of the tort (ie the Mexican tort law), this does not mean that the Ontario court shall automatically follow this connecting factor, irrespective of the content of Mexican law. Rather, in certain cases, the courts are entitled to intervene in the ordinary choice-of-law process on the basis of the above-mentioned doctrines. This intervention is highly exceptional and has been reserved for cases where the courts view the application of the foreign provision as incompatible with some 'deep-rooted tradition of the common weal',[31] and as 'shocking the morals of the forum'.[32]

B. Three Trends: Classification of Choice-of-Law, Party Autonomy and Most Significant Relationship Principles

1. Classification of Choice-of-Law Cases According to the Presence of a Foreign Element

The classification of choice-of-law according to the presence of a foreign element within the factual basis of the case would seem to define the division between purely private law cases and private *international* law cases and speaks to the very essence of the subject as a whole. For instance, would a situation of a contract drafted in Ontario between an Ontario resident and a New York resident with respect to delivery of goods in Ontario be considered a private law or private international law case? Or, consider an alternative situation of a tort committed by one Ontario resident against another in the US state of Idaho. Are these cases subject to choice-of-law analysis, as a precursor to the ordinary adjudication process? This form of classification tackles the distinction between purely domestic situations and private international law situations, where only under the latter does choice-of-law analysis enter the picture. **3.14**

This delineation between purely domestic and private international law situations bears a practical significance. Consider, for example, the party autonomy principle discussed in the following section, under which the parties can select the applicable law to adjudicate the litigation between them.[33] However, the contemporary choice-of-law doctrine excludes the application of this principle in purely domestic situations. This means that in order to be able to agree on an adjudicative framework, the parties must present some aspect of 'foreignness' in their situation.[34] Two English residents, for example, may not agree on the application of Norwegian law unless they can point **3.15**

[31] *Loucks v Standard Oil* 110 (Cardozo J).

[32] M G Paulsun and MI Sovern, 'Public Policy in the Conflict of Laws' (1956) 56 Colum L Rev 969, 970. For further discussion on the possibility of the substantive analysis in the context of the negotiable instruments' law choice-of-law rules, see Chapter VII section D.

[33] See Chap III, section B(2).

[34] See the text accompanying n 43.

to some 'foreign' element in their situation, one that need not be necessarily related to Norway.

3.16 As mentioned in section A, the majority of classical and contemporary literature distinguishes private international law cases from purely domestic cases based on the presence of a single 'foreign' element in the factual matrix of the case.[35] Thus, in the case of a contract between an Ontario resident and a New York resident signed in Ontario, the Ontario court shall treat the case as a private international law case due to the presence of the 'foreign element' in the factual matrix of the case—one of the parties to the contract is a foreign resident. By the same token, in the case of a tort committed by an Ontario resident against another Ontario resident in Idaho, the Ontario court would refer to the place of the tort (Idaho) as a foreign element leading to the application of choice-of-law analysis to this case.

3.17 Stated in these terms, the definition of 'international' within the 'private international law' phrase seems to be fairly loose and a careful examination and consideration of the interaction between the litigating parties can reveal a potentially unlimited number of 'foreign' connecting factors which constitute 'foreign elements'[36] and reference to a foreign territory might frequently be found in an evaluation of the parties' interaction.

3.18 Furthermore, in the era of technological progress and driven by COVID-19 era of internet commerce, it is hard to sustain a strict distinction between purely domestic cases and private international law. Cross-border commerce has become an ordinary practice of business, people travel around the globe and the digital age brings a wide spectrum of potential factors to interpersonal communications that would be classified under the traditional choice-of-law doctrine as 'foreign' elements. As one choice-of-law commentator has put it: 'Almost all cases in the world have links to more than one state.'[37]

3.19 Yet, it would appear that at the present time, the majority of contemporary choice-of-law literature seems to remain loyal to this traditional classification of choice-of-law cases according to the presence of a 'foreign element' in the factual basis of the case.[38]

[35] See the text accompanying nn 3–5.

[36] Indeed, one of the foundational fathers of the choice-of-law question already observed in 1849 that the list of the potential relevant connecting factors within choice-of-law analysis is 'unlimited'. See FC von Savigny, *A Treatise on the Conflict of Laws, and the Limits of Their Operation in Respect of Place and Time* (trans by W Guthrie, T& T Clark 1880) 140.

[37] See M Lehmann, 'Liberating the Individual from the Battles between States: Justifying Party Autonomy in Conflict of Laws' (2008) 41 Vand J Transnat'l L 381, 422.

[38] See eg Symeonides, *Choice of Law* 2 'The adjective *international* describes an important attribute of the disputes that fall within the scope of this subject—they are international (or interstate) in the sense that they have contacts with more than one country or state' (emphasis in original). In similar terms, Draft 2 of the American Restatement of the Law Third Conflicts of Laws (2020) https://www.ali.org/projects/show/conflict-laws/, accessed 20 December 2019 (hereafter 'Third Restatement Draft') starts with the following definition of the discipline 'Conflict of Laws is that part of the law of each state that is used to decide cases having connections to more than one state'. Similarly, art 1(2) of the Hague Principles on Choice of Law in International Commercial Contracts, 2015 https://www.hcch.net/en/instruments/conventions/full-text/?cid=135, accessed 20 December 2019 (hereafter Hague Principles) excludes from the definition of 'international commercial contract' (and subsequently from the application scope of the Hague Principles a purely 'domestic situation'. *Cheshire & North* 3 'Private international law is that part of English law which comes into operation whenever the court is faced with a claim that contains *a foreign element*' (emphasis added).

Because of the endless pool of potential connecting factors, technological progress and mobility of people, one can argue that the vast majority of private law cases can be classified as 'private international law' cases. The 'foreign element' seems to be easily found and nowadays only a few cases can be classified as truly 'domestic'.[39]

Furthermore, several scholars and choice-of-law legislative provisions have challenged the 'domestic'/'international' distinction altogether. By referring to the conceptual nature of the choice-of-law question, it has been argued that this shall always be a part of the adjudication process,[40] which challenges the clear cut definition of a 'foreign element' as a determinative factor for the application of choice-of-law analysis. Practically, it has been argued that the 'domestic'/'international' divide has been so blurred in contemporary reality that it is questionable whether one can support a sustainable division between purely domestic cases and private international law cases. For these approaches, all private law cases are private international law cases and vice versa. **3.20**

Without delving further into the conceptual debate between the predominant view (according to which private international law cases need still to be classified according to the presence of a single foreign element in the factual matrix of the case) and the minority view (which treats all private law cases as private international law cases), the practical application of the disagreement seems to be less crucial. Due to technological progress and an exploding web of commercial activity, the presence of 'foreign' elements under the predominant position classifies the vast majority of cases as warranting choice-of-law analysis given a similar result would be achieved under the minority view, which challenges the very existence of the divide in the first place. The practical conclusion is that the modern choice-of-law doctrine has opted for a fairly relaxed test (under the majority view) or an even non-existent test (under a more extreme position) as to the determination of whether a given case requires choice-of-law analysis. **3.21**

2. Party Autonomy: Beale's Challenge and Party Autonomy Triumph

(a) Party Autonomy and Beale's Challenge

In addition to blurring (or even eliminating) the boundaries between purely domestic cases and private international law cases, the second development within choice-of-law is the phenomenal success of the so-called 'party autonomy' principle. In fact, if one needs to single out one significant development in the choice-of-law doctrine of the twentieth century, most scholars would perhaps opt for the phenomenon of party autonomy. **3.22**

[39] See eg *Cheshire & North* 695 (offers a very relaxed understanding of the 'foreign element' according to which a purely domestic situation where one of the parties subsequently moves to another country, would meet the 'foreign element' requirement).

[40] Currie (n 5) 366; G Kegel, 'The Crisis on Conflict of Laws' (1964) 112 Recueil des Cours 95, 183–85; Peari, *The Foundation* (n 5) 85–90.

3.23 Party autonomy means the ability of the parties to choose the framework to adjudicate their dispute. For example, in a contract between an Ontario resident and a German resident with respect to delivery of goods in Brazil, the parties may incorporate a clause in their agreement indicating that their future rights and duties under the contract shall be governed by English contract law. Most systems around the globe would respect that clause.[41] For example, if an Ontario court was to acquire jurisdiction over this case, it would adjudicate in accordance with English law, honouring the parties' choice with respect to the identity of the applicable law.

3.24 Questions arise as to the source of the parties' ability to determine the framework to adjudicate their rights and duties; where does this ability come from and how does it relate to the states' apparent authority to legislate their laws or, at least, set legal precedents through their courts?[42] What is the relation between the traditional classification of the subject according to the presence of a single foreign element and the party autonomy principle, and is the application of the party autonomy principle restricted to what has traditionally been considered private international law cases?[43] How would it be possible for the parties to 'opt out' of the application of the forum's choice-of-law rules that would have been applied without the explicit choice-of-law clause?[44] What is the relation between the parties' ability to determine the applicable law, and the so-called 'mandatory rules' of the forum and/or the designated forum (ie the mandatory rules of the place that would have applied without the parties' agreement)?[45] On a similar note, what would be the reaction of the domestic legal system if the parties choose a law that violates some fundamental human rights, such as a law that discriminates against one of the parties?[46] Would the choice be valid in cases where the parties are situated in an inherently unequal bargaining position to one other, as in cases of consumer contracts?[47] Would it be possible for the parties to choose a law

[41] See eg SC Symeonides, 'The Scope and Limits of Party Autonomy in International Contracts: A Comparative Analysis' in F Ferrari and DPF Arroyo (eds) *Private International law: Contemporary Challenges and* the *Continuing Relevance of Private International Law and New Challenges* (Edgar 2019); A Mills, *Party Autonomy in Private International Law* 313–16 (Cambridge University Press 2018) (hereafter Mills, *Party Autonomy*); JF Coyle, *A Short History of the Choice-of-Law Clause* (2019) <https://papers.ssrn.com/sol3/papers.cfm?abstract_id=3420162>, accessed 20 December 2019.

[42] See eg R Michaels, 'Party Autonomy—A New Paradigm Without Foundation?' (2013) 15 Japanese Yearbook of Private International Law 288–90 (states the conceptual puzzle of party autonomy in terms of the relationship between states, adjudicators and litigating parties) (hereafter Michaels, 'Party Autonomy').

[43] Indeed, several choice-of-law provisions have provided an affirmative answer to this question and excluded the application of the party autonomy principle in cases that lack a single foreign element. See eg art 1(2) of the Hague Principles; art 3(3) of the Rome I and art 14 (2) of Rome II. On similar grounds, it has been argued that the distinction between 'private international law' and 'purely domestic' party autonomy exists in the USA, where the courts apply a more liberal test to the former. For a discussion of this point, see LJ Silberman, 'Lessons for the USA from the Hague Principles' (2017) 22 Unif L Rev 422, 424–26.

[44] See eg Michaels, Party Autonomy.

[45] See eg A Briggs, *Agreements on Jurisdiction and Choice of Law* (Oxford University Press 2008) 382 (mentioning that the 'mandatory rules' were traditionally immune from the scope of the party autonomy principle) [Briggs, *Agreements*]; Hague Principles, art 11.

[46] See eg Briggs, *Conflict of Laws* 210; SGA Pitel and NS Rafferty, *Conflict of Laws* (2nd edn, Irwin Law 2016) 272–74.

[47] See eg PJ Borchers, 'Categorical Exceptions to Party Autonomy in Private International Law' (2008) 82 Tul L Rev 1645, 1657–59; J Basedow, 'The Law of Open Societies-Private Ordering and Public Regulation of International Relations' (2013) 360 Rec des Cours 9, 189–93, 343–75; G Rühl, 'The Unfairness of Choice-of-Law Clauses' (2018) 5 Com Mar L Rev 201.

that does not have any relation to either of them?[48] And finally (and intriguingly), would it be possible for the parties to choose a framework to adjudicate their rights and duties that does not represent an official law at all—so-called 'non-state' law?[49] Religious laws (such as Sharia or Talmudic) or UNIDROIT principles are representative examples of such 'non-state' laws.[50] Further, even if the parties cannot explicitly incorporate non-state law, maybe they can override this difficulty by instead incorporating substantive provisions of the non-state law within the terms of the contract.[51] These questions pose serious conceptual and practical obstacles for the incorporation of party autonomy within the choice-of-law question.[52]

One of the earliest and fairly tentative attempts to tackle some of the above-mentioned questions can be witnessed in the works of one of the most influential figures of choice-of-law academic literature—Harvard Law School Professor Joseph Beale. Being the author of an influential treatise on the subject,[53] he was the figure behind the provisions of the First Restatement of Conflict of Laws,[54] a body of law that was once followed universally by all American courts.[55] The ensuing section provides some details on Beale's choice-of-law approach and his principal objection to party autonomy. **3.25**

(b) Beale's Choice-of-Law Approach and His Objection to Party Autonomy

Beale's work offered a theory of individuals' rights—the so-called theory of 'acquired rights', which stood at the basis of his subsequent account of choice-of-law doctrine. Beale insisted that the plaintiff's right is created or 'vested' by the state where the last element of liability occurred.[56] Relying precisely on this assumption, Beale's doctrinal analysis of choice-of-law rules primarily focused on the law of the place that Beale considered to be the last element within a given ground of liability. For example, since Beale's analysis of contract law regarded the place of contracting as the 'last element', he favoured the place of contracting as a choice-of-law rule in contract law.[57] Along **3.26**

[48] See Second Restatement § 187 (2); Hague Principles, art 2(4); Briggs, *PIL* 543–44.

[49] See eg K Boele-Woelki, 'Unifying and Harmonizing Substantive Law and The Role of Conflict of Laws' (2010) Rec Des Cours 275, 401–19); SC Symeonides, 'Party Autonomy in Rome I and II from a Comparative Perspective' in K Boele-Woelki et al (eds) *Convergence and Divergence in Private International Law* (Eleven International Publishing 2010) 513, 539–40.

[50] As *Cheshire & North* explains, Rome I excludes the possibility to apply non-state law. The draft proposal to apply 'the principles and rules of the substantive law of contract recognized internationally or in the Community' has been rejected. Accordingly, not just *lex mercatoria* has been rejected but also such well-established provision as the UNIDROIT principles, the UN Convention on the International Sale of Goods, and the Principles of European Contract Law. For discussion of these issues see eg *Cheshire & North* 713–15.

[51] Briggs, *Conflict of Laws* 238; *Dicey and Morris* 2058–61 (discusses the possibility of incorporating specific terms of Sharia within the parties' contract); *Cheshire & North* 715; *Halpern v Halpern* [Nos 1 and 2] [2008] QB 195.

[52] For recent attempts to answer some of these questions see Peari, *The Foundation* 90–106 and Mills, *Party Autonomy*.

[53] Beale, *Conflict of Laws*.

[54] *Restatement of Conflict of Laws* (1934) (hereafter First Restatement).

[55] See eg SC Symeonides, *The American Choice of Law Revolution: Past, Present and Future* (Martinus Nijhoff Publishers 2006) 10 (hereafter Symeonides, *Revolution*); SC Symeonides, 'The First Restatement Through the Eyes of Old: As Bad as Its Reputation?' (2007) 32 South Ill Univ L J 39.

[56] Beale, *Conflict of Laws* 45–47, 58, 62–63.

[57] ibid 1044–46; J Beale 'What Law Governs the Validity of a Contract' (1909) 23 Harv L Rev 73, 271 (hereafter Beale, 'Validity'). As Beale put it 'The phrase "place of contracting" and its equivalents, the place

similar lines, since he considered the place of 'damage'/'injury' to be the last element within the internal structure of tort law where the state 'vests' rights in the plaintiff, the First Restatement opted for the choice-of-law rule that follows the place of injury/damage.[58]

3.27 Whilst stated in terms of a theory of 'individuals' rights', Beale's theory was fundamentally based on the ideas of state sovereignty and state authority under which the states execute their power and apply their laws at the moment when the 'last element' of liability takes place.[59] For example, a contract between German and English parties signed in Ontario would be subject to the application of Ontario law as the contractual relationship between the parties was completed in Ontario and the contractual rights were 'vested' by the Ontario government.

3.28 This state-based account of choice-of-law explains Beale's principal objection to the party autonomy principle. Indeed, this principle is simply incompatible with Beale's state-based vision of the subject. For him, party autonomy was no less than a betrayal of the very essentials of choice-of-law as a discipline, which are based on states' authority to 'vest' or grant their law according to the place where the last element of liability is formed. Accordingly, Beale conceived party autonomy as no less than 'permission to the parties to do a legislative act',[60] and that granting 'so extraordinarily a power in the hands of any two individuals is absolutely anomalous'.[61]

(c) The Criticism and the Triumph of Party Autonomy

3.29 Much ink has been spilt to expose the conceptual and practical flaws of Beale's theory of rights and his subsequent account of choice-of-law. Conceptually, it has been argued that Beale's theory lacks foundation and fails to explain the very nature of its key concept of 'vested' rights. It is not clear why, within the interaction between individuals, one must focus specifically on the last element of liability, rather than on others, such as the nature of the wrong (and subsequently the place of the wrong) committed within the tort law category, or the nature of contractual performance (and subsequently the place of contractual performance) within the contract law category.[62] Stated in these terms, criticism has been levelled at the 'individuals' rights' language of the theory, pointing to its state-based foundation and the unexplained focus on the

of making or the place where the contract was made, properly meant the place in which the final act was done' (Beale, *Conflict of Laws* 1045).

[58] First Restatement 377. Beale, *Conflict of Laws* 1286–88.

[59] For this reading of Beale's work, see eg P Dane, *Vested Rights, 'Vestedness' and Choice of Law* (1987) 96 Yale L. J. 1191 at 1194–96; Brilmayer, *Conflict of Laws* 20–25.

[60] Beale, 'Validity' 260; Beale, *Conflict of Laws* 1079, 1941. See also HE Yntema, 'Autonomy' in Choice of Law at 343 (which mentions the inconsistency of the positivistic state-based conception of law with the party autonomy principle as reflecting the parties' 'power to legislate').

[61] Beale, 'Validity' 261.

[62] See eg K Roosevelt, 'Resolving Renvoi: The Bewitchment of Our Intelligence By Means of Language' (2004) 80 Notre Dame L Rev 1821, 1830–41; EE Cheatham, 'American Theories of Conflict of Laws: Their Role and Utility' (1945) 58 Harv L Rev 361, 365; R Michaels, 'EU Law as Private International Law? Reconceptualising the Country-of-Origin Principle as Vested Rights Theory' (2006) 2 J Private Int'l L 195, 226–34.

last element of liability. Furthermore, it has been argued that Beale's analysis of specific grounds of liability is puzzling and presumes certain universal conceptions as to the internal structures of the categories of private law. One can challenge Beale's point that the 'last act' within the contract law category is the place of contract formation, rather than the subsequent place of contractual performance.[63]

The biggest flaw of Beale's choice-of-law account has been a practical one. The courts have struggled to follow the single connecting territorial factor of Beale's choice-of-law account, which frequently led to the application of a law that was arbitrary given the factual matrix of the case.[64] Founded on the organizing basis of the 'vested' rights theory, Beale's (and subsequently the First Restatement's) choice-of-law rules were overly rigid. Thus, the single territorial rule of the place of contracting underpinned the choice-of-law rule in contracts, regardless of other territorial factors (such as the place of contractual performance), personal factors (such as the residence of the parties or the place of their business), and regardless of whether a given rule supports the application of that law which would sustain the validity of the contract.[65] The same point applies to the tort law category: the application of a rigid rule of the place of injury/damage disregards other potentially relevant connecting territorial and personal factors such as the residence of the parties and the place of the wrong. **3.30**

The actual practice of the courts has demonstrated the inherent difficulty of following a single territorial connecting factor, which in many cases looks quite arbitrary in the actual factual situation of the case. Thus, in the case of a contract for delivery of goods in Ontario signed in Germany between two Ontario residents during a brief meeting, the place of contracting—Germany—seems to be notably arbitrary in the factual matrix of the case. Indeed, in response to the rigidity of Beale's choice-of-law approach, the courts have developed an arsenal of so-called 'escape devices' or 'manipulative techniques' to avoid the actual implementation of Beale's rules.[66] Thus, a broad reading of the public policy doctrine and the miscategorization of private law categories were used as common devices to 'escape' the application of Beale's theory.[67] **3.31**

The call from the judiciary was heard by academics in the introduction of the Second Restatement[68] in 1971, which discarded Beale's rigid rules in favour of a much more flexible approach. Representing a complete antithesis to Beale's approach and the First **3.32**

[63] For an alternative to Beale's vision of the contract law category that perceives the place of contractual performance as the 'last component' of the contract law category, see eg EJ Weinrib, 'Private Law, Punishment, and Disgorgement: Punishment and Disgorgement as Contract Remedies' (2003) 78 Chi-Kent L Rev 55, 65–70; A Ripstein, *Force and Freedom* (Harvard University Press 2009) 107–45.

[64] See eg WW Cook, *The Logical and Legal Bases of the Conflict of Laws* (Harvard University Press 1942) 17, 203, 450; Currie 138–39; L Brilmayer, 'The Role of Substantive and Choice of Law Policies in the Formation and Application of Choice of Law Rules' (1995) 252 Recueil des Cours 1, 23.

[65] For further discussion on choice-of-law rules that sustain the validity of the contract, see Chapter VII section A.

[66] See eg Brilmayer and Anglin 1133–35. See also AA Ehrenzweig, *A Treatise on the Conflict of Laws* (West Publishing Co 1962) 326–28.

[67] ibid.

[68] Second Restatement.

Restatement's predictability, the Second Restatement became fairly popular among American courts.[69] First, in contrast to Beale, the Second Restatement adopted the party autonomy principle in the area of contract law and granted the parties the ability to set the identity of the applied law to adjudicate the dispute between them.[70] Second (and following the European experience[71]), the Second Restatement adopted a flexible principle of presumptions of certain connecting factors which can be overturned through an analysis of other connecting factors. Under this principle, called the 'most significant relationship' (MSR) principle, the courts shall evaluate the situation as a whole, taking into consideration not one, but a multitude of relevant connecting factors.

3.33 The issues that arose from the over-flexibility of the MSR principle are considered in section 3, but, on the point of incorporation of the party autonomy principle, Beale's defeat seems to be definitive. Indeed, a heated debate has been taking place over the normative foundations of the principle, its relation to such concepts as states' sovereignty and states' authority to execute power over their territories and residents, and further extensive practical questions on the scope and limits of the principle.[72] Yet, it is hard to challenge the popularity of party autonomy around the globe.[73] As one choice-of-law commentator has put it, 'Nowadays, party autonomy is deemed the "most universally observed" and "the most widely accepted private international rule' ".[74]

3.34 The party autonomy principle has been globally adopted in the area of contract law and various choice-of-law frameworks have explicitly incorporated it within their provisions.[75] It has become common practice for contracting parties to include a choice-of-law clause.[76] Furthermore, in addition to its global recognition in the area of contract law, the party autonomy principle has been rapidly expanded to other categories: tort law and the law of unjust enrichment,[77]

[69] On the popularity of the Second Restatement, see Symeonides, *Revolution* 88.

[70] Second Restatement § 187.

[71] On the European tradition of flexible connecting factors, see eg B Hayward, *Conflict of Laws and Arbitral Discretion* (Oxford University Press 2017) 234 (hereafter Hayward, *Discretion*); R Plender and M Wilderspin, *The European Private International Law of Obligations* (4th edn, Sweet & Maxwell 2014) 7.076.

[72] See the text accompanying nn 41–52.

[73] See eg Borchers 1646.

[74] M Zhang, 'Rethinking Contractual Choice of Law: An Analysis of Relation Syndrome' (2015) 44 Stetson L Rev 831, 843 (footnotes omitted); Mills, *Party Autonomy*; Coyle.

[75] See eg Rome I, art 4 (1); Rome II, art 14; Second Restatement § 187.

[76] While statistical data is missing in the context of state courts, a reference can be made to the context of international commercial arbitration where it has been found that in 2015, more than 85% of international arbitration agreements included a choice-of-law clause. See Hayward, *Discretion* 14.

[77] Rome II art 14(a) (extends party autonomy to the tort and unjust enrichment categories); Third Restatement Draft , § 6.08(2) (extends the party autonomy principle to the area of tort law); Zhang 845 (expansion of party autonomy to non-contractual obligations). Indeed, within the tort law and unjust enrichment categories (and in contrast to the contract law category), the parties usually do not engage in previous engagement/relationships prior to their interaction. Yet, the principle recognizes that the parties can agree, after the start of the litigation, on the identity of the framework to adjudicate the dispute between them.

succession,[78] movable property,[79] and even such traditionally state-influenced areas as family law.[80]

3.35 Indeed, in such categories as tort and unjust enrichment (and in contrast to the contract law category), the parties generally have not had any prior interaction. Yet, the principle recognizes that the parties can agree, after the start of litigation, on the identity of the framework to adjudicate the dispute between them. Reflecting the value of autonomy and choice of the parties to freely choose the applicable law, the party autonomy principle challenges the classical rationales of the choice-of-law question, grounded on states' considerations. The party autonomy principle has received almost a universal recognition. The future of choice-of-law doctrine seems to belong to this principle.

3. The Advances of the MSR Principle

(a) The Nature of the MSR Principle and Its Centrality Within Contemporary Choice-of-Law Frameworks

3.36 Advances in the MSR principle may be considered as the third major development of the choice-of-law doctrine in recent decades. The classical definition of the MSR principle in the Second Restatement, which refers to the application of the law of the state that 'has the most significant relationship to the occurrence and the parties'.[81] Stated in these terms, the MSR principle instructs the courts to provide a comprehensive look at the factual basis of a particular case, to examine the parties' interaction as a whole, and to trace within this interaction a place or territory that according to the court's view has the most significant relation or relationship to the 'occurrence' and the 'parties'.

3.37 Take, for example, an instance of a contract between two Ontario residents signed in Germany with respect to delivery of goods in Ontario. The judicial analysis of this case, under the MSR principle, would direct to the application of Ontario law: the litigating parties are from Ontario and the territory of Ontario has been set as the place of the contractual performance under their contract. In other words, in this case the connecting factors of the plaintiff's and defendant's residence at the time of contract formation, and the place of contract performance outweigh, the other connecting factor—the place of contract formation, which refers to Germany.

3.38 The words 'occurrence' and 'parties' within the classical definition of the MSR principle deserve elaboration. As a matter of fact, they directly relate to the division

[78] S Symeonides, 'The Hague Principles on Choice of Law for International Contracts: Some Preliminary Comments' 3, n 10 <https://papers.ssrn.com/sol3/papers.cfm?abstract_id=2256661>, accessed 20 December 2019.

[79] Thus, recent developments within Chinese law have incorporated the party autonomy principle in the area of movable property, see The Statute on the Application of Laws over Foreign-Related Civil Relations of the People's Republic of China (2011), arts 37–38: 'The parties concerned may choose the law applicable to the right over movable property by agreement' (hereafter Civil Relations Statute]; DJB Svantesson, *Private International Law and the Internet* (3rd edn, Kluwer Law International 2016) 313–15.

[80] See eg S Peari, 'Choice-of-Law in Family Law: Kant, Savigny *and the* Parties' Autonomy. Principle' (2012) 4 Neth J Priv Int'L L 597.

[81] Second Restatement § 145 (1) (emphasis added).

between the above-mentioned 'territorial' and 'personal' connecting factors.[82] While the word 'occurrence' represents a territorial connecting factor, the word 'parties' represents a personal one. In this way, the classical formulation of the MSR principle refers to both connecting factors: 'territorial' and 'personal'.

3.39 The last point is important. The contemporary reference of the MSR principle to both types of factors is a relatively new development within the modern doctrine of choice-of-law. Underpinned by the sovereignty-based vision of the subject, the traditional doctrine of choice-of-law has focused almost exclusively on the territorial connecting factors and viewed choice-of-law as a vehicle and means for promotions of such notions as states' sovereignty and states' interests.[83] The traditional old choice-of-law contract law rule referred to the place of contract formation,[84] representing the given state's inherent interest to be involved in acts (such as contract formation) that took place within its territorial borders. The Beale's vision of choice-of-law rules follows precisely this notion, and by focusing on the mysterious 'last act' of liability for each one of the legal categories, this vision of the subject has fundamentally linked the choice-of-law process to states' interests and the execution of states' authorities over acts that occur within their territories.[85]

3.40 Modern choice-of-law doctrine has abandoned this state-central vision of the subject and does not view it as exclusively governed by the considerations of states' sovereignty anymore. Instead of focusing on the sovereignty-based underpinnings of a single given act that takes place within states' territories, the MSR principle offers a fundamental re-evaluation of choice-of-law considerations. It crystalizes the normative notion of the 'parties' reasonable expectations', which in turn offers an alternative to the traditionally predominant state-based vision of the subject.[86]

3.41 The notion of the parties' reasonable expectations can clearly be traced within the underpinnings of many contemporary choice-of-law rules. Common law contract choice-of-law provides that in the absence of parties' explicit choice to identify the applicable law, the court should objectively evaluate the entire nature of the parties' interaction and ascertain their reasonable expectations.[87] In similar terms, the centrality of the concept of parties' reasonable expectations can be traced within other areas of choice-of-law rules: tort, unjust enrichment and movable property.[88]

[82] See the text accompanying nn 13–25.

[83] For a discussion of these matters, see Chap III section B(2)(b).

[84] SGA Pitel and NS Rafferty, *Conflict of Laws* (2nd edn, Irwin Law 2016) 285 ('The early English and American choice of law rule for contract was the *lex loci contractus*- the law of the place of contracting'); *Bondholders Securities Corp v Manville et al* [1933] SJ No 75 [1933] 4 DLR 699 [38] (applying the proper law of that time—the place of contract formation—to the case of promissory notes).

[85] See Chap III section B(2)(b).

[86] For an argument regarding the primary centrality of the concept of 'parties' reasonable expectations' in choice-of-law thought, see *Clarkson & Hill* 9–19; PE Nygh, 'The Reasonable Expectations of the Parties as a Guide to the Choice of Law in Contract and in Tort' (1995) 251 Rec Des Cours 273, 294–96; Hayward, *Discretion* 42, 44–46; Svantesson 501.

[87] See *Vita Food Products Inc v Unus Shipping Co* [1939] AC 277 (ibid at 290–91); see also Briggs, *Agreements* 429–40; SGA Pitel and NS Rafferty, *Conflict of Laws* (2nd edn, Irwin Law 2016) 285–95 .

[88] For an argument in this direction, see PE Nygh, 'The Reasonable Expectations of the Parties as a Guide to the Choice of Law in Contract and in Tort' (1995) 251 Rec Des Cours 273, 294–296.

This is exactly where the MSR principle enters the picture. By re-shifting the focus of choice-of-law doctrine from sovereignty-based considerations towards 'parties' reasonable expectations', it embraces a broad pool of potentially relevant factors within its operational mechanics. It requires the adjudicator to consider the parties' specific interactions, and then to evaluate the significance of various factors within this interaction. During this process, the adjudicator should consider both 'territorial' (that could include such factors as the place of contract formation, the place of contractual performance, the place of the wrong and the place of the damage/injury) *and* 'personal' connecting factors (that could include such factors as the parties' residence, parties' business and the parties nationality). This evaluation should not be a simple quantitative assessment of various factors. Rather, it requires a careful evaluation and analysis of the entire scope of the parties' interaction and the various factors according to their relative significance.[89] **3.42**

In this way, the MSR principle does not just reflect the normative notion of parties' reasonable expectations, but also follows the dramatic changes in modern choice-of-law doctrine that incorporated personal connecting factors into choice-of-law analysis, alongside territorial connecting factors. Similar to the Second Restatement, modern European choice-of-law legislation incorporates both territorial and personal connecting factors. Rome I, for example, sets as its general rule the personal connecting factor of the place of residence as the party who should perform the so-called 'characteristic performance' of the contract.[90] Rome II sets a territorial connecting factor of the place of injury to govern tort law disputes.[91] **3.43**

Arguably criticism of the 'rigidity' of the First Restatement's strict territorial rules, was because the Restatement focused exclusively on single territorial rules and disregarded the personal connecting factors.[92] The introduction of the Second Restatement, with the MSR principle at its heart,[93] has provided a solution to this rigidity by incorporating personal connecting factors alongside the territorial ones. **3.44**

The introduction of the MSR principle has therefore challenged both stances of the traditional choice-of-law doctrine: (1) it has challenged the notion that choice-of-law rules should be based on a single connecting factor; (2) it has challenged the notion that choice-of-law rules should exclusively be based on territorial connecting factors. The MSR principle has offered a multiplicity of connecting factors and has linked its **3.45**

[89] Second Restatement §§ 145, 187.

[90] Rome I , art 4(2). The specific choice-of-law rules for the sale of goods and provision of services follow this rule of characteristic performance as well (See Rome I, arts 4(1)(a) and 4(1)(b)). For further discussion and analysis of the 'characteristic performance' concept under the Rome I, see Chapter VI, the text accompanying nn 130, 177–78.

[91] Commission Regulation 864/2007, on the Law Applicable to Non-Contractual Obligations (Rome II), 2007 OJ (L 199) 40 (EC) art 4 (2).

[92] As Brilmayer and Anglin state on this point 'Close examination, however, reveals that the nature of the trigger factor—the territorial last act—was not the problem. The results dictated by the first Restatement were arbitrary not because of the nature of the single trigger [single connecting factor], but rather because they relied on a single, stand-alone trigger.' See Brilmayer and Anglin 1138 (footnote omitted).

[93] For a discussion regarding the decisive role of the MSR principle within the provisions of the Second Restatement, see eg SC Symeonides, *American Private International Law* (Kluwer Law International 2008) 33, 104–05.

operational mechanics to a combination of both personal and territorial factors. The words 'occurrence' and 'parties' in the classical definition of the MSR principle, indeed, reflect those features of the principle.

3.46 A few words can be said about the popularity of the MSR principle, alongside, the party autonomy principle, within the contemporary choice-of-law doctrine. Thus, the MSR principle appears to represent the most central rule within the provisions of the Second Restatement, which is popular amongst the courts.[94] A review of the Second Restatement's various provisions reveal the centrality of this principle to the following legal categories: tort,[95] contract,[96] movable property,[97] unjust enrichment,[98] and family law.[99] Not surprisingly, the MSR principle has been named as the 'intellectual heart of the Second Restatement'.[100]

3.47 The popularity of the MSR principle goes way beyond the American landscape and is well-established in other jurisdictions. Scholars around the globe have noted the paramount significance of this principle within contemporary choice-of-law doctrine and practice. They have pointed out that these 'are structured to lead to the application of a law which has a close connection with either the parties or the cause of action'.[101] Similarly, empirical work on the nature of choice-of-law rules in the area of international arbitration has found that the MSR principle governs the vast majority of cases where an explicit choice has not been stated under the party autonomy principle.[102]

3.48 The same popularity of the principle can be witnessed on a legislative level. Consider the European Rome Regulations. Article 4(4) of the Rome I and Article 4(3) of Rome II have specifically adopted a reference to the MSR principle with relation to contract, tort, and unjust enrichment categories, as referring to the law of the 'country with which it is most closely connected'.[103] Article 3(2) of Rome II[104] seems to crystalize the

[94] Second Restatement. For empirical studies indicating the significant popularity of the Second Restatement among American courts, see eg Symeonides, *Revolution* 48–49; CA Whytock, 'Myth of Mess? International Choice of Law in Action' (2009) 84 NYU L Rev 719, 745–76.

[95] Second Restatement §§ 145 (1), 146–49, 152.

[96] ibid §§ 188 (1), 189–97.

[97] ibid §§ 222, 244, 250, 251, 254, 256–58.

[98] ibid § 221.

[99] ibid §§ 154, 283(1), 284, 287(1), 288.

[100] WM Richman and WL Reynolds, 'Prologomenon to an Empirical Restatement of Conflicts' (2000) 75 Ind L J 417, 420–21.

[101] See eg *Clarkson & Hill* 9. As Clarkson and Hill state, 'The examples demonstrate the prevailing approach adopted by English law to the issue of choice of law: in the absence of party choice, the parties can be deemed reasonably to expect their relationships and transactions to be governed by the law with which those relationships and transactions are most closely connected' (ibid at 12). See also SC Symeonides, 'Codification and Flexibility in Private International Law' in K Brown and D Snyder (eds) *General Reports of the XVIII Congress of the International Academy of Comparative Law / Rapports Généraux du XVIIIeme Congrés de L'Academie Internationale de Droit Comparé* (Springer Pubs 2012) 167.

[102] Hayward, *Discretion* 84. See also PE Nygh, 'Choice of Forum and Law in International Commercial Arbitration' (1997) 24 Forum Internationale 1, 21 ('the closest connection principle has been recognized with "near unanimity" in international arbitration').

[103] Rome I, art 4(4); Rome II, art 4(4). See also R Fentiman, 'The Significance of Close Connection' in J Ahern and W Binchy (eds) *The Rome II Regulation on the Law Applicable to Non-Contractual Obligations* (Brill 2009) 85. For an interpretation of this principle, not as an exception but rather as a central part of the operational mechanism of Rome I and Rome II, see *Clarkson & Hill* 230–35.

[104] Rome II, art 3(2).

MSR principle in the sense that it overturns the general rule of the place of damage set in Article 4(1) in the case of a common residence of the parties. The case law on this matter, it can be argued that Article 3(1) of the Rome I[105] reflects the MSR principle in the sense that it refers to the so-called doctrine of 'inferred choice' under which choice-of-law analysis refers to such circumstances of the parties' interaction as the language of the contract and the identity of the stated currency of payment.[106] In China, the recent Chinese Foreign-Related Civil Relations Statute has warmly adopted the MSR principle as the governing principle for a wide range of categories, including the category of movable property.[107]

(b) The Over-Flexibility Charge

Since the MSR principle requires counting and weighing of the various connecting factors, it has been accused of leading to great unpredictability in the implementation of the Second Restatement.[108] The MSR principle has been criticised as being a 'no rules approach'[109] and 'unabashedly open-ended',[110] as well as overly flexible and lacking the ability to provide the courts with a clear guide as to the nature of the pool of relevant connecting factors and as to the process of how the connecting factors are to be evaluated.[111] **3.49**

Indeed, the MSR principle is inherently flexible. No one denies that. It requires the court to consider the essence of the parties' interaction. Taking into account both personal and territorial connecting factors, the MSR principle instructs judges not to simply count them, but rather to evaluate them according to their relative significance. As the Second Restatement states: 'These contacts [connecting factors] are to be evaluated according to their relative importance with respect to the particular issue.'[112] Yet, in our view, this inherent process of counting and weighting does not represent a doctrinal deficiency of the principle but in fact reflects the normative significance of the principle and its linkage to the notion of the parties' reasonable expectations. **3.50**

There are arguments as to why the criticism of 'over-flexibility' against the MSR principle is exaggerated. The changing social and technological landscape presents challenges to the traditional choice-of-law doctrine, whether it be to place of contract **3.51**

[105] Rome I, art 4(4).

[106] For a discussion of these issues see eg *Cheshire & North* 716–22. For further discussion on the point of accommodating art 3(1) of the Rome I under the auspices of the MSR principle, and a rejection of the somewhat artificial distinction between objective factors (such as place of the parties' residence) and subjective factors (such as the language of the contract), see Chapter VI, the text accompanying n 70.

[107] Civil Relations Statute, arts 47–48. See also Svantesson, 313–15.

[108] See eg RJ Weintraub, 'At Least, To Do No Harm: Does the Second Restatement of Conflicts Meet the Hippocratic Standard?' (1997) 56 Md L Rev 1284, 1288–89; K Roosevelt III, 'The Myth of Choice of Law: Rethinking Conflicts' (1999) 97 Mich L Rev 2448, 2466.

[109] AA Ehrenzweig, 'A Counter-Revolution in Conflicts of Laws' (1966) 80 Harv L Rev 377, 381.

[110] LE Little, 'Hairsplitting and Complexity in Conflict of Laws: The Paradox of Formalism' (2004) 37 UC Davis L Rev 925, 958.

[111] As Friedrich Juenger once sarcastically put it, 'But even a juggler, not to mention a trial judge, can only cope with a finite number of balls in the air. FK Juenger, *Contract Conflicts: The E.E.C. Convention on the Law Applicable to Contractual Obligations: An American Assessment* (ed by PM North) 295 at 300 (North-Holland Publishing Co 1982).

[112] Second Restatement §§ 145 (2)(c), § 188 (2 (e), 221 (2).

formation, where location is a host server, or place of injury/harm when it applies to the case of online defamation, where the place of harm (such as the place where the defamatory material has been downloaded) seems too hard to track and appears to be completely irrelevant to factual situation? As will be considered in Chapter VIII, the inherent flexibility of the MSR principle is essential if we want to meet the challenges of technology.[113]

3.52 Second, it would not be correct to say that the case law and the literature have not imposed *any* limitations on judicial analysis under the MSR principle. One of the central features of the MSR principle's operational mechanics relates to the notion that the pool of relevant connecting factors should be restricted to the time of the relevant event occurring—ie the time when the relevant components of contract/tort liability have taken place. In the case of a contractual transaction that would mean that the connecting factors of the parties' residence, the place of contracting, the place of performance, and the place of business were evaluated based on the time when each one of the constitutive elements of contractual liability took place. Accordingly, connecting factors such as the place of the forum[114] and subsequent changes in one of the parties' residence[115] should be excluded from the potential pool of relevant connecting factors under the operational mechanics of the MSR principle. This incorporation would defeat the notion of the parties' reasonable expectations, a notion that underpins the MSR principle.[116]

3.53 Third, and fundamentally, the critics of the MSR principle have frequently overlooked that its operation, usually goes alongside the establishment of flexible pre-built presumptions. These presumptions set flexible points of departure for its operation and eliminate much of the traditional criticism targeting the inherent flexibility of the MSR principle. In other words, the critics of the MSR principle have missed the point that within choice-of-law doctrine, the MSR principle does not come alone, but together with flexible pre-built presumptions.

3.54 Consider an instance of a car accident between Ontario and Florida residents, which has happened in the state of New York. The contemporary choice-of-law doctrine would classify this case as a tort law case. The operation of the MSR principle directs to various laws and territories, such as Ontario (the place of the plaintiff's residence at the time of the accident), Florida (the place of the defendant's residence at the time of the accident), and New York (the place of the defendant's negligent driving and the plaintiff's injury). Yet, the legal doctrine may take one of the connecting factors as a point of departure for its judicial analysis. And, if the analysis under the MSR principle does not clearly direct to the application of a law with the most significant relationship, the application of the law of the point of departure shall follow. Thus, in the above-mentioned example, if the place of the wrong (ie the place of the defendant's

[113] Indeed, Chapter VIII of our book demonstrates how the MSR principle can be coherently situated within the notion of electronic negotiable instruments. See Chapter VIII section F(2).

[114] See eg Currie 141.

[115] Second Restatement ch 7, topic 1, intro note.

[116] See eg Kegel 191–92; Currie 621; Mills, *The Confluence* 237.

negligent driving) serves as a presumption for tort law category, the law of New York shall govern this case.

The MSR principle does not operate in empty space, but usually works together, in syllogism with a pre-determined point of departure of one of the connecting factors. Critics have ignored the European and American tradition of so-called 'soft connecting factors'[117] (which we define as 'presumptions') that can be overturned by other connecting factors. We argue that in the relationship between the presumptions and the MSR principle, the former are not 'fixed' but rather present 'loose' starting points that can be overturned by relevant connecting factors of particular circumstances within the MSR analysis. **3.55**

A review of traditional and contemporary choice-of-law provisions reveals the centrality of the various presumptions within the operational mechanics of the MSR principle. Consider the provisions of the popular Second Restatement. Sections146 and 147 set a preliminary point of departure of the place of the plaintiff's injury in the area of tort law. Section 188(3) of the Second Restatement indicates that an instance of overlap between the places of contract negotiation and performance sets a presumption on that place.[118] Section 195 sets a preliminary point of departure of the place of the loan re-payment in the case of a loan contract, and § 196 establishes the point departure of the place of the service performance in the case of a contract for performance of services.[119] These and other points of departure can be overturned through an examination and evaluation of other connecting factors of the MSR analysis, such as the residence of the parties, the place of their business, their nationality, the place of contract formation and the place of the contract performance.[120] **3.56**

A similar tendency of combining the MSR principle with flexible points of departure can be traced on the other side of Atlantic. Thus, the traditional common law approach has viewed the place of contractual performance and enrichment as the point of departure for contract law and unjust enrichment categories, respectively.[121] The pre-Rome I instrument, the Rome Convention, clearly placed a combination of the MSR principle with flexible presumptions in the heart of its operational mechanics.[122] Even within the general rigidity of the provisions of Rome I and II, the application of the MSR principle can be seen. Thus, under Rome II the personal connecting factor of the common residence of the parties overturns the presumption of the place of injury.[123] Further, one can argue that Articles 4(4) of Rome I and Rome II crystalize the MSR principle as well. By referring to the application of the law of that country that **3.57**

117 See eg J Zekoll, 'A Review of Choice of Law and Multistate Justice' in PJ Borchers and J Zekoll (eds) *International Conflict of Laws for the Third Millennium* (Ardsley 2001) 9, 14.
118 Second Restatement §§ 146, 147, 188 (3), 195 and196
119 ibid § 196.
120 ibid § 188 (2).
121 See eg R Leslie, 'Unjustified Enrichment in the Conflict of Law' (1998) 2 Edin L Rev 233, 235–41.
122 For a discussion on the Rome Convention as a reflection of flexible presumptions in combination with the MSR principle, see eg *Cheshire & North* 734–35 'under the traditional common law rules and Rome Convention it was clear that the presumption of characteristic performance is weak and could be easily overturned through the application of the closest connection [MSR] principle'.
123 Rome II, art 4(2).

is 'manifestly more closely connected',[124] these articles enable the court to overturn the various presumptions set in the Rome Regulations for contract, tort and unjust enrichment categories. This reading of Articles 4(4) of Rome I and Rome II favour the interpretation of the Regulations, which do not view the various connecting factors as affixed points but rather as flexible rebuttable presumptions. This reading attributes a central role to those articles and views them as an integral part of the choice-of-law process, under the Regulations.[125] But even if we follow a restrictive reading of Articles 4(4) of the Rome Regulations, it can be argued that the reference to the parties' choice, which is 'clearly demonstrated by the circumstances of the case' under Article 3(1) of Rome I,[126] provides another route to overturn the Regulation's presumptions and apply the MSR principle.

3.58 The ascendancy of the MSR principle over Beale's over-rigidity has not been absolute and there is a noticeable tendency towards the value of predictability on both sides of the Atlantic has been noticed. It is clear that the MSR principle cannot operate on its own and shall be applied through presumptions. The MSR principle served as a basic principle of the pre-Rome II Regulation,[127] but its unpredictability led to the introduction of fairly stringent presumptions. Yet, it would appear that the application of the MSR principle on both sides of the Atlantic and beyond is still fairly central, and will perhaps grow with the UK's departure from the European Union and the return to the traditional English choice-of-law rules inspired by the MSR principle.[128]

C. The Need for Choice-of-Law Harmonization in Rules relating to Negotiable Instruments

3.59 What are the choice-of-law rules applicable to negotiable instruments? Chapter IV of this book demonstrates a significant divergence between the various choice-of-law rules amongst global systems. The effect of that divergence should not be underestimated and underpins arguments in favour harmonization of choice-of-law rules in various areas of law.[129] Given international political trends against globalization and the failure of systems to agree on unification of the substantive law,[130] it seems to be essential to reach a consensus on the identity of the choice-of-law rules. In other words,

[124] Rome I, art 4(4).

[125] For a debate on the point of the status of the 'manifestly more closely connected' phrase within the Rome Regulations, asking whether this phrase refers to an inherent flexible analysis of the MSR principle (which would be preferable from our point of view) or views it as a radical exception, see eg *Clarkson & Hill* 230–35; *Cheshire & North* 723.

[126] Rome II, art 3(1).

[127] Indeed, prior to the Rome Regulations, the MSR principle served as an organizing principle of the Rome Convention (Convention on the Law Applicable to Contractual Obligations 80/934/EEC, 1980 OJ (L266) 1 art 4. See also Hayward, *Discretion* 234; Plender and Wilderspin 7.076).

[128] On the paramount centrality of the MSR principle within traditional English rules, see eg *Clarkson & Hill* 9, 12; A Dickinson, 'Back to the Future: the UK's EU exit and the conflict of laws' (2016) 12 JPIL 195.

[129] See eg FC von Savigny, *A Treatise on the Conflict of Laws, and the Limits of Their Operation in Respect of Place and Time* (trans by W Guthrie, T& T Clark 1880)136–37; TM de Boer, 'Living Apart Together: The Relationship between Public and Private International Law' (2010) 57 NILR 183, 196.

[130] For some substantive unification projects within the area of private law, see eg *Cheshire & North* 8–15.

while the project of the substantive unification of the law has been hard to reach, the harmonization of choice-of-law needs to be effected in the immediate term.

Given the multitude of possible ways for the plaintiff to acquire jurisdiction over the defendant,[131] the diversity in the identity of choice-of-law rules means that the plaintiff may potentially unilaterally determine the identity of the choice-of-law rules and subsequently the applicable law. The phenomenon of 'forum shopping' is unfortunate, negates the value of fairness embedded in the parties' interaction, and is inconsistent with the demands of international commerce and business. The harmonization of choice-of-law rules would ensure that the same litigated case is decided according to the same substantive law, regardless of the identity of the forum. **3.60**

This point is particularly applicable in the case of negotiable instruments. Given their historical origins and practical operation, the frequency of private international law litigation within this area may potentially be more common than other areas of law.[132] Furthermore, as we have seen in Chapter I,[133] the substantive law of the various systems diverge. Despite unification efforts,[134] the law differs between the major systems that have been modelled on the UK Bills of Exchange Act 1882 (BEA)[135] and the Geneva Conventions.[136] The divergence is remarkable, even within various systems that even come from the same 'family' of origin, and affects the litigating parties' rights and duties to a significant degree. Although, for example the Canadian BEA[137] **3.61**

[131] Indeed, a glance at the contemporary jurisdictional rules reveals a multitude of potential bases of jurisdiction under the principal division between: (1) the presence-based basis of jurisdiction, such as the defendant's present location (see eg Brilmayer, *Conflict of Laws* 268–75; (2) specific jurisdictional bases, such as place of tort or contract formation (see eg Regulation (EU) No 1215/2012, OJ 2012 L351/1, ss 2 and 7 (hereafter Brussels I Recast); and (3) choice-based jurisdiction basis, such as the parties' choice of forum (see eg Brussels I Recast, art 7).

[132] See eg EG Lorenzen, *Cases and Materials on the Conflict of Laws* (5th edn, St Paul Minn 1946) 510 (mentions that 'Because of its commercial function- to effect payment in foreign countries- the bill of exchange raises more conflicts questions than any other type of contract') (hereafter Lorenzen, *Cases and Materials*). See also Chapter II sections A and F.

[133] See Chapter I sections D and E.

[134] On the unification efforts of substantive law within negotiable instruments, see eg Lorenzen, *Cases and Materials* 510 (mentions the unification efforts and divergence between 'two principal systems'—the 'Anglo-American group' and the Continental Geneva Convention. As Lorenzen put it: 'It is only natural that the commercial world should have begun trying a long time ago to overcome the obstacles to commerce caused by a diversity of local bills of exchange laws, and should have striven towards unification of laws relating to the bills of exchange'; E Balogh, 'Critical Remarks on the Law of Bills of Exchange of the Geneva Convention' (1935) 9 Tul L Rev 165, 165–68; HE Yntema, 'Unification of the Law Respecting Negotiable Instruments' (1951) 4 Int'l L Q 178; HC Gutteridge, 'The Unification of the Rules of Conflict Relating to Negotiable Instruments' (1934) 16 J Comp Legis & Int'l L 53, 54 ('The substantive or material law of negotiable instruments presents difficulties which must at present be regarded as insuperable'); CM Schmitthoff, *Selected Essays on International Trade Law* (Brill 1988) 84–86; MO Hudson and AH Feller, 'The International Unification of Laws Concerning Bills of Exchange' (1931) 44 Harv L Rev 333, 338–47; M Lehmann, 'Bill of Exchange' in J Basedow et al (eds) *Encyclopaedia of Private International Law* (Elgar Publishing 2017) 192: 'Uniform substantive law would clearly be preferable. In almost no other area of the law is there such a need for legal harmonization as in the regulation of bills of exchange.' See also Chalmer's replica in 1912 about the 'failure of the unification efforts, for the generations to come' (*The Report of Sir Mackenzie Chalmers to the Economic Committee of the League of Nations*, League of Nations Series, C. 487. M 203. 1923 II. E. 106, 106).

[135] 1882, c 61 (Regnal 45_and_46_Vict) (hereafter BEA).

[136] 143 LNTS 257 (7 June 1930), Annex I (hereafter UBL); 143 LNTS 355 (19 March 1931), Annex I.

[137] Bills of Exchange Act, RSC 1985, c B-4.

and (indirectly) Article 3 of the Uniform Commercial Code[138] have originated from the BEA, they diverge between themselves and in relation to the BEA on several key points.[139] Finally, our comparative analysis has revealed the divergence of BEA legislation in legal systems that are not part of the common law world such as Israel and South Africa.[140]

3.62 The frequency of private international law litigation in the area of negotiable instruments, the deep divergence between the systems, and the detrimental effect of 'forum shopping' all suggest that the further harmonization of the choice-of-law rules of negotiable instruments is highly desirable. Such harmonization would lead to more justice and fairness between the litigating parties, enhance the value of predictability, and promote international commerce and business. From this perspective, it seems to be of paramount significance to find a common ground as to the identity of the choice-of-law rules among the systems.

3.63 The choice-of-law question tackles the identity of the law to be applied by the court or other adjudication tribunal to adjudicate a given dispute. Our comparative findings have revealed a significant difference between the substantive laws of various systems underlies the contemporary significance of the choice-of-law question for negotiable instruments law.

3.64 Chapter IV provides a comprehensive outline of the choice-of-law rules relating to negotiable instruments. The examination is descriptive and analytical in its nature. It is critical only to the extent of the application and interpretation of the existing rules. It does not question existing rules but endeavours to enhance their understanding. Chapters V–VIII offer a reassessment of the existing rules outlined in Chapter IV,[141] challenge the orthodoxy, and offer an alternative set of rules to serve as a basis for a global harmonized framework of the choice-of-law rules relating to negotiable instruments.

[138] Uniform Commercial Code.
[139] See Chapter I sections D and E.
[140] See Introduction, text accompanying n 13.
[141] See Introduction, text accompanying n 13.

IV
Negotiable Instruments Choice-of-Law Rules in the Various Systems

A. Introduction

As discussed in Chapter I, in the absence of a universal adoption of one statute, such as one modelled on the United Nations Convention on International Bills of Exchange and International Promissory Notes (UNIBNC),[1] diverse statutes govern negotiable instruments in the various jurisdictions. This chapter examines the specific choice-of-law rules applicable to negotiable instruments in principal legal systems. Examination is comparative but critical only to the extent of the interpretation and application of the rules. Applicable sources of choice-of-law provisions to be considered are: **4.01**

1. Section 72 of the Bills of Exchange Act (BEA),[2] being the statute governing negotiable instruments in the UK. Similar provisions as part of a similar statute exist in Canada (CBEA)[3] and Australia (ABEA),[4] as well as in other jurisdictions sometimes collectively referred to here as BEA jurisdictions or countries;[5]

[1] UN Doc A/RES/43/165, 42 Yearbook of the United Nations 1988 (UN 1988) 834 (hereafter UNIBNC). Obviously, universal adoption will not preclude choice-of-law questions relating to '[a]spects of general law governing negotiable instruments [that] form "the law of bills and notes in the wide sense"' as pointed out in Chapter I section B, n 73.

[2] 1882, chapter 61, 45, and 46 Vict (hereafter BEA).

[3] RSC 1985, c B-4 (hereafter CBEA).

[4] Bills of Exchange Act 1909, C2012C00128 (hereafter ABEA).

[5] Listed by AW Rogers, *Falconbridge on Banking and Bills of Exchange* (7th edn, Canada Law Book 1969) 431–32 (hereafter Rogers, *Falconbridge on Banking*).

2. The Restatement Conflict of Laws, Second (Second Restatement)[6] in the USA, where in the various states the statue that governs negotiable instruments is Article 3 of the Uniform Commercial Code—Negotiable Instruments (UCC Article 3)[7]; two Geneva Conflict Conventions (GCCs), namely,

   i) The Convention for the Settlement of Certain Conflicts of Laws in Connection with Bills of Exchange and Promissory Notes, signed at Geneva 7 June 1930 (BNCC)[8] and
   ii) The Convention for the Settlement of Certain Conflicts of Laws in Connection with Cheques, signed at Geneva 19 March 1931 (CCC);[9]

   and finally,

   iii) Inter-American Convention on Conflict of Laws Concerning Bills of Exchange, Promissory Notes, and Invoices, 1975 ('IACC')[10].

4.02 In general, signatories to the BNCC, CCC and the IACC[11] are countries whose negotiable instruments statutes are based to one degree or another on the Convention Providing a Uniform Law for Bills of Exchange and Promissory Notes (UBL)[12] and/or the Convention Providing a Uniform Law for Cheques (UCL)[13] (both addressed in Chapter I section B). Neither the USA nor Canada is a signatory to the IACC.

4.03 Under the BEA, the cheque is a specie of the 'bill of exchange'[14] and the provisions applicable to bills of exchange ('bills') govern with necessary modifications, and subject to specific exceptions, promissory notes ('notes') as well.[15] The choice-of-law rules in BEA s 72 cover bills, cheques, and notes. Under the IACC, provisions governing bills apply to notes[16] as well as to 'invoices… that are considered to be negotiable instruments'.[17] The BNCC covers bills and notes and the CCC cover cheques. Choice-of-law questions arise even among UBL and UCL countries, as well as among countries that modelled their statues on the BEA. This is because, as indicated in Chapter I, there are local variations within each group. Unfortunately, there is no one body of choice-of-law rules covering conflicts between the major legal systems, namely, the BEA, UCC, and UBL and UCL countries. Stated otherwise, in the

[6] *Restatement of Conflict of Laws, Second* (1971, revised 1986 and 1988, American Law Institute) (hereafter Second Restatement).
[7] ALI and NCCUSL, 2002 (hereafter UCC).
[8] 143 LNTS 319 (7 June 1930 143 LNTS 407 (19 March 1931) (hereafter BNCC).
[9] 143 LNTS 407 (19 March 1931) (hereafter CCC).
[10] 1438 UNTS 211 (1975) (hereafter IACC).
[11] For signatories to the BNCC, CCC, IACC, UBL and UCL visit (in this order): <https://treaties.un.org/pages/LONViewDetails.aspx?src=LON&id=550&chapter=30&clang=_en>; <https://treaties.un.org/pages/LONViewDetails.aspx?src=LON&id=551&chapter=30&clang=_en;http://www.oas.org/juridico/english/sigs/b-33.html>; <https://treaties.un.org/pages/LONViewDetails.aspx?src=LON&id=552&chapter=30&clang=_en>; and: https://treaties.un.org/pages/LONViewDetails.aspx?src=LON&id=553&chapter=30&clang=_en, accessed 20 December 2019.
[12] 143 LNTS 257 (7 June 1930), Annex I (hereafter UBL).
[13] 143 LNTS 355 (19 March 1931), Annex I (hereafter UCL).
[14] BEA s 73.
[15] BEA s 89.
[16] IACC art 9.
[17] ibid, art 10.

normal course of events, a BEA-type jurisdiction will apply BEA s 72 (or its counterpart in that jurisdiction) in connection with a conflict with a UBL and UCL or UCC (as well as another BEA) jurisdiction. Conversely, in a dispute between a BEA or UCC jurisdiction, or another UBL and UCL country, a UBL and UCL country, depending on the convention to which it is a signatory, will apply either the BNCC or IACC for bills and notes, and the CCC for cheques. For its part, a court in the USA will apply the Second Restatement to determine choice-of-law questions with BEA, UBL and UCL jurisdiction countries and, in the few occasions where there are local variations, among American states.

The various frameworks show very little evidence of the three major developments outlined in Chapter III. Generally, the frameworks have remained loyal to the classical choice-of-law doctrine of stringent territorial connecting factors. There is almost no trace of party autonomy or the most significant relationship principle. The requirement of a 'foreign element' presence in the factual matrix of the case seems is a fundamental precondition to choice-of-law analysis. Thus, BEA's choice-of-law provisions, set forth in s 72, apply only '[w]here a bill drawn in one country is negotiated, accepted, or payable in another'. This is unfortunate on two counts. First, as we will see in greater detail in Chapter V, this provision is not sensitive to contemporary developments in the choice-of-law doctrine and may lead to undesirable results. Second, the meaning of 'drawn' is unclear. It could mean written, written and signed, or issued—meaning written, signed, and delivered. In principle, as further discussed in section C, unless signed and delivered so as to be issued, the instrument does not carry with it any liability.[18] The meaning of 'drawn' has not been judicially determined.[19] **4.04**

The discussion in this chapter proceeds as follows. Section B examines the principle, now universally accepted, under which each aspect of an instrument may be governed by a separate legal system so that there is not necessarily a single law governing each instrument. Section C deals with the choice-of-law rules governing intrinsic validity—that is, the effects of obligations as a matter of substantive law. Section D is concerned with the application of intrinsic validity rules to selected issues. Section E discusses rules governing extrinsic validity (ie form), while section F covers rules relating to specific cheque situations. Section G discusses choice-of-law rules affecting transfers, while section H addresses rules concerning formalities and other performance duties. Lastly, the conclusion in section I points out that the Second Restatement, although not flawless, sets up the most comprehensive and responsive scheme. **4.05**

[18] BEA s 21(1).

[19] In *Canada Life Insurance Co. v Canadian Imperial Bank of Commerce* (1979), 98 DLR 670 (SCC) at para 22, Estey J was inclined to read 'drawn' 'in the manual sense of the term'. So as effectively to dispense with the delivery requirement. Crawford disagrees: B Crawford, *The Law of Banking and Payment in Canada*, vol. 3 (Canada Law Book, Looseleaf, 2014 edition) § 21:20.110(3) (hereafter Crawford, *Law of Banking and Payment*). In BEA s 55(1) 'drawing' must be read as 'issuing' as it entails liability on the instrument for which delivery is required (BEA s 21(1), discussed further in section C).

B. Single or Several Laws?

4.06 As discussed in Chapter I, parties liable on a negotiable instrument are either primary or secondary. The acceptor of a bill, being the drawee who indicated his or her consent to comply with the drawer's order,[20] and the maker of a note, being the promissor thereunder,[21] are primary parties. For each, liability on the engagement is according to its tenor. The drawer, being the order giver,[22] and each indorser, being the transferor of an instrument payable to him,[23] are liable only upon the dishonour of the instrument, and usually upon the holder's compliance with presentment and notice requirements, which may be required to be formalized. The 'avalist' signs as a guarantor to a party liable on the instrument.[24] There is no 'avalist' under the BEA and the UCC; thereunder, a signer who is not a party to the underlying transaction is an accommodation party.[25] Under the BEA, he or she could also be taken to be an anomalous indorser.[26]

4.07 There have been two fundamental approaches in the selection of the law that applies to a contract on an instrument. The first is the 'several laws' doctrine. It is premised on the view that each one of the contracts on one instrument, such as that of the drawer, acceptor, maker, or indorser, is separate and independent.[27] Within this array, the dynamics of the enforcement mechanism provides the instrument's holder with a choice to sue each one of the signatory parties on the instrument.[28] The liability of each one of the signatory parties is determined within a framework that focuses on the specific interaction between the signatory party and the instrument's holder.

4.08 The opposite approach is that of a 'single law' governing all obligations on a given instrument which focuses on the unity of the instrument incorporating all such contracts. It is said[29] to go back to Pothier, although he did not provide reasoning for it, and made his broad statement as to its existence in connection with a discussion

[20] BEA s 54(1): UBL art 28; UNIBNC art 40.
[21] BEA s 88(1): UBL art 78; UNIBNC art 39.
[22] BEA s 55(1); UBL art 9 (in conjunction with arts 43–45); UCL art 12 (in conjunction with art 40); UNIBNC art 38.
[23] BEA s 55(2); UBL art 15 (in conjunction with arts 43–45); UCL art 18 (in conjunction with art 40); UNIBNC art 44.
[24] UBL arts 32 and 39; UCL art 27; UNIBNC arts 46–47.
[25] BEA s 28; UCC § 3-419.
[26] BEA s 56. In Canada where the corresponding provision (CBEA s 130) contains a variation, the aval contract was read into the statute in *Gallagher v Murphy* [1929] SCR 288. For further discussion of the 'avalist' see Chapter V, the text accompanying nn 30–38.
[27] See eg AG Gleeson, *Chalmers and Guest on Bills of Exchange, Cheques and Promissory Notes* (18th edn, Sweet & Maxwell 2016) 461, para 7-028 (hereafter Gleeson, *Chalmers and Guest*). See also E McKendrick (ed), Goode on Commercial Law (5th edn, Penguin 2016) (hereafter McKendrick, *Commercial Law*) 487.
[28] Indeed, only the holder can enforce payment on the instrument. Subsequently, a payee who ceases to be a holder of the instrument through its indorsement, loses his or her right of the instrument's enforcement. For a discussion of this point, see eg McKendrick, *Commercial Law* 534, 544–45.
[29] See eg EG Lorenzen, 'The Rules of the Conflict of Laws Applicable to Bills and Notes—III. Interpretation and Obligation—A. The Governing Law—2. Relationship of the Different Contracts' (1917) 1 Minn L Rev 320, 322 (hereafter Lorenzen, 'Relationship').

on the formalities required to trigger the liability of a secondary party.[30] For his part, treating a secondary party as a surety or guarantor[31] to the primary party, Westlake rationalizes a 'single law' to apply to all contracts on an instrument as follows:[32]

> Since the drawer or indorser ... are sureties for the due performance of the obligation incurred by accepting or making ... the law of the place where the bill or note is payable according to the terms in which it is drawn or made, as regulating such due performance, indirectly affects their obligation by affecting that of the acceptor or maker.

It is thus a single law, that of the place of payment (referred in Latin as *lex loci solutionis*) by the acceptor of a bill and maker of a note, which according to Westlake governs the liability of all parties to an instrument. Neither the law of the territorial connecting factors of the place of the issue of a bill or cheque nor the execution of any contract (referred in Latin as *lex loci contractus*) governs. **4.09**

A 'single law' approach provides simplicity; however, it may not lead to a resolution of issues such as one arising between two immediate parties, an indorser and indorsee, located outside the country in which payment is to be made. Also, an instrument may not state where it is to be paid, so that indorsers may not have any knowledge as to which law is applicable to their obligations. Furthermore, the 'single law' theory is premised on doctrinally disputed grounds. **4.10**

For example, by reference to a contract of suretyship (not on an instrument), under the Second Restatement, '[t]he validity of a contract for suretyship and the rights created thereby are determined, in the absence of an effective choice-of-law by the parties, by the law governing the principal obligation'.[33] Under English law, this is less straightforward. True, 'it may be inferred that the parties to a guarantee of obligation ... intended that [it] should be governed by the same law governing the guaranteed obligation'. Such is the case 'especially where the guarantor and [the principal debtor] are connected'.[34] However, parties to a negotiable instrument are typically not 'connected' to each other the way a guarantor and principal debtor are. Despite an inference of an intended single law in certain circumstances,[35] there is no universal rule in the absence of an agreement as to the application of a single law to a guarantee. This **4.11**

[30] RJ Pothier, *Traitè du contrat de change, Nouvelle Édition par M. Hutteau* (Letellier 1809) Premiere Partie ch V art I §V, 99, para 155.

[31] A 'person who makes [a] promise to be answerable for the debt or obligation of another is called [a] guarantor or [a] surety'. J O'Donovan and JC Phillips, *The Modern Contract of Guarantee* (2nd English edn by JC Phillips, Sweet and Maxwell 2010) 9, paras 1–19 (hereafter, O'Donovan and Phillips, *Guarantee*). The two terms (as well as related terms such as 'guarantee' and 'suretyship') are used here interchangeably.

[32] J Westlake, *A Treatise on Private International Law* (7th edn by N Bentwich, Sweet & Maxwell 1925) 320, § 230 (hereafter Westlake, *Private International Law*).

[33] Second Restatement § 194.

[34] Collins, Harris (eds) *Dicey, Morris and Collins on the Conflict of Laws*, vol 2 (15th edn, Sweet & Maxwell 2012) 1811, Rule 222 at paras 32–061. See eg *Emeraldian v Wellmix Shipping Ltd* [2010] EWHC 1411 [167] (Comm).

[35] *Samcrete Egypt Engineers v Land Rover* [2001] EWCA Civ 2019; *Commercial Marine & Piling Ltd v Pierse Contracting Ltd* [2009] EWHC 2241 (TCC). See O'Donovan and Phillips, *Guarantee* 932–33, paras 14–55.

is so even where there is an alleged 'connectedness' between the guarantor and the principal debtor. For example, under the European Rome I Regulation[36] the surety's contract is prima facie governed by the surety's place of residence and not by the law of 'the country in which the surety has to make payment to the creditor'.[37] 'Single law' presumption does not exist in a guarantee; neither between the less or non-'connected' parties to a negotiable instrument.

4.12 Both the BEA[38] and the UCC[39] speak of the drawer and indorser as becoming liable to pay upon the dishonour of the instrument, rather than guaranteeing payment (or acceptance thereof). While it is said that the relationship between parties secondarily liable on an instrument and the party primarily liable on it is one of suretyship,[40] it is more accurate to speak of that relationship as merely 'analogous'[41] to, or 'in the nature of',[42] but not strictly suretyship.[43] One reason is that between the primary and a secondary party to an instrument 'there is strictly speaking, no contract of suretyship'[44] existing between the surety and the creditor either alone or jointly with the principal debtor,[45] and under which 'personal responsibility for [a] debt [owed by the principal debtor] is assumed' by the surety.[46] Indeed, the drawer enters the transaction instructing the drawee to pay; each indorser is then deemed to be a drawer of a new bill.[47] Neither the drawer nor the indorser becomes a party to an instrument for the purpose of guaranteeing payment by another; rather he or she becomes a party on his or her account, instructing payment on a transaction on which he or she is a principal. Any 'suretyship' of a secondary party is by law and not by agreement. Moreover, there

[36] Regulation (EC) No 593/2008 of the European Parliament and the Council of 17 June 2008, on the law applicable to contractual obligations (Rome I) Official Journal of the European Union, L 177/6, of 4.7.2008 (hereafter Rome I)

[37] GM Marks and G Moss (eds) *Rowlatt on Principal and Surety* (6th edn, Sweet & Maxwell 2011) 278, para 18-02 (hereafter Marks and Moss, *Rowlatt*).

[38] BEA s 55.

[39] UCC §§ 3-414 and 3-415.

[40] *Rowe v Young* (1820) 2 Bligh 391 [467], 4 ER 372 [407]; *Roquette v Overmann* (1875) LR 10 QB 525 [537]. See Gleeson, *Chalmers and Guest* 461, para 7-021.

[41] WH Loyd, 'The Surety' (1917–18) 66 U Pa L Rev 40 [57] (hereafter Loyd, 'The Surety'), as well as Marks and Moss, *Rowlatt* 5 at para 1-07, where secondary parties are also characterized as 'quasi-sureties' and further see 157 at para 7-07. See also *Re Conley* [1938] 2 All ER 127 [130], 158 LT 323.

[42] Gleeson, *Chalmers and Guest* 606, para 12-024.

[43] *Duncan, Fox & Co. v North and South Wales Bank* (1880) 6 App Cas 1 [13], [14], [19], [1874-80] All ER Rep Ext 1406 (HL) (hereafter *Duncan, Fox & Co v North and South Wales Bank*); *Re Conley* [1938] 2 All ER 127 [131], 158 LT 323.

[44] *Duncan Fox & Co. v North and South Wales Bank* [13].

[45] ibid [11].

[46] *Re Conley* [1938] 2 All ER 127 [130], 158 LT 323. It is also said that while compared to suretyship, at its inception, the secondary party's obligation on an instrument is conditional and triggered only upon dishonour and the observance of formalities, 'when the conditions required by ... law are fulfilled', the secondary party's liability 'becomes absolute, and is that of a principal' and not surety: *Duncan, Fox & Co. v North and South Walest Bank* [13]. However, along lines set out by Loyd, 'The Surety' 50 and 54–56 with respect to suretyships the distinction between principal and secondary liability of a secondary party to an instrument looks to us as hair splitting and thus unhelpful.

[47] *Anon* (1694) Holt KB 115, 90 ER 962. For US cases see J Daniels, *A Treatise on the Law of Negotiable Instruments*, vol II (7th edn, Baker, Voorhis 1933) 1136–37 at § 1052 and cites in n 16 (hereafter Daniels, *A Treatise*).

is no obligation to be guaranteed on an unaccepted bill;[48] a drawee of a bill who has not accepted, which is typical in the case of a personal cheque, is not liable thereon.[49]

In fact, the analysis under both the UBL and UCL is quite similar. Both speak of the drawer and indorser *guaranteeing* payment, and in the case of a bill, also acceptance.[50] This, however, ought not to be taken literally. Certainly, the drawer of a cheque or an accepted bill does not guarantee any payment obligation. Rather, a secondary party undertakes to pay upon the occurrence of dishonour, which may or may not be in breach of the drawee's undertaking to the drawer, which on its own does not run in favour of the holder.[51] **4.13**

Accordingly, the position of a secondary party to an instrument may not be exactly the same as that of a surety. Hence, the law governing suretyships does not automatically apply in its entirety to the secondary's party position. Indeed, payment by a surety discharges the principal debtor so as to enable him or her to use it in defence to a subsequent action by the creditor. However, it was held that 'to [the holder's] action against the acceptor [of a bill], payment by the drawer is no plea'; rather, such payment 'only converts the holder into a trustee of the drawer when the holder afterwards recovers of the acceptor'.[52] Also, notwithstanding views to the contrary,[53] and whatever the position regarding the surety's engagement, under the law of negotiable instruments, a secondary party is said to undertake to pay 'at the place where [he or she] ... entered into the contract'[54] and not where the instrument was to be honoured by its principal party.[55] As Lorenzen explains, it is inconceivable that secondary parties made their respective contracts by reference to the law applicable in the place of the issue of the instrument,[56] its place of payment, or the place in which the principal party made his or her own contract.[57] **4.14**

The prevailing approach is that of 'several laws', each governing an 'independent contract' of a party to the instrument.[58] Under this approach, the law applicable to each of the various contracts on the instrument is selected by reference to facts relevant to **4.15**

48 The general rule is that a signature is a necessary requirement for liability on an instrument. See BEA s 23; UBL arts 7–8; UCC § 3-401; UNIBNC art 33.

49 See UCC § 3-408; BEA s 53(1).

50 UBL arts 15 and 19 and UCL arts 12 and 18.

51 For further discussion and objection to drawing a parallel between the liability of the secondary parties and the law of surety/guarantees, see Chapter VI, the text accompanying nn 172–94.

52 *Cook v Lister* (1863) 18 CBNS 543 [579], 143 ER 215 [230].

53 Set out by Daniels, *A Treatise* 1139, § 1054 who argues that the several laws doctrine 'does not bear the test of searching analysis' but nevertheless acknowledges that his view is dissenting to the one 'sustained by great weight of opinion, and an overwhelming current of authorities'. ibid. See 1134–1140, §§ 1051–1054 for his summary of case law in both directions.

54 J Story, *Commentaries on the Conflict of Laws* (Hilliard 1834; Rep Arno Press 1972) 262, § 315 (hereafter Story, *Conflict of Laws*).

55 *Allen v Kemble* (1848) 6 Moo PC 314 [21–22], 13 ER 704 [707] (hereafter *Allen v Kemble*)

56 While this is the same as the place of the maker's contract on a note, this is not necessarily the place of acceptance of a bill. For a brief discussion on the inappropriateness of the law of the place of issue see HC Gutteridge, 'The Unification of the Rules of Conflict Relating to Negotiable Instruments' (1934) 16 J Comp Legis & Int'l L 53, 68. (hereafter Gutteridge, 'Rules of Conflict')

57 Lorenzen, 'Relationship' 325–27.

58 ibid.

that contract only and not to the instrument as a whole,[59] nor to facts relevant to the primary's party's contract.

4.16 Lescot and Roblot address criticisms to the several laws doctrine that even under that doctrine, each clause inserted by a party binds a subsequent one under the law that governs the party who inserted the clause. Lescot and Roblot conclude that this argument is contrary to BNCC art 4 (we suggest CCC art 5 too) and ought to be rejected. One exception that they point out exists where two countries have different rules where there is inconsistency between the expression of the sum in figures or words. In such a case, payment made by the drawee (we suggest also from a maker) forfeits to the holder any right to the difference where a law applicable to the contract of an intervening party would have given him or her a higher amount. However, Lescot and Roblot acknowledge that this exception is 'more apparent than real'[60] as it goes to the distinction between a discharge of an instrument and that of a party thereto,[61] with the former being governed by the law pertaining to such discharge, which is the place of payment. Accordingly, the law governing 'effects of . . . obligations' under BNCC art 4 (and similarly under CCC art 5) covers both scope of liability on an obligation as well as defences to it (including discharge).[62]

4.17 Regarded as 'one of the few aspects of the conflict of laws in which there exists a widespread consensus of opinion throughout the world', [63] the several laws approach accepts on a fundamental level that the drawee's, drawer's, and indorser's contracts could potentially be governed by different laws. Representing a different type of relationship, each one of the contracts crystalizes the conceptual and practical separation between them—a separation that flows from the analysis of the internal structure of negotiable instruments law. Under this vision of negotiable instruments law, each one of the contracts is governed by a separate set of considerations and factors. The choice-of-law considerations applied to the drawee's, drawer's, and indorser's contracts are different and, potentially different laws may govern each one of the contracts. Considerations that are relevant to one contract may not affect others.

4.18 This view of choice-of-law rules of negotiable instruments law has received broad support. Commentators have stated that, 'many problems within conflict of laws relating to negotiable instruments could have been avoided would the single law theory be rejected'.[64] Nowadays, all major choice-of-law frameworks accept this insight about

[59] See eg JD Falconbridge, 'Bills and Notes' in *Essays on the Conflict of Laws* (2nd edn, Canada Law Book 1954) 316, 340–41 (hereafter Falconbridge, 'Bills and Notes') and a detailed discussion by Lorenzen, 'The Relationship'. For the pros and cons of each approach, see eg P Lescot and R Roblot, *Les Effets de Commerce*, vol 2 (Rousseau 1953) 574–76, §§ 1070–71 (hereafter Lescot and Roblot, *Les Effets de Commerce*). See also Gutteridge, 'Rules of Conflict' 67–68.

[60] ibid.

[61] For the discharge of the bill, see eg BEA s 59.

[62] Lescot and Roblot, *Les Effets de Commerce* 582, § 1077. BNCC art 4 and CCC art 5 are discussed in Chapter IV section C.

[63] Collins, Harris (eds) *Dicey, Morris and Collins on the Conflict of Laws*, vol 2 (15th edn, Sweet & Maxwell 2012) 1309, 2075–76.

[64] Collins, Harris (eds) *Dicey, Morris and Collins on the Conflict of Laws*, vol 2 (15th edn, Sweet & Maxwell 2012) 1309, 2075–76 . See also BEA s 51(4). For a different view, supporting the 'single law theory', see Westlake, *Private International Law*.

the nature of choice-of-law rules under the instrument,[65] for example, BEA's choice-of-law provision provided in s 72.[66] While this provision does not make a conceptual delineation between primary and secondary parties under the instrument and insists on applying a single choice-of-law rule of the place of contract formation to all contracts under the instrument, it does not apply a single law to all the contracts. The use of the term 'supervening contracts', recognises the internal structure of a negotiable instrument and that different laws can potentially govern each one of contracts within that structure.

The several laws doctrine is popular amongst many jurisdictions. The American courts, have repeatedly emphasized the distinctive nature of the indorsement contract, which is 'entirely distinct from the contract of the maker to pay the note and from the debt arising against the maker by reason thereof', [67] and therefore constitutes a 'new contract'.[68] While stressing the point that this contract conceptually diverges from the drawee contract, they have explained this divergence through the concept of parties' reasonable expectations under each contract.[69] In a similar vein, the English courts in the pre-BEA's days provided unequivocal support to the several laws doctrine through conceptually separating the various contracts under the instruments, for purposes of choice-of-law analysis.[70] **4.19**

The several laws doctrine is important in the sense that it defends the conceptual independence of each one of the contracts under the instrument and insists that each one of them can potentially be governed by a different law. This doctrine is also important in a sense that it delineates the distinctive nature of each relationship and provides us with invaluable insight that different choice-of-law considerations and factors apply to each one of the contracts. This is, indeed (as we will see in Chapters V–VII), an important insight for potential reform within choice-of-law rules relating to negotiable instruments.[71] **4.20**

C. Law Governing Intrinsic Validity or Effects of Obligations

In dealing with the question of applicable law for an obligation on a negotiable instrument, both the Second Restatement §§ 214-215 and IACC art 3 point to the law that **4.21**

[65] See section B of this chapter.
[66] BEA s 72.
[67] *Mackintosh v Gibbs* (1909) 79 NJL 40, 43 .
[68] *Walling v Cushman* (1920) 238 Mass 62, 68; *Everett v Vendryes*, (1859) 19 NY 436, 438.
[69] *Hyatt v Bank of Kentucky* (1871) 71 KY 193, 198 'A party may know when he indorses a paper in Kentucky executed in Louisiana that the law of the latter state imposes a different liability from the law of Kentucky, and still his assignment, being of itself an independent contract'.
[70] See *Allen v Kemble* (commenting on the conceptual separation between the various contracts under the negotiable instrument); *Lebel v Tucker* (1867) LR 3 QB 77, 17 LT 244 [80–81] (commenting on the status of the endorsement as a new contract); *Rothschild v Currie* (1841) 1 QB 43, 113 ER 1045 [1048] (commenting on the status of endorsement as a new contract).
[71] For centrality of the several laws doctrine within the normative framework of choice-of-law rules that we suggest, see Chapter V section B and Chapter VI section B(2).

governs parties' 'obligations'. For its part, BEA s 72(2) designates the law that determines the 'interpretation' of contracts on an instrument'. Lastly, BNCC art 4(1), CCC art 5, and BNCC art 4(2), respectively, point to the laws that determine '[t]he effects of the obligations' of primary parties to a bill or note, the 'effect' of 'obligations' on a cheque, and '[t]he effects of the signatures' of secondary parties on a bill or note. All address intrinsic validity.

4.22 Examining the implications of the several laws approach to the selection of law to govern each obligation, Lorenzen points out 'there is a possibility that one party may be liable under the law governing his or her contract, and yet because of a difference in the law governing the other contracts, have lost, without any personal fault of his own, all rights of recourse against prior parties'.[72] Lorenzen nevertheless concludes that '[w]ith reasonable limitations ... cases of actual hardship will arise only under exceptional circumstances'.[73] Indeed, all sources subject to the present discussion adhere to the several laws approach, albeit not applying it in an identical manner.

4.23 In rejecting the single law approach, both the BEA and the IACC nevertheless provide for a 'single rule'—that of *lex loci contractus*. This rule applies to each party liable on an instrument, although the law to govern each contract depends on the surrounding facts. This is not the case under the GCCs and the Second Restatement, which reject both a 'single law' and a 'single rule'. For its part, BEA s 72(2) provides that, subject to a proviso allowing a payer to have the indorsement of an inland bill interpreted according to UK law, the general rule is that the interpretation of the drawing, indorsement, acceptance, or acceptance supra protest of a bill is determined by the law of the place where such contract is made.

4.24 As to the scope of the proviso, under BEA s 4(1), an inland bill, to which the proviso applies, is 'a bill which is or on the face of it purports to be' 'drawn' within the British Islands, and either payable within the British Islands or 'drawn' upon some person resident therein.[74] It is unclear whether 'drawn' includes 'delivered'.[75]

4.25 To determine under BEA s 72(2), 'the place where the contract is made', the starting point under BEA s 23 is that '[n]o person is liable as drawer, indorser or acceptor of a bill who has not signed it as such'. Accordingly, the position of the drawee, for example, who has not signed as an acceptor, towards the drawer, and in fact vis-à-vis any party to the instrument, is not governed by the choice-of-law rules under BEA s 72(2).

4.26 However, although a signature is a necessary condition to trigger liability on an instrument, it is not sufficient on its own. Under BEA s 21(1):

> Every contract on a bill, whether it is the drawer's, the acceptor's or an indorser's, is incomplete and revocable until delivery of the instrument in order to give effect

[72] Lorenzen, 'Relationship'322. But cf at 326–27 where he points out (by reference to limitations of actions) that 'such a contingency would not be removed completely' under the single law approach. See also Gutteridge, 'Rules of Conflict' 67.

[73] Lorenzen, 'Relationship' 327.

[74] For further discussions (and criticism) of the 'inland'/'foreign' bills division, set in BEA s 4(1), see Chapter V section A(2).

[75] See the text accompanying nn 18–19.

thereto, but where an acceptance is written on a bill and the drawee gives notice to, or according to the directions of, the person entitled to the bill that he has accepted it, the acceptance then becomes complete and irrevocable

Specifically, 'indorsement means an indorsement completed by delivery' and 'issue means the first delivery of a bill or note, complete in form, to a person who takes it as a holder'. In turn, 'holder means the payee or indorsee of a bill or note who is in possession of it, or the bearer thereof'.[76] As well, in common law jurisdictions, an enforceable obligation on an instrument is required to be supported by consideration.[77] 'The mere signature does not make a contract. To constitute a contract on an instrument there must be a delivery over the instrument by the [signer] for a good consideration: and as soon as these circumstances take place the contract is complete.'[78] The sequence of events is of no importance: 'the place of contracting properly means the place in which the final act was done which made the promise or promises binding'.[79] **4.27**

Nonetheless, the final act is typically delivery. Thus, other than for the alternative option of notification for acceptance, each contract on a bill is made by the delivery of the bill,[80] signed by the contracting party to the holder against consideration. For its part, 'delivery' is defined in BEA s 2 to mean the 'transfer of possession, actual or constructive, from one person to another'. It is the acquisition of possession by the transferee[81] that completes the delivery of the signed instrument. In turn, in addition to 'an antecedent debt or liability', 'any consideration sufficient to support a simple contract' suffices under the BEA to constitute '[v]aluable consideration'.[82] Effectively, the consideration requirement is typically complied with upon completion of delivery, which is the final step for the contract to become binding. **4.28**

For acceptance to be binding, it must be 'completed by delivery or notification'[83] to the person who presented the instrument for acceptance. Practically, he or she is either the holder or the drawer. Surely, 'it is not the mere act of writing on the bill, but the making a communication of what is so written, that binds the acceptor; for the making the communication is a pledge by him ... [that] enables the holder to act upon it'.[84] There is, however, ambiguity as to compliance with the 'notification' requirement, namely, whether it occurs upon either dispatch by the acceptor or receipt by the receiver. As **4.29**

[76] BEA s 2.

[77] They are subject to the general rule under which all 'contracts in writing ... [which are] merely written and not specialties ... are parol and require consideration'. *Rann v Hughes* (1778) 7 TR 350n, 101 ER 1014, n (a).

[78] *Abrey v Crux* (1869) LR 5 CP 37 [42], 21 LT 327.

[79] JD Falconbridge, 'Contract' in *Essays on the Conflict of Laws* (2nd edn, Canada Law Book 1954) 316, 375–76, citing Beale, *A Treatise on the Conflict of Laws* (Baker, Voorhis & Co.1935) 1045. On this point see National Exchange Bank of *Baltimore v Rook Granite Co.*, 155 NC 43 (1911).

[80] Notwithstanding *Snaith v Mingay* (1813) 1 M & S 87, 105 ER 33 (as was also understood but not criticized by Story, *Conflict of Laws* 240, § 289) where, albeit for stamping purpose, the bill was taken to be drawn where it was merely signed.

[81] We are borrowing the language of s 68(1) of the *Ontario Securities Transfer Act*, SO 2006, C 8, which is to the same effect, even as it is clearer. Thereunder, '[d]elivery of a certificated security to a purchaser occurs when ... the purchaser acquires possession of the security certificate'.

[82] BEA s 27(1)(a).

[83] BEA s 2.

[84] *Cox v Troy* (1882) 5 B & Ald 474 [478–79], 106 ER 1264 [1266].

a matter of consistency with compliance with the delivery requirement, we contend that what counts is receipt—which completes notification and thus the acceptor's contract. Needless to say, between distant parties located in different countries, the completing event, subject to compliance with the consideration requirement, being either delivery for all contracts or notification for acceptance, thus takes place in a location, and hence a country, other than that where the signature occurred.[85]

4.30 While adhering to the 'several laws' approach, both the Restatement and the GCCs do not adopt the 'single rule' path. Thereunder, different rules determine which law applies to the liability of primary and secondary parties.

4.31 Thus, in the USA, under the Second Restatement § 214 (1), the general rule is that:

> The obligations of the maker of a note and of the acceptor of a draft are determined . . . by the local law[86] of the state designated in the instrument as the place of payment.

4.32 Otherwise, under Second Restatement § 214 (2):

> In the absence of a designated place of payment, the obligations of a maker or acceptor are determined . . . by the local law of the state where he delivered the instrument.[87]

4.33 As for secondary parties, in the general rule under Second Restatement § 215 (1):

> The obligations of an indorser of a draft or note, and of a drawer of a draft, are determined . . . by the local law [of the state] where he delivered the instrument.

4.34 Also, under both §§ 214 (2) (for primary parties) and 215 (1) (for secondary parties) of the Second Restatement, as to the identification of the state where delivery was made:

> That state is presumptively the state where the instrument is dated, if such state is indicated, and in the absence of notice to the contrary on the instrument, this presumption is conclusive with respect to a holder in due course.

4.35 Other than with respect to a holder in due course this presumption can thus be rebutted. There is, however, no provision to deal with the case where the place of dating is not indicated on the instrument.

4.36 As under BEA s 23, 'signature' is a prerequisite for liability on an instrument in the US under UCC § 3-401(a). At the same time, unlike the BEA, UCC Article 3 does not expressly designate 'delivery' as a requirement of a contract on an instrument, in addition to a 'signature'. However, UCC Article 3 makes possession a prerequisite for an entitlement to sue a party liable on an instrument.[88] Possession is acquired lawfully

[85] But cf Story, *Conflict of Laws* 263, § 317, whom we understand to read *Lewis v Owen* (1821) 4 B & Ald 654, 106 ER 1076 as treating the place of signature as the place of acceptance. We read the case as considering the place of payment as the place of the acceptance.

[86] 'Local law' under the Second Restatement excludes state choice-of-law rules. See Comments to the various provisions.

[87] The provision goes on to lay down the presumption that this state is 'the state where the instrument is dated' as well as that 'in the absence of notice to the contrary on the instrument, this presumption is conclusive with respect to a holder in due course'.

[88] UCC §§ 3-412–415 the obligation of each party liable on an instrument 'is owed to a person entitled to enforce' it, defined in § 3-301 primarily by reference to having (or having lost) possession.

either by the 'issue'[89] or 'transfer'[90] of the instrument, both of which require 'delivery'. As under the BEA s 2, for an instrument, 'delivery' under the UCC is 'the voluntary transfer of possession'. [91] Accordingly, to incur liability on an instrument, even if it is signed and sent, 'delivery' must have been completed. Hence, under the Second Restatement, the law selected to govern the 'obligation' of a secondary party, is the same as that under the BEA for 'interpretation', *viz.*, the law of the place where the contract is made. The same is true for primary parties but only '[i]n the absence of a designated place of payment'. This creates a problem in the case of acceptance, which under UCC § 3-409, once signed, an instrument may be made not only when 'the accepted draft is delivered'; but alternatively, in the footsteps of BEA s 2, also 'when notification pursuant to instructions is given'. Thus, where the place of payment is not designated, the law applicable to a signed acceptance completed by notification is not provided for by the Second Restatement.

A large number of cases is cited by Story[92] and the Second Restatement,[93] as well as by Daniels,[94] in support of the 'several laws' doctrine. A cornerstone of this doctrine is the identification at the place of the delivery of an instrument as the place in which the contract thereunder was made. However, careful reading of these cases reveals that **4.37**

[89] Under UCC § 3-105(a), '"Issue" means the first *delivery* of an instrument by the maker or drawer, whether to a holder or nonholder, for the purpose of giving rights on the instrument to any person'. Emphasis added.

[90] Under UCC § 3-203(a), '[a]n instrument is transferred when it is *delivered* by a person other than its issuer for the purpose of giving to the person receiving *delivery* the right to enforce the instrument'. Emphasis added.

[91] UCC § 1-201(b)(15).

[92] See Story, *Conflict of Laws*. Cases cited are: *Potter v Brown* (1804) 5 East R 123, 102 ER 1016; *Hicks v Brown*, 12 John R 142 (NY SC 1815); *Powers v Lynch*, 3 Mass R 77 (1807); *Prentiss v Savage*, 13 Mass R 200 (1816).

[93] Cases cited are: *Coulter v Stewart*, 379 P 2d 910 (Ariz). 1963); *Hyatt v Bank of Kentucky*, 71 Ky 193, 8 Bush (1871); *Mackintosh v Gibbs*, 79 NJL 40, 74 A 708 (1909), *aff'd* and modified, 81 NLJ 577, 80 A 554 (1911); *Hennenlotter v De Orvananos* 114 Misc 333, 186 NYS 488 (NY SC, 1921).

[94] Cases cited in Daniels, *A Treatise* (n 47), 1134–35, § 1051, n 10 are: *Freese v Brownell*, 35 NJL 286 (1871); *Everett v Vendryes*, 19 NY 436 (1859); *Hunt v Standard*,15 Ind 33 (1859); *Raymond v Holmes*, 11 Tex 54 (1854); *Kuenzi v Elvers* (1859), 14 La Ann 391 (1859); *Lennig v Ralston*, 23 Pa St 137 (1854); *Price v Page*, 24 Mo 65 (1856); *Bonedon v Page*, 24 Mo 595 (1859); *Page v Page*, 24 Mo 596 (1857); *Bank of the United States v United States*, 2 How 711 (1844); *Ex parte Heidelback*, 2 Low 526 (1876); *Story v McKay* (1888) OJ No 181, 15 OR 169; *Hazelhurst v Kean*, 4 Yeates 19 (1804); *London and San Francisco Bank v Moore*, 128 Cal 650 (1900); *Amsinck v Rogers*, 189 NY 252 (1907). Further cases cited in Daniels, *A Treatise* 1136–38, § 1052, nn 15–17 include: *Guernsey v Imperial Bank of Canada*, 188 F 300 (8th Cir 1911); *Phipps v Harding*, 70 F 468 (7th Cir 1895); *Dundas v Bowler*, US App LEXIS 383 (1844); *Clanton v Barne*, 50 Ala, 403 (1874); *Greathead v Walton*, 40 Conn 226 (1873); *Yeatman v Cullen*, 5 Blackf, 240, 1839 Ind. LEXIS 123 (1839); *National Bank of Michigan v Green*, 33 Iowa 140 (1871); *Short v Trabue*, 4 Metc (Ky) 299 (1863); *Trabue v Short*, 18 La Ann 257 (1868); *Trabue, Davis & Co. v R.H. Short & Co.*, 45 Tenn 293 (1868); *Baxter Nat. Bank v Talbot*, 154 Mass 213 (1891); *Mackintosh v Gibbs*, 81 NJL 577, 80 A 554 (1911); *Lee v Selleck*, 33 NY 615 (1865); *Cook v Litchfield*, 9 NY 280 (1853); *Aymar v Sheldon*, 12 Wend 443 (1834); *Colonial Nat'l Bank v Duerr*, 95 NYS 815 (1905); *Dow v Rowell*, 12 NH 49 (1841); *Grimes v Tait*, 21 OKl 361 (1908); *Artisans' Bank v Park Bank*, NY App Div LEXIS 30 (1864); *Hunt v Standart*, 15 Ind 33 (1860); *Lowry's Adm'rs v Western Bank*, 7 Ala (NS) 120 (1844); *Holbrook v Vibbard*, Ill LEXIS 87 (1840); *Brook v Van Nest*, 58 NJL 162 (1895); *Slacum v Pomery*, 6 Cranch 221 (US SC, 1810); *Spies v National City Bank*, 61 LRA 193 (1903); *Williams v Wade*, 1 Metcalf 82 (Mass, 1840); *Glidden v Chamberlin*, 167 Mass 486 (1897); *National Exchange Bank of Baltimore v Rook Granite Co.*, 155 NC 43 (1911); and *Douglas v Bank of Commerce*, 97 Tenn 133 (1896). See also *Queensboro Nat. Bank of City of New York v Kelly*, 48 F 2d 574 (1931) (liability of transferor by delivery of an unindorsed instrument); and *Weil v Sturgis*, 23 Ky L Rptr 644 (1901) (assignor's liability on a contract of assignment of an instrument). Another cited case, *Currier v Lockwood*, 40 Conn 349 (1873), strikes us as irrelevant.

their resolution mostly turned on the distinctiveness of the contract made by the secondary party in relation to other contracts. The same is true for *Allen v Kemble*[95] in England. True, there was some emphasis in case law on the delivery requirement for the secondary party's contract,[96] and even mention of delivery being a distinctive element in the contract on an instrument.[97] Nevertheless, case law has not focused on a situation under which the place of delivery was other than at the place of the signature. Moreover, Story himself treated the cases he cited as speaking of the place in which a secondary party 'entered into the contract';[98] in theory this may be the place in which the party signed and sent the instrument, prior to becoming irrevocably bound by it upon subsequent receipt by the holder. At the same time, such a fine distinction was raised neither by Second Restatement authors nor in any judicial and scholarly discussions of which we are aware. We will thus endeavour to go along with the position of the Second Restatement authors, which is consistent with the language of the BEA choice-of-law provision. Thereunder, the place of the completion of the delivery, namely, the receipt of the instrument by the holder, is the place where a secondary party incurs liability on a signature that might have be entered elsewhere.

4.38 It is quite common in trade finance for an exporter to draw on the importer a bill payable to the exporter and discount the bill with a bank. In such a case, the bill is not 'issued' until it is indorsed and delivered to the discounting bank so that there is no drawer's contract thereon and the exporter is liable as an indorser and not drawer.[99] However, as long as the discounting bank is located in the place of the exporter, which is the usual case, and as long as the same choice-of-law rule applies for a drawer's and indorser's contract, there are no practical implications to mischaracterizing the exporter's liability as that of a drawer.

4.39 In a face-to-face transaction, signature and delivery are likely to occur in the same place. However, once delivery is made between distant parties, and their contract is silent on the point of delivery, but rather contemplates, even implicitly, the use of a carrier, the plot thickens. Where the carrier is under the exclusive control of the sender, delivery is at the recipient's location. By the same token, where delivery is to a carrier who is under the exclusive control of the recipient, 'delivery' occurs at the recipient's location.

4.40 Analysis is less straightforward when the carrier is a third party available to the public at large, such as the post office. In such a case, according to Chalmers,[100]

> By the regulations of the English Post Office, a letter once posted cannot be reclaimed. If, then, the indorsee of a bill authorises the indorser to transmit it to him by post, the

[95] *Allen v Kemble*. The drawer and payee resided in the same country. Presumably (though the report does not say so) in addition to the drawer's signature, delivery to the payee also took place there.

[96] See eg *Mackintosh v Gibbs*.

[97] Cf *Ex parte Heidelback* *1021, where it was argued that '[a] bill or note takes effect as a contract, not at the place where it is written, drawn, or indorsed, but where it is delivered'.

[98] See text at n 93.

[99] This point is overlooked by Daniels, *A Treatise* 1134–36, § 1052, dealing with the conflict of law rules governing the drawer's contract.

[100] DAL Smout, *Chalmers on Bills of Exchange* (13th edn, Stevens & Sons 1964) 54 (being an update, rather than a revision, of the original work) (hereafter Smout, *Chalmers on Bills*).

> property in the bill passes to the indorsee, and the indorsement becomes complete as soon as the letter which contains the bill is posted.

In such a case, '[t]he [indorser's] contract was complete by delivery when the letter was put in the post, for the indorser lost all control over it',[101] so that not only property passes but also possession. The key is the loss of control by the sender without which delivery would not occur. For example, under French postal regulations, a person could recover a letter he had posted at any time before it was dispatched from the office where it had been posted. One case dealt with a letter containing bills of exchange indorsed to the person to whom the letter was addressed and posted in a French post office. It was held that the property in the bills did not pass to the indorsee until the letter had left the office where it had been posted.[102] **4.41**

Chalmers' postal delivery rule, focusing on loss of control by the sender, appears to be in line with the 'postal acceptance' doctrine under the law of contract which provides for an offer to be accepted to become a binding contract, the addressee of a letter of acceptance does not require to physically receive it; rather, a demonstration that a letter was stamped in the postal office is sufficient for the purposes of acceptance and contract formation.[103] **4.42**

Similarly, in connection with the carriage of goods for delivery from a seller to a buyer, under the UK Sale of Goods Act (SGA) s 32(1): **4.43**

> Where, in pursuance of a contract of sale, the seller is authorised or required to send the goods to the buyer, delivery of the goods to a carrier (whether named by the buyer or not) for the purpose of transmission to the buyer is prima facie deemed to be a delivery of the goods to the buyer.

By elevating 'send' to mean 'deliver', this rule effectively recognizes the carrier's actual possession is tantamount to the constructive possession of the buyer. While 'constructive delivery' is not unfamiliar in the law of negotiable instruments,[104] the reach of the rule of SGA s 32(1) is not universal even in connection with goods. For example, under SGA s 45(1), for the purpose of the right of an 'unpaid seller who has parted with the possession of the goods' to stop them in transit to an insolvent buyer: **4.44**

> Goods are deemed to be in course of transit from the time when they are delivered to a carrier ... for the purpose of transmission to the buyer, until the buyer or his agent in that behalf takes delivery of them from the carrier...

The seller's right to stop goods in transit is forfeited only upon actual delivery to the buyer, given that under SGA s 32(1) the carrier is deemed to be the buyer's agent. It is true that the rule under s 45(1) can be treated as an exception to the general rule under **4.45**

[101] *Sichel v Borch* (1864) 2 H & C 954 [956], 159 ER 395 [396].
[102] *Ex Parte Cote, In Re Devez* (1873) LR 9 Ch App 27.
[103] *Henthorn v Fraser* [1892] 2 Ch 27, [1891–4] All ER Rep 908. For further discussion on the apparent implementation of the Postal Acceptance Rule within the modern legislation on electronic communication, see Chapter VIII, the text accompanying nn 80–89.
[104] Crawford, *Law of Banking and Payment* § 21:20.50(6).

SGA s 32(1), but at the same time the former demonstrates that the latter does not apply universally.

4.46 In the final analysis, all three rules are not said to be absolute. Thus, for the 'postal acceptance doctrine' to apply, the crucial question is whether the interacting parties have intended or contemplated to use post as a means for communication letters.[105] Standing on its own, and regardless of SGA s 45(1), the rule under SGA s 32(1) is taken to be only presumptive so as to be displaced where circumstances reveal different intention.[106] Finally, so far as Chalmers' postal delivery rule is concerned, it was held that without a direction[107] or request from the creditor to make payment by sending a cheque by mail, '[t]he post office cannot be said in any sense to be an agent of the [creditor]' to whom the cheque had been mailed. This was so no matter how long such method of payment had been practiced. The fact that for a long period the creditor had not objected to this method of payment did not amount to the assumption by the creditor of the risk of loss in transit.[108]

4.47 The BEA does not have a rule similar to that of SGA s 32(1). Also, unlike under the law of bills, cheques, and notes, possession is not a key factor in relation to the acceptance of a contract offer as well as to rights to goods. Hence, flexibility in addressing possession that exists in these two contexts need not necessarily be imported into the discussion on the delivery requirement for an instrument. In the final analysis, even if a sender lost control of a letter delivered to the post office, it is hard to see how the destination party thereby acquired it. Therefore, we contend that no delivery presumption ought to apply. Rather, it is the converse presumption that should apply.

4.48 It appears that Chalmers' original proposition that an authorization to send a cheque by mail suffices to shift the responsibility away from the sender is too broad even by reference to case law just discussed and has not been repeated in recent editions.

4.49 Indeed, such an authorization may be given by the designated receiver to the sender merely for the sender's own convenience. Additionally, the post office, as well as any third-party carrier, can be seen as an agent for a limited purpose, if at all. The loss of possession by the sender upon the delivery to the carrier does not amount to its transfer to the designated receiver. In general, it is up to the debtor to deliver at the designated place of payment, and in the absence of such a designation, it is the debtor who must seek the creditor.[109] Indeed, when a debtor uses the banking system to make payment risk of loss does not shift to the beneficiary-creditor prior to the arrival of funds to the beneficiary's bank.[110]

4.50 As acknowledged in a recent edition of Chalmers' work, it is inconceivable that the delivery by a debtor to the post office of a cheque payable to the creditor will be treated

[105] *Adams v Lindsell* (1818) 1 B & Ald 681, 106 ER 250.

[106] MG Bridge, *Sale of Goods* (3rd edn, Oxford University Press 2014) 311–12.

[107] As is eg in *Warwicke v Noakes* (1791) Peake, 98, 170 ER 93 (NS)

[108] *Pennington v Crossley & Son* (1897) 1 LDAB 249, 77 LT 43 [44] (CA).

[109] Bowen LJ in *The Eider* (1893) P 119 (CA). For further discussions of this point, see Chapter VI, the text accompanying nn 193–204.

[110] See *Tenax Steamship Co. v The Brimnes (Owners)* [1973] 1 WLR 386; [1973] 1 All ER 769 (QBD).

as conditional payment to the creditor.[111] It is equally inconceivable that the debtor's delivery of such a cheque to the post office will entitle the creditor to sue on it as a holder.[112] Nonetheless, both are inescapable conclusions from Chalmers' proposition. Hence, the presumption ought to be that delivery takes place when either the destination party or his or her exclusive agent acquires the possession of an instrument.[113] In normal circumstances, while the sender loses possession once the instrument leaves his or her own sphere of exclusive control, the receiver gets possession only once the instrument enters his or her own sphere of exclusive control.

In effect, a third-party carrier acts under a contract with the sender and not the destination party, even if under that contract the sender has no right to stop the delivery. Certainly, there may be cases where the destination party instructs, rather than suggests or authorizes, the sender to send an instrument via a specific route, such as through a designated third-party carrier. It is plausible to argue that in such a case the risk of loss in transit falls on the instructing destination party. However, we contend it does not follow that possession is transferred to the destination party prior to actual delivery to that party by the designated carrier. The assumption of risk of loss in transit, whether by the sender or destination party, indicates neither continuation of possession by the sender nor its acquisition by the destination party.[114] **4.51**

The deposit of a cheque in a bank account can be treated as governed by the contract of indorsement, albeit supplanted by other terms,[115] even where by law no signature is required.[116] According to the preceding analysis, a deposit of a cheque sent by a depositor from one country to his or her bank account in another country is governed by the law of the latter country.[117] This is of course true as long as the cheque is dispatched by mail or a third-party courier. The delivery of the cheque to the depositary bank and the posting of its value to the depositor's account, even if provisionally, completes the depositor's delivery obligation. Some complexity is introduced when a depositor located in one country sends a cheque for deposit to a bank account in another country through a correspondent of the depositary bank located in the depositor's **4.52**

[111] Gleeson, *Chalmers and Guest* 122–23, at 2–151. For conditional payment see eg *Re Charge Card Services* [1989] Ch 497; [1988] 3 All ER 702 (CA).

[112] Under BEA s 38(1).

[113] But cf *Hyde v Goodnow*, 3 NY 266 (1850) where a premium note together with an insurance application was delivered by the insurance applicant to the insurer/payee's agent in one state to be passed on to the insurer in another state, in circumstances under which the insured/maker incurred liability on the premium note only upon the approval of his application by the insurer in another state. Even if the agent acted exclusively for the insurer, no 'delivery' capable to create liability occurred until after the insurer's approval and hence in the insurer's state.

[114] Cf *Ose Gessellschaft v Jewish Colonial Trust* (1927) 43 Times L Rep 398, where the loss was held to fall on the customer when a cheque mailed by the banker on the customer's behalf to a third party did not arrive to said third party. It was not assumed that the mailing of the cheque passed possession to the third party. However, whether the third party had authorized the mailing of the cheque was not addressed in the judgement.

[115] *Bank of Nova Scotia v Sharp* [1975] BCJ No 1148, 57 DLR (3d) 260.

[116] Cheques Act 1957, 5 & 6 ELiz 2 CH 36, s 2.

[117] *Fourth Nat. Bank v Bragg*, 102 SE 649 (Va 1920), dealing with a deposit, is not to the contrary even as Daniels, *A Treatise* 1035, § 1051, n 11, understands it to apply 'the law of the State where the bank depositor resides'. In the facts of that case this was also the place where the (intra-state) deposit was made from beginning to end.

country. The correspondent bank is neither under the complete control of the depositary bank nor acting as an independent third-party courier. We, however, contend that the correspondent bank is sufficiently acting under the depositary's bank control and direction so that delivery by the depositor occurs at the depositor's country. Moreover, while provisional credit to the depositor's account may be posted only upon the arrival of the cheque to the depositary bank itself, 'any consideration sufficient to support a simple contract', which suffices under the BEA to constitute '[v]aluable consideration',[118] is already given to the depositor at the point of the delivery of the cheque to the correspondent. Such consideration is in the form of the depositary bank's undertaking to give such provisional credit. Of course, when a depositor located in a country other than that of the bank of deposit delivers the cheque to a facility or entity in the depositor's country that is under the full control of the depositary bank, the depositor's contract is concluded at the country where he or she (or in fact the facility) is located.

4.53 Unlike the BEA, the BNCC assigns different laws to the liability of primary parties and that of secondary parties. For a primary party, the rule is similar to that under the Second Restatement. For a secondary party, the BNCC introduces a variation. Thus, for primary parties, under BNCC art 4(1):

> The effects of the obligations of the acceptor of a bill ... or maker of a ... note are determined by the law of the place in which these instruments are payable

4.54 Under the UBL, a bill or note is required to contain, *inter alia*, '[a] statement of the place where the payment is to be made'.[119] Otherwise, '[i]n default of special mention, the place specified beside the name of the drawee shall be deemed to be the place of payment' of a bill[120] and 'the place where the instrument is made shall be deemed to be the place of payment' of a note.[121] However, while '[a] statement of ... the place where the ... note is issued' must appear in a note,[122] there is no corresponding requirement as to indicating the place 'besides the name of the [drawee]' of a bill.[123] Accordingly, there is no provision for the place of payment of a bill that includes neither a statement as to the place of payment nor the address of the drawee.[124] Similarly, it is not clear whether a 'note' that does not include a statement as to the place of its issue is valid as a promissory note once 'the place where the instrument is made' is proven. Stated otherwise, it is unclear whether a proof or presumption as to 'the place where the instrument is made'[125] cures a lack of statement as to 'the place where the promissory note is issued'.[126]

118 BEA s 27(1)(a).
119 UBL respectively, arts 1(5) and 75(4).
120 ibid, art 2(3).
121 ibid, art 76(3).
122 ibid, art 75(6).
123 ibid, art 1(3) requires the inclusion of '[t]he name of the person who is to pay' (the drawee) but not the address of that person.
124 But cf Lescot and Roblot, *Les Effets de Commerce* 10, § 574, n 3, discussing the effect of a change of address by the drawee.
125 UBL art 76(3).
126 UBL. As required under art 75(6). Under art 76(1), 'An instrument in which any of the requirements mentioned in ... article [75] are wanting shall be invalid as a promissory note, except in the cases specified in the following paragraphs.'

Compared to the Second Restatement, and in fact also the BEA, the BNCC contains a few additions. Specifically, under art 7, the law of the country in which the bill is payable also governs the question as to 'whether acceptance [of a bill] may be restricted to part of the sum' as well as 'whether the holder [of a bill or note] is bound to accept partial payment'. **4.55**

On the other hand, under BNCC art 4(2): **4.56**

> The effects of the signatures of the other parties liable on a bill ... or ... note are determined by the law of the country in which is situated the place where the signatures are affixed.

In light of the legislative history, what counts under art 4(2) is the actual place where the signature has been affixed, irrespective of any indication on the instrument. However, such an indication could serve as a presumption that, unlike under the Second Restatement, is rebuttable against even an innocent party.[127] **4.57**

While BNCC art 4(1) speaks of the effects of the 'obligations' of primary parties, BNCC art 4(2) provides for the effects of the 'signatures' of other parties. On its own, this appears to be an unfortunate drafting glitch. Further, the choice in BNCC art 4(2) to make the place of the signature affixation as determinative of effect brings a substantive difference between the two subsections and is potentially problematic. Thus, in a face-to-face transaction, signature affixation and delivery may occur simultaneously and in the same place. This, however, will not be the case in a transaction between distant parties, which is the case in an international setting. While the UBL is not as explicit as the BEA as to the necessity of delivery to bind a signing party, notwithstanding any statement to the contrary,[128] it has adopted the same rule, even if implicitly, as the entitlement to sue a party liable on an instrument being premised on lawful possession.[129] Hence, BNCC art 4 should not be read to override the delivery requirement; rather, it must be taken to assume that the affixation of the signature to an instrument that is subsequently delivered is the characteristic factor in assigning the applicable law to the liability.[130] However, selecting the place where the signature is affixed as determining the governing law is logical only where the signer departs from the instrument in that place. One can sign an instrument with the view of taking it with him to another country in order to deliver it. As long as the signed instrument is in his or her possession, s/he is not bound by his or her signature. Thus, the place of its affixation is no more instructive than that of writing a non-binding draft for a contract. On its own, 'signature' cannot be determinative. Therefore, according to its own approach of focusing on the critical contractual event, the real choice of the BNCC as **4.58**

[127] Lescot and Roblot, *Les Effets de Commerce* 580–81, § 1075.

[128] See eg Gutteridge 62–63; H Fischer, 'The Law Governing Capacity with Regard to Bills of Exchange' (1951) 14 Mod L Rev 144, 149 (hereafter Fischer, 'Law Governing Capacity').

[129] Under art 43 of the Geneva Bills and Notes Convention it is '[t]he holder [who] may exercise [the] right of recourse against the endorsers, the drawer and the other parties liable'. In turn under art 16, '[t]he possessor of a bill of exchange is deemed to be the lawful holder if he establishes his title to the bill through an uninterrupted series of endorsements'. See also eg arts 19, 28, 38, and 40.

[130] Unfortunately, in addressing the discussions that led to the choice of the law applicable to the place of signature Lescot and Roblot, *Les Effets de Commerce* 578–79, § 1073, do not shed any light on this aspect.

to law applicable to a contract on a signed instrument ought to have been between the loss of control by the signer and receipt of control by the destination party.

4.59 In the final analysis, neither art 4(1), speaking of the effects of the 'obligations', nor art 4(2), speaking of the effects of 'the signatures',[131] designates the law of the place where the obligation was incurred by the signature, as the applicable law.

4.60 In the footsteps of BNCC art 4(2), albeit using a slightly different language, CCC art 7(4) provides that '[t]he law of the country in which the cheque is payable shall determine ... [w]hether the holder may demand, and whether he is bound to accept, partial payment'. At the same time, the general rule of CCC art 5 is that '[t]he law of the country in whose territory the obligations arising out of a cheque have been assumed shall determine the effects of such obligations'. Under cheque law, the entitlement to sue a party liable on an instrument is premised on lawful possession,[132] such that delivery is essential to create liability. Accordingly, CCC art 5 departs from its counterpart under the BNCC and is to be read as selecting the law of the place of the delivery of the cheque by each signer to his or her immediate party as the law applicable to the signer's obligation.

4.61 For its part, IACC art 3(1) provides that:

> All obligations arising from a bill of exchange shall be governed by the law of the place where they are contracted

4.62 Unlike the BNCC, in applying a 'single rule', the IACC does not distinguish between primary and secondary parties. Furthermore, for each contract, it designates the territorial connecting factor of the place of contract, rather than signature, as determining the law applicable. For UBL jurisdictions IACC signatories, this means that, as under the BEA, in the case of delivery between distant parties, it is the law that applies in the place of delivery, and not signature, that governs each obligation.

D. The Scope of Intrinsic Validity: Specific Issues

4.63 The law selected under the Second Restatement is said to cover matters such as the signer's capacity to contract, as well as whether the instrument is 'negotiable' so as to forfeit 'personal defences'. It also determines the existence of a condition precedent to liability such as presentment and where it is to be made.[133] This law certainly covers all matters of intrinsic validity. As for BEA s 72, Falconbridge is of the view that 'interpretation' is to be narrowly read, in its natural sense,[134] as strictly limited to the

[131] For treating the language of art 4(2) as 'more exact' see J Stoufflet, *Instruments de Paiement et de Crédit* (8th edn, LexisNexis Litec 2012) 206, § 180 (hereafter Stoufflet, *Instruments*).

[132] Under UCL art 40, it is '[t]he holder [who] may exercise his right of recourse against the endorsers, the drawer and the other parties liable'. As well, under art 44, '[a]ll the persons liable on a check are jointly and severally bound to the holder'. In turn, under art 19, '[t]he possessor of an endorsable check is deemed to be the lawful holder if he establishes his title to the cheque through an uninterrupted series of endorsements'. See also eg arts 13, 19, 22, 23, 45, and 52.

[133] See Second Restatement 701 at § 214, 706 at § 215 and Comments at 703, 707–09.

[134] Effectively adopting the 'natural meaning' for statutory language, commended by Lord Herschell in *Bank of England v Vagliano Bros* [1891] AC 107, 1 LDAB 130, [1891-4] All ER Rep 93, 64 LT 353.

meaning or construction of words.[135] Conversely, Chalmers defines 'interpretation' to include the 'obligations of the parties as deduced from such interpretation' and thus to cover intrinsic (material) validity or effect.[136] Chalmers was cited in agreement by case law[137] and the broad reading of 'interpretation' is said to have 'most [judicial] support'.[138]

Some who read 'interpretation' in the BEA narrowly would nevertheless extend it by analogy to also cover substantive matters, thereby practically reaching the same result as the adherents of the broad meaning of 'interpretation' under the statute.[139] However, the controversy is otherwise arguably result-driven, with each position-holder fearing the outcome of accepting the opposite position. Thus, those who adhere to the broad meaning of 'interpretation' fear the vacuum that would result from the lack of any BEA provision addressing a choice-of-law rule for the legal effect of an obligation. Naturally, they do not count on analogy to fill in the vacuum. For their part, proponents of the narrow meaning of 'interpretation' are dissatisfied with the choice-of-law rule assigned under the BEA to the contracts of primary parties (that of the place of contract). Rather, they prefer the choice-of-law rule assigned to primary parties under the Second Restatement and the GCCs (that of the place of payment)[140] and consider it reachable under general principles of law[141] that apply in the absence of a statutory rule to the contrary.[142] However, the question of potential reform must be left for a separate normative analysis, one that we carry out in Chapters V–VII. For the purposes of understanding the existing law, our own view on the matter follows that of Crawford, who reluctantly supports the broad meaning. He argues that '[i]t seems highly unlikely that Parliament, having decided to legislate on the question of the conflict of laws ... would have failed to attempt a rule dealing with the intrinsic validity or legal effect'. Accordingly, he concludes, the dissatisfaction from the BEA solution is 'quite separate' issue from 'the meaning' of 'interpretation'.[143] **4.64**

In any event, the distinction between the two senses of 'interpretation' may be more tenuous than it appears. In fact, not much is left to be covered by 'mere' interpretation. **4.65**

[135] Falconbridge, 'Bills and Notes' 320, 337.

[136] Smout, *Chalmers on Bills* 241.

[137] See eg *Bank Polski v K J Mulder & Co* [1942] 1 KB 497, [1942] 1 All ER 396 (CA); *Nova (Jersey) Knit Ltd. v Kammgarn Spinnerei GmbH* [1977] 2 All ER 463, [1977] 1 WLR 713 [718] (HL); and *London and Brazilian Bank v Maguire* (1895) QR 8 SC 358 [9]. For a learned discussion see Crawford, *Law of Banking and Payment* § 33:40.20(1).

[138] Collins, Harris (eds) *Dicey, Morris and Collins on the Conflict of Laws*, vol 2 (15th edn, Sweet & Maxwell 2012) 2087, para 33-351 . See eg *Banco Atlantico SA v British Bank of the Middle East* [1990] 2 Lloyd's Rep 504 [507](CA).

[139] Collins, Harris (eds) *Dicey, Morris and Collins on the Conflict of Laws*, vol 2 (15th edn, Sweet & Maxwell 2012) 2087, para 33-351 .

[140] For the view that pre-BEA cases supporting the contracting place dealt with a situation which this was also the place of payment see Gleeson, *Chalmers and Guest* 596, para 12-013.

[141] See eg Falconbridge, 'Bills and Notes' 337 and Gleeson, *Chalmers and Guest* 589, at para 12-015.

[142] BEA s 97(2).

[143] Crawford, *Law of Banking and Payment* § 33:40.30. To the same effect see also Gleeson, *Chalmers and Guest* 598–99, para 12-015.

Thus, as strictly limited to the meaning or construction of words, 'interpretation' is said[144] to cover:

(i) the addition to an indorsement of the words '*für mich*',[145]
(ii) the use of the expression '*bon pour aval pour les tirés*' next to a signature on an instrument,[146]
(iii) whether the acceptance of a bill is to be interpreted as general or qualified,[147] and
(iv) the inclusion of the word 'order' in directing payment to the payee on a bill or note.

4.66 However, we believe that all four situations raise questions as to the legal effect of the language used; the fourth one also raises an issue that goes to the form of the instrument.

4.67 Case law that cannot be reconciled with the strict meaning of 'interpretation' has dealt with matters such as discharge,[148] damages upon default, and transfer of an instrument. The law applicable to transfer shall subsequently be addressed below in section G. As for 'the measure of damages recoverable under a bill or note', inasmuch as courts classify it 'as a matter of substantive law',[149] the subject certainly raises issues relating to 'obligations of the parties as deduced from [the] interpretation' of their contracts, per the broad meaning of 'interpretation'.[150] An inescapable result is that depending on the law applicable to his or her contract, each party liable may thus be held to a different measure of damages, so that, for example, an indorser may recover from a preceding party a different amount from what he paid.[151]

4.68 Lescot and Roblot endeavour to distinguish between the 'validity' and 'effects' of the obligation or signature, pointing out that only the latter are covered by BNCC art 4 and CCC art 5. In their view, validity relates to optional clauses, such as restricting liability or indorsement. They go on and argue that as a matter of freedom of contract or the parties' autonomy, the validity of such terms is governed under the law

[144] Collins, Harris (eds) *Dicey, Morris and Collins on the Conflict of Laws*, vol 2 (15th edn, Sweet & Maxwell 2012) 2085, para 33-347 ..

[145] Literally meaning in German 'for me' but held to mean in German law 'substitute for' or 'instead of' me—so as to render the endorsement open and not restrictive. See *Haarbleicher v Baerselman* (1914) 3 LDAB 113, 137 LT 564 (KB).

[146] Meaning undertaking an aval liability: *G&H Montage GmbH v Irvani* [1988] 1 WLR 1285 (QBD); *aff'd* [1990] 1 WLR 667 (CA).

[147] Under BEA s 19(2). 'A general acceptance assents without qualification to the order of the drawer. A qualified acceptance in expressed terms varies the effect of the bill as drawn'. Cf UCC § 3-410 addressing acceptance varying draft, as well as UBL art 26 under which '[a]n acceptance is unconditional, but the drawee may restrict it to part of the sum payable'.

[148] Story, *Conflict of Laws* 284, § 343.

[149] Collins, Harris (eds) *Dicey, Morris and Collins on the Conflict of Laws*, vol 2 (15th edn, Sweet & Maxwell 2012) 2087, para 33-352 .

[150] Under Chalmers' definition in Smout. *Chalmers on Bills* 241.

[151] See Story, *Conflict of Laws* 261-62, § 314;Collins, Harris (eds) *Dicey, Morris and Collins on the Conflict of Laws*, vol 2 (15th edn, Sweet & Maxwell 2012) 2089–90, paras 33-355—33-357 .

of the place of signature or contract (they do not appear to draw a distinction between the two).[152]

However, no distinction between 'validity' and 'effects' is mentioned by Stoufflet.[153] As well, the distinction is unknown in the common law, where the GCC language plays no role in the analysis. Thus, in the early years of the twentieth century, both Beale[154] and Lorenzen[155] invariably used 'intrinsic validity' and 'effects' interchangeably, as distinguishable from 'extrinsic (formal) validity' (to be discussed in section E). Additionally, Falconbridge juxtaposed the two terms as alternatives.[156] Indeed, under the common law, 'material or essential validity' and 'effect', together with 'interpretation' and 'discharge', are all said to constitute the 'proper law'[157]—namely, the law that governs every contract 'at its outset'.[158] **4.69**

We would have thought that if the two terms are to be distinguished, 'validity' goes to the binding effect or enforceability of an obligation, while 'effects' address the substantive law that governs a valid obligation. For example, while 'consideration' is a matter of 'validity', what constitutes breach, damages, and other remedies denote 'effects'. The distinction is, however, not infallible; for example, whether an obligation is voidable (eg for fraud) goes both to its 'validity' and 'effect'. In the final analysis, 'intrinsic validity and effects of contracts' have been dealt with as one category,[159] so that the two terms are to be treated as synonyms. **4.70**

Substantive matters pertaining to contractual engagements on instruments, to be governed by the law that applies to the obligation or its effect, include the nature and scope of liability as well as the availability of recourse. This is true under the GCCs, Second Restatement, as well as under the BEA if 'interpretation' is to be broadly construed. These matters include the range of defences available to a party sued on the instrument, whether or not by a holder in due course or 'lawful holder'. Such defences include partial failure of consideration in an unliquidated amount,[160] equitable defences,[161] set-off and compensation,[162] and limitation of action or prescription. **4.71**

[152] Lescot and Roblot, *Les Effets de Commerce* 581, § 1076 and internal references there.

[153] See eg Stoufflet, *Instruments* 206–07, § 180.

[154] JH Beale, 'What Law Governs the Validity of a Contract' Part I (1909) 23 Harv L Rev 1; Part II (1909) 23 Harv L Rev 79; Part II (Continued) (1910) 23 Harv L Rev 194; Part III (1910), 23 Harv L Rev 260.

[155] EG Lorenzen, 'Validity and Effects of Contracts in the Conflict of Law' Part 1: (1920–21), 30 Yale LJ 565; Part 2: (1920–21), 30 Yale LJ 655; Part 3: (1921–22) 31 Yale LJ 53.

[156] Falconbridge, 'Bills and Notes' 329.

[157] Collins, Harris (eds) *Dicey, Morris and Collins on the Conflict of Laws*, vol 2 (15th edn, Sweet & Maxwell 2012) 1778, para 32-008 . The term 'proper law' was coined by Westlake, *Private International Law* 304–05, §§ 213 and 213A.

[158] Collins, Harris (eds) *Dicey, Morris and Collins on the Conflict of Laws*, vol 2 (15th edn, Sweet & Maxwell 2012) 1777, para 32-006 .

[159] See subtitle so worded in Westlake, *Private International Law* (299.

[160] Such a defence is available against a holder not in due course under the UCC § 3-305 but not under the BEA. See eg *James Lamont & Co. v Hyland (no.2)* [1950] 1 KB 585; [1950] 1 All ER 929 (CA).

[161] *Ory v Winter*, La LEXIS 40 (ED 1826) and discussion in Story, *Conflict of Laws* 263, § 317.

[162] See *Allen v Kemble*, where the drawer and indorser were allowed to meet the holder's suit by invoking under the law that governed their obligations the acceptor's compensation (see para 4.72) against the holder so as to extinguish his or her right.

4.72 Not all of them may be available in each legal system, even against a holder not in due course or its equivalent. For example, at common law, being 'a personal privilege, and not an incident or accompaniment of the debt',[163] the right to *set off* a debt owed to the defendant is 'not a modification of [his or her] obligation, but an incident of its enforcement'.[164] Rather, unless agreed otherwise by contract, it is a matter of procedure, or 'a convenient mode of settling mutual accounts or preventing multiplicity of actions between the same parties'.[165] Hence, it 'is not a defence, but a cross action [which] concedes the validity of the plaintiff's claim, and is founded upon an independent cause of action in favour of the defendant, who may at his or her election assert it by way of set-off, or enforce it by a separate suit'.[166] In contrast, in civil law, 'compensation' operates automatically by the sole operation of law to extinguish mutual obligations.[167] Classification is then a matter to be determined by the law that governs the obligation[168] and not the *lex fori*. At the same time, the *lex fori* may permit a party liable to set off a debt he owes to the plaintiff (but not a prior holder) even where such right is not given by the law governing the obligation.[169]

4.73 Whether a *statute of limitations* operates to extinguish a right or only to bar an action is similarly not universally agreed. In *Jensen v Tolofson*, La Forest J acknowledged (even if unenthusiastically) that '[t]he common law traditionally considered statutes of limitations as procedural, as contrasted with the position in most civil law countries where [they have] traditionally been regarded as substantive'.[170] Either way, in a given case, the determination of the issue is to be made according to the law that governs the obligation and not the *lex fori*. Arguably, this position is supposed to be reflected in both BNCC art 5 and CCC art 6,[171] providing that:

> The limits of time for the exercise of rights of recourse shall be determined for all signatories by the law of the place where the instrument was created.

4.74 However, it is unclear whether 'created' means written, signed, or delivered. As well, 'limits of time for the exercise of rights of recourse' appear to be part of the 'effects' of obligations uncured on an instrument, so as to be governed by BNCC art 4 and CCC

[163] *Lincoln v Grant*, 47 DC App 475, 483 (1917–18).

[164] Falconbridge, 'Bills and Notes' 371.

[165] Rogers, *Falconbridge on Banking* 671.

[166] ibid. For characterizing both set-off and counterclaims as independent claims, see also *Stooke v Taylor* (1880) 5 QBD 569 [575], 43 LT 200 *per* Cockburn CJ. Under Rules of Practice a set-off may be either pleaded as a defence or set up by way of counterclaim: *A-G Ont. v Russell* (1921) 64 DLR 59, 49 OLR 103 (SC). Rogers, *Falconbridge on Banking* 437 claims that 'a set-off is by its nature a defence'. This, however, should be taken only to mean that Rules of Practice may allow its assertion by way of defence. In its nature, set-off is an action: *Campbell v Imperial Bank* (1924) 4 DLR 289, 55 OLR 318 (SC App Div).

[167] G Nicholls, 'The Legal Nature of Bank Deposits in the Province of Quebec' (1935) 13 Bar Rev 635, 647.

[168] Which is in line with the general rule of art 17 Rome I.

[169] See eg Ontario Courts of Justice Act RSO 1990, c C43, s 111.

[170] (1995) 120 DLR (4th) 289, 319 (SCC). See also R Garnett, *Substance-Procedure in Private International Law* (Oxford University Press 2012) (hereafter Garnett, *Private International Law*). For further discussion of this point, see Chapter VII, the text accompanying nn 70–71.

[171] Stoufflet, *Instruments* 209, § 183.

art 5. Indeed, there is no apparent reason for dealing with 'limits of time' under a separate, poorly identified 'single law'. There is no parallel to this provision in the other sources.[172]

4.75 Under pre-BEA case law, *illegality* of an obligation on an instrument is determined according to the law of the place designated for its payment.[173] This rule was also followed in the UK after the passage of the BEA.[174] Such law may not be under the BEA the same as that governing the obligation—the latter being under BEA s 72(2) the law applicable in the place where the obligation was incurred. As well, since secondary parties' obligations 'are somewhat in the nature of suretyship... they should be unenforceable if the principal contract is illegal', even under the 'several laws' theory,[175] and in our view even when the illegality is that of another secondary party for whom the sued party is a quasi-surety.[176] In the final analysis, as with regard to any type of contract,[177] illegality may be invoked under the law of the forum, the law of the place of performance, the law of the place of contracting, as well as under the 'proper law' of the contract.[178]

4.76 There is no consensus on the applicable law regarding *capacity*. Having reviewed legislation and scholarly works from the early twentieth century, Lorenzen identified two competing laws to govern capacity to contract on an instrument. These are on one hand, personal law, usually being that of the signer's residence and otherwise of his or her nationality, and on the other, the law of the place where the contract was made. Lorenzen then spoke of a possible compromise, being that of 'either the personal law or that of the place of contracting'. An alternative to the place of contracting is the law that governs the contract (which may be different than the law of the place of contracting). Yet, according to a third alternative, 'the law of the place of issue mentioned in the instrument is to govern [capacity], and only in the absence of such an indication, the law of the domicile, or, in the case of a merchant or a professional [person], the law of the ... place of business or office [of that person]'.[179]

4.77 As a reflection of similar lack of consensus, albeit for contracts other than on instruments,[180] capacity is not governed by Rome I art 12(1) and in effect is excluded altogether from the scope the uniform rules.[181] Nonetheless, under art 13:

> In a contract concluded between persons who are in the same country, a natural person who would have capacity under the law of that country may invoke his

[172] For further discussion on statutes of limitations, see Chapter VII, the text accompanying nn 70–71.

[173] *Robinson v Bland* (1760) 2 Burr 1077, 97 ER 717.

[174] *Moulis v Owen* [1907] 1 KB 746, 96 LT 596 (CA).

[175] Collins, Harris (eds) *Dicey, Morris and Collins on the Conflict of Laws*, vol 2 (15th edn, Sweet & Maxwell 2012) 2090, para 33-358.

[176] For example, an indorsee with recourse to the drawer may raise against a subsequent holder a defence based on the illegality of the drawer's contract.

[177] See eg SGA Pitel and NS Rafferty, *Conflict of Laws* (2nd edn, Irwin Law, 2016) 300.

[178] For further discussion on illegality, see Chapter VII section A(1).

[179] EG Lorenzen, 'The Rules of the Conflict of Laws Applicable to Bills and Notes—A Study in Comparative Law' (1917) 1 Minn L Rev 10 (hereafter Lorenzen, 'Study'). Quotes are from pp 22 and 22–23 respectively.

[180] For discussion of this point, see Introduction, the text accompanying nn 2–9.

[181] Art 1(2)(a) and (f). Comment 2 to art 10 of the Rome I.

incapacity resulting from the law of another country, only if the other party to the contract was aware of that incapacity at the time of the conclusion of the contract or was not aware thereof as a result of negligence.

4.78 The Second Restatement treats the law governing capacity as one incident of the law that determines the obligation of a party to an instrument.[182] For its part, the IACC designates in art 1(1) 'the law of the place where the obligation is contracted' as the law governing '[c]apacity to enter into an obligation by means of a bill [or note]'. However, under art 1(2), 'incapacity may not be relied upon [in a place in which] the obligation is valid'.

4.79 There is no special choice-of-law provision as to capacity under the BEA, where the general rule under s 22(1) is that '[c]apacity to incur liability as a party to a bill is coextensive with capacity to contract'. Case law appears to be inconclusive, either shifting from the law of the place of contract for instruments[183] to the signer's personal law for every purpose,[184] or possibly being satisfied with whatever law, among the two, which will validate the contract.[185]

4.80 For their part, echoing Lorenzen's summary, BNCC and CCC art 2 provides specific rules as to capacity as follows:

1. Capacity to bind oneself on an instrument is determined by the national law of the person to be obligated;
2. However, where the national law of the person to be obligated on an instrument 'provides that the law of another country is competent in the matter, this latter law shall be applied';
3. At the same time, and subject to the right of a country not to apply such a rule, where either national law or the law of the country referred by it denies capacity to the person to be obligated on an instrument, this person 'is nevertheless bound, if his signature has been signed in any territory in which according to the law in force there, he would have the requisite capacity';

4.81 It should, however, be pointed out that national law, to the extent that it is the law of the country of citizenship, does not serve as a good criterion for the personal law. This is because some people hold multiple citizenships, and conversely, others have none. Place of residence, and its equivalent for legal entities, serves a more appropriate choice for the personal law.

4.82 Finally, it should be noted that none of the sources discussed in this chapter address choice-of-law rules applicable in case of *fraud*. Fraudulent transfers are addressed in section G. Here, we consider the law determining liability in cases of theft of a complete unissued instrument by the designated payee, unauthorized completion of an instrument, and alteration of an instrument. In each case, the fraud is committed in a

[182] See Second Restatement 701 at § 214, 706 at § 215 and Reporter's notes at pp 703 and 707.
[183] *Male v Roberts* (1800) 3 Esp 163, 170 ER 574.
[184] Lorenzen, 'Study' 11–12.
[185] Fischer, 'Law Governing Capacity' 147. For further discussion on capacity and the Validation principle, see Chapter VII section A(1).

country other than the one in which the signature was made. We contend that the law where each signature was affixed determines which law governs that signer's liability. In turn, liability on a forged signature is governed by the law of the place in which the forgery was committed.

E. Law Governing Extrinsic Validity (Form)

4.83 The national and international law vary in provisions relating to formal requirements for an instrument. As pointed out in Chapter I section D, Grisoli goes as far as to argue that 'English law and the Uniform Law appear irreconcilably divided on formal requirements'.[186]

4.84 Under the Second Restatement, the law that governs an obligation covers also its form.[187] Similarly, under BEA s 72(1):

> The validity of a bill as regards requisites in form is determined by the law of the place of issue, and the validity as regards requisites in form of the supervening contracts, such as acceptance, or indorsement, or acceptance supra protest, is determined by the law of the place where such contract was made.

4.85 The same result occurs under IACC art 2, providing that:

> The form of the drawing, endorsement, guaranty, intervention, acceptance or protest of a bill of exchange shall be governed by the law of the place in which each one of those acts is performed.[188]

4.86 However, a variation is introduced by BNCC art 3(1), providing that:

> The form of any contract arising out of a bill ... or ... note is regulated by the laws of the territory in which the contract has been signed.

4.87 For the drawer and indorser, under all three schemes, the law that governs extrinsic validity is that which governs intrinsic validity. The same is true for the maker's or acceptor's obligation under the BEA, as well as under the IACC. However, under the BNCC, intrinsic validity of the obligation of a maker or acceptor who signs in Ruritania an instrument payable in Penguina is governed by the law of Penguina. At the same time, the extrinsic validity of that obligation is governed by the law of Ruritania. With regard to the primary parties, this scheme may unnecessarily give rise to difficult questions of classification between 'intrinsic' and 'extrinsic' matters in border cases.[189] It also strikes us as incongruous. For example, acceptance made in Ruritania on a bill payable in Penguina, which complies in form only with the law of

[186] A Grisoli, 'Uniform Law of Bills of Exchange from the Standpoint of Anglo-American Law' (1958–59) 33 Tul L Rev 289, 291. He also argues (in our view unpersuasively) to a fundamental difference in the theory of liability. ibid 293–96.

[187] Ssecond Restatement 703, Comments to § 214 and 707–08, Comments to § 215.

[188] 'Performance' is not of the contract but rather of the act of entering to it, hence, arguably, signature and delivery.

[189] Fischer, 'Law Governing Capacity' 148

Penguina, but not Ruritania, would not be an 'acceptance' under the law of Ruritania in the first place, and thus would be incapable of being governed by the law of Penguina as an 'acceptance'.

4.88 For its part, in the footsteps of BNCC art 3(1), CCC art 4(1) points at the place of signature as determining the form of 'any contract arising out of a cheque'. However, CCC art 4(1) goes on to provide that in case of non-compliance with the law of that place, 'it shall be sufficient if the forms prescribed by the law of the place of payment are observed'. For cheques, this eliminates the incongruity of BNCC art 3(1), except that there is no maker or acceptor for a cheque so as to benefit from this escape clause. However, the provision will 'validate' the liability of a drawer who signed in Ruritania a cheque payable in Penguina, which complies in form only with the law of Penguina, but not Ruritania. This flexibility supports the validation of contracts. In such a case, liability is governed by the law of Ruritania, while form need not necessarily comply with the law of Ruritania and would still be sufficient if it complied with the law of Penguina instead.

4.89 Similarly to the BEA, the BNCC supports the validation of a negotiable instrument. Under this approach, one of the purposes of choice-of-law rules is not just to follow certain connecting factors, but also to support the application of those rules that would not invalidate the instrument.[190] BEA incorporates two 'provisos' that disapprove possible invalidation of the instrument, specifically, BEA s 72(1)(a).[191] Additionally, BEA s 72(1)(a) provides further support of the validation principle and supports a validity of an instrument negotiated in England, despite its potential invalidity under the law of the place of its original issue.[192] Interestingly, both BEA's provisos have been drafted in somewhat paternalistic manner: while providing a support of document validation under the English law, this validation does not have effect in the opposite case when the instrument is invalid under the English law and valid under the foreign law.[193] The BNCC, however, rejects this one-sidedness. In contrast to the BEA, the application of this validation principle is drafted in a 'neutral' way: rather than supporting the validation rule of a particular place in a one-sided manner, the Convention adheres to a general rule that applies to all.[194]

4.90 In *G&H Montage GmbH v Irvani*,[195] Saville J surmised 'that it was the intention of the legislature to apply the special conflict rules [under BEA s 72] to bills as defined in the [BEA]'.[196] In the Court of Appeal,[197] both Mustill LJ[198] and Purchas LJ[199] seemed

[190] In Chapter VI of this book, we will say much more about this principle of validation and its consistency with choice-of-law and negotiable instruments law doctrine. See Chapter VI section A.
[191] BEA s 72(1)(a).
[192] ibid, s 72(1)(b).
[193] In Chapter VI we will return to this 'one-sidedness' of the BEA's provisions. See Chapter VI, the text accompanying nn 49–71.
[194] In Chapter VI we will say much more on the point of this disjunction between the BEA and the GCC. See Chapter VI, the text accompanying nn 49–71.
[195] [1988] 1 WLR 1285 (QBD), *aff'd* [1990] 2 All ER 225 (CA).
[196] ibid [1290].
[197] ibid.
[198] ibid [234].
[199] ibid [242]. For further discussion of this case, see Chapter VI, the text accompanying nn 30–38.

to agree. This *obiter* is, however, an unfortunate restriction.[200] Rather, for the proper application of choice-of-law rules, one should read BEA s 72(2) to apply to bills as defined by the law of the place of issuance.

When more than one contract exists on an instrument, compliance with formal requisites raises interesting issues. Indeed, under all systems it is possible for a drawer's contract on an instrument to be governed by the law of Ruritania while the acceptor's and indorser's respective contract on the same instrument to be governed by the law of Penguina. This is what the doctrine of the 'several laws' or 'independent contracts', discussed in section B, is all about. At the same time, suppose the drawer's formal validity of the contract is governed by the law of Ruritania and that of the acceptor or indorser is governed by the law of Penguina: for the acceptor or indorser to be liable as such, must the instrument comply with the formal requirements of the law of Ruritania as well? **4.91**

On one hand, it is arguable that an 'indorsement', as well as an 'acceptance', complying as to requisites of form with the law of Penguina, may not be an indorsement as well as acceptance under the law of Penguina if the instrument itself does not meet formal requirements under the law of Penguina. On the other hand, there is a precedent to the effect that an accepted (even invalid) 'bill' may be treated on its own as a (valid) note.[201] As well, there is case law under which each indorsement is tantamount to the issuance of a new bill.[202] From such perspectives, the past of an instrument is relevant only as to its effect on the liability of prior parties. In our scenario, as long as they comply with formal requirements under the law of Penguina as to making of a note and the issuance of a bill, acceptance and indoresment complying in form under that law will be held valid in case of non-compliance with formal issuance requirements under the law of Penguina. This remains true irrespective of possible non-compliance with the drawer's contract with formal requirements under the law of Ruritania. **4.92**

Two American cases, cited by Lorenzen,[203] appear to follow the former analysis and reject the latter. Each case deals with an instrument issued in Ruritania, in a form complying with the law of Ruritania, but not of Penguina, and 'indorsed' in Penguina in compliance with the formal requirements of the law of Penguina. It was held in each case that this was an invalid indorsement.[204] Lorenzen disapproves of this result,[205] arguing that 'the law of the place of issue must fix the character of the instrument throughout its life',[206] at least where formal requisites of the law of the place of issue have been complied with.[207] We take this to mean, by reference to the previous scenario, that had the instrument form been invalid under the law of Ruritania, Lorenzen would not have validated the subsequent, otherwise compliant in form, indorsement in Penguina. On that point, he thus **4.93**

200 Gleeson, *Chalmers and Guest* 591–92, para 12-006.
201 *Novaknit Hellas SA v Kumar Bros* [1998] 1 Lloyd's Rep Bank (CA). See D Tobias, 'The Invalid Bill becomes a Valid Promissory Note' (2000/01) 16 BFLR 113.
202 ibid.
203 Lorenzen, 'Relationship' 329.
204 *Hyatt v The Bank of Kentucky*, 71 Ky 193, 8 Bush 193 (1871); *Nichols v Porter*, 2 W Va 13 (1867).
205 Lorenzen, 'Relationship' 331–32.
206 ibid, 330.
207 ibid, 331–32.

adheres only in part to the second interpretation indicated here, under which the acceptance, as well as indorsement, are each treated as an instrument on its own, so that non-compliance with the formal requirements of the issuance may be ignored.

4.94 BNCC art 3(2) appears to reject Lorenzen's limitation and validate the indorsement—and acceptance—complying with the law of Penguina. Under this article, whether or not the issuance complied with the formal requirements under the law of Ruritania, as long as issuance would have been valid in form under the law of Penguina:

> If ... the obligations entered into by means of a bill ... or ... note are not valid according to [art 3(1)], but are in conformity with the laws of the territory in which a subsequent contract has been entered into, the circumstances that the previous contracts are irregular in form does [sic] not invalidate the subsequent contract.

4.95 Both the Second Restatement and the BEA do not address this point.

4.96 A separate Geneva Stamp Convention precludes the invalidation, albeit not the suspension of liability, on a bill or note on the basis of non-compliance with stamping requirements.[208] There is no comparable CCC provision, presumably since such a question has not come up for cheques. However, the corresponding provision, BEA s 72(1)(a), does not exclude cheques. Thereunder:

> Where a bill is issued out of the United Kingdom, it is not invalid by reason only that it is not stamped in accordance with the law of the place of issue

4.97 A 'complementing' exception exists in Australia. Under ABEA s 77A, 'A bill issued in Australia which is presented for acceptance, accepted, or payable, outside Australia' is not invalidated by the violation of 'any law ... requiring that [instrument] to be stamped'. Accordingly, it 'may be received in evidence on payment'.

4.98 BEA s 72(1)(b) provides for another exception to the general rule of BEA s 72(1):

> Where a bill, issued out of the United Kingdom, conforms, as regards requisites in form, to the law of the United Kingdom, it may, for the purpose of enforcing payment thereof, be treated as valid as between all persons who negotiate, hold, or become parties to it in the United Kingdom[209]

4.99 For its part, rather than covering domestic transactions, even between foreigners as BEA s 72(1)(b) does, BNCC art 3(3) extends coverage to 'domestic' parties' transaction that take place abroad:

> Each of the High Contracting Parties [210] may prescribe that contracts by means of a bill ... and ... note entered into abroad by one of its nationals shall be valid in respect

[208] Convention on the Stamp Laws in Connection with Bills of Exchange and Promissory Notes, signed at Geneva, 7 June 1930 (No 3315).

[209] For extensive discussions of provisos (a) and (b) of s 72(1), see Chapter VI, the text accompanying nn 49–71 and Chapter VII, the text accompanying nn 35–40.

[210] In international law these are, the representatives of states who have signed or ratified a treaty. See eg <http://www.oxfordreference.com/view/10.1093/oi/authority.20110803095935812 >, accessed 20 December 2019. In the context of the GCC discussed here these are the states themselves.

> of another of its nationals in its territory, provided that they are in the form laid down by the national law.

CCC art 4(3) is almost verbatim with respect to a cheque. **4.100**

In being selective in its coverage, such a provision under the BEA, BNCC, and CCC, may result in the exoneration of a party covered by the provision from liability, as well as in depriving such a party from having recourse against a party not covered by it. Thus, suppose X issues an instrument payable to B, who indorses it to Y, who indorses it to C, who indorses it to Z. Suppose B and C are covered by the provision and X, Y, and Z are not. In this scenario, Z will not be able to enforce liability on the instrument. Suppose C manages to take possession of the instrument (though it is not clear how this could happen in the normal chain of events). Though effectively immune from liability, C may sue B, who is unable to recover from X. **4.101**

F. Laws Governing Specific Cheque Topics

As indicated in Chapter I section E, compared to other instruments, cheques give rise to a greater multiplicity of topics and consequently, to a greater diversity in statutory solutions. This is reflected in several CCC provisions, which do not have parallels in the other sources. Such provisions address both intrinsic and extrinsic validity and hence are dealt with on their own. **4.102**

Under CCC art 3: **4.103**

> The law of the country in which the cheque is payable determines the persons on whom a cheque may be drawn.
>
> If, under this law, the instrument is not valid as a cheque by reason of the person on whom it is drawn, the obligations arising out of the signatures affixed thereto in other countries whose laws provide otherwise shall nevertheless be valid.

CCC art 3(1) recognizes the multiplicity of approaches as to who can serve as the drawee of a cheque. For example, in the UK, under the BEA s 2, 'Banker', on which under BEA s 73 a cheque must be drawn, is defined to include 'a body of persons whether incorporated or not who carry on the business of banking'. By comparison, under CBEA s 164, a 'bank' on which under CBEA s 165 a cheque must be drawn, is defined to include 'every member of the Canadian Payments Association'. Membership in the Association is compulsory for chartered banks but open to a variety of other regulated financial institutions such as life insurance companies, securities dealers, credit unions, and trust companies.[211] Where the drawee of an instrument does not meet the required definition under the applicable law, the instrument is a bill but not a cheque. **4.104**

[211] Canadian Payments Act, RSC 1985, C C-21, s 4.

4.105 Rules relevant only to cheques, and hence with no counterpart in the BNCC, are provided for in CCC art 7, according to which the law of the country in which the cheque is payable shall determine:

(1) Whether a cheque must necessarily be payable at sight or whether it can be drawn payable at a fixed period after sight, and also what the effects are of the post-dating of a cheque;

...

(3) Whether a cheque can be accepted, certified, confirmed or visaed, and what the effects are respectively of such acceptance, certification, confirmation or visa;

...

(5) Whether a cheque can be crossed or marked either with the words 'payable in account' or with some equivalent expression, and what the effects are of such crossing or of the words 'payable in account' or any equivalent expression;

(6) Whether the holder has special rights to the cover and what the nature is of these rights;

(7) Whether the drawer may countermand payment of a cheque or take proceedings to stop its payment (opposition); [212]

...

4.106 These provisions address cheque facets pointed in Chapter I section E and are self-explanatory.

G. Transfer, Negotiation, and Assignment

4.107 For the purpose of our discussion, 'transfer', in its usual colloquial meaning, may occur with regard to the instrument, rights thereon, or a debt thereunder. 'Negotiation' involves the physical transfer of an instrument to a person who takes it as a holder. For its part, 'assignment' is associated with the transfer of a debt, whether or not on an instrument, under the general law of property.

4.108 The selection of law that applies to these matters is not addressed by the BEA. Conversely, under Second Restatement § 216:

(1) The local law of the state where a negotiable instrument was at the time of the transfer of an interest in the instrument determines the validity and effect of the transfer as between persons who were not both parties to the transfer.
(2) The local law of the state where the instrument was at the time of its transfer to a person determines whether that person holds the instrument in due course.

[212] Cover for a cheque is the same as *la provision* for a bill (see Chapter I (n 95)), hence, in fact there is a parallel to the subsection (6) in the law of bills. Similarly, in a legal system that does not recognize *la provision*, also an unaccepted bill may be stopped which is a parallel in the law of bills to subsection (7). Nonetheless, the BNCC does not address these issues.

Subsection (1) is limited to 'the validity and effect of the transfer' as between non-parties to the transfer. In turn, subsection (2) is limited to the acquisition of a holder in due course status. It is unfortunate then, that in contrast to Rome I[213] art 14 governing an ordinary assignment, Second Restatement § 216 does not provide for the 'validity and effect' of a transfer between the parties to it,[214] other than in subsection (2), as to whether the transferee becomes a holder in due course. Query as to whether a holder in due course overcomes claims and defences unavailable against him or her under the law of the place of the transfer which are nevertheless available against him or her under the law of an obligation when the latter is not apparent on the instrument. In the usual case of an instrument payable to order, the transfer is by indorsement completed with delivery.[215] Arguably then, as in connection with the indorser's contract discussed above in section C, the place of the transfer is where the transferee obtained possession. **4.109**

Effectively echoing Second Restatement § 216(1), Falconbridge characterizes the matter as 'primarily one of the transfer of the property in an obligation to pay money which is in effect merged in a tangible document'.[216] Accordingly, relying *inter alia* on *Alcock v Smith*,[217] he submits that under the BEA 'the simplest and most satisfactory solution ... is to treat the subject as analogous to the transfer of a movable thing and therefore to be governed by the *lex rei sitae* at the time of the transfer'.[218] **4.110**

For their part, the GCCs do not identify a law that governs 'the validity and effect' of a transfer in general and to the acquisition of a holder in due course status in particular. Rather, under BNCC art 6: **4.111**

> The question whether there has been an assignment to the holder of the debt which has given rise to the issue of the instrument is determined by the law of the place where the instrument was issued.

No direct parallel provision exists in the CCC except that, under its art 7(6), the law of the country in which the cheque is payable shall determine '[w]hether the holder has special rights to the cover and what the nature is of these rights'. Effectively, this means that the law of the designated place of payment determines the assignability of the cover to the holder. **4.112**

IACC provisions are of an even more limited effect. art 8 is limited only to the identification of the 'jurisdiction over disputes arising from the negotiation' of an instrument, being '[t]he courts of the State Party in which the obligation is to be honoured **4.113**

213 Rome I art 14.
214 Under Rome I art 14(1) that law is 'the law that applies to the contract between the assignor and assignee'.
215 See eg BEA s 2, and in general section C.
216 Falconbridge, 'Bills and Notes' 342.
217 [1892] 1 Ch 238, 66 LT 126.
218 Falconbridge, 'Bills and Notes' 342.

or the courts of the State Party in which the defendant is domiciled, at the option of the plaintiff'.

4.114 In the final analysis, only Second Restatement § 216 is clear as to the effect of a forged indorsement placed in a Geneva Convention country on an instrument issued in a BEA jurisdiction. Such forgery does not preclude the instrument transfer under the UBL,[219] as well as the UCL,[220] but is ineffective under the BEA[221] and the UCC.[222] In fact, *Embiricos v Anglo-Austrian Bank*[223] applied this principle, albeit to a cheque issued and stolen in Romania, collected (and taken by the court to be indorsed) in Austria,[224] and payable in England. More generally, and perhaps by extension, in our view of the existing law, any fraudulent transfer which under the law of the place where it has been made is effective to confer title, will be taken to pass title to an instrument, regardless of where it has been originally issued. Accordingly, in a BEA or UCC jurisdiction, whether a fraudulent indorsement passes title to an instrument payable to order ought to depend on whether, under the law of the place where the indorsement is made, the instrument is treated as payable to a fictitious person.[225]

4.115 For its part, IACC art 7 covers 'the measures to be taken in case of robbery, theft, forgery, loss, destruction, or of the instrument deteriorating to the point of becoming useless'. Such measures are determined by the law of the place where the instrument is payable. Both BNCC art 9 and CCC art 7(8) are to the same effect, albeit only in connection with the 'loss or theft' of the instrument. Arguably, this language addresses merely the means to protect an ex-holder out of possession—where protection is otherwise provided for. However, such a provision does not seem to cover the validity and effect of a transfer by means of a forged indorsement.

H. Formalities and Other Performance Duties

4.116 As indicated in Chapter I section C, in principle, under all laws, liability of a secondary party on a negotiable instrument arises upon the dishonour of the instrument, namely, the failure to accept or pay by a primary party or the drawee in response to its presentment by the holder. Under the GCCs and for foreign bills under the BEA, protest is also required. In all systems, albeit with different consequences as to the failure

219 UBL art 16.
220 UCL arts 19 and 21.
221 BEA s 24.
222 UCC § 3-403.
223 [1905] 1 KB 677 *affn'g* [1904] 2 KB 870.
224 This was a pre-UCL case and the judgement does not provide information about the laws of those two countries. Both have been civil law jurisdictions.
225 See BEA s 7(3) and UCC § 3-404 (as well as § 3-405). For the allocation of 'loss resulting form the forgery of the payee's endorsement' as the key issue in determining whether an instrument is payable to a fictitious person see *Canada Life Assurance Co. v Canadian Bank of Commerce* (1974), 3 OR (2d) 70 [1].

to comply, a notice of dishonour or default is required to be given by the holder to the secondary party to be charged with liability.

As discussed in section C, depending on the legal system and its type, an obligation on an instrument may be governed by the territorial connecting factors of the place of delivery, signature, or payment. Whether, and to what extent, a separate law governs formalities and their execution is the subject of this section. **4.117**

> BEA s 72(3) provides the following rule for the law applicable in connection with required formalities:
>
> The duties of the holder with respect to presentment for acceptance or payment and the necessity for or sufficiency of a protest or notice of dishonour, or otherwise, are determined by the law of the place where the act is done or the bill is dishonoured

The obscure language of this subsection has been subject to criticism.[226] In our view, the provision ought to be read as limited to the mechanisms for performing formalities, such as presentment, protest, and notice of dishonour, which are to be exercised by the holder. At the same time, whether formalities are required to trigger liability is a question addressing the existence of, or conditions for, liability. As such, it is determined under the law that governs the obligation itself,[227] as selected under BEA s 72(2). **4.118**

The same applies to the range of beneficiaries of a notice of dishonour,[228] as well as to the circumstances under which a formality or a delay in performing it is excused.[229] Also, the law of the obligation also determines the consequences of breaching the holder's duty to pursue a required formality. Such consequences may either be liability for damages[230] or loss of the cause of action.[231]The law applicable to all such matters is to be determined under BEA s 72(2) and not 72(3). **4.119**

To read BEA s 72(3) as proposed here requires the insertion of 'performance of' before 'duties' and the deletion of 'necessity for or' before 'sufficiency'. The provision should accordingly be read to address 'the *performance* of the duties ... and the ... sufficiency of a protest or notice of dishonour'. For its part, protest as a condition to liability is to be required or dispensed with under the law of the obligation selected under BEA s 72(2). **4.120**

Needless to say, while the proposed insertion of 'performance' could be read into the language of the provision as it stands now, this is not the case for the proposed deletion of 'necessity for or'. Accordingly, we propose to read 'the necessity for or sufficiency of a protest or notice of dishonour' as an additional requirement, which is triggered under BEA s 72(3) only once the 'necessity' is established under BEA s 72(2). Stated otherwise, the law selected under BEA s 72(3) can excuse compliance with 'a protest **4.121**

[226] For a summary see eg Falconbridge, 'Bills and Notes' 365–66.
[227] *Bank Polski v K J Mulder & Co* [1941] 2 KB 266; *aff'd* [1942] 1 KB 497. We do not share the criticism of Gleeson, *Chalmers and Guest* 614, para 12-031.
[228] See eg BEA s 49(3) and (4).
[229] See eg BEA ss 46 and 50; UCC § 3-504.
[230] See eg UBL art 45(6); UCL art 42(6).
[231] See eg BEA ss 45 and 48; UCC § 3-503.

or notice of dishonour' required under the law selected under BEA s 72(2) but not to require compliance where it is excused under the law selected under BEA s 72(2).

4.122 Our proposed interpretation to BEA s 72(3) disagrees with Falconbridge's insofar as it is 'obvious' to him that the necessity for protest, as opposed to that for a notice of dishonour, is to be determined under 'the law of the place where the [instrument] is payable'.[232] True, the law of the obligation is likely to designate the place of payment for the performance of the protest and thus to select the law applicable there. However, this is not the same as saying that the law of place of payment, on its own, determines whether protest is either required or dispensed with.

4.123 *G & H Montage GmbH v Irvani*[233] addressed the question as to whether formality steps are required to crystallize the liability of an avalist who signed outside the UK a foreign bill payable in the UK. In the Court of Appeal, the separate concurring judgements of Woolf LJ and Purchas LJ are reconcilable with our analysis as to the relationship between BEA ss 72 (2) and (3). In their judgements, they dispensed with the satisfaction of the formality requirements by the holder, since under relevant foreign law, applied through BEA s 72(2), such steps were not required to charge the avalist. A discussion as to the scope of BEA s 72(3) and its relationship with BEA s 72(2) was thus not required.

4.124 Unfortunately, we submit, in delivering the Court of Appeal principal judgment, Mustill LJ unnecessarily confused the matter. To find a party liable, and not being 'sure that s 72(2) does provide the correct route to the foreign law', he required 'the rights which are sought to be enforced ... [to be] capable (even if governed by a foreign law) [of being] assimilated to the concepts of English commercial law'. Having found the aval contract to be analogous to that of the indorser, he brought in BEA s 72(3) to 'apply English law as the law of the place where payment was due'. He then concluded that since 'there is nothing in [BEA] ss 48 and 51(2) which addresses a liability said to accrue ... simply by signature with added words of aval', no formalities were required under the BEA to charge an avalist with liability.[234] To say the least, we submit that Mustill LJ's judgment is unclear. Certainly, it does not reflect the proper relationship between BEA s 72(2) and (3). He did not apply BEA s 72(2) where it should apply and misinterpreted BEA s 72(3) by wrongly applying it to where it should not apply.

4.125 Compared to BEA s 72(3), BNCC and CCC art 8 is clearer in being limited to the manner, including the time limits, in which the formalities are to be pursued. Thereunder:

> The form of and the limits of time for protest, as well as the form of the other measures necessary for the exercise or preservation of rights concerning [instruments], are[235] regulated by the laws of the country in which the protest must be drawn up or the measures in question taken.

[232] Falconbridge, 'Bills and Notes' 367.

[233] [1988] 1 WLR 1285 (QBD), *aff'd* [1990] 2 All ER 225 (CA). The case is extensively discussed by B Crawford, 'Montage v. Irvani: Conflict or Harmonization of Laws?' (1991) 7 BFLR 85.

[234] ibid, quotes and reasoning are from pp 235–236. BEA ss 48 and 51(2) respectively deal with notice of dishonour and protest requirements.

[235] Replaced by 'shall be' in the CCC.

However, for cheques, in the footsteps of BEA s 72(3) on the point of necessity of protest, CCC art 7 adds that: **4.126**

> The law of the country in which the cheque is payable shall determine:
>
> ....
>
> (9) Whether a protest or any equivalent declaration is necessary in order to preserve the right of recourse against the indorsers, the drawer and the other parties liable.

Under BEA s 51(6), in principle, '[a] bill must be protested at the place where it is dishonoured'. No location for the protest is specified under the UBL, UCL, and the UCC. However, in practice, 'the country in which the cheque is payable' under CCC art 7 will be 'the country in which the protest must be drawn up' under CCC art 8. Nonetheless, BNCC and CCC art 8 address the regulation of the form and time limits for a protest and other measures, and not their necessity. In short, in following the plain meaning of BEA s 72(3) on the necessity of a protest, as supported by Falconbridge, the language of CCC art 7(9) is equally problematic. **4.127**

Both the Second Restatement and the IACC are to a similar effect to that of BNCC and CCC art 8 (without the 'overload' of CCC art 7(9)) except that each broadens the scope of the corresponding rule to also cover the performance of the payment obligation by the party liable. **4.128**

Place of payment is at least the default place for presentment under BEA s 45(4) and UCC § 3-501(b)(1).[236] Along these lines, Second Restatement § 215(2) provides that 'the local law' of the state 'designated in the instrument as the place of payment', if any, 'determines in which state, or states, presentment may be made'. As for method for presentment and other acts, under Second Restatement § 217: **4.129**

> Details of presentment, payment, protest and notice of dishonor are determined by the local law of the state where these activities take place.

Similarly, under IACC art 6: **4.130**

> The procedures and time-limits for acceptance, payment and protest shall be governed by the law of the place where such acts are or should be performed.

In line with our view as to BEA s 72(3), the Comment to Second Restatement § 217 specifically states that whether an obligation is triggered upon the compliance with a formality is a matter determined under the law that governs the obligation itself. In contrast, along the lines of our analysis, according to the Comment: **4.131**

> The law selected by application of the rule of [§ 217] governs such questions as whether payment must be made on a Sunday or other legal holiday, the number of days of grace, if any, to which the obligor is entitled, and the time and manner for making presentment and protest and for giving notice of dishonour

[236] The GCCs do not provide for the place for presentment for payment. Cf UBL arts 21 and 38(2) and UCL art 31 (presentment for acceptance at the domicile as well as presentment for payment in a clearing-house is permissible).

4.132 The Comment further acknowledges that the rule of Second Restatement § 217 'is a specific application of the rule of [Restatement] § 206'. The latter is a rule under general contract law, which designates the law of the place of performance as the law applicable to the determination of issues relating to details of the performance of any type of contract.

4.133 We submit that the inclusion in IACC art 6 of 'procedures and time-limits for acceptance' is unfortunate. Acceptance is a form of obligating oneself and not performing and hence its 'procedures and time-limits' ought to be governed by the law of the obligation, primarily that relating to the extrinsic validity. At the same time, as a matter of principle, it is not all that obvious whether the place and time limits within which formalities are to be performed is a matter to be determined under the law of the obligation or the law that governs the mechanics of performing the formalities. As indicated, Second Restatement § 215(2) designates the law of the place of payment as determining the place of presentment; this, however, may not go as far as to designate that law as governing the presentment to be made at that place. We are inclined to think that it is the law of the obligation that ought to determine the existence of the obligation to present, including the place in which it is to be performed. The law of that place is the law that at most determines the details, namely, the mechanics of presentment.[237]

4.134 BEA s 48, UBL art 45, UCL art 52, and UCC § 3-501(a), each require the holder to 'give' a notice of dishonour or default to a secondary party to be charged with liability. It is tempting to argue that in choosing a word conjugating 'give' rather than 'deliver' the drafters sought to distinguish between these two words and indicate that in 'giving', unlike in 'delivering',[238] compliance is required at the sender's, and not recipient's, place. However, in excusing the sender from complying where under prescribed circumstances the notice did not reach the recipient for example, BEA s 50(2)(a) demonstrates that the duty is not otherwise complied with until the recipient gets the notice. At the same time, compliance with the law of each recipient's place would be impractical in case of multiple indorsements. On that point, we agree with Falconbridge that compliance with the obligation to give a notice of dishonour is required according to the law of the sender's place.[239]

4.135 In turn, there is a partial consensus in relation to the selection of the law that determines time limits to perform formalities. As indicated, according to the Comment to Second Restatement § 217, 'the time and manner for making presentment and protest

[237] Conversely, it may be argued that even details, namely, mechanics of the presentment, are to be determined by the law of the obligation. Nowadays issues of procedure are fairly limited and relate to operational mechanics of the courts. The rest is considered to be issues of substance. See Garnett, *Private International Law*. From this perspective the mechanics of presentment can be viewed as a matter of substance. For further discussion of this point, see Chapter VII, the text accompanying nn 70–71.

[238] For which see extensive discussion in section C.

[239] Falconbridge, 'Bills and Notes' 367.

and for giving notice of dishonor' is a 'detail' determined under Second Restatement § 217 'by the local law of the state where these activities take place'. Along these lines, CCC art 7(2) provides that:

> The law of the country in which the cheque is payable shall determine:
>
> ...
>
> (2) The limit of time for presentment

To that same end, BEA s 72(5) states: **4.136**

> Where a bill is drawn in one country and is payable in another country, the due date thereof is determined according to the law of the place where it is payable.

The provision should not be read as merely addressing the time differences among different geographical locations. Rather, in the footsteps of the Comment to Second Restatement § 217, it must be taken to also cover the issue of whether a given statute provides for days of grace, and their number, during which payment can still be lawfully made after the date marked on the instrument as the date on which payment is due. **4.137**

Unfortunately, the various choice-of-law provisions as to the law applicable to formalities and other performance obligations are not clear on the relationship between the place required or authorized for performance and that of actual performance. Thus, BEA s 72(3) speaks of 'the law of the place where the act is done or the bill is dishonoured', while BEA s 72(5) speaks of the 'the law of the place where [the bill] is payable'. For its part, BNCC and CCC art 8 speaks of 'the laws of the country in which the protest must be drawn up or the measures in question taken'. CCC art 7 speaks of '[t]he law of the country in which the cheque is payable'. In turn, Second Restatement § 217 speaks of 'the local law of the state where [relevant] activities take place'. Finally, IACC art 6 speaks of 'the law of the place where such acts are or should be performed'. In the final analysis, we argue formalities and other performance duties are to be carried out at the place identified by the law governing the intrinsic validity of the obligation, in a manner determined by the law of the place in which they are accordingly to be carried out. **4.138**

A particular performance obligation relates to the payment of an instrument denominated in a foreign currency. Two questions arise in this context. First, can the obligation be performed and enforced in the foreign currency?[240] Second, if payable in the domestic currency of the forum, is the exchange rate to be determined at the day of breach or upon actual payment? **4.139**

We are inclined to think that under choice-of-law rules, the starting point for determining the law applicable to each question is the law governing the obligation. However, an answer in the affirmative to each question under this law will be reversed **4.140**

[240] This question may be governed by foreign currency regulations, which are outside the scope of the present discussion.

by either policy considerations under the law of the place of payment or, if only in connection with enforcement, by the *lex fori*.

4.141 On these questions, CBEA s 162 provides that:

> Where a bill is drawn out of but payable in Canada and the sum payable is not expressed in the currency of Canada, the amount shall, in the absence of an express stipulation, be calculated according to the rate of exchange for sight drafts at the place of payment on the day the bill is payable.

4.142 This provision differs from all other conflict provisions in not selecting a law applicable; rather it provides for a substantive rule of law to address a single situation relating to an instrument involving a specific international element. It corresponds to BEA s 72(4), which was repealed in the UK[241] in the footsteps of the reversal of its rule under the law of contract in *Miliangos v George Frank (Textiles) Ltd*.[242] So far as payment in domestic currency of a contractual debt obligation is denominated in a foreign currency, the decision rejected the 'breach date rule'—effectively applying the rate existing on 'the day the bill is payable'. Instead, the House of Lords replaced it with the 'payment date rule', thereby, contrary to old BEA s 72(4) (and present CBEA s 162), allocating the domestic currency depreciation losses that had been incurred between the two dates to the breaching debtor.[243]

4.143 UBL art 41 is similar to the repealed BEA s 72(4). However, it adds that the applicable rate of exchange is that prevailing in the country of payment. At the same time, it specifically provides that a stipulation for actual payment in foreign currency as money of payment is binding. For its part, UNIBNC art 75(1) provides that in principle, '[a]n instrument must be paid in the currency in which the sum payable is expressed.'

I. Conclusion

4.144 Among the schemes discussed in this chapter, none is perfect—even as the Second Restatement may be in the least need of improvement. Otherwise, the discussion highlighted the global adherence to the 'several laws' approach, the advantage of avoiding a 'single rule' for the selection of a law applicable to a contract, and the desirability of having the same law governing both intrinsic and extrinsic validity for each party. In relation to payment between distant parties, it was contended that the choice between the law applicable in the place of 'signature' and that of 'delivery' is problematic. Rather, it was pointed out that in selecting the law applicable, under the existing law, the better choice is between the law of the place where the sender loses control (point of irrevocability) and the law of the place in which the recipient gains it (point of achieving a binding contract). Finally, it was submitted that the existence of and

241 *Administration of Justice Act* 1977, c 38, s 4(2)(a)(3) (UK).

242 [1976] AC 443, [1975] 3 All ER 801 (HL).

243 *Miliangos* was codified in Ontario in s 121 of Courts of Justice Act RSO 1990, c C43 Arguably, however, so far as negotiable instruments are concerned, it does not supersede CBEA s 162 since the latter is *lex specialis* passed under federal power.

compliance with formality requirements are two distinct issues not necessarily to be governed by the same law.

The broader normative questions as to choice-of-law rules relating to negotiable instruments are left to the ensuing chapters. For now, let us nevertheless make a few observations. **4.145**

First, the systems diverge as to the identity of the choice-of-law rules in the area of negotiable instruments. Following traditional choice-of-law doctrine, the various connecting factors generally focus on various territorial links and do not incorporate personal connecting factors, such as the place of the parties' residence or their place of business. Yet, the choice-of-law provisions stand in remarkable disagreement as to identity of territorial factors: while some of the systems focus on the connecting factor of the place of contract formation, others opt for the place of signature or the place of payment. As we have seen, only one of the provisions incorporates a non-territorial rule—that of the parties' nationality. Second, the provisions seem to cover different areas and components within negotiable instruments law.[244] Some of the provisions incorporate choice-of-law provisions to cover issues of the parties' capacity, while others do not. The lack of consistent uniform approach extends to other areas, such as: the possible incorporation of the validation principle within choice-of-law analysis; the scope of application of mandatory rules; the identity of choice-of-law rules applicable to the case of instrument transfer; the rules governing the limitation period on the instrument; and the rules governing the procedural requirements of the instrument holder. Third, there appear to be matters within negotiable instruments law that are not covered by any framework, such as the question of the law governing the issue of illegality[245] and the damages. **4.146**

[244] See eg Gutteridge, 'Rules of Conflict' 75–76 (discussing matters that are not covered by the Geneva Conflicts Convention); Gleeson, *Chalmers and Guest* (discussing matters that are not covered by BEA s 72).

[245] Thus, the pre-BEA case law followed the connecting factor of the place of designated payment (see *Robinson v Bland* (1760), 2 Burr 1077, 97 ER 717). This rule seems also to have been followed in the UK after the passage of the BEA (see *Moulis v Owen* [1907] 1 KB 746, 96 LT 596 (CA)).

V
The Foreign Element and Party Autonomy in Negotiable Instruments Law

5.01 Chapter IV considers the developing trends within the the choice-of-law doctrine: (1) the relaxation of the 'foreign element' requirement (section A); and (2) the advances of the party autonomy principle (section B).

A. The 'Foreign Element' in Negotiable Instruments

5.02 Chapter III considered the many reasons for a significant relaxation or even elimination of the 'foreign element' requirement. We contend that where the matter of the foreign element is raised in the context of negotiable instruments it can be classified as a private international law case that will benefit from choice-of-law analysis.

5.03 A review of the choice-of-law provisions in the American Second Restatement (Second Restatement),[1] the Geneva Conflicts Conventions[2] (GCC), and the Inter-American Convention on Conflict of Laws (IACC)[3] does not reveal particular requirements as to the scope of their application. These follow the general requirements of the systems with regard to the presence of a 'foreign element' as a precondition to choice-of-law analysis. Thus, for example, the application of §§ 214–17 of the Second

[1] Restatement of Conflict of Laws, Second (1971; revised 1986 and 1988, American Law Institute) (hereafter Second Restatement).

[2] The Convention for the Settlement of Certain Conflicts of Laws in Connection with Bills of Exchange and Promissory Notes, signed at Geneva 7 June 1930; The Convention for the Settlement of Certain Conflicts of Laws in Connection with Cheques, signed at Geneva 19 March 1931.

[3] Inter-American Convention on Conflict of Laws Concerning Bills of Exchange, Promissory Notes, and Invoices, 1438 UNTS 211 (1975). For an outline of these provisions, see Chapter IV.

Restatement seems to hinge on the general provision of the Second Restatement that refers to a single foreign element requirement.[4] The relaxation in this requirement naturally leads to an adequate relaxation in the area of negotiable instruments. From this perspective, the major development that occurred amongst the systems with respect to mitigating or even eliminating the barriers for choice-of-law analysis extends to negotiable instruments law.

The United Nations Convention on International Bills of Exchange and International Promissory Notes (UNIBNC)[5] and the Bills of Exchange Act (BEA)[6] by contrast incorporate provisions that define the application scope of choice-of-law rules in relation to negotiable instruments. Thus, Article 2 of UNIBNC refers to a broad range of potential connecting factors that can trigger the convention application. Amongst these factors, the UNIBNC mentions the 'place where the bill is drawn', 'the place indicated next to the signature of the drawer', 'the place indicated next to the name of the drawee', 'the place indicated next to the name of the payee', and 'the place of payment'. This list seems be broad and it reflects the contemporary tendency of choice-of-law jurisprudence to consider a wide range of potential connections for the purposes of meeting the requirement of the presence of a 'foreign element'.[7] Furthermore, UNIBNC incorporates both territorial connecting factors (by referring to such places as the place of payment and signature) and personal factors (by referring to 'place indicated next to the name of the drawee and payee', which suggests, in turn a reference to the places of residence/business of the drawee/payee) into choice-of-law analysis.[8] 5.04

The approach of the BEA was briefly discussed in Chapter IV.[9] Under the BEA, a given factual circumstances should be classified into two-fold situations: (1) purely domestic situations; and (2) foreign situations. Specifically, the 'domestic'/'foreign' divide is sourced within the following two provisions of the BEA: (1) the beginning of s 72, which determines the scope of the application of choice-of-law provisions within this section;[10] (2) s 4, which goes further and differentiates between two types of negotiable instruments: the so-called 'inland' bills (or as we shall call it throughout the book 'domestic' bills); and the so-called 'foreign' bills.[11] As the BEA's provisions are the foundation of many national instruments and against the background of the 5.05

[4] As § 1 of the Second Restatement states 'The world is composed of territorial states having separate and differing systems of law. Events and transactions occur, and issues arise, that may have a significant relationship *to more than one state*, making necessary a special body of rules and methods for their ordering and resolution' (emphasis added). See Second Restatement §§ 214–17.

[5] UN Doc A/RES/43/165, 42 Yearbook of the United Nations 1988 (UN 1988) 834. For a discussion of this convention, see Chapter I, the text accompanying notes 77–78.

[6] 1882, Chs 61, 45, and 46 Vict (hereafter BEA).

[7] For a discussion of these issues, see Chapter III section B(1).

[8] For a discussion on the 'territorial' connecting factors related to the event (such as tort) or institution (such as contract and marriage), as opposed to 'personal' connecting factors, such as place of parties' residence or business, see Chapter III, the text accompanying nn 13–25.

[9] See Chapter IV, the text accompanying nn 14–19.

[10] BEA s 72.

[11] BEA s 4.

remarkable unpopularity of the UNIBNC,[12] the discussion in this section focuses on those provisions.

1. The Scope of Choice-of-Law Analysis Set in s 72 of the UK BEA

5.06 The beginning of s 72 of the UK BEA determines the application scope of choice-of-law rules set in this section in the following terms: 'Where a bill drawn in one country is negotiated, accepted, or payable in another'.[13] Stated in these terms, the provision provides a clear-cut definition of a 'foreign' situation and therefore draws a sharp line between private international law cases (which involve choice-of-law analysis) and purely domestic cases (which do not). The literal reading of this provision suggests that situations which are not 'foreign' according to its definition are simply not cases of private international law and preclude the application of the choice-of-law provisions specified in s 72.

(a) Four Prescribed Territorial Factors

5.07 Section 72 determines which territorial connecting factors are important and which are not. Specifically, it focuses on the territorial location of the instrument itself, rather than on the territorial location of the parties. For example, the instrument can be drawn by a German resident in the name of a German resident, and yet, those factors are irrelevant for the purposes of the classification enterprise under s 72. No matter how incidental and arbitrary the territorial connecting factors related to the instrument are (or how central other connecting factors related to the parties may be), the BEA's classification focuses exclusively on what has been coined in choice-of-law literature as 'territorial' connecting factors (such as places where the instrument is drawn, negotiated, accepted and payable) rather than 'personal' connecting factors (such as the places of parties' residence and business at the time of the various events).

5.08 As we saw in Chapter III, contemporary choice-of-law thinking provides equal status to 'territorial' and 'personal' connecting factors and treats them *prima facie* on equal grounds for the purposes of choice-of-law analysis.[14] Indeed, Article 2 of the UNIBNC has incorporated both types of factors. Despite this tendency in choice-of-law thought, the BEA's scope of classification clause has remained strictly loyal to territorial connecting factors that track the physical location of the instrument. It directs the analysis to the place where the document is drawn by the drawer, transferred to the holder (ie 'negotiated'), accepted by the drawee and the place where the instrument is payable by

[12] For a discussion of these issues, see Chapter I section B.

[13] BEA s 72; AG Gleeson, *Chalmers and Guest on Bills of Exchange, Cheques and Promissory Notes* (18th edn, Sweet & Maxwell 2016) 583–84 (hereafter Gleeson, *Chalmers and Guest*).

[14] See Chapter III, the text accompanying nn 13–25.

the drawee/acceptor to the holder. None of the above-mentioned factors refers to the residence of any of the parties under the instrument or to the place of their business.

In contrast to UNIBNC, s 72 of the BEA not only rejects the significance of personal connecting factors, but it concentrates on a few territorial connecting factors further limiting the potential pool of 'foreign' situations. Under this section, the list of possible territorial factors is a closed one naming four factors: (1) the place where the instrument is drawn; (2) the place where the instrument has been transferred; (3) the place where the instrument has been accepted; and (4) the place where the instrument is payable. The list excludes other possible territorial factors, such as the place where the instrument is issued (ie drawn and completed by delivery[15]), the place of the signature, the place of the instrument's indorsement, or the place of the instrument's presentment. As the language of s 72 stands, it stipulates absolute priority to four territorial connecting factors, and only if they are not situated in the same place, does choice-of-law analysis apply. **5.09**

(b) The Language of s 72 Excludes an Entirely Foreign Situation

The scope of choice-of-law analysis in s 72 does not cover a straightforward case of an entirely foreign situation. The beginning of s 72 accepts the basic insight of traditional and contemporary choice-of-law literature, according to which it is sufficient to have a single 'foreign' element to classify the case as a private international law case and to proceed to choice-of-law analysis. This indeed follows a literal reading of the provision according to which the application of the choice-of-law analysis requires that at least one (out of four) specified territorial connecting factors must diverge from others. Yet, the formulation is unfortunate, as its scope excludes a factual situation where *all four* crucial connecting factors are foreign to the domestic forum. In other words, s 72 has excluded from its application what appears to be an entirely 'foreign situation', which paradoxically is supposed to be the most straightforward situation for private international law rules and subsequent choice-of-law analysis. **5.10**

A representative example of this anomaly can be seen in the *Karafarin Bank*[16] case in which the plaintiff had drawn several cheques payable to the defendant, as a part of the security for a loan that the defendant provided to the plaintiff. At the time of the loan and the issue of the cheques, all matters connecting to the cheques and the parties took place in Iran: the plaintiff lived and operated a business in Iran and the defendant operated a bank there.[17] Since the plaintiff subsequently moved to the UK, the UK court had the authority to adjudicate the case based on his present residence.[18] **5.11**

The court recognized that since all connecting factors of the case referred to Iran, its factual matrix fell outside of the scope of s 72.[19] Indeed, none of the four crucial factors mentioned in s 72 (places of instrument's drawing, acceptance, payment, and transfer) **5.12**

15 BEA s 2.

16 *Karafarin Bank v Gholam Reza Mansoury Dara* [2009] EWHC 3265 (Comm) [2010] 1 Lloyd's Rep 236 (hereafter *Karafarin Bank*).

17 ibid [10].

18 ibid [1].

19 ibid [10].

took place in different countries. They all took place in a single country—Iran. This explains why the court reached the conclusion that the factual situation of the case lay outside s 72.

5.13 The question is what the court should do in situations that fall outside of the determined scope of s 72? One obvious option would be that given a factual situation not falling within the definition of s 72, the matter should not be treated as a private international law situation at all, and the domestic law (*lex-fori*) should apply. However, we think that conclusion is problematic. In *Karafarin Bank* the factual situation was entirely 'foreign' to the UK system, all factors, territorial and personal connected to the state of Iran. To refer the matter to *lex-fori* in this situation seems to be undesirable, as it may encourage the discredited phenomenon in choice-of-law literature referred to as 'forum shopping'.[20] Indeed, it seems to be unfair to the defendant in *Karafarin Bank* that despite the foreign factual matrix of the case, the plaintiff had recourse to the application of domestic UK law, just because of the defendant's subsequent move to UK.

5.14 Indeed, in *Karafarin Bank* the court did not turn to the *lex-fori* solution and chose another path to address the situations which did not fall under the scope of s 72.[21] While recognizing that the factual situation did not fit the wording of s 72, the court simply decided to set a new rule and to adjudicate the case based on Iranian law, without providing a reasoning or rationale as to the application of that law.[22] *Karafarin Bank* has been referenced in the leading choice-of-law text book, *Dicey and Morris*. After stating the four territorial connecting factors of s 72,[23] the textbook has added the following replica: 'In other cases, the law of the country where the bill is drawn, negotiated, accepted and payable will apply to the bill and all supervening contract'.[24]

5.15 Without delving at this point into the potential significance and implications that could follow from the application of Iranian law in UK courts,[25] it would appear that the problem lies in the wording of s 72, which in its present formulation puzzlingly excludes its application to an 'single foreign country' situation, such as *Karafarin Bank*. The confusion could have been easily resolved had the BEA followed the

20 For the traditional objection to forum shopping in the context of *lex-fori*, see Chapter III, the text accompanying nn 5–12.

21 In section B of this chapter we will say much more on the courts' treatment of the situations and issues which do not fall under the explicit language of BEA's section 72. See section B(2).

22 As Blair J put it, 'since the cheques were both issued by the drawer in Iran, and payable in Iran, it is unnecessary to decide whether Iranian law applies as the law of the place of issue (*lex loci contractus*), which is Chalmers' preferred analysis, or as the law of the place of payment (*lex loci* solutions) which is Dicey's preferred analysis', *Karafarin Bank* [26] (italics in original).

23 See eg Collins, Harris (eds) *Dicey, Morris and Collins on the Conflict of Laws* (15th edn, Sweet & Maxwell 2012) 2075 (Rule 240 (1) (hereafter *Dicey and Morris*).

24 ibid, Rule 240 (2) (reference to *Karafarin* case has been omitted). In other parts of their work Dicey and Morris have stated the relation between s 72 and the *Karafarin* case in the following terms 'section applies only if a bill is drawn in one country, is negotiated, accepted or payable in another country. In other cases . . . the law of the country where the bill is drawn, negotiated, accepted and payable will apply to the bill and all supervening contracts' (ibid, 2077, reference to *Karafarin* has been omitted).

25 Indeed, in *Karafarin* the court had no problem relying on the expert's testimony and applying a foreign law, specifically Iranian law in an UK court. The UK judge did not delve into the substantive content and qualities of Iranian law and its comparison with UK negotiable instrument law, with further potential questions on which law is 'better'. Later in this book, we will say more on this decision and/or any substantive assessment of the involved provisions within choice-of-law process. See Chapter VII section D.

contemporary and predominant definition of the choice-of-law question, which classifies private international law cases based on a relaxed test of a single foreign element. Had this definition been applied, the UK court would have immediately recognized the 'foreign' nature of the situation in *Karafarin*, which was full of 'foreign elements' (or more precisely was based only on foreign elements), without the need for judicial acrobatics and the need to design a special rule that would capture situations where all elements are foreign.

Accordingly, one can argue that the present scope of choice-of-law analysis determined in s 72 is disappointing. First, the territorial connecting factors are rooted in the sovereignty foundation of choice-of-law thought. This foundation is based on the insight that a sovereign is interested in applying its laws to acts (such as instrument's drawing/issue/transfer/acceptance/payment) that take place within its territory.[26] Nevertheless, as we have seen in Chapter III,[27] this foundation is not predominant anymore within choice-of-law doctrine. This is particularly true with respect to the case of negotiable instruments' law, which is deeply rooted in the practice of international commerce and as such seems to be immune from the sovereigns' intervention and the sovereign's interests.[28] Second (and as we have already seen), the provision excludes from its wording a clearly private international law situation when all connecting factors are foreign. **5.16**

Accordingly, based on the earlier discussion, we would recommend eliminating the choice-of-law scope definition within s 72 altogether or, alternatively, replacing it with a different provision that would adopt a simple (and relaxed) test that triggers choice-of-law analysis in situations with the presence of a single foreign element within the factual matrix of the case. **5.17**

2. Foreign Negotiable Instruments versus Domestic Negotiable Instruments

Other private international law provisions within the BEA differentiate between domestic and foreign situations and can be found in s 4, which defines two types of instruments: (1) the so-called 'domestic' bills; and (2) 'foreign' bills.[29] **5.18**

[26] Indeed, Joseph Beale's justification of the place of contract formation connecting factor was based on the state's territoriality and as reflection of the states' sovereignty principle. See J Beale, 'What Law Governs the Validity of Contract' (1909) Harv L Rev 1, 271 ('This doctrine [place of contract formation] gives full scope to the territoriality of law, and enables each sovereign to regulate acts of agreement done in his own territory') (Beale, 'Validity').

[27] On the regression of the sovereignty-based approaches within modern choice-of-law thought, see Chapter III section B(2).

[28] See Chapter II.

[29] BEA s 4. Throughout this section we use the term 'bill', rather 'negotiable instrument', to distinguish the former from other types of negotiable instruments—notes and cheques. As we will see in a moment, we will challenge the necessity of the mandatory requirement of the procedure called 'protest' on dishonoured foreign negotiable instruments. And yet, under the provisions of the BEA, the requirement of this procedure does not extend to 'foreign notes' ((BEA s 89(4)). Similarly, while the Canadian BEA follows the division between 'foreign' and 'domestic' notes (RSC 1985, c B-4, s 177), the requirement of formal protest of a foreign note extends only to the question of the indorser's liability, rather than to the 'foreign' note's maker (see Canadian BEA, s 187); B Crawford, *The Law of Banking and Payment in Canada*, vol 3 (Canada Law Book

5.19 According to s 4, a bill shall be classified as a 'domestic bill', if it meets one of the following conditions: (1) to be drawn and payable in UK; or, alternatively, (2) it should be drawn in UK for an UK resident. In other words, the BEA's criterion for determining that a given bill is purely domestic takes as a point of departure that the bill needs not just to be drawn by the drawer in UK, but it also shall meet one of the following additional two requirements: (1) be payable in UK; or (2) be drawn upon an UK payee. Bills that do not meet one of the two options shall be classified, under s 4, as 'foreign bills'.[30]

5.20 This classification departs from the traditional doctrine of private international law.[31] This doctrine treats all factual situations as 'domestic' cases unless a foreign element is present. Section 4, however, takes an opposite approach: all bills are foreign, unless the requirements under the two above-mentioned options (which, in turn, each requires the presence of two significant domestic factors within the factual matrix of the case) are met.

5.21 Perhaps the different point of departure reflects the historical origins of negotiable instruments as representing a legal institution to meet the demands of international commerce, at least with respect to bills of exchange.[32] On the face of it there is a presumption that the common case of the instrument would involve a foreign bill, rather than a domestic bill. To add complexity to the 'domestic'/'foreign' divide, s 4(2) establishes a presumption according to which all bills shall be treated as domestic 'unless the contrary appears on the face of the bill'.[33] This presumption underlies the paramount centrality of the physical face of the bill.[34] It also signifies a return to the traditional choice-of-law doctrine, which takes the 'domestic' case as its point of departure and perhaps reflects the inherent tension within the BEA's principal division between 'domestic' and 'foreign bills'.

5.22 There are two implications to the 'domestic'/'foreign' divide. The first concerns the mandatory procedure called 'protest'. In contrast to the case of a 'domestic' bill, the classification of a given bill as a 'foreign' means that the holder must undergo this procedure in a case where the bill is dishonoured by the drawee. This procedure requires the holder to go to a notary who needs to make a formal announcement under a stamp and signature, stating that the given bill was duly presented, and yet dishonoured by

2008) 21–23 (hereafter Crawford, *Law of Banking and Payment*). A similar point applies to the other type of negotiable instruments—cheques: while the requirement of 'protest' applies to foreign cheques (BEA s 73), in the commercial reality regarding the drawer (as opposed to indorser) of the foreign cheque, this requirement can be usually waived under ss 50(2) and (4) (5), 51(9) of the BEA. See also Gleeson, *Chalmers and Guest* paras 2-032 and 5-154. These fairly mitigated requirements of mandatory protest of foreign notes and foreign cheques explain why we choose to focus on the 'bill' type of negotiable instruments in this section.

30 BEA s 4(1) ('Any other bill is a foreign bill').

31 For a discussion of this point, see Chapter III section B(1).

32 See Chapter II, the text accompanying nn 6–7.

33 BEA s 4(2).

34 On the significance of the physical face of the instrument see eg E McKendrick (ed), *Goode on Commercial Law* (5th edn, Penguin 2016) (hereafter McKendrick, *Commercial Law*) 538–39 (mentions the centrality of the physical appearance of the document for the purposes of the HDC's status determination); *Arab Bank Ltd. v Ross* [1952] 2 QB 216, 226 (Lord Denning).

the drawee by non-acceptance or non payment.[35] This procedure usually takes place in the location where the bill is dishonoured.[36] The procedure of 'protesting' is a mandatory requirement only for 'foreign' bills (rather than domestic), to preserve the holder's right to sue the drawer and/or indorser who undertook the obligation of honouring the bill.[37] This distinction is a significant one: it protects the drawer and/or indorser from a possible claim of the holder, despite their obligations to the bill. In other words, the 'foreign' bills[38] impose an additional burden on the holder in relation to his or her relationships with the secondary parties on the instrument.

The second implication of the 'foreign'/'domestic' divide is relevant to the operation of the BEA s 72(2). This section states: 'Provided that where an inland bill is endorsed in a foreign country the indorsemnet shall as regards the payer be interpreted according to the law of the United Kingdom.'[39] A domestic bill will be governed by law of the United Kingdom even where it is indorsed abroad.[40] The BEA applies a domestic law—the *lex-fori* on the question of indorsement of domestic bill in a foreign state. **5.23**

Our aim in the next sections is to make a case against the 'foreign-domestic' bills' division. For this purpose, we describe in more detail the implications of that division. Our strategy will be: (1) to demonstrate the shaky grounds and problematic nature of both implications; and (2) to consider the origins of the distinction and to challenge its relevance to modern reality. **5.24**

(a) Implication I: The Application of *Lex-Fori* on Bills Indorsed Abroad Under s 72(2)

BEA s 4 and the division between domestic and foreign bills stood at the heart of the decision of the Supreme Court of Canada in *Canada Life v CIBC*.[41] In this case a Canadian insurance company prepared in Toronto, Canada thirty-one cheques, drawn on CIBC, New York agency and payable to New York customers. The latter neither claimed nor were entitled to these payments. Rather their names were provided to the insurance company in Toronto by the company's representative in **5.25**

[35] Gleeson, *Chalmers and Guest* paras 6-144 and 6-145 (frames the notion of protest in the following terms: 'Protest is a declaration, in solemn form, that a bill has been dishonoured. It must normally be made by a notary public. It derives from the ancient customs of merchants and in many legal systems it is required upon the dishonour of any bill of exchange or promissory note.' See also *Convention Providing a Uniform Law for Bills of Exchange and Promissory Notes*, 143 LNTS 257 (7 June 1930), Annex I, ss 33 and 77 (hereafter UBL). For further discussion on the procedure of protest, see Chapter I, the text accompanying nn 144–45.

[36] Gleeson, *Chalmers and Guest* para 6-158. See also EG Lorenzen, *The Conflict of Laws Relating to Bills and Notes* (Yale University Press 1919) 43 40 (stresses the point that within the Anglo-American system, the requirement of protest applies only with respect to foreign bills) (hereafter Lorenzen, *Bills and Notes*).

[37] BEA s 51(1). For further discussion on the nature of the drawer/indorser obligation in relation to guarantee's law, see Chapter IV (the text accompanying nn 29–56) and Chapter VI (the text accompanying nn 172–192).

[38] BEA s 51(1); See also Gleeson, *Chalmers and Guest* para 6-147 ('It is not necessary to protest a dishonoured inland bill or cheque in order to preserve the recourse against the drawer or indorser').

[39] BEA s 72(2).

[40] Crawford, *Law of Banking and Payment* paras 21–24 ('An inland bill is entirely governed by Canadian law even where it is endorsed abroad').

[41] [1979] 2 SCR 669 (hereafter *Canada Life*). More specifically, the case dealt with the corresponding provision of the Canadian Bills of Exchange Act, RSC 1985, c B-4, s 24 (hereafter CBEA).
CBEA s 24

New York with the fraudulent intent to collect the cheques made payable to these customers for his personal gain. Upon receiving from Toronto the cheques for distribution to the customers, the fraudulent company representative in New York forged the payees' indorsement and collected the cheques.[42] How should the cheques be classified—foreign or domestic bills—and which law shall govern the liability of the CIBC bank that honoured the cheques with forged indorsements? This determination mattered in this case in light of the divergence between Canadian and New York substantive law. If the Canadian negotiable instruments law been applied, the loss would fall on the CIBC bank.[43] If the New York negotiable instruments law on fake A indorsement been applied, the loss could have fallen on the insurance company that acted as the drawer of the cheques.[44] Which law should have been applied to this situation?

5.26 The legal analysis in *Canada Life* followed the distinction between foreign and domestic bills in s 4 BEA and the subsequent question regarding whether the *lex-fori* provision of s 72(2) BEA applied to this case. After analysing the factual situation of the case, Estey J reached the conclusion that the instruments had been drawn in Canada, which met the first condition of s 4. Also, it was clear that the bills were payable in a foreign country—New York, USA. Accordingly, the classification of the cheques in this case fell on the determination of whether the cheques were drawn upon a 'Canadian resident'.[45] For these purposes the court had analysed what is considered to be a 'resident', for the purposes of s 72(2). The court held that, despite the fact that CIBC bank had a head office in Canada, it did not satisfy the Canadian 'residency' requirement of s 72(2).[46] New York law applied and the loss fell on the Canadian insurance company.[47]

5.27 Several observations can be made with respect to the court's analysis in *Canada Life*. First, the determination regarding the question of whether CIBC bank shall be classified as a Canadian or foreign resident seems to be difficult and fairly formalistic. Indeed, it has been noted in the literature how unpredictable and flexible the definition of 'residency' can be and how it can vary for the purposes of various statutes.[48] The determination of 'residency' is made more difficult by the contemporary reality of international commerce and transnational corporations with a multiplicity of

[42] ibid 669.

[43] iIbid 670; CBEA s 21(5) corresponding to BEA s 7(3). See also Crawford, *Law of Banking and Payment* paras 21–24.

[44] Indeed, as trial judge found, had New York law been applied, the provisions of § 3-405(1) of UCC would have applied, the drawee bank would have had a complete defence against the insurance company. See *Canada Life* 670. For a comparison between the Anglo Canadian and American loss allocation rules, see Benjamin Geva, *Bank Collection and Payment Transactions* (OUP 2011) at 465–73, 507–11.

[45] ibid, 674–75. For further discussion on the question whether the term 'drawn' includes 'delivery' of the instrument, see Chapter IV, the text accompanying nn 18–19.

[46] ibid, 683: 'It is not sufficient, in my interpretation of the section [s 4], to say that the bank to whom the direction is issued has its head office in Canada . . . Clearly all the parties to the transaction recognize that the cheque was directed to the New York Agency because the commerce in question was centered exclusively in the State of New York.' The corresponding CBEA provision is s 160.

[47] ibid, 683–84.

[48] See eg WW Cook, *The Logical and Legal Bases of the Conflict of Laws* (Harvard University Press 1942) 194–211; WLM Reese, 'Does Domicile Bear a Single Meaning?' (1955) 55 Colum L Rev 589, 594.

branches. Indeed, despite the fact that the head office of CIBC bank was in Toronto, Ontario,[49] the court reached the conclusion that for the purposes of this particular interaction between the insurance company and the bank's specific agency that resided in New York it could not be classified as a Canadian resident. However, one could also see how the court could have reached the opposite conclusion with respect to the above-mentioned 'residency' classification.

Secondly, it seems that what really stood at the heart of the court's decision in the *Canada Life* was not a certain formalistic classification of the residency requirement of s 4. Rather it was a somewhat vague version of the most significant relationship (MSR) principle discussed in detail in Chapter III,[50] which focused on the particular relationship between the parties and the evaluation of this relationship, which directed to application of New York law. Thus, the court stressed that the cheques were denominated in US dollars drawn on the New York agency of the bank, rather than generally to the bank itself.[51] As the court put it: **5.28**

> In the cheques here issued by Canada Life [the insurance company], the direction is not to the Imperial Bank of Commerce at large but TO THE AGENCY, CANADIAN IMPERIAL BANK OF COMMERCE, 20 Exchange Place, New York ... The cheque is payable on demand to joint payees who, on the evidence here, have been found concurrently by the courts below to be business organizations in the State of New York. Payment is of course to be in United States Currency.[52]

This justification clearly refers to the operational mechanics of the MSR principle. The evaluation of the parties' interaction as a whole determined the application of New York law. The court pointed out that the instruments were made out in US dollars, and payable in New York. Also, the court stressed that the instruments were directed to the New York agency of the Canadian bank.[53] The application of New York law represented, in this case, an application of a law with the MSR to the parties and the event. What seems to underpin the court's reasoning in the *Canada Life* case was in fact MSR principle analysis, and a rather formalistic definition of the term 'residency'.[54] **5.29**

This analysis of *Canada Life* illustrates the problematic nature of the BEA's s 72(2). For the purposes of deciding whether a given factual situation falls within the scope of this section, the court engaged the classification enterprise between 'foreign' and 'domestic' bills under s 4 and the subsequent definition of 'residency' under s 72(2). The **5.30**

[49] Interestingly, but within the traditional choice-of-law literature, the place of residence of corporations has been precisely determined by the place of their head office or the place of the corporation's incorporation. See eg A Briggs, *Private International Law in English Courts* (Oxford University Press, 2014) 803–04 (hereafter Briggs, *PIL*); SGA Pitel and NS Rafferty, *Conflict of Laws* (2nd edn, Irwin Law 2016) 26–27.

[50] See Chapter III, section B(3).

[51] *Canada Life* 672, 682–83.

[52] ibid, 682–83 (emphasis in original).

[53] ibid, 672, 682–83.

[54] Later in this book, we will say more on this decision and/or any substantive assessment of the involved provisions under the choice-of-law process. See Chapter VII section D.

court's line of reasoning is plainly unconvincing and the decision seems to be based on different grounds.

5.31 The application of the *lex-fori* solution under s 72(2) is also untenable. This strict choice-of-law rule has been criticised in modern choice-of-law literature as negating the parties' reasonable expectations and for providing an unfair advantage to the plaintiff.[55] Yet, under s 72(2), *lex-fori* governs the liabilities of the parties under a domestic bill, despite the bill's subsequent indorsement in the foreign state. As such, *lex-fori* seems to be based on the notion of a state's sovereignty that follows the place of the bill's initial creation—United Kingdom. According to this reading of the underlying grounds of s 72(2), the creation of the bill in United Kingdom reflects an act of sovereign UK authority which remains to govern the bill, despite its subsequent indorsement abroad. However, this 'sovereignty' reasoning seems to be incompatible with the modern developments within the choice-of-law doctrine, the transnational origin of the bills of exchange and the intellectual developments of the negotiable instruments law.

(b) Implication II: The Protest Requirement on Foreign Bills Under s 51

5.32 The second implication of the 'domestic'/'foreign' bills division refers to the procedural requirement of 'protest', which applies solely to the case of 'foreign' bills. As it has already been mentioned,[56] under s 51 BEA, the holder is required to undertake this procedure as a precondition to liability imposition on the secondary parties to the instrument.

5.33 A review of the literature with respect to the mandatory protest requirement suggests that this has been presented through the lens of such terms as 'comity' and 'respect' that the domestic system owes to the foreign systems. More specifically, it has been argued that since the requirement of protest has a sound historical trace within the so-called 'ancient customs of merchants',[57] and has a strong hold within the provision of the continental UBL,[58] the BEA shall follow this procedure out of 'respect' and 'comity' of foreign systems. Crawford made a reference to the protest requirement as 'borne out by the text of the 1930 Geneva Convention' and mentioned that the 'formality of a documented notarial protest is at least a *courtesy* to a foreign court'.[59] In a similar vein, Chalmers has adopted a comparable justification for the protest requirement of foreign bills by referring to Articles 44 and 77 of the UBL,[60] and by mentioning the 'strict rules governing protest of bill of foreign legal systems'.[61]

[55] For a discussion of this point, see Chapter III, the text accompanying nn 6–12.

[56] See the text accompanying nn 36–37.

[57] See eg Gleeson, *Chalmers and Guest* para 6–144 (makes a reference to 'ancient customs of merchants' as standing at the basis of historical roots of the 'protest' requirement).

[58] UBL arts 44 and 77 (states that 'default of payment or acceptance must be evidenced by an authentic act'). The requirement of protest under ULB seem to be generally more relaxed in the case of cheques (see ULB arts 40 and 41); See also Gleeson, *Chalmers and Guest* para 6-144, n 621.

[59] Crawford, *Law of Banking and Payment* paras 21–23 (emphasis added).

[60] Gleeson, *Chalmers and Guest* para 6-144.

[61] ibid, para 6-149. A similar rhetoric of 'comity'/'courtesy' towards foreign states can found in the Comment to § 3-305 of Article 3 of the Uniform Commercial Code—Negotiable Instruments, ALI and NCCUSL, 2002 (hereafter UCC): 'Protest is generally required by the laws of foreign states and that cannot be altered by the domestic statutes of other states'.

5.34 Both Chalmers and Crawford suggest extending the protest requirement beyond the definition of the 'foreign' bills set out in s 4 of the BEA.[62] Based on the rhetoric of comity, prudence and courtesy towards foreign systems, they suggest extending this requirement to domestic bills cases where the signatory party resides abroad.[63]

5.35 One can argue, however, that the reference to the notions of 'comity' and 'respect' of foreign systems in the context of the *choice-of-law* question[64] is flawed. Indeed, Story made a reference to these notions as a key for grasping the nature of the choice-of-law question.[65] According to this approach, choice-of-law cases shall be resolved on the basis of a 'courtesy' between states.[66] Yet, Story's 'comity' approach has been conceptually and practically disapproved. Thus, conceptually, it has been argued that *choice-of-law* question has nothing to do with public international law and the inter-state relationships between sovereign states.[67] Accordingly, the argument that the choice-of-law process shall follow the potential acts of 'courtesy' that one state executes (based on the vision of the domestic court as a long-arm representative of the sovereign) towards another, goes awry with the very conceptual foundations of the subject.

5.36 Practically, it has been shown that the 'comity' and 'respect' terms have not much to contribute to choice-of-law analysis: even if the domestic system owes 'respect' and 'comity' to another system, it is still not clear which law should apply to cases that include a foreign element in their factual basis. Consider, for instance, a contract signed in Japan between an Ontario resident and a German resident with respect to delivery of goods in Brazil. How can the notions of 'respect' and 'comity' between states help us address the question of applicable law to this situation?

5.37 The objections to the 'comity' and 'respect' terms, along these lines, can be traced throughout the various texts of the modern choice-of-law literature. Consider the frequently quoted passage from *Cheshire & North*[68] on the rejection of 'comity' as irrelevant to the nature of choice-of-law:

> Although the term [comity] has been often used, analysis of it reveals that it has been employed in a meaningless or misleading way. The word itself is incompatible with the judicial function, for comity is a matter of sovereigns, not for judges

62 See BEA s 51(1); Gleeson, *Chalmers and Guest* para 6-147 ('It is not necessary to protest a dishonoured inland bill or cheque in order to preserve the recourse against the drawer or indorser').

63 Gleeson, *Chalmers and Guest* para 2-032 ('if any party is resident abroad, it should, as a matter of prudence, be protested').

64 Indeed, these notions play a fairly central role within the other questions of private international law-that of jurisdiction and recognition. See DE Childress III, 'Comity as Conflict: Resituating International Comity as Conflict of Laws' (2010) 44 UC Davis L Rev 11.

65 J Story, *Commentaries on the Conflict of Laws* (4th edn, Little, Brown and Company 1852) 7.

66 ibid, 38–40.

67 See eg A Nussbaum, *Principles of Private International Law* (Oxford University Press 1943) 22; CL von Bar, *The Theory and Practice of Private International Law* (trans by GR Gillespie, W Green & Sons 1889) 6.

68 Thus, eg this passage has been cited by A Briggs, 'The Principle of Comity in Private International Law' (2012) 354 Rec Des Cours 65, 80–81 who rejected the 'reciprocity' vision of 'comity' (p 89).

> required to decide a case according to the rights of the parties. Again, if the word is given its usual meaning of courtesy it is scarcely consistent with the readiness of English courts to apply enemy law in time of war. Moreover, if courtesy formed the basis of private international law, the judge might feel compelled to ignore the law of Utopia on proof that Utopian courts apply no law but their own, since comity implies a bilateral, not a unilateral, relationship. If, on the other hand, comity means that no foreign law is applicable in England except with the permission of the sovereign, it is nothing more than a truism. The fact is, of course, that the application of a foreign law implies no act of courtesy, no sacrifice of sovereignty. It merely derives from a desire to do justice.[69]

5.38 This quotation envisages judicial authority not as a vehicle of the sovereign for promoting its internal policies or for addressing sovereign policies in the sovereign's interaction with other states. Rather, the choice-of-law process is deeply engaged with such terms as 'justice', litigating parties' rights and duties, and their reasonable expectations. As *Cheshire & North* explains, the nature of the subject has nothing to do with international relationships between the states, which explains 'the readiness of English courts to apply enemy law in time of war'. The question of 'courtesy' is simply irrelevant for the choice-of-law process and it does not matter whether the foreign court does or does not apply a domestic law in the same way as the domestic court does. The notion of comity as a key for grasping the nature of the subject has been coined here as no less than a 'truism'.

5.39 Presented in these terms, there seems to be no reason for negotiable instruments law to incorporate the 'comity' and 'courtesy' rhetoric. These have been fiercely criticised in modern choice-of-law literature. Indeed, systems significantly diverge on the question whether the procedure of protest is required to protect the rights of the secondary parties on the instrument. Yet, this departure touches upon the fundamental question of the discipline; whether or not choice-of-law doctrine shall take this substantive law divergence into consideration as a matter of principle. The short answer according to the traditional and contemporary choice-of-law doctrine to this question is, 'no'.

5.40 On a fundamental level, choice-of-law doctrine abstracts itself from the content of the applied laws. It acknowledges that the contemporary international order is comprised of a multiplicity of states that are governed by different positive laws. With the exception of some radical cases, it avoids executing a judgment on the quality of the applied laws and does not analyse their content.[70] This means that continental law, for good reasons, may consider the procedural requirement of protest as an important requirement to protect the rights of the secondary parties on the instrument. Other systems may have a different view on this matter (and for good reasons, as well[71]), and consider

[69] J Fawcett and JM Carruthers (eds), *Cheshire, North & Fawcett: Private International Law* (15th edn, Oxford University Press 2017) 5 (hereafter *Cheshire & North*).

[70] For a generally formal structure of choice-of-law mechanics, see Chapter III (the text accompanying nn 26–32) and Chapter VII section D.

[71] See eg Lorenzen, *Bills and Notes* 43 (this seems to make a point about the internal balance between the continental and Anglo-American systems: while the former focuses more on the procedural requirement of protest, the latter more focus on the procedural requirement of the notice of dishonour).

the institution of mandatory protest as over-protective requirement that undermines the holder's rights. The traditional and contemporary choice-of-law doctrine is simply disinterested in the debate on whether the procedure of protest is 'good' or 'bad' and does not enter into this analysis in the first place, as a matter of principle.

There seems to be no reason for the BEA to continue executing this act of 'courtesy' towards foreign systems. It appears to negate the very nature of the choice-of-law doctrine, which does not attribute a normative significance to the considerations of 'comity' and 'courtesy'. Indeed, the choice-of-law literature has commented about the need to eliminate the need of protest with respect to foreign bills within UK jurisprudence.[72] The UK *Review Committee on Banking Services and Practice* recommended that the requirement of protest on foreign bills under s 51 shall be abolished.[73] In a similar vein, the American negotiable instruments' law does not distinguish between foreign and domestic bills.[74] While acknowledging the existence of the protest requirement within foreign systems, this law simply disapproves of it as a mandatory rule to uphold the position of the secondary parties.[75] **5.41**

(c) The Origins of the Distinction

Our observations have suggested that the two central implications of BEA's s 4 'inland'/'foreign' distinction are problematic and seem to be untenable. It follows that *Canada Life* was in fact decided on the MSR principle's analysis. In a similar vein, the requirement of protest under BEA s 51, specifically designed for 'foreign' bills, seems to be superfluous. These are all a challenge to the validity of the 'inland'/'domestic' distinction set in BEA's s 4. If so, how was this distinction made in the first place? **5.42**

Chalmers refers to the *Amner v Clark*[76] case as the leading authority for the original distinction between domestic and foreign negotiable instruments.[77] At the basis of this decision stood a notion according to which the taxation power of UK government cannot extend over negotiable instruments that are 'foreign'.[78] The situation involved an instrument drawn in London, upon a merchant residing in Paris, payable in London, and accepted in London. It was decided that although the payee was a foreign resident, this instrument shall be classified as a domestic instrument. **5.43**

[72] As Chalmers put it, 'it is difficult to see why the protest of a foreign bill should be mandatory in the sense that a failure to protest will discharge the drawer and indorsers' (Gleeson, *Chalmers and Guest* para 6-144).

[73] Gleeson, *Chalmers and Guest* para 6-144.

[74] See Second Restatement Second ss 214–17.

[75] The official comment to § 3-505 UCC states as follows: 'Protest is no longer mandatory and must be requested by the holder. Even if requested, protest is not a condition to the liability of indorsers or drawers. Protest is a service provided by the banking system to establish that dishonour has occurred. Like other services provided by the banking system, it will be available if market incentives, inter-bank agreements, or governmental regulations require it, but liabilities of parties no longer rest on it. Protest may be a requirement for liability on international drafts governed by foreign law which this Article cannot affect.'

[76] (1835) 2 C.M. & Rosc. 468; 150 ER 202 (hereafter *Amner v Clark*).

[77] See eg Gleeson, *Chalmers and Guest* para 2:033, n 178.

[78] *Amner v Clark* 202.

5.44 The reason for the need of the 'domestic'/'foreign' classification in *Amner v Clark* lay in UK laws' stamp duties requirement, which applied to negotiable instruments. Since the court considered the stamp duties to be fiscal in their nature and a reflection of the UK sovereign's taxation power, it was thought that it would be problematic to extend this duty to instruments originated in the foreign territory. As the court put it, 'The legislature never intended to impose stamp on bills drawn abroad; it was not in their power to do so'.[79] The distinction originated in the context of the domestic/UK stamp duties and was made in the context of an argument about the inability to extend this duty to certain types of instruments.

5.45 Indeed, there is a long standing position within private international law that has challenged the application of foreign tax law within domestic courts. This position has applied primarily to the point of the possibility of recognizing a foreign judgment with relation to a tax statute[80] and also, with respect to the possibility of application of foreign tax law as a part of the choice-of-law analysis.[81] The latter has been considered as an 'extra-territorial application of revenue statues'.[82] This notion seems to closely relate to the sovereignty principle and that a sovereign state cannot exercise its sovereign authority over the territory of another state.[83]

5.46 Yet, over the decades a call has been made in the literature for a relaxation of the traditional position. It has been argued that the foreign revenue law exclusion shall not apply in an absolute manner,[84] and that private international law cannot 'totally ignore'[85] foreign tax provisions. The criticism has explicitly targeted the exclusion of stamp duties requirements from the choice-of-law process. The position according to which the stamp requirements of a given system could be presented as of a 'fiscal nature', and therefore not-recognizable for the purposes of the choice-of-law analysis, has been long criticised.[86] Lorenzen once referred to the exclusion of the stamp duties from choice-of-law analysis as 'condemned by the great majority of text-writers; both continental and Anglo-American'.[87] Accordingly, one can argue that an incorporation of choice-of-law analysis towards foreign revenue law (and specifically stamp duties)

[79] ibid, 203 (Lord Abinger). For a historical reference to the stamp duty as a reflection of the sovereign power, see B Geva, *The Payment Order of Antiquity and the Middle Ages* (Hart 2011) 133 (hereafter Geva, *Payment Order*).

[80] See eg *Holamn v Johnson* (1775) 1 Cowp. 341; 98 ER 1120, 1211.

[81] See eg *Cheshire & North* 115–19; SGA Pitel and NS Rafferty, *Conflict of Laws* (2nd edn, Irwin Law 2016) 37–39.

[82] See Lorenzen, *Bills and Notes* 10. See also J Daniels, *A Treatise on the Law of Negotiable Instruments*, vol II (7th edn, Baker, Voorhis 1933) 923 (which mentions the traditional approach of the various systems to disregard the stamp requirements of foreign systems within choice-of-law analysis).

[83] See *Cheshire & North* 116.

[84] Hans W Baade, 'Operation of Foreign Public Law' in K Zweigert and Ulrich Drobnig (eds) *International Encyclopedia of Comparative Law* (Brill 1970) c 12, 52.

[85] *Cheshire & North* 119.

[86] See Lorenzen, *Bills and Notes* 103. See also Daniels, *A Treatise* (n 82) 923.

[87] See Lorenzen, *Bills and Notes* 103 (references omitted). Indeed, in contrast to the BEA's provisions, Lorenzen supported a position that validates foreign stamp law, even if the application of that law would mean an invalidation of the contract. See ibid.

has been long overdue, in the same way this analysis has been extended to other traditionally 'public' areas, such as antitrust and financial regulations.[88]

Furthermore, stamp duties requirements on negotiable instruments do not exist anymore. While this requirement existed in United Kingdom at the time of the *Amner v Clark* case, it has never been popular outside of United Kingdom,[89] and now it has been abolished in the UK as well.[90] In the same way as a 'regular' contract does not require a stamp, the legislature has acknowledged that the law of negotiable instruments shall not serve as vehicle for taxation. Accordingly, the originating basis for the 'domestic'/'foreign' distinction is no more relevant. Modern systems simply do not view the negotiable instrument's stamp duty as a legitimate vehicle for taxation of commercial private activity.[91] **5.47**

The shaky foundations of the originating basis of the 'domestic'/'foreign' distinction, in combination with the problematic nature of each one of its two implications that this distinction has created (ie ss 51 and 72(2)), suggests that it should be re-considered and perhaps abolished. **5.48**

Accordingly, we would opt for an elimination of the 'inland'/'foreign' distinction set in BEA s 4, and removal of its two implications: (1) the application of lex-fori rule under s 72(2); and (2) the implication of the mandatory 'protest' requirement under s 51. **5.49**

B. Party Autonomy Principle as a Governing Principle of Choice-of-Law Cases of Negotiable Instruments

1. Preliminary Remarks: Four Justifications

In light of the extensive inroads made by the party autonomy principle within modern choice-of-law doctrine outlined in Chapter III,[92] its absence from the law of negotiable instruments is striking. Consider the following set of related **5.50**

88 See eg K Knop et al, 'From Multiculturalism to Technique: Feminism, Culture, and the Conflict of Laws Style' (2012) Stan L Rev 589; A Riles, *Managing Regulatory Arbitrage: A Conflict of Laws Approach*, 47 Cornell Int'l LJ 63 (2014).

89 See Lorenzen, *Bills and Notes* 58. It would appear that the stamp duties of certain countries stood at the basis of the several conventions that require the parties to make amendments to their domestic law of negotiable instruments to avoid a situation when the failure to meet the stamp requirements would mean an invalidation of the document. See *Geneva Convention of June 7, 1930, On Stamp Laws in Connection with Bills of Exchange and Promissory Notes*; *Geneva Convention of March 19, 1931, on the Stamp Laws in Connection with Cheques*. See also MO Hudson & AH Feller, 'The International Unification of Laws Concerning Bills of Exchange' (1931) 44 Harv L Rev 333, 373.

90 Finance Act 1970, sch 7, para 2. See also *Dicey and Morris* 2082.

91 We will return to the stamp requirement in Chapter VII of this book, in the context of the so-called proviso a of s 72, which supports the validation of a foreign instrument, despite being inconsistent with stamp requirements of the foreign system (see Chapter VII, the text accompanying nn 35–40).

92 On the remarkable success of the party autonomy principle within a wide range of private law categories, see Chapter III section B(2).

justifications for the introduction of the party autonomy principle as a governing principle of choice-of-law cases of negotiable instruments: it would (1) serve the important goal of negotiable instruments' law regarding the promotion of predictability and stability of transactions; (2) be consistent with the general spirit of negotiable instruments' law that already seems to be informed by the value of party autonomy; (3) be consistent with the general spirit of negotiable instruments' law that is not just informed by the party autonomy principle but also seems to reflect a particular form of this principle—that which allows the parties to determine their rights and duties; and finally, and above all else; (4) be consistent with the conceptual foundations and historical development of negotiable instruments law. Specifically, this area of law seems to be immune from the criticism invoked in the choice-of-law literature against the introduction of party autonomy. The ensuing discussion addresses each one of the justifications, in turn.

(a) Market Stability and Predictability Promotion

5.51 As to providing predictability to the actual form of the instrument, the introduction of party autonomy would serve the ultimate goal of negotiable instruments law. One can wonder whether the wide spectrum of potential connecting factors (such as the place of the instrument's formation, the place of payment, the place of the instrument's issue, the residence of the parties, and so on) really sheds light on the question of the applicable framework to adjudicate the parties' rights and duties. Indeed, some of the aforementioned connecting factors are fairly easy to ascertain due to the commercial practice to record details such as the place of the instrument's issue and payment on the face of the instrument.[93] Other connecting factors can be traced with a significant amount of certainty as well, in light of the hierarchy of certain presumptions that the law sets to clarify the places of certain events and deeds under the instrument.[94] Yet (and crucially), it is not clear why the predictability on the point of, say, the place of instrument's payment, sheds light on *the question of applicable law*.

5.52 Consider a case of negotiable instruments signed in Ontario, delivered in Brazil (which means that the place of contract formation is Brazil[95]) and specifying New York as the place of payment. How did the knowledge of the place of the instrument's formation in Brazil lead to the conclusion that the parties had in mind to employ Brazilian law to adjudicate their rights and duties? How would the application of Brazilian law in this case correlate with the parties' reasonable expectations as to the identity of the applicable law? In other words, one can inquire about the unexplained gap in choice-of-law literature between the identity of the connecting factor (regardless of how predictable is it and how easily it can be ascertained) and the ultimate object of choice-of-law inquiry—which law applies?[96]

[93] See eg McKendrick, *Commercial Law* 527–31.

[94] Thus, eg negotiable instruments law sets several traceable presumptions to shed light on the place of the instrument's payment when this place is not specified on the face of the instrument. See §§ 217 and 218 of the Second Restatement; § 3-311 of UCC.

[95] For a discussion of this point, see Chapter IV section C.

[96] In Chapter VI we will say more about this puzzle within the choice-of-law literature. See Chapter VI section A(2)(b).

This unexplained gap suggests that the principle of party autonomy should be considered the 'bread and butter' of choice-of-law analysis. In contrast to uncertainty and possible speculations on what question the various connecting factors shed light on and to which degree they are relevant to address the question of the *applicable law*, the introduction of party autonomy as a general rule would greatly eliminate this difficulty. An explicit specification on the face of the instrument would provide a direct answer to the ultimate question of our inquiry: which law applies? Thus, it would provide much needed predictability for negotiable instruments' law.[97] **5.53**

The significance of the value of predictability cannot be underestimated within the internal structure of negotiable instruments law. It has been noted for a long time that one of the most central aspects of this law is to provide predictability and stability to the transferability of the instrument, in a way akin to the easiness and 'worry-free' transferability of money.[98] This aspect of predictability within the internal structure of negotiable instruments' law is well exemplified through the so-called 'substantive'[99] aspect of the notion of negotiability, under which the Holder in Due Course (HDC) acquires the document free from defects and potential defences ('free from equities'[100]) that his or her predecessor might have had.[101] As such, it protects the position of those merchants who have purchased the instrument in good faith and for value, and ensures that a wide range of potential defences could not be invoked against them. In its essence, this feature of negotiability reflects the demands of the market and commerce which aim to ensure the stability and predictability of commercial transactions.[102] It has been coined as a 'major privilege'[103]and 'a bed-rock'[104] of negotiability. **5.54**

A review of negotiable instruments law reveals the centrality of the value of predictability, reflecting the needs of business and the desirability of a smooth operation of commercial transactions. It explains, for example, the importance that this area of law attributes to the physical appearance and physical examination of the instrument for the purposes of determination of the parties' rights and duties;[105] the strict **5.55**

[97] Of course, things may not be as simple and later in this section we will say more on the scope and limits of party autonomy within negotiable instruments law. See section B(2).

[98] DV Cowen and L Gering, *Cowen The Law of Negotiable Instruments in South Africa Vol. One: General Principles* (5th edn, Juta 1985) 9, 47–49 (hereafter Cowen and Gering, *Negotiable Instruments*). See also McKendrick, *Commercial Law* 518–19.

[99] Cowen and Gering, *Negotiable Instruments* 39.

[100] ibid, 22.

[101] For a discussion on the substantive aspect of negotiability, see Chapter I, the text accompanying notes 6–22. See also UBL art 17.

[102] Cowen and Gering, *Negotiable Instruments* 21–22, 32, 43, 52, 96–97, 106–07. See also Gleeson, *Chalmers and Guest* 585 (states the object of the negotiable instrument's law in terms of 'to secure to the holder payment of the amount stated in the instrument'); A Barak, 'The Nature of the Negotiable Instrument' (1983) 18 Isr L Rev 49, 51–52 ('the underlying theory of negotiable instrument: the transfer of a document is enough to give right to it and also, the holder receives a better title under certain conditions. It is important to give people faith in negotiable instruments and to increase use of it as means of payment'); A Barak, 'The Requirement of Consideration for Bills or Notes in Israel' (1967) 2 Isr L Rev 499, 500 (hereafter Barak, 'Consideration').

[103] Cowen and Gering, *Negotiable Instruments* 22.

[104] ibid, 34 (reference omitted).

[105] See eg ibid, 23. Indeed, the physical appearance of the instrument is central for determining the HDC status. In order to inquire as to its status, the physical form of the document must be 'regular' on the face

requirements as to the form of the instrument to be considered a 'negotiable instrument';[106] the support of the instrument's validity in case of its potential challenge on the grounds of the parties' incapacity.[107] It is of paramount significance for negotiable instruments law to make the instrument easily transferrable, to ensure the predictability as to its terms, and to provide a fairly strong status to the HDC. In shedding light on the identity of the applicable law, party autonomy as a general rule of choice-of-law analysis appears, to perfectly serve this underlying goal of the negotiable instruments law.[108]

(b) The Consistency with the General Spirit of Party Autonomy Within Negotiable Instruments Law

5.56 An analysis of negotiable instruments' law reveals that this law has already been informed by the principle of autonomy of the parties. Two aspects of negotiable instruments law require further attention. First, one can argue that the various provisions seem to be preoccupied with the task of verifying that the parties' choice with respect to their obligations is 'relational', rather than 'one-sided'. This ensures that party autonomy is respected in the sense that the internal structure of negotiable instruments law requires an expression of choice from *both* sides of the transaction and that the obligation is not imputed in a one-sided manner by either party to the instrument.

5.57 Second, the other set of provisions of negotiable instruments law seems to reflect another side of party autonomy: after insuring that the parties' rights and duties are set in a relational way and express a relational choice of both parties, the law inquiries as to authenticity of such a choice. Accordingly, a wide range of provisions seems to engage in verifying this authenticity or genuineness of the parties' choice with respect to the content and scope of their obligations under the instrument. This ensures that party

of it, without signs to arouse suspicion. See eg McKendrick, *Commercial Law* 538–39; *Arab Bank Ltd. v Ross* [1952] 2 QB 216 [226] (Lord Denning). Similarly, *Dicey and Morris*, in the older edition, stated as follows: 'The characteristic of a negotiable instrument is that it intended to circulate, and that, for this purpose, anyone becoming a party to it should be able to see from the instrument itself what are going to be his rights and his obligations. Agreements which do not appear on the face of the instrument should therefore not be allowed to affect the rights and duties of those who are parties to it.' See Collins (ed) *Dicey and Morris on the Conflict of Laws* (11th edn, Sweet & Maxwell 1987) 1311.

[106] BEA s 3; UBL art 1. Similarly, Goode has characterized the negotiable instrument as a document which is 'traditionally concise and no greater in size that enables it to be conveniently carried and transferred; its terms are limited to payment obligations'. (McKendrick, *Commercial Law* 517). For further comparative analysis of the form requirements amongst the systems, see Chapter I, the text accompanying nn 131–34, 162.

[107] See eg BEA s 26(2); McKendrick, *Commercial Law* 561 (mentions the BEA's presumptions against lack of capacity). For further discussion of this point in the context of Validation Principle, see Chapter VII section A.

[108] Yet, as we will see in Chapter VI, the upholding of the holder's rights is not absolute and it is balanced with the rights of the signatory party to a significant degree. Accordingly, it is more accurate to speak of a 'balanced' structure of negotiable instruments law which accommodates within its provisions a certain equilibrium between the interests of the instrument's holder and those of the signatory parties. It would be inaccurate to speak about the internal structure of the negotiable instrument's law, as completely pro-holder. At least with respect to the rights of the instrument's holder who is not HDC. For further discussion on the relation between the internal structure and policies of the negotiable instruments law and the underlying values of the choice-of-law question, see Chapter VI section A(2).

autonomy is respected in a sense that once the relational choice is proved, there has to be verification that it is 'real' and 'genuine'.

5.58 A wide range of rules, doctrines, principles, and concepts crystallize these two aspects of the party autonomy principle, which seem to be already deeply embedded within the internal structure of negotiable instruments law. For example:

the requirement for the drawee's acceptance as a fundamental precondition of his liability,[109] with further provisions that aim to ensure the genuineness of the acceptance;[110]

the requirement of delivery as a crystallization of the authenticity of the signatory party choice;[111]

the various provisions addressing parties' capacity, as a reflection of the understanding that the parties must have the capacity to make a choice and this choice shall be a genuine one;[112]

the requirement of a signature as an ultimate precondition to liability imposition;[113]

the requirement for consideration, as a doctrine for verification of the genuineness of party's choice;[114]

the linkage of the 'good faith' doctrine to such notions as 'duress' and 'fraud', as a reflection of the defectiveness of the party choice;[115] and

the provision according to which an alteration of the bill requires a consent of all parties.[116]

These examples demonstrate how deeply the contemporary negotiable instruments law has been informed by the principle of party autonomy.

5.59 Furthermore, as we have seen throughout Chapter I, one can see the clear centrality of the party autonomy principle within the historical development of the various ancient and medieval payment mechanisms, including under Jewish, Islamic, Roman,

[109] BEA s 17 ('The acceptance of a bill is the signification by the drawee of his assent to the order of the drawee') and 39. UCC § 3-409; UBL art 25. Similarly, Goode speaks about the internal structure of the negotiable instruments law in terms of the 'web of contracts' 'Thus, for example the drawee would not be liable on the instrument if he simply refuses to accept it and in this case the payee's/holder's remedy would be not against the drawee, but against the drawer'. (See McKendrick, *Commercial Law* 518).

[110] BEA s 44(2) (a provision that clarifies that the scenario of 'qualified acceptance' cannot be imputed on the drawer in a one-sided manner, and therefore without his or her consent, it would be considered as an interference with his or her autonomy); UBL art 27.

[111] BEA s 21 ('Every contract on a bill, whether it be the drawer's, the acceptor's, or an indorser's, is incomplete and revocable, until delivery of the instrument'). This essential requirement for each one of the instrument's contracts formation can be presented through the lens of party autonomy: the physical delivery the document singles out a positive action of the signatory party to demonstrate the genuineness of his choice and his willingness to enter into a binding obligation.

[112] BEA s 22; UBL art 22.

[113] BEA ss 23 ('No person is liable as drawer, indorser, or acceptor of a bill who has not signed it as such'), 30 (1), 32. See also McKendrick, *Commercial Law* 542; UBL art 8; UCC § 3-401. Stated in these terms, the requirement of a signature can be presented as inherent doctrine within the structure of negotiable instruments law that reflects a physical act on the part of a signatory party and signifies the genuineness of his choice to enter into a binding obligation.

[114] BEA s 27.

[115] BEA s 29.

[116] BEA s 64(1).

and early European laws. Consider the discussions within Jewish law on the debtor–creditor–drawee three-fold relationship.[117] The requirement, according to which all parties must be physically present at the time the agreement is made (*Ma'amad Shloshtam*),[118] seems to illustrate the principles of the party autonomy under which Jewish law is predicated ensuring that all parties on the instrument make their choice in a relational and genuine manner. The provisions within Jewish law with respect to the debtor's liability release on the part of the creditor,[119] seems to precisely address the point of the nature and scope of creditor's choice.

5.60 By the same token, the structure of the 'mandate' doctrine (which underpinned the payment mechanism of Roman law) followed a relational structure of party autonomy under which one person provided other instructions to do something for him.[120] The institution of the Islamic *Hawale* was fundamentally based on the three-part agreement between the parties.[121] Or, consider the cheque document that emerged in medieval Europe that followed Jewish law on the point of the requirement of the payer-banker-payee to be present at the time the relationship was established.[122] Finally, this was precisely the notion of party autonomy and its scope in the Justinian reform which affected the development of negotiable instruments law.[123]

(c) Party Autonomy in the Context of Parties' Rights and Duties

5.61 One can invoke the following point of objection about the inherent presence of party autonomy within the internal structure of negotiable instruments law: the above-mentioned instances of party autonomy apparently belong to 'ordinary' contractual arrangements. An example of such arrangements would be contractual arrangements that establish such aspects of the parties' relations as the consideration, the timing of delivery, the nature of goods, and so on. One can argue that these arrangements should be delineated from other contractual arrangements that deal with the parties' rights and duties, such as contractual provisions that set a restriction on potential compensation in the case of breach, provisions in relation to possible contract termination, and waiver of contractual rights. The choice of applicable law seems to precisely belong to these sort of arrangements. We contend that there is a paradigmatic difference between an agreement to purchase, say, a kilo of tomatoes in the local store and an agreement to govern future disputes under, say, French law.[124] Can one trace

[117] Chapter II section B.
[118] iIbid. See also B Geva, 'Liability on a Cheque: A Legal History' 33 https://papers.ssrn.com/sol3/papers.cfm?abstract_id=2767542, accessed 20 December 2019 (hereafter Geva, 'Liability on a Cheque').
[119] ibid. See also Geva, *Payment Order* 165.
[120] See Chapter II section D(1). See also Geva, *Payment Order* 201–02.
[121] Geva, *Payment Order* 47–49.
[122] Chapter II section D(2). See also Geva, *Payment Order* 55.
[123] ibid, 232.
[124] For a somewhat related distinction within choice-of-law literature between a 'regular contract' and a contract which addresses parties' rights and duties, see eg A Briggs, 'The Nature or Natures of Agreements Relating to Jurisdiction and of Governing Law' <https://www.asil.org/sites/default/files/pdfs/Which%20Law%20Governs%20Forum%20Selection%20Clauses.pdf>, accessed 20 December 2019.

within the negotiable instruments law provisions that determine the nature and scope of the parties' rights and duties?

The answer to this question is positive. A review of the negotiable instruments law suggests that these are not limited to the 'ordinary' contractual arrangements, but precisely determine the nature and scope of the parties' obligations. It is to this group of arrangements that the choice-of-law clause belongs. Indeed, negotiable instruments law generally enables the parties to give up/waive (or, in the language of the BEA, 'dispense with') their rights and duties under the instrument or alternatively, to extend them. **5.62**

Several examples can be mentioned on this point. First, the parties have the ability to determine their rights and duties in relation to the most essential feature of negotiable instruments- the feature of negotiability.[125] Thus, both the formal and substantive aspects of the document's negotiability can be excluded through the appropriate wordings on the face of the instrument.[126] Under the provisions of the law, the drawer may simply draw an instrument which precludes negotiability.[127] Second, negotiable instruments law allows the drawer or indorser to insert an express stipulation excluding or limiting his or her own liability to the holder, for example, by adding words such as 'sans recours' or 'without recourse to me' after his or her signature words.[128] This stipulation is fairly common in commercial practice and has been coined as 'forfeiting'.[129] **5.63**

Third, the parties' autonomy with respect to the rights and duties extends to the various procedural requirements under the instrument.[130] Thus, the right to presentment can be waived, by simply writing on the bill 'presentment for payment waived'.[131] As we have seen in Chapter I,[132] when an instrument is dishonoured by non-acceptance or non-payment, the holder needs to provide the so-called 'notice of dishonour' to the secondary parties as a precondition to his or her ability to sue them. And yet, similar to the case of presentment, this holder's duty to send a notice of dishonour can be waived.[133] Similarly, the secondary party may insert an express stipulation waiving **5.64**

[125] For a discussion on the formal and substantive aspects of negotiability see, Chapter I section A; Chapter II section F(3).

[126] BEA ss 6(3), 6(5) and 32; UBL arts 31 and 32. *Standard Bank of South Africa Ltd. v Sham Magazine Cenre* [1977] (1) SA 484 (AD). See also Cowen and Gering, *Negotiable Instruments* 62 ('One or both of the two distinguishing characteristics of negotiability, namely transfer of title by mere delivery and the acquisition of a title free from equities, may be excluded in respect of bills, cheques and notes without depriving them of their statutory character as bills, cheques or notes').

[127] BEA s 8(1).

[128] BEA s 16(1). See also UBL art 9 (the drawer can release him or herself from liability) and art 15 (liability release with respect to the indorser).

[129] McKendrick, *Commercial Law* 550, n 157.

[130] On the various procedural requirements in relation to negotiable instruments law, see Chapter I, the text accompanying nn 102–03 and 144–50. See also EP Ellinger et al, *Ellinger's Modern Banking Law* (5th edn, Oxford University Press 2011) 418–22.

[131] BEA s 46(2)(e). See also Gleeson, *Chalmers and Guest* para 6-153; McKendrick, *Commercial Law* (553.

[132] See Chapter I, the text accompanying nn 102–03 and 144–50. See also BEA, ss 49 and 50(2)(b); Gleeson, *Chalmers and Guest* para 6-161.

[133] BEA ss 48 and 50(2)(b). Gleeson, *Chalmers and Guest* para 6-161, 86–89; McKendrick, *Commercial Law* 533.

him or herself of the holder's duty to protest a dishonoured foreign bill[134] and/or waiving or limiting their other liabilities to the holder.[135]

(d) The Consistency with the Historical and Intellectual Development of Negotiable Instruments Law

5.65 Above all, and crucially, the introduction of party autonomy would be consistent with the historical and intellectual foundations of negotiable instruments law. The conceptual origins of this area of law within the foundations of the traditional contracts and movable property categories[136] suggests that the phenomenal success of party autonomy in these categories[137] could be extended to negotiable instruments.

5.66 Indeed, compared to other clauses that deal with parties' rights and duties, the choice-of-law clause appears to be a horse of a different colour. Not only does it permit the parties to set the limitations and extensions of their rights and duties through their choice of the applicable law, but such a choice displaces the state's positive law provisions that would have applied otherwise. A provision limiting the parties' right to terminate the contract seems to be different from the provision setting French law to govern the contract. The latter seems to not just deal with the parties' rights and duties, but also raises a conceptual question about the role of the sovereign in the choice-of-law analysis.[138]

5.67 Yet, unless one follows some grand underlying theory of the choice-of-law question, which focuses on states' sovereignty or states' interests, there is no reason to distinguish between parties' choice of applicable law and other private arrangements as to their rights and duties. As we have seen in Chapter III,[139] while the sovereignty-based approaches to choice-of-law had their hold in the past, they have been losing their ground, precisely because of the advances of the party autonomy principle as a primary rule of the choice-of-law process.

5.68 Choice-of-law thought has simply moved away from the classical *a-la* Beale type of argument, according to which the identity of choice-of-law rules should be grounded on the considerations of states' sovereignty and states' interests. As we have seen,[140] conceptually and practically the criticism has targeted Beale's basic premise, according to which the plaintiff's right can be 'granted' or 'vested' by the law of that state which represents the 'last element' of liability. A similar line of objections has been raised against

[134] BEA s 51(9). See also Gleeson, *Chalmers and Guest* paras 6-153 and 6-161.

[135] BEA ss 16(2) and 51(9). See also Gleeson, *Chalmers and Guest* paras 6-153 and 6-161.

[136] See Chapter II. See also Barak, 'Consideration' 500 (mentions the internal structure of negotiable instruments in terms of an 'amalgam of contract and property doctrine').

[137] On the adoption of party autonomy in the areas of contract and movable property, see Chapter III section B(2).

[138] On the conceptual challenges of for the party autonomy principle from the standpoint of sovereignty-based conception of choice-of-law, see Chapter III section B(2)(a).

[139] On the regression of the sovereignty-based accounts within the modern choice-of-law literature, see Chapter 3 section B(2).

[140] See Chapter III section B(2)(c).

other sovereignty-based accounts of choice-of-law that have favoured the impossible process of tracking the extra-territorial scope of states' legislation interests[141] or have favoured the application of the domestic law–the *lex-fori*.[142]

5.69 The point about the sovereignty-free basis of the choice-of-law question is particularly true with respect to the law of negotiable instruments. As we have seen in Chapter II, the development of this area of law has been rooted in the interaction and transformation of legal values between legal systems and societies. The birth, development, and maturity of this area of law can be attributed to the basic needs of commerce, human interaction and the promotion of transnational values such as predictability and convenience of commercial activity, parties' reasonable expectations, and ease of negotiability of negotiable instruments, rather than related to the interests of a given state.

5.70 The sovereignty-free vision of choice-of-law rules of negotiable instruments would support a dramatic introduction of the party autonomy principle as a governing principle of the choice-of-law process. For this view, the fact that a given act occurs within a territory of a certain sovereign,[143] would not mean that the law of that sovereign shall govern the case. Beale, for example, characterized his support of place of contract formation rule precisely around these lines: 'This doctrine [place of contract formation] gives full scope to the territoriality of law, and enables each sovereign to regulate acts of agreement done in his own territory.'[144] By the same token, the counter-sovereignty position would reject the position that domestic judges shall always apply the sovereign's own law (*lex-fori*) in domestic courts, as a long-arm representative of the sovereign.[145]

2. Party Autonomy in Negotiable Instruments Literature

5.71 Interestingly, but despite the above-stated strong reasons for an introduction of the party autonomy principle as a primary vehicle for choosing the applicable law, the negotiable instruments literature and private international law literature hesitate on this matter. While acknowledging the strong conceptual reasons to introduce this principle within negotiable instruments law, the literature reflects some doubt. Perhaps this literature became aware of the phenomenal success of the party autonomy

141 See eg L Brilmayer, 'Interest Analysis and the Myth of Legislative Intent' (1980) 78 Mich L Rev 392.

142 On the principal objection in choice-of-law literature to *lex-fori*, see Chapter III, the text accompanying nn 5–12.

143 On the various aspects of the traditional states' sovereignty principle, see eg B Simma et al, *The Charter of the United Nations: A Commentary*, vol1 (Oxford University Press 2012) 121–65.

144 See Beale, 'Validity' 271. Accordingly, Beale justified the place of contract formation as the governing choice-of-law rule for negotiable instruments 'It follows that the place of contracting of a contract on negotiable instrument, be it the obligation of the maker, the drawer, or the indorser, is the place where, after signature, the document is first delivered for value.' See JH Beale, *A Treatise on the Conflict of Laws* (Baker, Voorhis & Co 1935) 1048.

145 See eg P Dane, 'The Natural Law Challenge to Choice of Law' in DE Childress (ed) *The Role of Ethics in International Law* (Oxford University Press 2012) 142, 154.

principle within the contract choice-of-law rules and other areas of law. Consider the intriguing discussions on this matter in what are considered to be the two leading textbooks in English-speaking literature on negotiable instruments and choice-of-law: Chalmers[146] and Dicey and Morris[147] outlined in the following sub-sections (a) and (b).

(a) The Possibility of Party Autonomy in Chalmers

5.72 The possibility of incorporating the party autonomy principle within the choice-of-law rules of negotiable instruments law has been introduced in the leading text on negotiable instruments in the following terms:

> It would no doubt in theory be possible for a party to stipulate expressly on the instrument that his rights, duties and liabilities are to be governed by a law other than that mentioned in s. 72 [reference to choice-of-law section within UK BEA], and effect might then have to be given to this choice [footnoting reference to *Centrax* case]. But such stipulations are never encountered.[148]

5.73 One notices some hesitation in the above-mentioned statement. On the one hand, it says that, in principle, the party autonomy principle can be introduced into the choice-of-law analysis in a way that the parties' explicit choice would prevail over the ordinary choice-of-law rules set in the BEA. It seems that the author acknowledges that such a choice would be consistent with the very nature of the negotiable instruments law and would acquire a predominant status over the statutory choice-of-law provision set in s 72. Yet, on the other hand, the statement mentions that the court only 'might' honour such choice and it uses fairly strong language about the absence of the party autonomy principle in practice.

5.74 Furthermore, it would appear that the possibility of expressed choice of applicable law has been limited in the author's wording to cases where the applicable law is stipulated on the negotiable instrument itself ('stipulate expressly on the instrument'[149]) rather than having a choice-of-law clause within the underlying agreement under which the negotiable instrument is issued. Finally, it should be noted that Chalmers favourably acknowledges the possibility of the parties to stipulate on the instrument a non-state provision such as the UNIBNC.[150]

5.75 *Centrax*[151] is a case that merits attention. Paradoxically, this case represents a situation where the explicit stipulation of the applied law has been made precisely within the underlying contract to govern parties' rights and duties with respect to the negotiable instrument. In this case the negotiable instruments (cheques) accompanied the underlying agreement. This agreement stipulated both the law governing the

146 Gleeson, *Chalmers and Guest*.
147 *Dicey and Morris*.
148 See Gleeson, *Chalmers and Guest* para 12-004.
149 ibid. Later in the quoted passage Chalmers also says 'It is submitted that ... nor could any express choice of law outside the instrument be regarded as valid' (ibid, 586).
150 ibid, 586–87. For further discussion on the UNIBNC see Chapter I, the text accompanying nn 73–75.
151 *Centrax Ltd v Citibank NA* [1999] EWCA Civ 892 (hereafter *Centrax Ltd v Citibank 1999*).

underlying agreement (New York) and the law governing the negotiable instruments (England).[152]

Without delving into the debate about the scope and the linguistic interpretation of the above-mentioned negotiable instrument's choice-of-law provision (which directed the application of English law) and its relation to the choice-of-law provision of the underlying agreement (which directed the application of New York law), it would appear that the court in *Centrax* had no difficulty with the negotiable instrument's provision as a matter of principle. Indeed, the negotiable instrument's choice-of-law clause appeared within the provisions of the underlying agreement, rather than on the face of the instrument itself. And yet (and in contradiction to Chalmers' principal objection), the trial judge[153] and the Court of Appeal[154] in *Centrax* seem to have clearly acknowledged the possibility for the *immediate parties* (ie within the relationship between drawer-drawee and drawer-payee[155]) to agree which law would govern the various aspects of the negotiable instrument in their underlying agreement, including such aspects as the instrument's validity and effect.[156] Since in this case the underlying agreement took place between immediate parties (ie within the relationships between the drawer and drawee), the negotiable instrument's choice-of-law provision was validated. **5.76**

(b) The Possibility of Party Autonomy in Dicey and Morris

The possibility of incorporating the party autonomy principle into negotiable instruments law has been acknowledged in the leading textbook on choice-of-law as well. The authors have stated their position about this possibility in the following terms: **5.77**

> There is nothing in the Bills of Exchange Act 1882 which expressly prevents the parties from choosing the law to govern an instrument, but there is nothing which permits it either. However, though it may be rare or non-existent in principle, unacceptable (at least for issues to which s.72 does not apply) if it appears on the face of the instrument [reference to *Chalmers*] ... Providing [sic] anyone becoming a party to the instrument can see from the instrument itself what are going to be his rights and obligations (and these can be ascertained by reference to the law chosen on the face of it) there is no compelling reason why such a choice should not now be accepted [reference to *Zebrarise*], but such a proposition is controversial.[157]

[152] ibid, 559–60. According to this negotiable instrument's provision, 'any action or dispute between the parties regarding any Payment Instrument shall be governed by and interpreted according to the laws of the country or state in which the Drawee of such Payment Instrument is located'.

[153] *Centrax Ltd v Citibank NA* [1998] Royal Courts of Justice Strand WC2A 2LL (1998) [15] (Clarke J) (hereafter *Centrax Ltd v Citibank 1998*).

[154] *Centrax Ltd v Citibank 1999.*

[155] This point has been stressed by the trial judge (See *Centrax Ltd v Citibank NA 1998* [15]). For further discussion on the immediate/remote parties divide under the instrument, see the text accompanying n 171.

[156] *Centrax Ltd v Citibank NA 1999* 563 (Ward LJ), 565 (Roch LJ). In a similar vein, more recently the Singapore Court of Appeal held that an arbitration clause to adjudicate dispute over the negotiable instrument would be valid if expressly made within the provisions of the underlying agreement between the parties. See *Rals Internaiotnal Pte Ltd v Cagsa Bi Risparnio di Parma Piacenza Spa* [2016] SGCA 53.

[157] *Dicey and Morris* 2078. It should be noted that although the factual situation in the *Zebrarise* case (*Zebrarise Ltd and another v de Nieffe* [2004] EWHC 1842 (Comm)) does not involve an explicit choice-of law clause, the court in *obiter dictum* made some supportive comments about the possibility of

5.78 As we can see, Chalmers' ambivalence with respect to the party autonomy principle can be witnessed in Dicey and Morris, as well. Although being somewhat enthusiastic about the possibility of the principle's incorporation, the authors are self-reserved and allow the doubts to speak. In fact, Dicey and Morris' analysis of the party autonomy principle seems to be of a more restrictive character than that of that Chalmers. While similar to Chalmers, Dicey and Morris acknowledge the conceptual validity of the argument about the incorporation of the party autonomy principle on the instrument itself, they restrict the possible scope of its application to issues that are not covered by s 72[158] and also mention that such an incorporation would be 'controversial'.

5.79 The more restrictive position with respect to the party autonomy principle can also be witnessed in Dicey and Morris' treatment of non-state law. Thus, the authors explicitly reject Chalmers' proposition regarding the potential possibility of the parties to agree on the UNIBNC as a legitimate framework to adjudicate their dispute.[159] In pointing out that the UNIBNC does not represent an obligatory law in United Kingdom,[160] the authors seem to refer to the state's sovereignty principle and the conceptual difficulty that it creates in applying non-state law in domestic courts. This vision of choice-of-law question rules excludes the possibility of non-state law application.

5.80 Finally, it is worth mentioning that the older edition of *Dicey and Morris* from 1987[161] had a more significant discussion on the possibility of applying party autonomy to negotiable instruments law. While acknowledging the possibility of incorporating the party autonomy principle, the authors have limited the scope of the parties' potential choice to the following two connecting territorial factors: (1) place of contracting; and (2) place of contractual performance.[162] This position imposes a significant burden on the parties and restricts the pool of potential adjudicative frameworks to a two-fold option.

3. The Scope of Party Autonomy: A Proposal

5.81 We suggest that there is no reason to exclude the party autonomy principle from the choice-of-law rules of negotiable instruments. Our suggestion would be to name this principle as a *primary rule* of the choice-of-law process. Indeed, the incorporation of the party autonomy principle into negotiable instruments law might sound 'unnatural' to the current practice of commerce and could be met with somewhat dogmatic opposition from scholars who have traditionally simply discarded this possibility.

incorporating the party autonomy principle to negotiable instruments, expressly referring to the mentioned replica in *Dicey and Morris* [36]).

158 Later in this chapter, we will say more on the scope of s 72 and the relation of this section to the developments within the modern choice-of-law doctrine. See section B(3).

159 *Dicey and Morris* 2078, n 1565.

160 As the authors have pointed out, the position to incorporate UNIBNC under the party autonomy principle 'This view cannot, however, be accepted given that the United Kingdom is not a party to the Convention, which is not in any event yet in force' (ibid).

161 Collins (ed) *Dicey and Morris on the Conflict of Laws* (11th edn, Sweet & Maxwell 1987) 1311.

162 ibid, 1311.

Thus, for example, in the 1993 edition of *Cheshire & North*, the authors simply, and without much elaboration, stated 'There is no right of the parties to select their own governing law'.[163]

There are no conceptual or practical reasons why negotiable instruments law, underpinned by traditional contract law and movable property categories, would not follow these categories and warmly adopt this principle. In fact, as we have contended, the internal structure and purposes of negotiable instruments law would be well served through the introduction of party autonomy. The incorporation of this principle clearly sets up parties' expectations as to the framework to govern their relationships and thus promotes the value of predictability and certainty, which is so deeply embedded in the internal structure of this area of law to enhance the negotiability and circulation of the instrument. **5.82**

The literature on the negotiable instruments law has rightly indentified that the internal structure of this law involves not one, but several contracts: not just the contract of drawer to serve as a type of a guarantee on the instrument, but also a contract of the acceptor to honour it.[164] Similarly, the nature of the indorsement creates a new contract under which the indorser (similar to the drawer), through his or her signature and delivery, creates a new contract.[165] **5.83**

The internal structure of negotiable instruments law has been explicitly recognized by the various choice-of-law frameworks: the BEA, Geneva Conventions, and Article 3 of UCC.[166] Subsequently, the party autonomy principle can potentially be applied on each one of the possible contracts. In other words, it is submitted that the drawer can stipulate the identity of the applied law in the original contract between him or her and the payee and the acceptor might not agree to that applicable law and offer another. The same point applies to the payee who becomes the indorser of the instrument and who can stipulate a different applicable framework on the instrument than what was specified by the drawer. **5.84**

Given the history and underlying nature of negotiable instruments law, we see no reason why the drawer, for example, would not be able to write the following phrase 'to be governed by UK Law' or 'UK law applies' on the instrument, and the payee by receiving the document would agree to that term. The same point applies with respect to the relationship between the payee and drawee: if the drawee accepts the document with an indication 'to be governed by UK law', that means that his or her relationship with the payee is to be governed by UK law. Indeed, the nature of the negotiable instrument requires predictability and hence we accept the point that the choice-of-law provision must be drafted to a strict form which 'does not leave room for any ambiguity of **5.85**

163 *Cheshire & North* 123. In similar vein Lord Wilberforce in the *Nova* case (*Nova (Jersy) Knt Ltd v Kamgarn Spinnerei GMBh* [1977] 1 WLR 713) briefly commented that a potential arbitration clause on the face of the bill would not be given effect ('The bills themselves of course contained no arbitration clause (they would not be valid bills if they did') (ibid, 716).

164 See Chapter IV section B.

165 For an exposition and discussion of the drawer's, acceptor's, and indorser's contracts within the internal structure of negotiable instruments, see Chapter I section C. See also Chapter IV sections B and C.

166 For a discussion of this point, see Chapter IV sections B and C.

interpretation'.[167] The above-mentioned statements—'to be governed by UK Law' or 'UK law applies'—appear to meet this requirement.

5.86 The above-suggested specification on the face of the instrument does not undermine any of its essential features.[168] It shall not be considered to be a part of the formal requirements of the instrument.[169] Rather, choice-of-law autonomy would find its place alongside other provisions of negotiable instrument law that allow the parties to determine the scope (by limitation or extension) of their rights and duties under the instrument, such as the possibility of excluding the various aspects of negotiability, the holder's requirements, and the practice of forfeiting.[170] Also, a choice-of-law clause would not challenge the 'unconditional' feature of the instrument.[171]

5.87 Similar to other legitimate arrangements between the parties under the existing law, the party autonomy principle determines parties' rights and duties. It specifies the applicable law to govern their potential dispute under the instrument. The physical face of the instrument is the primary place for such a specification. While the underlying contract between the immediate parties[172] may include a choice of the applicable law, such a choice cannot affect the position of the remote parties who might not be aware of the provisions of the underlying contract. As long as the language of the choice-of-law clause is not limited to a specific party, the creator of the instrument (that is either drawer or maker) can bind the subsequent parties to the applicable law. After all, the subsequent parties have the option of reviewing the instrument and making a choice as to whether to accept the obligations under it or not.

5.88 Finally, it does not seem that the presence of the choice-of-law clause on the face of the instrument shall affect the status of the HDC. From this perspective, the choice-of-law clause would be similar to other provisions that affect the parties' obligations under the existing law. While the presence of these provisions does not affect the good faith status of the holder, the same rule must apply to the choice-of-law clause. These provisions simply set a framework for parties' future obligations and do not necessarily suggest or indicate that the instrument would not be honoured.

5.89 One can object to the suggested proposal by reference to formalistic reasoning, arguing that the incorporation of the party autonomy principle has not been explicitly

[167] See eg McKendrick, *Commercial Law* 517 (comments about the form of the instrument in the following terms 'the document is traditionally concise and no greater in size that enables it to be conveniently carried and transferred'. See also Collins (ed) *Dicey and Morris on the Conflict of Laws* (11th edn, Sweet & Maxwell 1987) 1311.

[168] For a presentation of the essential features of the instrument, see Chapter I sections A and C.

[169] For the formal requirements under the instrument, see BEA s 3(2). For further discussion (and a comparative analysis) on the form requirements within various systems, see Chapter I sections C, D, and E.

[170] For a discussion of these provisions, see section B(1)(c).

[171] For a discussion of the 'unconditional' feature of the instrument, see Chapter I section C.

[172] The term 'immediate parties' means parties with a direct relation between them. Crawford, for example, has characterized the division between 'immediate' and 'remote' parties under the instrument in the following terms 'The maker and the payee of a note are usually immediate parties, as are the drawer & the payee of a cheque.... However, the payee & the drawee of a cheque are ordinarily remote parties, as would be the indorser and endorsee, or the acceptor & payee'). See Crawford, *Law of Banking and Payment* para 26-5. See also B Geva, *Financing Consumer Sales and Product Defences in Canada and the United States* (Carswell 1984) 81–164.

mentioned within the BEA's choice-of-law provision s 72 and suggest that it had been considered and consequently rejected.[173] Indeed, according to this line of reasoning, the scholarship has tended to avoid the application of modern choice-of-law thought to the area of negotiable instruments.

Consider, for example, the possibility of implementing the MSR principle, which we discuss in Chapter VI. This principle has not been mentioned under the provisions of s 72 of the BEA. Accordingly, in order to justify its application, it has been argued that the MSR principle needs to be explicitly mentioned within the section's provisions.[174] Furthermore, since this section is based on the precedents of judicial decisions prior to the BEA's legislation, it has been argued that it would be implausible to draw an analogy to the developments within the contract and movable property doctrines[175] where the advances of the MSR principle are vivid. **5.90**

Without delving into how much this objection holds with respect to the MSR principle,[176] it would appear that the literature on the question of objections to potentially incorporating new choice-of-law rules, alongside those set in BEA s 72 are inconsistent. This leaves room for incorporating party autonomy as a governing rule of the choice-of-law process. It has been acknowledged that s 72 is not an exhaustive provision to govern all aspects of negotiable instruments law and that other choice-of-law rules could be developed.[177] **5.91**

In fact, sometimes, the ambivalence in the literature on this point is striking. While hesitating about the possibility of applying choice-of-law rules of the contract law doctrine,[178] at the same time it acknowledges and explicitly leaves the door open for a direct incorporation of the party autonomy principle: 'That is not to say, however, that the way in which those rules [contract law doctrine] have developed (eg as to recognition of party autonomy) may not be a useful source of inspiration in this context.'[179] Indeed, as we saw earlier,[180] both leading textbooks on choice-of-law and **5.92**

[173] See eg C Nyguist, 'A Spectrum Theory of Negotiability' (1995) 78 Mary L Rev 897, 899 ('Negotiable instruments law is viewed as self-contained and self-sufficient').

[174] Collins (ed) *Dicey and Morris on the Conflict of Laws* (11th edn, Sweet & Maxwell 1987) 1310.

[175] See eg *Dicey and Morris* 2078 (mentions that 'filling of the gaps in the conflict of laws' provisions of the 1882 Act, to date, been largely carry out on the basis of drawing analogies from s 72 of that Act rather than applying the more flexible approaches [MSR principle]'. Or, as the authors put it in a different place, 'choice of law rules for contracts in general cannot be applied with ease to bills of exchange, it is suggested that the appropriate course in such cases is to provide analogy with the provisions of s 72, at least because these provisions to a considerable extent reproduce the effect of decided cases' [ibid, 2080, reference to *Irvani* case omitted].

[176] We will return to the discussion on the clear trace of this principle within negotiable instrument's case law and the possibility of incorporating the MSR principle within this area of law, see Chapter VI section, A.

[177] See eg *Dicey and Morris* 2077; see also Gleeson, *Chalmers and Guest* 584 (acknowledges that s 72 does not purport to cover all matters within negotiable instruments law).

[178] See *Dicey and Morris* 2077 (mentions that 'Nor can appropriate principles always be found in common rules developed in contracts generally').

[179] See *Dicey and Morris* 2077, n 1563 (emphasis added). Chalmers also seems to leave room for incorporating the party autonomy principle. As he stated with respect to areas that are not covered by choice-of-law provision of BEA, 'The law to be applied in such cases has to be delivered by analogy from the express provisions of the section, or *from the general principles of the conflict of laws applicable to contractual obligations*, or from judicial decisions' (Gleeson, *Chalmers and Guest* 584, emphasis added).

[180] See section B(2)(b).

negotiable instruments acknowledge the possibility of incorporating the party autonomy principle, despite the fact that it does not explicitly appear within the provisions of BEA s 72.

5.93 At this point, allow us to return to the conceptual and practical puzzles of the party autonomy principle which has emerged in choice-of-law literature, outlined in Chapter III.[181] The reference to the underlying nature and historical evolution of the negotiable instruments law addresses the various sovereignty-based conceptual objections to party autonomy.[182]

5.94 As to the debate on non-state/state law in the choice-of-law literature,[183] our position can be stated as follows. We acknowledge the tendency of the choice-of-law thought[184] to grant the litigating parties an option to choose an adjudicative framework that does not represent an official law of any state. At the same time, we recognize that the literature has been fairly cautious about such an incorporation. Indeed, the lessons of reality have shown that even where the parties are free to make a choice of a non-state provision, they do it on exceptionally rare occasions.[185]

5.95 Specifically, it has been proposed that the incorporation of the non-state provisions under the party autonomy principle should be limited to those frameworks that are predictable enough and comprehensive enough in a way that would operate similarly to 'regular' legislative provisions or, alternatively, similar to the mechanism of judicial precedents in common law. As one of the choice-of-law commentators put it with respect to the possibility of incorporating the non-state law: 'the ultimate test ought to be to ask whether the system of rules chosen is specific and clear enough for a court to be able to apply it to the issues which arise between the parties'.[186]

5.96 These thresholds of 'predictability' and 'comprehensiveness' as requirements would probably exclude from choice-of-law analysis the application of the amorphous merchant law (*lex mercatoria*)[187] and perhaps would accept the fairly comprehensive

[181] On the conceptual and practical puzzles involved in the application of the party autonomy principle, see Chapter III section B(2)(a).
[182] ibid.
[183] ibid.
[184] See eg Hague Principles on Choice of Law in International Commercial Contracts, 2015 art 3 <https://www.hcch.net/en/instruments/conventions/full-text/?cid=135>, accessed 20 December, 2019 (hereafter Hague Principles).
[185] Thus, the lessons of the field of international arbitration teach us that, despite the theoretical possibility to incorporate a non-state framework to adjudicate their dispute, the arbitrating parties generally avoid this option. Thus, the statistics speak to only 1% of cases in which the parties have opted for a non-state framework (see B Hayward, *Conflict of Laws and Arbitral Discretion* (Oxford University Press 2017) 208).
[186] A Briggs, *Agreements on Jurisdiction and Choice of Law* (Oxford University Press 2008) 388. See also J Basedow, 'The Law of Open Societies-Private Ordering and Public Regulation of International Relations' (2013) 360 Rec des Cours 9, 171–73 (discusses the strong opposition that non-state party autonomy has raised in the academic community).
[187] This would explain, for example, the unpopularity of the Inter-American Convention on the Law Applicable to International Contracts. Article 10 of this Convention mentions the 'general principles of international commercial law', and therefore seems to refer to *lex-mercatoria*. For a discussion on this point, see eg R Michaels, 'Non-State Law', 7 < https://scholarship.law.duke.edu/faculty_scholarship/3227/>, accessed 20 December 2019. For further discussion on the mythical *lex-mercatoria* within the specific context of negotiable instruments law, see Chapter II section F(1).

provisions of the UNIDROIT Principles of International Commercial Contracts[188] as potential candidates for non-state law under the party autonomy principle. In a similar vein, it would be possible to incorporate several comprehensive and fairly predictable frameworks of religious law that through the centuries have created a body of law that has been comparable with common law in comprehensiveness and sophistication.[189]

Within the field of the negotiable instruments law the obvious candidate for such incorporation (in line with Dicey and Morris and opposing Chalmers[190]) would be the UNIBNC. As we have seen earlier in this book,[191] this body of law provides a comprehensive framework for a wide range of situations within negotiable instruments law. Furthermore, as we have also seen, it can be argued that the present substantive structures of negotiable instruments' provisions around the globe could be roughly classified between two major principal camps: the Anglo-American camp and the Continental camp.[192] As a means to avoid what would be considered by one of the parties as a harsh concession of his or her substantive law to the other party law,[193] the parties can employ a third substantive framework—the UNIBNC—as tie-breaker between the two rival camps.[194] **5.97**

How about the possibility of incorporating the various frameworks of payments' mechanisms, which existed during the historical development and intellectual maturity of the negotiable instruments law, outlined in Chapter II? We are hesitant on this point. Our detailed analysis of the payment mechanisms within Jewish, Islamic, Roman, and medieval European law has suggested that by and large they may not meet the requirements of predictability and comprehensiveness to provide a suitable framework to adjudicate the parties' rights and duties in the contemporary reality. While providing the ultimate basis for intellectual development and maturity of the contemporary negotiable instruments law, these mechanisms are not matured enough, too debatable within their own framework, and too distinct to be applied in contemporary reality of negotiable instruments. **5.98**

Consider the tripartite relationship between employer, employee, and the money changer, and the potential impact of this relationship on the contemporary law of negotiable instruments, within Jewish law.[195] Generally Jewish law has a rule that prohibits **5.99**

[188] UNIDROIT Principles of International Commercial Contracts. See <https://www.unidroit.org/instruments/commercial-contracts/unidroit-principles-2016 >, accessed 20 December 2019.

[189] A representative example of such sophistication could be traced, for example, in the Jewish law of unjust enrichment. See eg EJ Weinrib, 'Planting Another's Field: Unrequested Improvements Under Jewish Law' in J Neyers and M McInnes (eds), *Understanding Unjust Enrichment* (Hart Publishing, 2004) 221.

[190] See section B(2)(b).

[191] See Chapter I, the text accompanying nn 76–78.

[192] See Chapter I sections C, D, and E.

[193] This is in fact a common practice within the field of international arbitration—We are thankful to Dr Johannes Landbrecht for raising this point with us.

[194] Accordingly, we would follow on this point the general tendency of the systems to eliminate the so-called 'connection' requirement (see Chapter III, the text accompanying n 48), which imposes on the parties an obligation to demonstrate some 'relation' to the chosen law/framework. For liberalization (and even elimination) tendencies with respect to this requirement, see eg G Rühl, 'Party Autonomy in the Private International Law of Contracts: Transatlantic Convergence and Economic Efficiency' in E Gottschalk et al (eds) *Conflict of Laws in a Globalized World* (Cambridge 2099) 153, 155–76; Hague Principles art 3.

[195] See Chapter II section B.

an employer from delaying his or her payments to the employee.[196] Yet, the case where the employer directs the employee to receive payment from a money changer seems to provide an exception to this rule. In the extensive debates that have taken place over the centuries, Jewish law thinkers have debated the nature of the tripartite relationship (employee, employer, and money changer) involving complex questions such as the employee's explicit and implicit consent to the tripartite arrangement, the legal status of the money changer towards the employee, and the question of the continued liability of the employer. How does it relate to the contemporary sophisticated mechanism of negotiable instruments law under which the debtor ('drawer') delegates his or her obligation towards the creditor ('payee') to a third party (drawee bank)? Can it be brought to the contemporary reality of a non-agrarian society? What is the significance of the labour law aspect in the above-mentioned tripartite relationship, which has not been addressed by Jewish law thinkers? The context seems to be very different. The underlying rationale appears to be easily debatable, unclear, and, as such, it seems to be hard to grasp and implement for particular cases of present-day reality.

5.100 Ceasing looking at the question of choice-of-law through the prism of sovereignty-based accounts would allow us to view the party autonomy principle in a similar way to other private arrangements between the parties with respect to their rights and duties, arrangements that are already present within the internal structure of negotiable instruments law. The incorporation of this principle would be consistent with its advances in other areas of law. And finally, its introduction as a primary rule of the choice-of-law process would correlate with the sovereignty-free origins and development of negotiable instruments law. Having originated within the practice of international commerce and commercial practice, rather than as a reflection of the sovereign's will and promotion of particular sovereign's interests, the party autonomy principle seems to be a natural home for negotiable instruments. Accordingly, our suggestion would be an incorporation of the following general principle for choice-of-law rules of negotiable instruments:

> The governing principle of choice-of-law rules shall be party autonomy. It can appear on the face of the document or within the provisions of the underlying contract between immediate parties. The party can choose a non-state law, given this framework is predictable and comprehensive enough, akin to a 'regular' law.

[196] See Chapter II section B. See also Geva, *Payment Order* 159–86; Geva, 'Liability on a Cheque'.

VI

Choice-of-Law Rules in the Absence of Party Autonomy

The Most Significant Relationship Principle

We hope that, in the near future, commercial practice and scholarship will adopt our suggestion to incorporate the party autonomy principle as the primary vehicle of choice-of-law rules relating to negotiable instruments. However, cases need to be decided in the meantime. Which law should apply to adjudicate the parties' rights and duties when the parties have not selected one? This chapter aims to answer this question. **6.01**

Similar to Chapter V, our analysis challenges the basic presumptions and underpinnings of traditional choice-of-law rules, which have not changed much over the last three centuries. We challenge the traditional orthodoxies, expose their flawed foundations, and suggest a reconsideration of the choice-of-law rules derived from them. In this way, our adherence to the 'radical overhaul' call in the area of negotiable instruments is not limited to the introduction of the party autonomy principle but extends to scenarios where the parties have not expressly agreed on the identity of the law to be applied. **6.02**

Our discussion in this chapter proceeds as follows. First, we favour the extension of the popular 'most significant relationship' (MSR) principle to negotiable instruments law. We contend that a careful evaluation of the nature of this principle and the objections raised against it point towards its incorporation into this area of law. We reveal clear examples of the MSR principle within the traditional and contemporary case law of negotiable instruments, which suggest that this principle has always played a role in the choice-of-law mechanics of the field (section A). Second, we make some suggestions as to the operational mechanics of the MSR principle. Specifically, we propose that the principle should not operate alone but in combination with flexible presumptions, which provide points of departure for choice-of-law analysis (section B). **6.03**

A. The Extension of the MSR Principle to Negotiable Instruments Law

6.04 Notwithstanding the evident popularity of the MSR principle as a governing principle in the various areas of law outlined in Chapter III,[1] so far negotiable instruments law has remained immune from its application. On the basis of its alleged 'special nature', it has been argued that the intellectual development and conceptual foundations of negotiable instruments law depart from the essentials of the traditional private law categories of contract and movable property. Consequently, the contemporary choice-of-law doctrines of contract and movable property are considered non-applicable to negotiable instruments law.

6.05 Yet, as we saw in Chapter II, the premise of the 'special nature' of negotiable instruments law and its departure from the underpinnings of the laws of contract and property can be challenged and reconsidered. In the same manner that the MSR principle has been incorporated within other private law categories, there is no reason to exclude its operation from negotiable instruments law. The opposite is true: the historical development of the field and its internal structure support such incorporation.

6.06 Two related objections have been raised in the literature against the incorporation of the MSR principle into negotiable instruments law. First, its incorporation is at odds with contemporary choice-of-law frameworks and case law. Second, the incorporation of the principle would jeopardize predictability and undermine negotiability of the instrument. The ensuing sections examine these objections and demonstrate their flaws.

1. Assessing Objection 1: Inconsistency with Existing Law and Case Law

(a) Inconsistency with Contemporary Choice-of-Law Frameworks

6.07 It has been argued that the MSR principle cannot be incorporated within choice-of-law analysis as it has not been explicitly mentioned within the provisions of the UK choice-of-law provision, that is, Bills of Exchange Act (BEA) s 72. By referring to legislative history and raising the point that the section's categories were based on judicial determinations, pre-BEA scholars have pointed out that an incorporation of the MSR principle would be considered a deviation from an established precedent.[2] Accordingly, it has been argued that although it is central to other private law categories, the MSR principle cannot serve as a guiding principle for matters and issues that have not been covered by the BEA's provisions. As Dicey and Morris put it,

[1] See Chapter III section B(3).

[2] See Collins (ed) *Dicey and Morris on the Conflict of Laws* (11th edn, Sweet & Maxwell 1987) 1310. For a discussion on BEA as a reflection of pre-existing case law, see Chapter I, the text accompanying nn 40–47.

> choice of law rules for contracts in general cannot be applied with ease to bills of exchange, it is suggested that the appropriate course in such cases is to provide analogy with the provisions of s.72, at least because these provisions to a considerable extent reproduce the effect of decided cases.[3]

This justification for ignoring the general contract choice-of-law rules, underpinned by the MSR principle, is plainly unconvincing. As we have seen in the introductory section to this book,[4] Dicey and Morris frankly admits the need for a 'dramatic overhaul' of the choice-of-law rule. This is indeed one of the main aims of this book. While we do not suggest deviating from the existing law, a comprehensive reform is required. It is puzzling why, in contrast to their willingness to incorporate the principle of party autonomy that is entirely foreign to s 72,[5] Dicey and & Morris do not extend this line of reasoning to another popular principle—the MSR principle. They put it in slightly different terms: **6.08**

> Otherwise, as appears below, the filling of the gaps in the conflict of laws provisions of the 1882 Act, to date, have been largely carried out on the basis of drawing analogies from s.72 of that Act rather than by applying the more flexible approaches inherent in the developed 'proper' doctrine [MSR principle].[6]

But why refute the MSR principle? Having accepted the possibility of an incorporation of the party autonomy principle into negotiable instrument law, the authors should have considered a further logical development of the field—the incorporation of the MSR principle. The full stop after the introduction of party autonomy suggested by the authors is puzzling. The strong call in the literature for a dramatic overhaul of the subject seems to be fatal to this line of reasoning. **6.09**

(b) Inconsistency with Case Law

Traces of the MSR principle are evident throughout choice-of-law decisions in the area of negotiable instruments. This challenges the second part of the objection regarding the absence of the MSR principle from case law. Consider, first, the American *Hyatt v Bank of Kentucky*[7] (1871) case, cited in the Second Restatement as supporting the rigid connecting factor of place of delivery for the secondary parties on the instrument.[8] In this case, the maker executed a promissory note payable to the plaintiff in Louisiana. Subsequently, the plaintiff changed his residence to Kentucky and indorsed the note there to a local Kentucky indorsee, the note holder and the defendant in this case. The court stressed that the reasonable expectations of the parties under the indorsement contract diverged from the reasonable expectations of the parties under the primary **6.10**

[3] Collins, Harris (eds) *Dicey, Morris and Collins on the Conflict of Laws* (15th edn, Sweet & Maxwell 2012) 2078 (hereafter *Dicey and Morris*).

[4] For authors' support of the radical overhaul, see Chapter III section C.

[5] For a discussion of this point, see Chapter V section B(2).

[6] *Dicey and Morris* 2078 (make reference to *Robinson* and *Moulis* cases). For our discussion of the *Robinson* and *Moulis* cases as grounded on the MSR principle, see the text accompanying nn 23–29.

[7] *Hyatt v Bank of Kentucky*, 71 Ky, 193 (1871) (hereafter *Hyatt v Bank of Kentucky*).

[8] *Restatement of Conflict of Laws* (1971; revised 1986 and 1988, American Law Institute) § 215, Reporter's Note (hereafter Second Restatement).

contract.[9] It had followed the connecting factor of the place of delivery, which is now set in Article 214 of the Second Restatement. Kentucky law was applied as reflecting the place where the instrument was delivered to the indorsee. Yet, the court made reference to what appears to be the MSR principle by mentioning the residency of the parties at the time of their interaction, the place of indorsement and the place where the money was received.[10]

6.11 *Hennenlotter v De Orvananos*[11] (1921) is another case cited by the Second Restatement in support of the rigid rule of the place of delivery for the secondary parties under the instruments.[12] This case involved cheques signed by Mexican drawers (the defendants) to the order of Mexican payees (the plaintiffs), delivered in Mexico and payable in New York.[13] While mentioning the rule that the obligation of the drawer of a bill of exchange is determined by the place of delivery, the court once again made comments in direction that very much resemble the MSR principle: 'it was a Mexican transaction as to all parties except the drawee'.[14] The language (Spanish) in which the instruments were written was also mentioned.[15] Based on this reasoning, Mexican law was applied.

6.12 *Hyatt* and *Hennenlotter* are not exceptions. Traces of the MSR principle can be found within other decisions cited by the Second Restatement, despite the fact that these have been cited in the context of supporting the Second Restatement's rigid rules.[16] Thus, for example, in *Walling v Cushman* (1920),[17] the court made it clear that the connecting factor of the place of delivery to determine the liability of the secondary party under the instrument can potentially be overturned and is 'not applicable when it appears from the special circumstances that the parties intended otherwise'.[18] Similarly, in *Greenlee v Hardin* (1930),[19] the court commented that the connecting factor of the place of payment to determine the liability of the primary party under the instrument is not a rigid rule and only serves as a point of departure for judicial analysis of the circumstances of the case. In the court's words:

> This presumption [the place of payment], however, is not absolute. And will be controlled by the actual truth of the case, when ascertained, or, in other words, by

[9] *Hyatt v Bank of Kentucky* 198: 'A party may know when he indorses a paper in Kentucky executed in Louisiana that the law of the latter state imposes a different liability from the law of Kentucky, and still his assignment, being of itself an independent contract.'

[10] *Hyatt v Bank of Kentucky* 200: 'In the present case the Bank of Kentucky [the indorsee/holder] at the date of the assignment was and now corporation in this state. Hyatt [the indorser] was a resident of this state, and the indorsement made at the bank in Louisville [Kentucky], and the money there received for it.'

[11] *Hennenlotter v De Orvananos*, 114 Misc 333 (1921) (hereafter *Hennenlotter v De Orvananos*).

[12] Second Restatement § 215 (Reporter's Note).

[13] *Hennenlotter v De Orvananos* 334.

[14] ibid, 336.

[15] ibid, 334. For observations on the significance of the language within the operational mechanics of the MSR principle, see Chapter III, the text accompanying nn 103–07.

[16] Second Restatement §§ 214 and 215 (Reporter's Note).

[17] 238 Mass 62 (1920) (hereafter *Walling v Cushman*).

[18] ibid, 68.

[19] *Greenlee v Hardin*, 157 Miss 229 (1930) (hereafter *Greenlee v Hardin*).

the intention of the parties, to be collected from the contract itself, and all the surrounding circumstances.[20]

There is a similar trajectory underlying judicial reasoning in Canada. A leading Canadian decision, *Canada Life v CIBC*,[21] can be explained on the MSR principle. Technically, the decision was based on a problematic distinction between 'inland' and 'foreign' bills and a somewhat vague discussion of the 'residency' requirement under the BEA s 4. Both justifications were plainly unconvincing and did not reflect the court's underlying reasoning in this case. Rather, the decision appears to be based on the nature of the particular relationship between the parties and the evaluation of this interaction, and the surrounding circumstances.[22] **6.13**

The MSR principle can be traced to one of the earliest choice-of-law decisions of the English courts—*Robinson v Bland*[23] (1760). This case involved a bill of exchange ('bill') given in Paris by one English resident to another in relation to a gambling debt. Clearly adopting the MSR principle, Lord Mansfield commented that, 'The parties had a view to the laws of England'[24] and that 'the payment is to be in England: it is an English bill of exchange, and so intended by the parties'.[25] Stated in these terms, this early vision of the choice-of-law rules of negotiable instruments links itself to the notion of the parties' reasonable expectations. Having nothing to do with state sovereignty and state interests or considerations, it disconnects the choice-of-law analysis from France, the place of the contract formation, and the interests of France to govern acts that occur within its territory. This understanding of the case has been recognized in the contemporary choice-of-law literature. While rejecting the application of the MSR principle to negotiable instruments law, it has admitted the MSR principle's basis of *Robinson v Bland*.[26] **6.14**

Lord Mansfield's observations in *Robinson v Bland* on the nature of choice-of-law rules in negotiable instrument's law have been explicitly followed in *Moulis v Owen*[27] (1907), which involved similar facts: a cheque issued in Algeria by one English resident to another, in relation to a gambling debt.[28] Despite the place of the contract formation (Algeria), the court followed the MSR principle, mentioning *Robinson v Bland* and pointing out that all other connecting factors referred to England: both the plaintiff and the defendant were English residents, and the cheque was payable in England.[29] One could wish Lord Mansfield's insightful comments on the nature of the field would have been followed more **6.15**

[20] ibid, 230.
[21] [1979] 2 SCR 669 (hereafter *Canada Life*).
[22] For a discussion of these issues, see Chapter V, the text accompanying nn 50–54.
[23] (1760) 2 Burr 1077; 97 ER 717 (hereafter *Robinson v Bland*).
[24] *Robinson v Bland* 718.
[25] ibid, 719.
[26] See eg *Dicey and Morris* 2078, n 1567.
[27] (1907)1 KB 746 (hereafter *Moulis v Owen*).
[28] ibid, 753–54.
[29] ibid, 750.

often. They remain relevant today and should be taken seriously by judiciary and academics.

6.16 *Robinson v Bland* and *Moulis v Owen* do not stand alone in the English landscape as demonstrating judicial support of the MSR principle. *G & H Montage G.m.b.H v Irvani*[30] do so as well. This case dealt with the status of the well-established continental 'aval' form of liability on a negotiable instrument, which does not exist under the BEA.[31] An Iranian resident signed several bills by way of 'aval' issued by an Iranian drawer to a German payee/holder.[32] The trial judge noticed[33] the fairly arbitrary nature of the place of contract formation in this case: while the defendants signed the bills in Iran, the bills were delivered in Germany. Based on BEA s 72, the place of contract formation (ie Germany) was supposed to be the determinative factor in identifying the applicable law.

6.17 The difficulty of basing choice-of-law analysis on the place of contract formation is even more evident in the judicial reasoning of the Court of Appeal in *Irvani*.[34] By tracking the 'last step' of the contractual arrangements between the parties, the Court of Appeal needed to name the place of the instrument's actual delivery.[35] It recognized the situation as an anomaly under which the potentially arbitrary connecting factor of place of delivery determined the applicable law. In that case, the court characterized the application of this connecting factor as an 'adventitious route',[36] as a factor that fortuitously 'should depend upon whether one course was taken rather than another'.[37]

6.18 Interestingly, as a solution to this difficulty, the Court of Appeal made an explicit reference to the MSR principle. In addition to the 'adventitious route' of the place of contract formation that pointed to Germany, the MSR principle provided an alternative justification for applying German law. As the court stated:

> the fact that the centre of gravity [ie the MSR] of the transaction on the bill between the defendant and the plaintiffs does seem to me to have been in Germany is at least a reason for believing that the solution obtained by a totally different route [ie the place of contract formation] is not too far wide of the mark.[38]

[30] [[19901 WLR 82 (hereafter *Irvani*). For previous discussion of this case, see Chapter IV, the text accompanying nn 196–201 and 234–36.

[31] For a discussion on 'avalist' form of liability, see Chapters I and IV, the text accompanying nn 105–07 (Chapter I) and 24–25 (Chapter IV).

[32] *Irvani* 1288–89.

[33] ibid, 1297.

[34] *G & H Montage G.m.b.H v Irvani* [1990] 1 WLR 667 (hereafter *Irvani, Court of Appeal*).

[35] ibid, 685: 'Much attention was devoted during the argument to the location of the last contractual step, on the suppositions that the relevant contract was created by the bare signature of the defendant, that this was in the nature of an indorsement, and that one must therefore consider when the indorsement was completed by delivery (section 2), namely by "transfer of possession, actual or constructive", from the defendant to plaintiff.'

[36] ibid, 686.

[37] ibid, 685.

[38] *Irvani, Court of Appeal* 685. In section B (see the text accompanying nn 212–13) we will return to the *Irvani* case and the Court of Appeal's justification mode in the context of the discussion on the pre-built presumptions for negotiable instruments.

The MSR principle is also found in other English UK cases. For example, in the *Karafarin Ban*,[39] discussed in Chapter V,[40] the court made reference to the MSR principle in support of applying Iranian law by noting, 'In the present case, all matters connected with the cheques took place in one country, namely Iran'.[41] Similarly, in *Zebrarise*,[42] the court exercised what appears to be an MSR principle analysis. Addressing the question of the law applicable to a promissory note, it supported the application of that law which it viewed as 'connecting' the particular plaintiff, the particular defendant and their interaction.[43] **6.19**

However, it was argued that the MSR principle cannot be traced to older English 'decided cases', which the BEA's choice-of-law provisions are said to reproduce 'to a considerable extent'.[44] This objection is, however, flawed. *Robinson v Bland*[45] is a pre-BEA case, and it provides support for the application of the MSR principle. **6.20**

In fact, the underlying reasoning of the MSR principle is clear in the pre-BEA jurisprudence that served as an originating basis for its choice-of-law provisions. Earlier in this book, we examined this pre-BEA case law. In Chapter V, our discussion focused on the 'inland'/'foreign' distinction set in s 4 of the BEA, with several further implications with relation to ss 72(2) and 51.[46] We contended that the 'inland'/'foreign' distinction was based on shaky foundations. Through an examination of the pre-BEA basis of this distinction—the *Amner v Clark*[47] case—we sought to demonstrate the irrelevance of this case for contemporary reality and outlined the problematic nature of the 'inland'/'foreign' distinction.[48] **6.21**

The ensuing paragraphs continue to examine the foundational basis of the BEA's choice-of-law provisions and demonstrate evident traces of the MSR principle. Specifically, consider s 72(2)(b) of the BEA, mentioned in Chapter V,[49] which reads as follows: **6.22**

> Where a bill, issued out of the United Kingdom, conforms, as regards requisites in form, to the law of the United Kingdom, it may, for the purpose of enforcing payment thereof, be treated as valid as between all persons who negotiate, hold, or become parties to it in the United Kingdom.[50]

Stated in these terms, this provision (proviso b) deserves consideration. Two points can immediately be raised. First, the provision clearly supports a form of validation of the instrument. It makes it easier to negotiate[51] instruments issued abroad in the **6.23**

39 *Karafarin Bank v Gholam Reza Mansoury Dara* [2009] EWHC 3265 (Comm) (hereafter *Karafarin Bank v Gholam Reza Mansoury Dara*).
40 See Chapter V, see the text accompanying nn 16–25.
41 *Karafarin Bank v Gholam Reza Mansoury Dara* para [10].
42 *Zebrarise Ltd and another v de Nieffe* [2004] EWHC 1842 (Comm) (hereafter *Zebrarise*).
43 ibid [33].
44 *Dicey and Morris* 2078. See also Chapter I, the text accompanying nn 40–47.
45 *Robinson v Bland.*
46 See Chapter V section A.
47 Amner v Clark *(1835)*2 C.M. & Rosc. 468; 150 ER 202.
48 See Chapter V section A(2).
49 ibid.
50 BEA s 72(2)(b).
51 Collins (ed) *Dicey and Morris on the Conflict of Laws* (11th edn, Sweet & Maxwell 1987) 1315.

United Kingdom and seems to support 'business purposes'.[52] For example, an instrument issued in France should be treated by a UK court as a valid instrument if it has been negotiated in UK, and despite the fact that it might not be valid under French law. We will discuss this point in detail in Chapter VII.[53]

6.24 Second, proviso b seems to be at odds with the value of equality. In this section we focus on this aspect of the provision. Specifically, proviso b[54] does not neutrally support the instrument's validity. In fact, it violates the value of equality by not discriminating, for example, against foreign residents as opposed to UK residents.[55] Thus, a UK resident who issued the instrument abroad may not benefit from proviso b. Nor does the provision discriminate within the relationship between the particular plaintiff and the particular defendant.[56] This is so because both the plaintiff and defendant can potentially benefit from the instrument's validity.

6.25 Rather, the provision does something else. It simply applies itself in a one-sided manner. It implies that only UK law of negotiable instruments can validate an instrument issued abroad. This supports the view that by virtue of proviso b, UK law is considered superior in quality to any other potential law. The support of the instrument's validity is limited to a case where the instrument meets the form requirements of UK law, which suggests that proviso b blatantly violates the value of equality.

6.26 This type of quality assessment has been rejected within the literature and judicial decisions in the strongest way possible. These have demonstrated very little tolerance[57] for domestic judges exercising substantive judgment about the quality of a foreign system or foreign law and deciding on their own whether the foreign law is 'good' or 'bad'. Such a practice would violate the very structure of the international order, an order based on such values as 'diversity', 'tolerance', and 'comity' between states and their public legal institutions. Exercising quality judgments on foreign law has

[52] *Dicey and Morris* 2082.

[53] See Chapter VII section D.

[54] To be sure, the charges that we lay out in this paragraph apply equally to BEA's proviso a (s 72(2)(a)) and proviso b. As the practice of the systems is to remove the stamp requirements from negotiable instruments (see eg Finance Act 1970, sch7, para 2), we chose to focus our criticism in this section on proviso b.

[55] For unequivocal objections made in the choice-of-law literature, disapproving of unequal treatment of local residents vis-à-vis foreigners, see eg EG Lorenzen, 'Rules of the Conflict of Laws Applicable to Bills and Notes' (1917) Minn L Rev 10, 16 (criticizing on these grounds art 84 of the German Law of Exchange) (hereafter Lorenzen, 'Rules'); HC Gutteridge, 'The Unification of the Rules of Conflict Relating to Negotiable Instruments' (1934) 16 J Comp Legis & Int'l L 53, 63–64. Within the contemporary choice-of-law framework the value of equal treatment between local residents and foreigners has been adopted on a declarative level within several international conventions, see eg JJ Fawcett et al, *Human Rights and Private International Law* (Oxford University Press 2018) 433–65 (hereafter Fawcett, *Human Rights*).

[56] For a traditional reluctance of choice-of-law thought to provide one of the litigating parties an advantage over another, such as the ability to determine the identity of the applied law, see eg F von Savigny, *A Treatise on the Conflict of Laws, and the Limits of Their Operation in Respect of Place and Time* (trans by W Guthrie, T & T Clark 1880) 145 (disapproving the potential ability of the plaintiff to 'shop' for a law preferable for him as 'very dangerous') (hereafter Savigny, *Conflict of Laws*).

[57] For for an example of reluctance to give an advantage to one litigating party over another, see Chapter VII section D.

been coined as 'dangerous'[58] and as inconsistent with the very essentials of private international law.[59]

6.27 Furthermore, the practice of exercising quality judgments on foreign law challenges the basic vision of contemporary international order, an order comprised of a multiplicity of states. Since the states are situated in equal relation to each other, there is equal relation between the states' public institutions and their products.[60] A substantive content evaluation of foreign law challenges international order.[61]

6.28 A parallel between proviso b and the family law context may be suggested. In this context, the general choice-of-law rule says that the parties' capacity to marry should meet the residency requirements of both parties.[62] The choice-of-law literature, however, has suggested an exception to this rule. This exception validates a marriage that takes place in England, despite the incapacity of one of the parties to marry under its own law of residency. Similar to BEA proviso b, the exception applies in a one-sided manner: it supports marriage validation only for marriages that take place in England, excluding from its scope marriages that take place elsewhere. Not surprisingly, Cheshire and North commented on this exception as follows:

> This suggested rule [the exception] has been stigmatised as 'anomalous' and as 'unworthy of a place in a respectable system of the conflict of law', as well as being criticised by the Law Commission. It is xenophobic in that it gives to the law of the place of celebration of the marriage of that is English, but not if it is foreign. It is likely to lead to 'limping' marriages, valid in England but not in the country of the domicile of one spouse. Thus, the case for the abandonment of the rule seems clear.[63]

6.29 The harsh criticism expressed here is understandable and applies with similar force to proviso b. The very legitimacy of this provision should be challenged on the grounds that it is inconsistent with the very fundamentals of private international law and international order.

6.30 The literature names the decision *In re Marseilles Extension Railway and Land Company* (1885)[64] as the source of proviso b. Both Chalmers and Dicey and & Morris referred precisely to this case as a pre-BEA basis for proviso b.[65] This case involved several bills drawn in France by a French resident on an English drawee, payable in

[58] J Fawcett and JM Carruthers (eds) *Cheshire, North & Fawcett: Private International Law* (15th edn, Oxford University Press 2017) 34–35: 'it [the quality judgment] is a dangerous factor to use in the choice of law process because it confuses the issue of the reform of the substantive law of one country which is that of choosing the most appropriate law to govern a dispute with links with two or more countries. It is certainly not the task of a judge in one country to try to reform the law in another' (hereafter *Cheshire & North*).

[59] See eg A Briggs, 'The Principle of Comity in Private International Law' (2012) 354 Rec Des Cours 65, 80–81; Fawcett et al, *Human Rights* 48.

[60] See eg B Roth, *Sovereign Equality and Moral Disagreement* (Oxford University Press 2011) 54; UN Charter, art 2, § 1. For further discussion of this point see Chapter VII section D.

[61] For an argument in this direction, see eg D Laycock, 'Equal Citizens of Equal and Territorial States: The Constitutional Foundations of Choice of Law' (1992) 92 Colum L Rev 249.

[62] See eg *Cheshire & North* 918–19.

[63] ibid.

[64] 30 Ch D 598.

[65] See eg AG Gleeson, *Chalmers and Guest on Bills of Exchange, Cheques and Promissory Notes* (18th edn, Sweet & Maxwell 2016) 590–91 (hereafter Gleeson, *Chalmers and Guest*); *Dicey and Morris* 2082.

England. The bills were subsequently indorsed in England to the bills' holder who was an English resident. The drawee challenged the validity of the indorsement in England and the holder's entitlement to the instrument, arguing that this should be determined based on the French law.[66]

6.31 The court opted for the application of English law. A close look at the court's reasoning reveals how deeply affected it had been by such considerations as the parties' intentions and their reasonable expectations:

> when I come to look at this bill, I find that the bill though drawn in the French language, drawn by M. Barry [the drawer] in Marseilles, is in all other respects an English bill of exchange. It speaks of English current money and not of French current money, and it is drawn in a form which according to the French law would make the bill itself an invalid bill ... I come therefore to the conclusion that this was intended to be, although expressed in the French language, an English bill of exchange for all purposes, at all events as regards the acceptors of the bill[67]

6.32 The reasoning follows, in its essence, the MSR principle. Instead of focusing on the considerations of state sovereignty and the physical location of formation of one of the contracts under the instrument, the judge focused on the parties' interaction as a whole and analysed this interaction in light of such factors as the language of the bills, the currency of the payment, and the bills' form. Without considering, at this point, such matters as the choice-of-law rules for validity of indorsements,[68] the parties' intention to draw a valid instrument,[69] and the question of the centrality of such factors as the bills' language, form and payment currency for an MSR analysis,[70] the court's

[66] Gleeson, *Chalmers and Guest* 601.

[67] ibid, 602

[68] See Chapter VII section B(1)(c).

[69] See Chapter VII section A.

[70] Indeed, in addition to the *In re Marseilles* decision, a review of choice-of-law decisions in the area of negotiable instruments law reveal that courts have in their analysis considered such factors as the instruments' form, the language used and the payment currency as indicators of the parties' reasonable expectations. See eg *Hennenlotter v De Orvananos* 334 (referring to the factor of the instrument's language; *Canada Life* 682 (referring the factor of currency of payment). Can these factors be integrated within the MSR principle's analysis, suggested in this chapter? With respect to this question, our position would be as follows. First, as a matter of principle, we favourably support the integration of these factors as a part of the MSR analysis. We reject a view expressed in the literature according to which it is possible to delineate a sharp line between so-called 'objective' and 'subjective' factors within the MSR principle's analysis (see eg *Cheshire & North* 716–22), offering to draw a sharp line (and in contrast to choice-of-law judicial practice) between the 'inferred choice' circumstances of art 3(1) of Rome I and the MSR principle stated in art 4(4) of this Regulation). See Regulation (EC) 593/2008 of the European Parliament and of the Council of 17 June 2008 on the Law Applicable to Contractual Obligations (Rome I), 2008 OJ (L 177) 6 (EU) (Rome I). Rather, the operation of the MSR principle is based on combination of *both* objective (such as the place of the parties' residence and business) and subjective factors (such as the language used in the instrument and the instrument's form). Both types of factor refer to the notion of parties' reasonable expectations and provide a fertile ground for the judiciary to provide a meaning to parties' deeds and actions. For a similar argument rejecting the sharp distinction between subjective and objective factors within various legal doctrines see eg TW Bell, 'Graduated Consent in Contract and Tort Law: Toward A Theory of Justification' (2010) 61 Cas W Res L Rev 17, 34–40). Secondly, we must say that the considerations of the instrument's language, form, and the payment currency shall be executed in a cautious manner, bearing in mind the underlying purpose of our inquiry—the identity of the applicable law. Thus, depending the circumstances,

reasoning evidently considered the parties' intentions and expectations in light of the particular circumstances of the case.

Not only does this reasoning not refer to considerations such as state sovereignty and interests, it fundamentally departs from the language used in BEA proviso b. There is nothing in this case to support the two-tier rule of proviso b, under which the validity of indorsement in France (which was not valid under French law) would be still enforceable in England if it (1) has been negotiated in England, and (2) is valid according to English law. The facts in this case could easily be the opposite: the bills could have been drawn in England and then negotiated in France. Would this factual basis support a rule that if the bills are valid under French law, the court should disregard the form requirements under English law? The answer to this question is, of course, no.[71] Pearson J had no intention of setting a rule resembling proviso b in the *In re Marseilles* case. To say that the ruling or justification in the pre-BEA *In re Marseilles* case in some way correlates with proviso b set in BEA s 72(1)(b) would be a notable exaggeration. 6.33

2. Assessing Objection 2: Challenging the 'Predictability and Certainty' Thesis

The second line of objection takes a different path and refers to what seems to be the underlying value of negotiable instruments law—the value of predictability/certainty. It argues that incorporating the MSR principle would undermine that value. The values of predictability/certainty, the argument continues, aim to give predominant status to the instrument's holder and enhance the smooth transferability of the instrument, akin to money.[72] The MSR principle, on the other hand, directs the adjudicators to apply the law of that place which represents the most significant relationship to the 'parties' and the 'event'. The inherently flexible nature of the MSR principle seems to epitomize the direct antithesis of the stated goal/value of negotiable instruments law—the values of predictability and certainty. The provisions of the Second Restatement and (especially) the official commentaries that accompany them are an excellent illustration of this point. 6.34

such factors as the instrument's language and the currency of payment are more likely to relate to the matters of convenience and to shed little light on the question of parties' reasonable expectations as to the identity of the applicable law.

[71] Indeed, Chalmers, while drawing the parallel between the *In re Marseilles* case and proviso b, frankly mentioned the 'different grounds' (compared to proviso b) on which the case was decided (see Gleeson, *Chalmers and Guest* 601, n 1609).

[72] On the centrality of the value of predictability within the internal structure of negotiable instruments' law to ensure security of transactions and enhance the transferability/negotiability of the instrument, in a manner alike to transferability of money, see eg E McKendrick (ed), *Goode on Commercial Law* (5th edn, Penguin 2016) 518–19, 571 (hereafter McKendrick, *Commercial Law*); *Nova (Jersey) Knit Ltd v Kammgarn Spinnerei G.m.b.H.* [1977] 1 WLR 713, 727 (Lord Salmon: 'Negotiable instruments shall be treated very much alike as "money" '). See also *Quaker City Nat'l Bank v. Showacre*, 26 WV 48 (1885) [52] (noting with respect to negotiable instruments law, as: 'always careful to protect the rights of innocent holders').

(a) The 'Clear-Cut Rules Thesis' and the Return of Beale's Rhetoric in the Provisions (and Commentaries) of the Second Restatement

6.35 The 'over-flexibility' charge mounted against the MSR principle explains much of the unwillingness of the negotiable instruments literature and the choice-of-law frameworks to accept it. The official comments to §§ 214–17 of the Second Restatement clearly follow this path. In striking contradiction to its underlying spirit of providing much more flexibility to defeat the stringent spirit of the First Restatement,[73] the Second Restatement explicitly denies its own stated goal with respect to negotiable instruments. Arguably, due to the special nature of the field, the Second Restatement simply rejects its main vehicle for promoting flexibility—the application of the MSR principle. In this way, the law of negotiable instruments is left outside the general spirit of the Second Restatement and its ultimate goal. In direct contradiction to the broad application of the MSR principle within the Restatement's provisions,[74] there was no room left for this principle in the case of negotiable instruments law.

6.36 From this perspective, negotiable instruments law has been effectively equated with another area of law—real/immovable property. The latter has been traditionally governed by a single connecting factor—the *lex-situs* rule of place of property.[75] Conceptually, this factor is based on the notion that foreign land physically represents part of foreign territory, suggesting a direct application of the sovereignty principle to immovable property.[76] The other justification for the *lex-situs* or 'land-tabu' rule[77] is practical—the area of immovable property is usually heavily regulated, requires registration, and as such is governed solely by the law of the location of the property.[78] Similarly to immovable property, negotiable instruments law has been excluded from the underlying rationale of the Second Restatement.

6.37 Let us take a closer look at the Second Restatement and its commentaries on negotiable instruments law. Beginning with brief observations on the nature of the subject, the text rightly mentions its contractual and property foundations.[79] It acknowledges the principal structure of negotiable instruments law as comprising various contractual obligations made by the parties to the instrument—the acceptor, the drawer, and the indorser.[80] Similar to other choice-of-law frameworks, [81] the Second Restatement accepts the 'separate contracts' theory, under which each one of these obligations shall be conceived as a separate contract, unrelated to other obligations.[82] What follows is that the choice-of-law rules of each one of the obligations under the negotiable instrument shall be determined by a distinct analysis. The Second Restatement explicitly

[73] For a discussion of this point on the historical background and underlying spirit of the Second Restatement as an antithesis to First Restatement, see Chapter III section B(3).

[74] ibid.

[75] *Second Restatement* §§ 225–32.

[76] On the conceptual justification of the *lex-situs* rule, see *Cheshire & North* 1251–63.

[77] See eg SC Symeonides, *Choice of Law* (Oxford University Press 2016) (hereafter Symeonides, *Choice of Law*) 581–83.

[78] On the practical justification of the *lex-situs* rule, see eg *Cheshire & North* 1251–63.

[79] Second Restatement Ch 8, Introductory Note ('Negotiable Instruments').

[80] ibid, § 214, Comment f.

[81] For a discussion of this point, see Chapter IV section B.

[82] Second Restatement § 214, Comment f.

acknowledges the similarity between a 'regular' contract and the internal structure of negotiable instruments by saying that, 'Like other contracts, negotiable instruments present a variety of problems, involving their validity and effect, the manner or mode of their performance'.[83] In a similar vein, by delineating the physical aspect of the instrument involved in its transfer, the Second Restatement acknowledges the property foundations of the subject and draws a parallel between the transfer of negotiable instruments and the transfer of 'tangible things' and 'ordinary chattels'.[84]

Despite these promising statements about the conceptual foundation of negotiable instruments law in the essentials of the law of contract and movable property, the Second Restatement explicitly refuses to draw a direct analogy between these areas of private law and negotiable instruments law. By referring to the qualities and underlying policies of negotiability of the instruments, the Second Restatement explicitly rejects the possibility of applying to negotiable instruments law the intellectual heart[85] of the Second Restatement—the MSR principle. Despite the overall application of the MSR principle to such areas as contract law, tort law, family law and even movable property (which is fairly unusual even for contemporary movable property doctrine, which adheres to the traditional rule of the place of property[86]), the area of negotiable instruments has been left behind. **6.38**

While drawing a parallel with contract choice-of-law rules and the centrality of the connecting factor of the place of payment within these rules,[87] the Second Restatement does not fully follow the contractual doctrine, under which the place of performance of contractual obligations serves only as a presumption and flexible point of departure for analysis of the MSR principle. Rather, the Second Restatement sets the connecting factor of the place of payment as a rigid rule (*à la* Beale) based on the following justification: **6.39**

> Certainty and predictability are values of paramount importance in this field [the field of negotiable instruments], and there is need for simple, hard-and-fast rules of choice of law. For this reason, only one contract [connecting factor] is considered[88]

Thus, the Second Restatement states that the liabilities of the primary parties of the instrument (ie the liabilities of the acceptor of a bill and of the maker of a note) shall be determined by the connecting factor of the place of payment specified on the face of the instrument.[89] The Second Restatement follows its 'hard-and-fast rules' rationale of negotiable instruments and sets the place of payment as the *only* connecting factor that 'will always furnish the applicable law'.[90] We describe this position of the Second Restatement as a 'Clear-Cut Rules' Thesis. **6.40**

[83] ibid.
[84] ibid.
[85] See Chapter III section B(3).
[86] J Carruthers, *The Transfer of Property in Private International Law* (OUP 2004).
[87] Second Restatement § 214, Comment b.
[88] ibid; see also § 216, Comment a.
[89] ibid, § 214 (1).
[90] ibid, § 214, Comment b.

6.41 Ironically, the Second Restatement's justification follows Beale's 'vested rights' theory. Thus, when the place of the payment is not specified on the face of the instrument, the Second Restatement refers to the connecting factor of the place of the instrument's delivery as representing the 'final act necessary to impose liability'.[91] This reasoning effectively follows Beale's vision of the subject, against which the Second Restatement came into existence in the first place—to counterbalance Beale's theory and the Beale-inspired rigid choice-of-law rules.[92] As we have seen in Chapter III, it was precisely Beale's theory of rights that favoured the application of the law of the place where the last act of liability occurs.[93] In other words, negotiable instruments law represents a case where Beale's discredited rhetoric and his rigid rules have entered through the back door of the Second Restatement.

(b) Challenging the Clear-Cut Rules Thesis

6.42 However, one can challenge the application of the 'clear-cut rules' thesis according to which negotiable instruments law must follow rigid connecting factors. This thesis rests on the fundamental premise of a correlation between the underlying goals and internal structure of a particular legal category and the nature of the choice-of-law process. Consider tort law, for example. According to this premise, the underlying rationales of tort law—deterrence and compensation—should underpin the identity of tort choice-of-law rules.[94] When applied to the context of negotiable instruments law, the premise means that the entire choice-of-law process and its mechanics should be subordinated to the alleged underlying values of negotiable instruments law—predictability and certainty. In other words, since the values of predictability and certainty underpin the internal structure of negotiable instruments law, these values should ultimately determine the identity of its choice-of-law rules.

6.43 In the following paragraphs, we address the following: (i) the fundamental premise of the thesis that negotiable instruments law is, in fact, based *solely* on the values of certainty and predictability; (ii) the premise that there has to be a *complete* correlation between the underlying goals of a given legal category and the choice-of-law process (iii) the related notion that the application of 'clear-cut' rules to the context of negotiable instruments law has actually served the values of certainty; and (iv) the operational result which de-facto places negotiable instruments law in the same camp as immovable property law. And finally, we

[91] ibid, § 214, Comment b.

[92] ibid, Ch 7, topic 1, intro note; Ch 8, topic 1, intro note.

[93] Chapter III section B(2).

[94] Indeed, some choice-of-law scholars have made suggestions in this direction and have offered to base tort choice-of-law rules on the underlying rationales of this legal category,- compensation and deterrence. See eg Symeonides, *Choice-of-Law* 155–72. For discussion on the practical difficulty of such approach, see WC Perdue, 'A Reexamination of the Distinction between "Loss-Allocating" and "Conduct-Regulating Rules' (2000) 60 La L Rev 1251.

comment on the inherently unpredictable nature of the MSR principle. As we saw in Chapter III, the charges regarding the over-flexibility of the MSR principle have been overstated.[95]

(i) The Values of Certainty and Predictability as the Only Two Underlying Values of Negotiable Instruments Law

While it was held that free circulation facilitating negotiability requires certainty and predictability,[96] we saw in Chapter II[97] that negotiability has not been the cornerstone in the evolution of the law of bills, notes and cheques. Indeed, this area of law encompasses a complex combination of various values drawn from contract and movable property laws. These values reflect inherent inquiries into the relational structure of the particular parties' interaction under the instrument and the questions of the genuineness of the parties' consent within this interaction.[98] **6.44**

Negotiability has been curtailed and counterbalanced in several ways. For example, 'real defences' are available even against a holder in due course.[99] Also, with respect to an instrument payable to the order, negotiability has not been extended in English law to protect a *bona-fide* taker for value from a thief.[100] Furthermore, in Canada[101] and the US,[102] the holder in due course does not have a defence-free position in relation to consumer bills and notes. For its part, case law reveals a hardening attitude to the compliance requirements for holding in due course so as to curtail negotiability and balance it with other policies.[103] **6.45**

(ii) The Complete Correlation Between the Underlying Goals of a Given Legal Category and the Choice-of-Law Process

We challenge another fundamental premise of the thesis according to which the underlying goals of a given legal category and the choice-of-law process shall *always* coincide. The underlying rationales of the choice-of-law process such as the 'parties' reasonable expectations', 'justice', and 'predictability'[104] sometimes correlate with the underlying goals of negotiable instruments law and sometimes depart from it. As we **6.46**

[95] See Chapter III section B(3)(b).
[96] See eg *Carlos v Fancourt* (1794) 5 TR 482; 101 ER 272.
[97] See Chapter II.
[98] For a discussion of these issues in the context of the party autonomy principle, see Chapter V section B(1).
[99] Even as their availability is now limited after *Saunders v Anglia Building Society* [1971] AC 1004 (HL).
[100] See eg *Mead v Younge* (1790) 4 TR 28, 100 ER 876, discussed in Chapter II (the text accompanying nn 225–28).
[101] *Bills of Exchange Act* (RSC 1985, c B-4) Part V (hereafter Canadian BEA).
[102] Federal Trade Commission Holder-in-due-course Regulations, 16 CFR Part 433.
[103] For curtailing negotiability along all such lines, see eg B Geva, *Financing Consumer Sales and Product Defences* (Carswell Legal Publications 1984).
[104] See eg Clarkson and Hill, who structure their comments on the nature of the discipline around the following notions: (1) justice as a reflection of such notions as 'conflict justice', 'party autonomy', 'parties' reasonable expectations'; (2) uniformity of results; and (3) promoting public interest. See J Hill and MN Shúilleabháin (eds), *Clarkson & Hill's Conflict of Laws* (5th edn, Oxford University Press 2016) 9–19 (hereafter *Clarkson & Hill*).

have seen on the point of possibly introducing the party autonomy principle into the law of negotiable instruments,[105] such an introduction seems to be well suited to the underlying goals of both negotiable instruments law and choice-of-law.

6.47 Nonetheless, the underlying goals of the choice-of-law process in matters concerning negotiable instruments and negotiable instruments law do not necessarily need to coincide. Even if they coincide, they may operate on different levels of legal analysis and at different strengths. Accordingly, we disagree with the point that the *choice-of-law process* of negotiable instruments law shall submerge itself into the underlying goals of this area of law. Even if negotiable instruments law had been solely founded on the underlying values of certainty and predictability (and as we have seen, it is not), this would mean that the *choice-of-law rules* of negotiable instruments law should be subjected *solely* to these values. In other words, we argue that the underlying values of negotiable instruments law may depart from the underlying values of the choice-of-law rules in this area of law.

6.48 The disjuncture between the underlying values of a given legal category (such as contract law, torts, and unjust enrichment) and that of the choice-of-law question is supported in the literature[106] and evident in choice-of-law provisions. Thus, various systems apply the same set of choice-of-law rules to a broad range of legal categories. For example,[107] the Second Restatement applies the MSR principle to categories of tort, contract, movable property and family law. No attempt has been made to distinguish between the underlying values of each category and set a separate choice-of-law rule for each category. By the same token, as we saw in Chapter III,[108] many systems apply the party autonomy principle to categories of family law, succession, tort, contract, and unjust enrichment. The choice-of-law doctrine has simply refused to say that the choice-of-law process shall be completely equated with the adjudication process of a given legal category.

6.49 The potential division between the underlying values of the choice-of-law process and those of the various legal categories has also not slipped under the radar of legal scholarship. Thus, Kegel, one of the twentieth-century giants of choice-of-law thought, refused to accept the notion that the choice-of-law question shall completely collapse into the adjudicative process of a given legal category. For Kegel, the choice-of-law question requires a different conceptual and practical analysis, which should be determined before the adjudicative process and as such should be decided based on a distinctive type of considerations.[109] In this book, we accept the notion of the independence of the choice-of-law question from the adjudicative process of a

[105] See Chapter V section B.

[106] See J Singer, 'Real Conflicts' (1989) 69 Bos Univ L Rev 1.

[107] For a broad application of the MSR principle, within the American Second Restatement, see Chapter III section B(3).

[108] For a broad application of the party autonomy principle, see Chapter III section B(2).

[109] G Kegel, 'The Crisis on Conflict of Laws' (1964) 112 Recueil des Cours 95, 183 (hereafter Kegel, 'Conflict of Laws').

given legal category, a notion that challenges the basic premise of the 'clear-cut rules thesis'.

(iii) The Application of 'Clear-Cut' Rules to the Context of Negotiable Instruments Law Enhances the Values of Certainty and Predictability

An essential stance of supporters of the 'clear-cut rules' thesis is that its application leads to more certainty and predictability, which serves the ultimate goal of negotiable instruments law. But does the application of the 'clear-cut' choice-of-law rules in the context of negotiable instruments law truly enhance certainty and predictability? **6.50**

If a bill is signed in Germany by an Australian resident, payable to the order of a New York resident and sent to from Germany to New York. How can one argue, for example, that the BEA's clear-cut rule of the place of contract formation[110] serves the certainty and predictability values in this case? The doctrine of negotiable instruments law follows the place of the instrument's delivery to determine the place of the contract formation between the drawer (Australian resident) and the payee (the American resident). However, what should the place of contract formation be? Is it the instrument's location at the time of its delivery (ie New York), or is it the location of the post office that the package with the instrument is posted from (ie Germany)? **6.51**

By the same token, a review of the case law reveals that the application of the clear-cut choice-of-law rules has frequently not enhanced the values of certainty and predictability. The opposite is true. The judges have acknowledged the inherent difficulty in tracking the rigid place of contract formation in common cases of transactions between distant parties.[111] In this context, the place of contract formation is frequently hard to detect.[112] **6.52**

The rigid connecting factor of the place of contract formation is often quite arbitrary and simply irrelevant to the parties' interaction. Thus, the Court of Appeal in *Irvani*,[113] has recognized the notably fortuitous nature of the place of contracting and offered an alternative route for the application of German law. This route explicitly adopted the MSR principle. The arbitrariness of the place of contract formation and the need to use legal doctrines to identify that place, challenges the point made by the 'clear-cut rules' thesis supporters that the parties to the instrument can easily identify such a place. **6.53**

Contemporary phenomena of the digital age, online communication and online commerce, present an insurmountable challenge to the rigidity of such inflexible rules as the place of contract formation. For example, where is the place of the contract formation in the case of online transactions? In the place of the plaintiff's residence, the place of the **6.54**

[110] BEA s 72(1).

[111] See eg *Amin Rasheed Shipping Corp v Kuwait Insurance Co* [1984] AC 50, 62; *Fleming v Marshall* [2011] NSWCA 86 [64]; *ACCC v Valve Corporation* (No 3) [2016] FCA 196 [81].

[112] Thus, eg the Court of Appeal in the *Irvani* case explicitly refused to follow the traditional English postal rules: 'I do not think that recourse to the idiosyncratic rules of English law about the status of posting as delivery are of much help here, relevant though they may be to the question whether indorsement has been completed by delivery.' (ibid, 685).

[113] See the text accompanying nn 30–38.

defendant's residence, or maybe in the place of the location of the Internet's server, which is often situated in a location which is completely unrelated to the parties' interaction? Where would the place of the instrument's delivery be in the near future of online communication of electronic negotiable instruments? Chapter VIII addresses these questions and makes further observations on the inapplicability of the traditional rigid rule of contract formation to when negotiable instruments may (hopefully) take their digital form.[114]

(iv) *Placing Negotiable Instruments Law in the Same Camp as Immovable Property Law*

6.55 We question the operational result of the 'clear-cut rules' thesis that essentially equalizes the categories of negotiable instruments and immovable property. Presently, the choice-of-law rules in the area of negotiable instruments law resemble the rules in the area of immovable property law; in the sense that they adhere to the rigid connecting factor and remain immune from the application of the MSR principle.[115]

6.56 One can contend that the equalization between the two is fundamentally flawed. The two areas of law diverge deeply on both conceptual and practical levels. As we saw in Chapter II, the mythical notion of the independent 'law of merchant' should be challenged.[116] The birth, development, and internal structure of negotiable instruments law direct us to draw an analogy with the areas of contract and movable law, rather than immovable property law. Developed over centuries through the Sisyphean work of commercial law adjudicators, these areas crystallize the convenience of commercial practice, the needs of merchants, and such notions as justice and parties' reasonable expectations.[117] These have been developed separately from states' interests and states' intervention.

6.57 The last point precisely delineates the difference between negotiable instruments law and another area left behind by the Second Restatement—immovable property law. The latter seems to be based on the states' interests and, as such, should be distinguished from other areas of law. The traditional choice-of-law rule of the place of the property, the *lex-situs* rule, has usually been explained through the lens of the principles of states' sovereignty and states' interests. Reaching a universal consensus,[118] this rule requires disputes over immovable property to be exclusively governed by the place of the immovable property.

6.58 The area of immovable property law must be distinguished from other areas of law. A dispute over an immovable property involves a fundamentally different type of consideration: a dispute over a part of a territory *itself* and, as such, it inherently links itself to the principles of states' sovereignty and states' interests.[119] A dispute over

[114] See Chapter VIII.

[115] See the text accompanying nn 73–83.

[116] See Chapter II section F(1).

[117] Cf Lewis J observations on the bill of exchange governed by such considerations as 'plain justice good faith'. See *Lennig v Ralston*, 23 Pa 137 (1854), 149.

[118] See eg *Clarkson & Hill* 471–73; A Briggs, *Private International Law in English Courts* (Oxford University Press 2014) 703–12 (hereafter Briggs, *PIL*).

[119] For a justification around these lines of the *lex-situs* rule in immovable property, see eg *Clarkson & Hill* 471–73; Briggs, *PIL* 703–12.

land in Germany involves a dispute over a part of Germany as a state. By targeting the states' constituents themselves—parts of their territories and their territorial integrity—a dispute over immovable property justifies an exclusive application of the *lex-situs* rule.

However, the law of negotiable instruments is different and cannot be subject to considerations applicable to the immovable property category belonging to the categories of contract and movable property, and subject to the significant developments that have taken place in choice-of-law rules within these categories. While Chapter V concentrated on one significant development in this direction—the introduction of the party autonomy principle—this chapter offers another significant step in this direction: the introduction of the MSR principle. **6.59**

We believe criticism against the application of the MSR principle to the area of negotiable instruments should be reconsidered. We contend that the principle *has* a strong application within the judicial reasoning of the courts. There is no reason to reject the implementation of the principle on the grounds of targeting its inherent flexibility. As argued, this inherent flexibility is normatively justifiable; the underlying values of negotiable instruments law do not necessarily need to overlap with the choice-of-law process; and the critics have overlooked an inherent feature of the principle—the various presumptions that set points of departure for the operation of the MSR principle. **6.60**

What set of presumptions could be applied to the specific context of negotiable instruments law that could operate together with the MSR principle? Is an operational combination of the MSR principle and flexible presumptions present within traditional and contemporary case law? And what is the operational scope of this combination? Does it apply to all issues within the internal structure of negotiable instruments law? These are the themes of Section B. **6.61**

B. The Operational Mechanics of the MSR Principle

1. Pre-Built Presumptions

As we saw in Chapter II, the birth, development, and internal structure of negotiable instruments law have not been premised on a mythical *lex mercatoria*. Rather, this area of law is based on the basic principles, concepts, and doctrines of traditional contract law and movable property law. The quest for presumptions in the area of negotiable instruments law must start with those in the areas of contract and movable property law. **6.62**

(a) The Presumption for the Category of Contract Law: Place of Contractual Performance

Consider, first, contract law. Which connecting factor should determine the MSR principle's point of departure for this category? In this respect, legal thinkers have noticed that some elements within its internal structure are more significant than others. Specifically, they have argued that the place of contractual performance is more **6.63** important than the place of contract formation.[120] According to this view, what stands at the heart of the contractual obligation is not the signing of the contract but rather the performance of the contractual obligation under that contract.

6.64 This point explains the popularity of the connecting factor of the place of contractual performance to serve as a flexible point of departure for judicial analysis under the MSR principle. Referring to the place of contractual performance, this connecting factor does not provide the answer to the ultimate question of choice-of-law analysis: Which law applies? It does not serve as a rigid, pre-determined connecting factor to provide an ultimate solution to the choice-of-law question. Yet, the place of contractual performance provides *a point of departure* for choice-of-law analysis. Representing a more central element within the internal structure of contractual liability, it suggests that the parties' reasonable expectations, as to the point of departure, would direct towards the application of the law of that place which is more central to the nature of their interaction. While this presumption could potentially be overturned through an analysis of other connecting factors of the parties' interaction, the judicial analysis begins with the place of contractual performance.

6.65 This was precisely the position of Savigny, the architect of the modern vision of the choice-of-law question. As both the founder of modern choice-of-law thought[121] and a great private law scholar,[122] he envisioned contract choice-of-law rules based on flexible presumptions. These presumptions were not set in an arbitrary way or on historical facts,[123] but on his rational analysis of the contract law category and the claim regarding the normative structure of this category.[124] Within this structure, the place of contractual performance represents what Savigny called the 'essence'[125] of the contractual obligation—a structure that not only provides insight into the basic underpinnings of contract law but also provides a flexible point of departure to address the question of the applicable law that accords with the parties' reasonable expectations.

6.66 The place of contractual performance as a presumption within the operational mechanism of the MSR principle and as a reflection of the internal structure of contract law can be traced in the commentaries of the Second Restatement. After acknowledging the paradigmatic significance of the concept of the 'parties' reasonable expectations',[126] the Second Restatement's commentaries acknowledge that 'Standing alone, the place

[120] See eg I Kant, *The Metaphysics of Morals (1798)* (trans by M Gregor, Cambridge University Press 1996) (Page citations will be of the Prussian Academy edition of Kant's works) [6:273] (hereafter Kant, *Doctrine of Right*); EJ Weinrib, 'Private Law, Punishment, and Disgorgement: Punishment and Disgorgement as Contract Remedies' (2003) 78 Chi-Kent L Rev 55, 65–70.

[121] See Savigny, *Conflict of Laws*.

[122] For Savigny's key works on private law, see FC von Savigny, *System of the Modern Roman Law* (trans by W Holloway, Hyperion Press 1979); FC von Savigny, *Jural Relations* (trans by WH Rattigan, Hyperion Press 1884).

[123] Accordingly, Ernest Lorenzen was simply wrong in his assertion that Savingy's presumption of the place of contractual performance was based on Roman Law (see Lorenzen, 'Rules' 243–56). In contrast to this assertion, Savigny's analysis of the contractual presumption was normative, rather than historical.

[124] Savingy, *Conflict of Laws* 194, 203.

[125] ibid, 198. For a discussion on the historical impact of Savigny's work on contract law choice of law rules, see Lorenzen, 'Rules' 251–52.

[126] Second Restatement § 188, Comment b.

of contracting is relatively insignificant contact'.[127] Rather, similar to Savigny's position, the commentaries justify the presumption of the place of service performance in service contracts and link this presumption to the parties' reasonable expectations:

> The rendition of the services in the principal objective of the contract, and the place where the services, or major portion of the services, are to be rendered will naturally loom large in the minds of the parties.[128]

By the same token, the commentaries follow this justification with respect to the presumption of the place of loan repayment in the case of loan contracts.[129] **6.67**

In this book, we reject the position of Rome I. Rather, we follow the position of the Second Restatement under which the place of contractual performance should serve as a starting point for judicial analysis under the MSR principle.[130] Originated in the great private law thinkers' observations about the very nature of the contract law **6.68**

[127] ibid, § 188, Comment e.

[128] ibid, § 196, Comment c. See also *Cheshire & North* 730 (mentions the place of service performance as a place of 'characteristic performance of the contract').

[129] Second Restatement § 195, Comment b. See also Report on the Convention on the law applicable to contractual obligations by Mario Giuliano, Professor, University of Milan, and Paul Lagarde, Professor, University of Paris I, Official Journal C 282, 31/10/1980 P. 0001–0050, paras 20–21 <http://eur-lex.europa.eu/LexUriServ/LexUriServ.do?uri=CELEX:31980Y1031(01):EN:HTML>, accessed 20 December 2019 (hereafter Giuliano & Lagarder Report); *Cheshire & North* 726, 730 (referring to the place of loan payment as usually representing the 'characteristic performance' of the contract).

[130] The presumption of the place of contractual performance is contrasted with the position of the Rome I. Articles 4(2) and 4(1)(a) and (b) of Rome I set the presumption of the place of so-called 'characteristic performance' to serve as a point of departure for the operation of the MSR principle under the Regulation (for the reading of the Rome I in a way that attributes a central role to the operation of the MSR principle, either through a broad reading of art 4(4) or art 3(1) of Rome I, see Chapter III, the text accompanying nn 103–07). While rightly following the notion that an analysis of the internal structure of the contract law category leads to the place of 'characteristic performance' of the contract, Rome I does not set this place as a point of departure. Rather, Rome I makes a twist and sets the residence of the party who 'is to effect' that performance as a connecting factor and a point of departure for contract law category. Thus, eg in the case of the contract of guarantee, the presumption would follow the connecting factor of the place of the guarantor's residence—the party who is usually set to perform the obligation under the guarantee contract (see Giuliano & Lagarde Report para 21). Similarly, the presumption of the characteristic performance names the place of residence of the service provider as a point of departure for judicial analysis for service contracts (art 4(2)). Originated in the Swiss tradition (see eg K Lipstein, 'Characteristic Performance- A New Concept in the Conflict of Laws in Matters of Contract for the EEC' (1981) 3 Nw J Int'l L & Bus 402, 405–09), the characteristic performance of Rome I has aimed to promote such values as 'business efficacy' and 'certainty' (see eg *Cheshire & North* 724, n 431) and to reflect 'the centre of gravity and the socio-economic function of the contractual transaction' (see Giuliano & Lagarde Report paras 20–21). We respectfully disagree. The internal analysis of the contract law category suggests that what stands at the heart of the contractual obligation is the performance of the service itself, rather than the residence of the party who is required to perform that service. While the identity of the latter might be easier to track, the former connecting factor is the one that correlates the parties' reasonable expectations. From this perspective, while the rhetoric of Giuliano & Lagarde's Report is tenable (mentioning eg that such connecting factors as the place of the payment and the place of product delivery represent the characteristic performance of the contract that 'usually constitutes the centre of gravity and the socio-economic function of the contractual transaction'. See Giuliano & Lagarde Report paras 20–21), its final product—the place of characteristic performance as a reflection of the party's residence who is to effect that performance—is disappointing. If anything, in this respect, we would be more favourable towards the connecting factor set out in art 6 of the Rome I, which deals with consumer contracts and sets the connecting factor of the consumer residence. Since the place of consumer residence frequently serves as the place of product delivery/service performance, this factor would have better approximated towards our position expressed here.

category, this notion has been transferred to the field of choice-of-law to serve as a point of departure for MSR principle analysis.

(b) The Presumptions in the Movable Property Category: The Place of Property

6.69 Similar to the category of contract law, an analysis of the internal structure of movable property can assist with deriving the MSR principle's presumption. Traditionally, disputes that involved movable property cases (or, more precisely, cases that involved disputes over entitlements to things/chattels[131]) have been considered by the courts as representing the execution of the states' authority over people and objects situated within their territories. This explains the traditional rigid choice-of-law rule, which directed towards the application of the *lex-situs* (the place of the location of the property) rule to govern disputes regarding movable property.[132]

6.70 In addition to state-sovereignty-based considerations, the *lex-situs* rule has also been justified as serving the value of predictability.[133] This justification of the *lex-situs* rule points out that the special nature of disputes over entitlements for things requires an application of fast, clear-cut rules that need to be easily ascertained. As Briggs has put it, 'Certainty and security of title are paramount and are best achieved by the general application of the *lex-situs* rule'. [134] By focusing on a single connecting factor of the place of the chattel at the relevant time,[135] the *lex-situs* rule greatly simplifies choice-of-law analysis. Yet, as we saw in Chapter III, the rigid *lex-situs* rule has received a significant blow in §§ 222, 244, 250, 251, 254, and 256–58 of the Second Restatement[136] and Article 2 of the Chinese Foreign-Related Civil Relations Statute.[137] A similar tendency can be witnessed in the scholarly literature, which has called for a reconsideration of the *lex-situs* rule with respect to movable property.[138]

6.71 Indeed, given the irrelevance of state-based considerations, and following the perspective of the parties' reasonable expectations, one can challenge the applicability

[131] One can distinguish movable property cases from contractual ones. When both cases involve issue of the transfer of chattels, only the latter involves disputes over entitlement. Therefore, disputes over movable property could be more accurately described as disputes over 'entitlements'.

[132] For a justification of the *lex-situs* rule based on the ideas of states' sovereignty, see *Cheshire & North* 1252.

[133] See A Briggs, *Conflict of Laws* (Oxford University Press 2013) 303–07 (hereafter Briggs, *Conflict of Laws*).

[134] ibid, 303.

[135] The phrase 'relevant time' here deserves attention. The position of the case law and the literature requires focusing on the choice-of-law analysis at the time when the given dispute over the title of the chattel arose. This timeline focuses on the time of the litigating parties' interaction and disregards the location of the chattel as relevant at the time of litigation. For a discussion of this point, see eg Stephen GA Pitel and NS Rafferty, *Conflict of Laws* (2nd edn, Irwin Law 2016) 350, n 4 (hereafter Pitel & Rafferty, *Conflict of Laws*); Briggs, *Conflict of Laws* 303 (referring to the relevant time as 'the date of the event which alleged to have affected title to it'); Symeonides, *Choice of Law* 590 (referring to the place where 'the critical transaction occurred').

[136] Second Restatement §§ 222, 244, 250, 251, 254, 256–58.

[137] See The Statute on the Application of Laws over Foreign-Related Civil Relations of the People's Republic of China (2011), art 2. See also Chapter III section B(3).

[138] Symeonides, *Choice of Law* 584–85; SC Symeonides, 'A New Conflicts Restatement: Why Not?' (2009) 5 J Priv Int L 383, 409 ('the time for rebuking the "situs taboo" is long overdue'); Carruthers, *Transfer in Property*, paras 9.48–9.49.

of the rigid *lex-situs* rule for contemporary reality. Consider the following facts: two academics from Perth, Australia travel to a private international law conference in Munich, Germany. During their layover in Singapore, a dispute arises between them as to the proprietary entitlement of a wallet, belonging to one of them. While the wallet had been carried by one of them, the other simply says that it belongs to him. Which law shall the Singaporean court apply to adjudicate the property right to the wallet?

Under the *lex-situs* rule (the place of the wallet), the application of Singaporean property law appears to be entirely arbitrary to the circumstances of this case: both academics are from Australia and they were heading to Germany. The application of Singaporean law seems to be merely incidental to the parties' interaction.[139] As with contract law, one can suggest analysing the internal structure of the parties' interaction in cases of disputes over movable property. In such disputes, the movable property represents the central object of the parties' inquiry, links the parties and lies at the heart of their interaction.[140] As such, it represents a starting point for judicial analysis under the MSR principle.[141] Under this vision of movable property choice-of-law rules, the chattel's location serves only as starting point that can be overturned by other circumstances of the case. In our case, the Singaporean law's point of departure should be overturned by the connecting factors of the parties' common residence. Accordingly, a Singaporean court should apply Australian property law in this case. **6.72**

In contrast to American and Chinese contemporary choice-of-law jurisprudence, English decisions and scholarship have generally remained faithful to the legal precedent set in *Cammell v Sewell*.[142] This judgment applied rigid *lex-situs* rule to a dispute over movable property's title. *Cammell v Sewell* involved a complex set of factual circumstances. A Russian seller shipped a cargo of timber from Russia on a German vessel to English merchants in England. While the vessel was badly damaged near the coast of Norway, the entire timber cargo was saved. The vessel's captain was a German resident. Without waiting, he sold the cargo in a public auction in Norway with a view to deliver the money to the English merchants. The cargo was purchased by Mr Clausen, whose place of residence was unclear. Subsequently, Mr Clausen sold the **6.73**

[139] Cf Roy Goode's sarcastic comments with respect to the question of applicable law to the case of the rights of the third parties in the case of assignment. While addressing the question on the proprietary relationship between the assignor, assignee, and the third parties, Goode dismisses the traditional *lex-situs* analysis of the subject that applies the *lex-situs* rule (ie the place of the debt in the case of assignment) and views it as completely arbitrary and irrelevant. R Goode, 'The Assignment of Pure Intangibles in the Conflict of Laws' in L Gullifer and S Vogenauer (eds) *English and European Perspectives on Contract and Commercial Law* (Hart Publishing 2017) 353, n 1; 355–56 (hereafter Goode, 'The Assignment').

[140] For this relational structure of the property law category, as a relation between a particular plaintiff's and defendant's rights and duties, through the object of property, see Kant, *Doctrine of Right* (n 120) paras 6:293–6:294; A Ripstein, *Force and Freedom* (Harvard University Press 2012) 86–107.

[141] For a somewhat related exposition of this point, see Savigny, *Conflict of Laws* 174–75, 188–89. See also *Cheshire & North* 1265 (mentioning that the *lex-situs* rule generally satisfies the reasonable expectations of the parties).

[142] (1858) 3 H & N 617.

cargo to English buyers. When the cargo arrived in England, the English underwriters of the cargo sued the buyers, claiming ownership of the cargo.[143]

6.74 The court did not apply itself to the location where the timber had ended up (England), but focused on where the disputed sale took place (in Norway, where Mr Clausen purchased the cargo). The English underwriters challenged the cargo sale in Norway arguing that the German captain acted in a hurry to sell the cargo and acted without their authorization.[144] The question of applicable law mattered a lot in this case: under Norwegian law, the captain had a right to act as an owner of the cargo; under German or English law, the cargo's sale to the English buyers would have been invalid.[145] The court applied Norwegian law, validated the sale, and the decision became the leading authority[146] on the question of disputes over title.

6.75 It is hard to see how this case can be seen as a determinative precedent for choice-of-law rules for movable property. The judgment is unclear due to its unusually complex factual basis and the many connecting factors that point to no less than four countries: Germany, England, Norway, and Russia. Under these circumstances, the application of the connecting factor of the cargo's location at the time of the disputed transaction seems to be a reasonable justification for application of Norwegian law.

6.76 Furthermore, the fact that the cargo was sold through a Norwegian *public auction* was pertinent. First, the seller and the buyer knew that the goods were sold through a pre-set public authority in Norway—which had an impact on their reasonable expectations as to the applicable law. Secondly, the act of public sale should have been conceptually and practically distinguished from the other acts and deeds situated within the borders of a given sovereign territory. The normative significance of such a sale meant that the foreign public institution had already executed its public authority through the sale of the cargo and declared that the sale was valid under its law.

6.77 The significance of the public auction draws an analogy with another area of private international law: recognition of foreign judgments. Similar to a public sale of goods, a foreign court's decision does not simply represent a deed made within a foreign territory or the mere fact of location for a certain person or thing within this territory. Rather, the international community views a foreign judgment as the execution of a foreign institution's authority. It views states as placed in equal relation to each other.[147] The products of their public legal institutions, such as judicial decisions, are also situated in equal relation to each other. This explains why under private international law doctrine, as a matter of principle, domestic courts view the normative status of foreign judgment as sound as theirs and avoid judging the substantive quality of their content. Accordingly, similar to the doctrine that directs domestic courts to recognize foreign judgments as a rule of thumb,[148] the fact that the sale of the goods

[143] ibid, 617–21.
[144] ibid, 621.
[145] ibid, 620.
[146] For authorities viewing this case as a leading case on the matters of movable property, see *Cheshire & North* 1268; Pitel & Rafferty, *Conflict of Laws* 348.
[147] For a discussion of this point, see the text accompanying nn 57–63.
[148] For this general position of the private international law scholarship, see eg Pitel & Rafferty, *Conflict of Laws* 168–77; A Reed, 'A New Model of Jurisdictional Propriety for Anglo-American Foreign Judgment

involved a public auction in Norway is a strong argument for this to be recognized by the English courts, regardless of the nature of the particular interaction between the parties. The principle of state equality is fundamental for private international law, and it supports this reading of *Cammell v Sewell*. The time for reconsideration of the strict *lex-situs* rule for movable property has come.

2. Built-In Presumptions for Negotiable Instruments Law

(a) Presumption for Obligations of the Primary Parties

Consider, first, the obligations of the primary parties under the instrument—that is, the obligations of the acceptor of a bill and the maker of a note. A primary party is liable to pay the holder the sum specified in the instrument unconditionally, namely, regardless of the holder's compliance with procedural requirements. Typically, payment by him or her discharges the instrument, that is, all other parties as well.[149] **6.78**

What should the nature of the presumptions for the primary parties be within the operational mechanism of the MSR principle? Following the observations made in section (B)(1) on this matter, one shall follow the insights of the general contract law doctrine. The internal structure of the contract law category suggests that the connecting factor of the place of the contractual performance shall serve as a point of departure for judicial analysis. Recall, however, this connecting factor serves only as a presumption. Representing a single constituent within the operational apparatus of the MSR principle, the place of contractual performance is mitigated through the analysis of the parties' interaction as a whole, including a careful evaluation of other factors of this interaction, such as the place of residence, place of business, and nationality. Even such factors as the instrument's form, specified currency and the language of the drafted instrument can potentially be taken into consideration for the purposes of MSR principle analysis.[150] **6.79**

The indicated place of payment seems to point clearly to the place of contractual performance between the primary party and the instrument's holder. By the very act of issuing the negotiable instrument, the drawer does not simply indicate that the payee will receive the specified amount from the drawee but also indicates that the payee will receive that amount from the drawee at a specific location. The acceptor, before accepting his or her obligations under the instrument, has the opportunity to revise the location of this payment.[151] **6.80**

Recognition and Enforcement: Something Old, Something Borrowed, Something New?' (2003) 25 Loy LA Int'l & Comp L Rev 243; *Dicey and Morris* 673–712; SI Strong, 'Recognition and Enforcement of Foreign Judgments in U.S. Courts: Problems and Possibilities' (2014) 33 Rev of Lit 45.

[149] See eg BEA ss 54 (1), 88(1), and 59; Chapter I, the text accompanying nn 144–50.

[150] For discussion about the possibility of incorporation of the factors of language, instrument's form, and the specified currency into the MSR principle's analysis, see the text accompanying nn 67–70.

[151] See eg Gleeson, *Chalmers and Guest* 98–101.

6.81 The Second Restatement suggests the connecting factor of the place of payment governs the obligations of the primary parties under the instrument and this has been incorporated in § 214 of the Second Restatement.[152] The Second Restatement makes a direct reference and draws an analogy to the centrality of place of payment in the context of general contract law.[153]

6.82 However, our position with respect to the connecting factor of the place of payment diverges on several key points from the choice-of-law rule stated in the Second Restatement.

6.83 First, we reject the Second Restatement's position to set the place of payment as a rigid connecting factor to determine the applicable law. Setting the place of payment as the *only* connecting factor betrays the Second Restatement's own *anti-Beale* rhetoric and departs from its own organizing principle of the MSR. As we have contended earlier in this chapter, the Second Restatement's justification of the 'special nature' of negotiable instruments law and the departure from the underlying structures of contract law and movable law is questionable. Relatedly, there was no reason to depart from the Second Restatement's fundamentals and essentially equalize negotiable instruments law with the category of immovable property.[154]

6.84 Second, the rigid view of the connecting factor of the place of payment ultimately fails to provide an answer to the question of *choice-of-law*. Instead of tackling the question of applicable law, it exclusively focuses on the question of *place of payment*. These are two different questions.[155] When the place of payment serves as an indicative starting point for tackling the question of the applicable law, setting the place of payment as a rigid connecting factor defeats the nature of choice-of-law analysis. The place of payment reflects the parties' reasonable expectations as to the identity of the applicable law only if it functions as a starting point. Then, this starting point needs to be mitigated and evaluated through other factors of the parties' interaction. Otherwise, the choice-of-law question would simply collapse into the question of the place of payment.

6.85 Finally, we reject the Second Restatement's position of addressing the case on its face where the instrument does not specify the place of payment. In this case, the Second Restatement favours a set hierarchy of connecting factors to determine the identity of such a place: the places of delivery and the instrument's dating.[156] The meaningful link between the place of payment and this hierarchical structure is minimal at best. It does not seem to be related to the underlying rationale of the choice-of-law process: what are the parties' reasonable expectations about which law would govern their potential future dispute? Clearly unrelated to this rationale, and without clear relation to the

[152] Second Restatement § 214.
[153] ibid. § 214, Comment b.
[154] See the text accompanying nn 115–20.
[155] For further discussion of this issues, see Chapter V section B(1).
[156] Second Restatement § 214 (2).

question of the place of payment, this hierarchical structure seems to simply serve the values of certainty and predictability.

This position, however, defeats the normativity of the choice-of-law question. As we have seen earlier in this chapter, the underlying justifications of the 'clear-cut rules' thesis should be reconsidered.[157] The alternative position would say that, in rare cases where the instrument does not specify place of payment,[158] the general structure of negotiable instruments law can establish the presumed place of payment of the acceptor. That is the place of the acceptor's location at the time of his or her acceptance. By accepting the obligation through his or her signature, the acceptor does not simply accept the obligation towards the holder to pay an amount stated on the face of the instrument, he or she also undertakes an obligation to make this payment at his or her location. In other words, it would appear that on the occasions when the place of payment is not clear, the internal structure of negotiable instruments law presupposes the place of the acceptor's location to be such a place.[159] The same point applies to the note maker. 6.86

In determining the location of the primary party, we suggest following the hierarchical structure of presumptions specified in several contemporary legislative frameworks. This structure takes the place of business as a point of departure. If the primary party has more than one place of business, the place of business is that which has the closest connection to the parties. If the holder does not have a place of business, it would be assumed that the primary party's location is the place of his or her residence.[160] It is true that because of the nature of the practice of negotiable instruments law, the place of payment will frequently coincide with the place of the primary party's business. This would naturally direct the MSR principle analysis towards the application of the law of the place of payment. Yet, this does not mean that the connecting factor of the place of payment operates exclusively to govern the obligations of the primary parties and that it cannot potentially be overturned. In fact, a close look at the case law supports this assertion. 6.87

Take, for example, *Greenlee v Hardin*.[161] The case is cited in the Second Restatement in support of the rigid place of payment rule to govern the obligations of the primary parties.[162] It involved a promissory note issued by a Florida corporation in the state 6.88

[157] See section A(2).

[158] On the commercial practice that usually specifies the place of payment on the face of the instrument, see McKendrick, *Commercial Law* 527–31.

[159] This suggestion seems to be consistent with the general common law choice-of-law rules applied to the banking contracts. Starting with party autonomy principle, and taking the place of the bank's habitual residence as a presumption, these rules proceed to the application of the MSR principle. See eg *Dicey and Morris* 2057–74. Also, it seems to be compatible with the general presumptions set in the negotiable instruments law with relation to the place of presentment. When the law takes the place of payment as the point of departure for presentment, in its absence it refers to the place of the drawee's residence and business. See eg Canadian BEA ss 84(1) and 88(m).

[160] This set of presumptions is based on the following list of contemporary and traditional legislative provisions: UCC § 3, ss 3-111; Canadian BEA s 87(c); UN Convention on the Use of Electronic Communications in International Contracts, art 6; Electronic Transactions Act 2011, s 15(2); Principles of European Contract Law 1995, art 2, 106.

[161] 157 Miss 229 (1930).

[162] Second Restatement § 214, Reporter's Note.

of Mississippi and payable in Florida. It was subsequently negotiated in Florida. The court made it clear that the connecting factor of the place of payment serves only as a point of departure for the judicial analysis. As the court put it:

> This presumption [the place of payment], however, is not absolute. And will be controlled by the actual truth of the case, when ascertained, or, in other words, by the intention of the parties, to be collected from the contract itself, and all the surrounding circumstances. [163]

6.89 This line of reasoning takes the place of payment as a point of departure, but it is not absolute and can potentially be overturned. In dealing with the question of the applicable law to liabilities of the primary parties under the instrument, the court refers to an ordinary contract law doctrine and the concept of the 'parties' reasonable expectations'. In this way, the court's line of reasoning effectively incorporates an MSR principle analysis. A similar reading of the MSR principle can be suggested with respect to other decisions on the question of the applicable law with respect to primary parties on the instrument.[164]

6.90 Accordingly, within the question of liability of the primary parties under the instrument (ie the bill acceptor and the note maker), we would opt for a rebuttable presumption of the place of the instrument's payment. Where the place of payment is not indicated in the instrument, the place of the primary party's location (to be determined by a hierarchical set of presumptions) shall serve as an indication of the place of payment.

(b) Presumption for Obligations of the Secondary Parties

(i) The Delineation from the Primary Parties

6.91 For secondary parties, the plot thickens. As we have seen in Chapter IV, the several laws doctrine[165] suggests that the obligations of the secondary parties are potentially governed by different choice-of-law rules. Respectively, different laws could potentially apply to govern the obligations of the primary and secondary parties. The principal distinction between primary and secondary parties under the instrument suggests that each case could potentially involve different considerations and be grounded on the different nature of the parties' reasonable expectations. Accordingly, the presumption applicable to the secondary party may differ from that of the primary party.

6.92 Indeed, a secondary party, namely the drawer and the indorser, undertake that the primary party will pay the sum specified in the instrument. As we saw in Chapter I, the secondary's own payment obligation in that sum arises only upon the holder's

[163] *Greenlee v Hardin* 234.

[164] See eg *McCornick & Co v Tolmie Bros.*, 46 Idaho 544 (1928) (this American case involved a note maker from Idaho delivered to the holder in Utah and payable in Utah. While applying the law of the place of payment (Utah), the court did not elaborate on the identity of other potential relevant factors, such as the residence of the parties); *Wragge v Sim Cooper and Company* (Australia) Pty Ltd [1933] HCA 59; 50 CLR 483 (in this Australian case, the place of payment coincided with the place of document's delivery—the Australian state of Victoria); *Banku Polskiego v Mulder & Company* 2 KB 266 (1941) (this English case dealt with a bill drawn in Poland and payable in Amsterdam. The application of the Dutch law followed the presumption of the place of payment and the residence of the bill's acceptors).

[165] For a discussion of the several laws doctrine, see Chapter IV section B.

presentment of the instrument, its dishonour, and the holder's dispatch of a notice of dishonour.[166] For its part, the secondary party undertaking to pay is not *at the same place* designated for the payment of the instrument by the primary party or the drawee.

Consider, for example, a bill issued by a German resident, addressed to an American drawee residing in New York and payable to a Mexican resident. In this case, the fact that the German resident undertook to pay the bill in the case of dishonour by the drawee does not mean that he or she undertook to pay in the exact same place mentioned for the drawee, regardless of whether the drawee accepted or not. We cannot say that the German resident undertook to make the payment in New York. **6.93**

The difference between the place of payment indicated on the instrument and the potential place of payment to be performed by the secondary party underlies the significance of the several contracts doctrine and conceptually distinguishes the secondary party's contract from the primary party's contract. The contractual obligation of the primary party to pay the holder in a certain location seems to be irrelevant within the spectrum of the secondary party's relationship with the holder. **6.94**

The fact that the principles governing the place of payment of a secondary party differ from that of a primary one was noted in the provisions of the various choice-of-law frameworks and the scholarly writings in the field. As Daniels puts it, 'the drawer of a bill does not bind himself to pay it specially where the acceptor is impliedly or expressly called on to pay it'.[167] Indeed, the status and the reasonable expectations of the secondary parties simply diverge from those of the primary parties. The acceptor's obligation to pay the instrument's sum at the location specified on the instrument or at his or her location does not extend to secondary parties. The secondary party simply does not expect to make payment in a place designated to the primary party. Accordingly, the place of the contractual performance (ie the place of payment) of the secondary parties in the case of the primary party's default requires a separate analysis. **6.95**

The various choice-of-law frameworks, other than that under the BEA, follow this conceptual division between primary and secondary parties. Thus, the Second Restatement explicitly sets a different choice-of-law rule with respect to the liabilities of secondary parties.[168] Rather than applying the connecting factor of the place of payment relevant to the primary parties, it applies the connecting factor of the place of document delivery.[169] The continental Geneva Conflicts Conventions follow a similar path. While the obligations of the primary parties are governed by the place of the instrument's payment, the obligations of the secondary parties are governed by the place of signature.[170] This way, the contemporary choice-of-law frameworks **6.96**

[166] See Chapter I, the text accompanying nn 144–50.

[167] See JW Daniel, *A Treatise on the Law of Negotiable Instruments* (5th edn, Baker, Voorhis & Company 1909) 909. A similar justification can be found within the provisions of the Second Restatement: 'the obligations of an indorser or drawer are governed by the local law of the state where he delivered the instrument and where, ordinarily at least, it must have been tacitly understood that any payment by him would be made'. Second Restatement § 215, Comment b.

[168] Second Restatement § 215 (1).

[169] ibid.

[170] The Convention for the Settlement of Certain Conflicts of Laws in Connection with Bills of Exchange and Promissory Notes 143 LNTS 319 (7 June 1930 143 LNTS 407 (19 March 1931), art 4.

acknowledge the different considerations involved in the choice-of-law analysis of secondary parties' obligations.

6.97 Where should the place of contractual performance of the secondary party be to the holder? The place of payment indicated with respect to the relationship between the primary party and the holder does not provide an answer to that question. The internal structure of negotiable instruments law does not suggest an inherent pre-designed place of the secondary party's payment that follows from the very nature of his or her obligation.[171] Where, then, should that place be set? One option for answering this question would suggest drawing an analogy with choice-of-law rules set in two related areas of law: (1) the law of suretyship; and (2) the law of assignments.

(ii) Potential Reference to Laws of Suretyship and Assignments

6.98 Consider, first, the law of suretyship. As we saw in Chapter IV,[172] the position of the secondary party under negotiable instruments law resembles that of the guarantor within suretyship law. This law has a tripartite structure of debtor, creditor, and guarantor. Within this structure, the contract of guarantee provides the creditor with security for the debtor's obligation. In the case of a debtor's default, the creditor holds the guarantor personally liable for the debt payment. In this sense, the obligations of the secondary party towards the instrument's holder in negotiable instruments law appear to mimic the relationship between guarantor and creditor in suretyship law.[173] Accordingly, it is possible to argue that the choice-of-law rules with respect to the obligations of secondary parties shall follow the choice-of-law rules set in the various frameworks of suretyship law.

6.99 The Second Restatement provides that the creditor–guarantor relationship shall follow what it calls the 'principal obligation'—the relationship between the debtor and the creditor.[174] Subject to an MSR principle analysis,[175] the two contracts within the internal structure of suretyship law are seen as intimately interconnected. For example, if the creditor-debtor agreement explicitly names the identity of the applicable law, this law shall govern the relationship between the creditor and the guarantor.[176]

6.100 The European jurisprudence on this matter is somewhat mixed. It follows the general notion of the characteristic performance concept,[177] which sets a presumption of the place where the party to perform the characteristic performance resides. Specifically,

[171] For discussion of this point, see the text accompanying nn 165–70.

[172] See Chapter IV, the text accompanying nn 40–57.

[173] See *Second Restatement* § 194.

[174] See eg MJ Oyarzaval, 'Guarantees' in J Basedow et al (eds) *Encyclopedia of Private International Law* (Elgar Publishing 2017) 861.

[175] For the centrality of the MSR principle's analysis in the context of the suretyship contracts, see eg *Johnson v Romamy Consumer Credit Corp.* 515 A 2d 682, 687 (Del, 1987); *Freestone Capital Partners LP. v MKA Real Estate Opportunity Fund* I, LLC, 155 Wash App 643, 643, 230 P 3d 625, 635–37.

[176] See eg *Empire Bank v Dumond*, 28 F Supp 3d 1179, 1185 (Okl, 2014).

[177] For a discussion (and criticism) of the 'characteristic performance' concept, see Chapter III, the text accompanying n 90.

in the context of the suretyship contract, this connecting factor would be the place of residence of the guarantor who needs to perform the characteristic performance.[178]

There is a clear correlation between the American and European positions on this point. In line with the Second Restatement, European jurisprudence has acknowledged the paramount significance of the 'principal obligation' within the internal structure of suretyship law. This significance comes into play under an MSR principle analysis of Article 4(4) of Rome I.[179] For example, in *Samcrete v Land Rover*,[180] the court has clarified that, under an MSR principle analysis, the law governing the principal obligation could potentially overturn the presumption of the guarantor's residence.[181] Thus, it would appear that European jurisprudence follows the Second Restatement's insight that choice-of-law analysis of the creditor–guarantor relationship shall be greatly affected by the law of principal obligation.[182] This is, at least, a point of departure 'in the absence of countervailing indications'.[183] **6.101**

A similar parallel can be drawn with assignment law. In the assignment of a simple debt a third party (the assignee) takes the place of the creditor as a claimant from the debtor. This way, the creditor transfers the benefit of the obligation to a third party—the assignee.[184] As such, the assignment inherently involves two contracts: (1) a contract between the debtor and the creditor; and (2) a contract between the creditor and the assignee. Translated to the context of negotiable instruments law, particularly where the assignment is with recourse, the position of the indorsee/holder resembles the position of the assignee. **6.102**

There is some correlation between choice-of-law rules in assignment and suretyship. Under the *Hague Principles*,[185] the contract between the debtor and the creditor shall be governed by the ordinary contract law rules of party autonomy and the MSR principle. The applicable law to the debtor–creditor relationship also determines the identity of the choice-of-law rules within the assignee–debtor relationship.[186] The Rome **6.103**

[178] See Giuliano & Lagarder Report para 21 (referring to suretyship contract where 'the characteristic performance is always that of the guarantor, whether in relation to the principal debtor or the creditor'). See also *Samcrete Egypt Engineers and Contractors v Land Rover Exports Limited* [2002] CLC 533 (hereafter *Samcrete v Land Rover*) [36] and [37]. Indeed, it seems to be clear that under the concept of the characteristic performance any obligation of payment would direct to the residence of the debtor. See eg *Ferguson Shipbuilders Ltd. v Voith Hydro GmbH & Co KG* 2000 SLT 229; *Ophthalmic Innovations International v Ophthalmic Innovations International Incorporated* [2004] EWHC 2948 Ch [26].

[179] Rome I art 4(4).

[180] *Samcrete v Land Rover.*

[181] ibid [47]. It should be noted that since the *Samcrete v Land Rover* was decided under the provisions of a more liberal Rome Convention, it is not entirely clear whether this would be the court decision under the framework of Rome I, which imposes a stricter vision of the characteristic performance presumption. For a discussion of this point, see eg CSA Okoli, 'The Significance of the Doctrine of Accessory Allocation as a Connecting Factor under Article 4 of the Rome I Regulation' (2015) 9 JPIL 448, 488–91.

[182] See eg *Aquavita International SA, Glendive Enterprose Limited v Ashapura Minecham Limited* [2014] EWHC 2806 (Comm) [17].

[183] ibid. See also Chapter IV, the text accompanying nn 33–38.

[184] See TC Hartley, 'Choice of Law Regarding the Voluntary Assignment of Contractual Obligations Under the Rome I Regulation' (2012) Int & Com L Qua 29, 31 (hereafter Hartley, 'Choice of Law').

[185] See Hague Conference on Private International Law, Principles on Choice of Law in International Commercial Contracts (adopted Mon 19 March 2015) art 10(a).

[186] ibid, art 10(b).

I follows a related path. The creditor and the debtor can set their relationship through an express choice of the governing law.[187] In the absence of such choice, Rome I follows the connecting factor of debtor's residence as a point of departure to govern his or her (debtor's) relationships with the creditor.[188] Based on the rationale of the debtor's protection and the notion that the change in identity of a creditor shall not affect the debtor's position, the relationship between the debtor and the assignee is governed by the same law.[189] Apparently, under the Rome I, the debtor and the assignee can agree on a different law under the party autonomy principle.[190] As mentioned, the underlying position of the European thinking is that the choice-of-law rules of assignment should aim to protect the debtor and avoid a situation where the debtor's position worsens as a result of the assignment. In other words, the underlying trigger of the choice-of-law rules is that the successor of the original creditor (the assignee) shall not have more rights than the assignor had.[191]

6.104 Despite the resemblance to negotiable instruments law, we do not suggest referring to the area of suretyship law as a model for designing and developing choice-of-law rules to govern the internal relationships within negotiable instruments law. Indeed, the position of the secondary party under negotiable instruments law is of a similar nature to the guarantor's position under the law of suretyship. Yet, fundamentally, the secondary party's contract lacks the degree of inherent connectedness or closeness to the primary party's contract as exists between the debtor-creditor and the creditor-guarantor in suretyship law.[192]

6.105 This 'connectedness' aspect of suretyship law explains why the applicable law to the principal agreement (ie the contract between the debtor and the creditor) plays a decisive role for the guarantor's contract (ie the contract between the creditor and the guarantor). The two contracts are interchangeably connected, which explains why the choice-of-law under the primary contract will usually affect the applicable law of the secondary contract.

6.106 Furthermore, the contract of guarantee lacks the negotiability aspect under which the guarantor's obligation towards the creditor can be easily transferred by the latter. This aspect affects the three-fold relationship between the parties where the identity of the parties is known to each other and their reasonable expectations as to applicable

[187] Rome I art 14(1). See also CE Tuo and MR Isidro, 'Assignability/Assignment of Claims' in J Basedow et al (eds) *Encyclopedia of Private International Law* (Edgar Publishing 2017) 141, 146 (mentioning party autonomy as 'normal connecting factor' in assignments) (hereafter Tuo and Isidro, 'Assignment').

[188] Rome I art 14(2). See also Hartley, 'Choice of Law' 39.

[189] Rome I (art 14(2). *Raiffeisen Zentralbank Osterreich AG v Five Star Trading* LLC [2001] EWCA CIV 68. See also Catherine Walsh, 'The Role of Party Autonomy in Determining the Third-Pary Effects of Assignment: of "secret Laws" and "Secret Liens"' (2018) 181 at 182; McKendrick, *Commercial Law* 359, mentioning the 'obvious reason that the debtor ought not to have its position affected by an assignment to which it is not a party'.

[190] See Tuo and Isidro, 'Assignment' 144: 'Nonetheless, the possibility that the assignee and the debtor choose the law applicable to their relations should not be excluded.'

[191] ibid, 146. The position of the Second Restatement is somewhat vague on the point of assignment. Thus, §§ 208–09 apply the MSR principle to various aspects of assignment. However, no presumptions or the possibility to apply party autonomy principle are mentioned.

[192] Thus, § 194 of the American Second Restatement acknowledges a close relationship within suretyship law. See also Chapter IV, the text accompanying nn 33–38.

law are different. Transferred into the negotiable instruments language, in the guarantee contract, the holder (ie creditor) knows or should have known the identity of the guarantor and such factors as his or her (guarantor's) residence. This fundamentally diverges from the inherent vision of the parties' reasonable expectations within the internal structure of negotiable instruments law where, due to the inherent negotiability of the instrument, the holder does not have knowledge (and should not have knowledge) of the guarantors of his or her payment—the secondary parties.

A more nuanced point can be made with respect to the law of assignment. In contrast **6.107** to the contract of guarantee, but similarly to the secondary party's engagement on a negotiable instrument, the assignor's contract with the assignee lacks the degree of inherent connectedness or closeness to the primary party's contract as exists between the debtor-creditor and the creditor-guarantor in suretyship law. Also, and again similarly to the position of a secondary party on a negotiable instrument, a debtor on a simple debt ought to be cognizant of the potential transferability of the debt to successive assignees. Yet, there is a distinction between the assignment of a simple debt and the negotiation of a negotiable instrument. Each indorsement is tantamount to the issue of a new bill which generates an autonomous relationship between each party liable and the holder at that time. At the same time, the assignment of a simple debt transfers to the assignee the original creditor's claim against the debtor. For his or her part, the debtor remains a primary party towards an assignee who steps into the shoes of the original creditor, rather than a secondary party in an independent relationship with a new holder of the negotiable instrument.

Unlike a debtor on a simple debt, a secondary party to a negotiable instrument be- **6.108** comes liable on an obligation which by nature of things is 'circulable'. This supports the conceptual distinction between negotiable instruments law and assignment law. Even as the assignee-assignor contract is distinct from that of the debtor-creditor one, the debtor–assignee relationship is intimately linked to the debtor–creditor original contract. Conversely, the secondary party's obligation on a negotiable instrument stands on its own.

Without delving further into the choice-of-law rules of suretyship and assignment,[193] **6.109** the important point for our purposes is this: to one degree or another, these laws are

[193] Naturally, the purpose of this book is to analyse the nature of choice-of-law rules of negotiable instruments, rather than the laws of assignment and suretyship. Yet, we can briefly say that on the one hand, we welcome such developments in these areas as the general application of ordinary contract choice-of-law rules (ie the incorporation of the party autonomy and MSR principles) and the point about an inherent connectedness within the internal structure of suretyship law. On the other hand, we doubt such phenomenon as the application of the characteristic performance presumptions in the way it applies (for a criticism of this presumption see n 130) to the guarantor contract and the submergence of the choice-of-law analysis of the assignments' law to the place of the debtor's residence. This one-sided focus on the debtor is not just questionable from the internal choice-of-law question standpoint (for discussion of this point, see Chapter V section B(1)) but also relates to the attempt to impose on the law of assignment the property law rule of the *lex-situs*. The connecting factor of the debtor's residence seems to crystalize that rule. For a recent discussion (and criticism) of this point, see Goode, 'The Assignment' 353, n 1 and 355–57. See also *Cheshire & North* 1280 (acknowledging that the traditional property law rule of *lex-situs* correlates with the connecting factor of the debtor's residence). See also *In re Banque Des Marchands De Moscou (No 2)* [1932] 1 WLR 1108, 1116 (affiliating the location of the debt with the place of debtor's residence).

incapable of shedding full light on the identity of the choice-of-law rules of the secondary parties under the instrument. Resorting to various choice-of-law rules frameworks set with respect to assignments and suretyship would fail to acknowledge the distinctive character of these areas of law. The key for grasping the nature of presumption to the secondary parties lies somewhere else.

Having rejected the laws of the secondary party's place of signature, delivery, or business (including incorporation or residence), we are left with two options. The first is the place of the next in line, namely subsequent, secondary party in the liability chain (the immediate or direct creditor of the liable secondary party). The second is the place of the holder, the ultimate creditor of the party secondary liable. On balance, focusing on the 'circulable' nature of the secondary party's engagement, we are inclined to prefer the location of the holder. However, we recgonize that this option entails a situation in which a signer would not know at the time of incurring liability which law will apply to it. We are further cognizant that in the eyes of many this may be too high a cost to pay in order to achieve what we believe is doctrinal consistency.

(c) The Suggested Point of Departure: Holder's Location

6.110 As a point of departure, we suggest referring to the general doctrine of the law of payments. The general rule of this law instructs that the debtor must seek after the creditor. The payment of the debt must be made in the place designated by the parties in the agreement between them. In the case where such an agreement is absent, the legal doctrine of payment sets the place of debt repayment as the creditor's location.[194] We suggest following the insight of this doctrine of the payment law. After all, the essence of the secondary party's obligation is that of debt payment to the holder. Negotiable instruments law creates this obligation of the secondary party to the holder without specifying the place of its fulfilment. Similar to the general law of payments, in the absence of an indication otherwise, the debtor must make the payment at the place of the creditor's location. The set of hierarchical presumptions discussed in paras 6.86–6.90 as to the location of such a place[195] apply.

6.111 To be sure, the suggested rule of the place of the holder's location focuses on the time when the relevant interaction between the parties takes place—the time when the instrument leaves the sphere of secondary party's control. This time represents the critical moment of the parties' interaction.[196] Recall, when an instrument is dishonoured

[194] See eg Bowen LJ in the *The Eider* (1893) P 199, 136–27. This seems to be the general position of English (*Browne v White* [1947] 1 WWR 622; *Soward v Palm* (1818) 129 ER 390; *Robery & Co v Snaefell Mining Co. Ltd* (1887) 20 QBD 152) and American (*Venetian Slami Co v Parthenais*, 554 So 2d 499, 502; *Sterrett v Stoddard Lumber Co*, 150 Ore 491, 505 (1935)) courts. See also C Proctor, *Goode on Payment Obligations* (2nd edn, Sweet & Maxwell 2009) at 24 (mentioning that 'prima facie it is for a debtor to seek out his creditor and pay him where he may be found' and that the place of the creditor's residence is just a presumption that can be rebutted by an explicit or implied terms of the contract or other circumstances).

[195] See the text accompanying nn 157–64. As we have seen in section 2(a), this point does not apply with respect to the payment of the primary party which inherently presupposes the location of this party as the place of payment (see nn 158–59 and the accompanying text).

[196] Cf 'critical transaction' timing mentioned in the context of the relevant timing for cases involved disputes over proprietary entitlements (see section B(1)(b). For discussion on the significance of the timing when the instrument leaves the sphere of secondary party's control, see Chapter IV, the text accompanying nn 100–33.

by non-acceptance or by non-payment, the holder must give the secondary party a notice of dishonour.[197] Yet, the parties' reasonable expectations are set at the time of their original interaction and their subsequent interactions are simply irrelevant for the purposes of the determination of the applicable law.[198] The fact, for example, that a party (or parties) changes his or her location at the time of the notice of dishonour cannot affect the identity of the applicable law to govern their adjudication process.

The instrument's holder sets his or her reasonable expectations with respect to the identity of the applicable law at the time he or she receives the instrument. The holder knows or should have knowledge of the applicable law at the time of his or her decision to acquire the possession of the instrument. The secondary party should expect to litigate his or her claim with a wide range of potential holders and applicable laws. Of course, to balance the situation, there is an option open to the signatory secondary party to write on the instrument 'without recourse'[199] or specifically (as suggested in Chapter V[200]) to indicate an applicable law. The secondary party knows or should have known about these legal devices available to him or her to limit the unpredictability of his or her potential position. If the secondary party fails to do so, he or she should expect to be sued under a framework of an unlimited number of laws.[201] **6.112**

On this point, the suggested point of departure coincides with the underlying rational of negotiable instruments law, which encourages the instrument's negotiability and enhances the position of the instrument's holder. The suggested rule indeed enhances the position of the instrument's holder. Whether he or she is holder in due course or not, the holder knows or should have known that his or her potential future litigation with the secondary party will be governed by the negotiable instruments law of his or her premises at the time of the instrument's transfer to him or her, at least as a point of departure. **6.113**

A careful review of the case law supports placing the connecting factor of the holder's location as the point of departure. The resolution of cases seems more attuned with the **6.114**

197 See eg Canadian BEA ss 95(1), 102(1) and (2).

198 It should be noted that this 'timing issues' (ie irrelevancy for the choice-of-law process of the parties' subsequent changes of residence or other circumstances) has been duly noted in the choice-of-law literature, see eg Kegel, 'Conflict of Laws' 191–92 (objecting to taking into consideration the interests of those who have helped the injured party after the accident); WA Reppy Jr, 'Eclecticism in Methods for Resolving Tort and Contract Conflict of Laws: The United States and the European Union' (2008) 82 Tul L Rev 2053, 2102.

199 Cf *Coulter v Stewart* 93 Arix 242, 243 (1963).

200 See Chapter V section B.

201 Indeed, the suggested presumption of the place of holder's location follows the internal rationale of the negotiable instruments law that underlies the value of predictability and the value of upholding the status of the instrument's holder (See eg Gleeson, *Chalmers and Guest* 585: 'the object of a bill, cheque or note is to secure to the holder payment of the amount stated in the instrument'. Yet, it is important to say that such coincidence is incidental. Our path for deriving the place of holder's location rule has been based on the insights of the general contract law doctrine (with respect to the centrality of the contractual performance within the internal structure of contract law) and the general payment law (with respect to the insight that the debtor must make the payment at the creditor's residence). Accordingly, nothing in our discussion here contradicts our principle position according to which choice-of-law analysis may sometimes confirm and sometimes disconfirm the underlying rationales of the negotiable instruments law. For discussion of these issues in the context of the party autonomy principle and the MSR principle, see Chapter V section B and Chapter VI section B(1).

distinctiveness of the contract made by the secondary party rather than defence of a particular choice-of-law rule applicable to the secondary party. The cases have simply focused on the support of the several laws doctrine and the distinctiveness between obligations of primary and secondary parties to the instrument.[202] Some cases simply do not mention the connecting factor of the holder's location.[203] The operational result of others is consistent with this presumption and the underlying reasoning of the MSR principle.[204]

6.115 In the case of *Hyatt v Bank of Kentucky*, a note maker made a promissory note payable to the plaintiff in the state of Louisiana. Subsequently, the plaintiff changed his residence to Kentucky and indorsed the note to a local Kentucky bank, the note holder and the defendant in this case. While stressing the point that the indorsement contract conceptually diverges from the primary contract,[205] the court followed the law of the place where the note was delivered to the Kentucky bank. Yet, the court added in the same sentence that the place of delivery coincided with the place of the holder's business residence—Kentucky.[206] Then, the court made reference to what would nowadays be called the MSR principle, mentioning the residence of each one of the parties, the place of indorsement, and the place where the money was received.[207]

6.116 *Hennenlotter v De Orvananos*[208] is another example. The case involved cheques signed and delivered in Mexico and payable in New York. The plaintiffs, who were cheque holders, sued the defendants, who were drawers. While mentioning the rule that the obligation of the drawer of a bill of exchange is determined by the place of delivery, the court once again engaged in what seems to be very much an MSR principle analysis, mentioning, as noted earlier, that 'it was a Mexican transaction as to all parties except the drawee',[209] and the language in which the instruments were written.[210] This presumption of the place of the holder's residence at the time of the relevant interaction between the parties pointed to Mexican law as well. Accordingly, this law was applied.

6.117 Finally, we return to the English case of *G & H Montage G.m.b.H v Irvani.*,[211] which involved a business relationship between German and Iranian corporations.

[202] See eg *Mackintosh v Gibbs* 98 NJL 40 (1909) 43 ('This contract of endorsement was entirely distinct from the contract of the maker to pay the note and from the debt arising against the maker'); *Allen v Kemble* (1848) 6 Moo PCC 314; 13 ER 704, 707 ('This argument, however, appears to us to be founded on a misapprehension of the obligation which the drawer and the indorser of a Bill incurs.... If this contract of the drawer might be broken by the drawee, either by non-acceptance, or non-payment, the drawer is liable for payment of the Bill, not where the Bill was to be paid by the drawee, but where he, the drawer, made his contract'); *Walling v Cushman* 68. See also Chapter IV, the text accompanying nn 93–99.

[203] See eg *Coulter v Stewart* 93 Ariz 242 (1963); *Allen v Kemble*; *Mackintosh v Gibbs* 79 NJL 40 (1909); *Mayfield v Equitable Trust Co.* 295 F 109 (1924).

[204] *Walling v Cushman* 68 (mentioning that the presumption of the place of delivery can be overturned when 'it appears from the special circumstances that the parties intended otherwise').

[205] ibid, 198: 'A party may know when he indorses a paper in Kentucky executed in Louisiana that the law of the latter state imposes a different liability from the law of Kentucky, and still his assignment, being of itself an independent contract'.

[206] ibid, 197.

[207] ibid.

[208] *Hennenlotter v De Orvananos.*

[209] ibid, 336.

[210] ibid, 334.

[211] *Irvani, Court of Appeal*. For a discussion of this case, see the text accompanying nn 30–39.

Several bills were issued by the Iranian corporation and the question was one of the legal status of the *aval* indorsement by the Iranian corporation's managing director. What is particularly interesting for our purposes here is the court's reference to the MSR principle and its assertion that the principle directs towards applying the German law in this case. In the court's words, 'the centre of gravity [an alternative term to MSR principle] of the transaction on the bill between the defendant and the plaintiffs does seem to me to have been in Germany'.[212] In light of the multiplicity of connecting factors in this case, one can, however, challenge this assertion. Under the operational mechanics of the MSR principle, the analysis should have relied on a certain presumption. Apparently, only the presumption of the instrument holder's location (ie Germany) would justify the application of German law in this case.

In order to elaborate on the suggested choice-of-law rules mentioned in sections 2(a) and 2(b), which are applicable to primary and secondary parties, consider the following. While on vacation in Mexico an Australian resident purchases a watch from a German resident. As a method of payment, the Australian resident issues to the German resident a bill payable in New York drawn on a New York resident. The bill is accepted in New York and negotiated in Egypt by the German resident to a Nigerian resident. Upon the dishonour of the bill, the Nigerian resident has an option to sue the US acceptor. In this case (and based on the suggested rule mentioned in section 2(a)), the US law would apply unless the US place of payment is arbitrary and the acceptor does not reside in New York, but rather in Nigeria. In this case, the analysis under the MSR principle would overturn the presumption of the place of payment and would direct to the application of the Nigerian law to govern the liability of the acceptor. **6.118**

The Nigerian holder may also choose to sue the Australian resident as a secondary party on the instrument. According to the above-suggested rule in section 2(b), this litigation should be governed by Nigerian negotiable instruments law. Indeed, this development seems to be unfavourable to the Australian resident. His or her position can potentially get worse. First, most likely the Australian resident would not be able to raise the defence he or she could have raised related to the underlying transaction had he or she been sued by the German resident. For example, he or she cannot argue that the watch stopped working after several days. This deterioration of the position of the Australian resident relates to the Holder in Due Course status under the negotiable instruments law, rather than to the choice-of-law process itself. Second, and perhaps worse, the Australian resident could now be potentially sued by a wide range of unfavourable negotiable instruments laws. However, the Australian resident should be viewed as undertaking the risk of such unfortunate developments: he or she could limit the negotiability of the instrument and could determine the identity of the applicable law. In this way, the suggested rule seems to be internally balanced in terms of the parties' expectations. In addition, it supports the underlying rationale of **6.119**

[212] ibid, 686

negotiable instruments law that enhances the position of the holder and the fluency of commerce at this point.

6.120 Accordingly, within the question of liability of the secondary parties under the instrument (ie the drawer and the indorser), we would opt for a rebuttable presumption of the place of the holder's location (to be determined by a hierarchical set of presumptions).

VII
The Boundaries of the Proposed Argument

This chapter addresses the scope and limits of the proposed extension of the party autonomy and most significant relationship (MSR) principles to negotiable instruments. Section A challenges the validation principle, being an apparent major limitation to the proposed broad scope argument. Section B discusses the relevance of the argument to such issues as the proprietary aspects of the instruments, remedies and limitation periods, and the holder's duties. Section C elaborates on the relevance of the proposed argument beyond bills of exchange (bills), promissory notes (notes), and cheques. Specifically, it explores whether our suggestions could be extended and applied to choice-of-law rules in areas where the notion of negotiability has traditionally played a role: investment securities and documents of title. Finally, section D sets a limit to the scope of the argument and explains in which cases the organizing principles of party autonomy and MSR shall not be applied. **7.01**

A. Challenging the Validation Principle

1. Form, Capacity, and Illegality as 'Particular Issues'

We begin our discussion with an apparently serious objection to the broad application of our contentions with respect to contractual aspects of the instrument. This objection, which we shall describe as the 'validation principle', supports an application of different rules to various aspects of contractual liability under the instrument. To add complexity to our task, the validation principle is far from being settled within the ordinary contract law doctrine of the choice-of-law rules. In the ensuing paragraphs, we challenge this principle in the context of general contract law and disagree with its application to negotiable instruments law. **7.02**

7.03 Over the years, the choice-of-law literature and judicial decisions have made suggestions and comments about a possible exclusion of several areas and instances from the application of ordinary contract choice-of-law rules. Specifically, it has been argued that issues such as form requirements, parties' capacity, and the issues of legality should be governed by a set of different or, at least, modified rules that would reflect the special nature of these issues. These have been described as 'particular issues'[1] of contract law.

7.04 The 'particular issues' of contract law inherently tackle the very validity of the contract. First, consider formal requirements. Various jurisdictions impose requirements on the form of the contract, making the validity of the contract dependent on the fulfilment of a certain formal requirement.[2] Among these are the requirements for certain contracts (such as insurance contracts) to be in writing, to be properly sealed (for instance, in cases where no consideration is required under the contract), or to have several witnesses physically present at the time of the contract formation.[3] Within common law, perhaps the most well known contract form requirement was set in the English Statute of Frauds[4] and in the re-enactment of some of its provisions around the Commonwealth.[5] This early piece of legislation requires the following types of contract to be in writing: contracts involving transfer of interest in real property, contracts involving the sale of goods beyond a certain amount, contracts lasting more than one year, and contracts responsible for someone else's debt.[6]

7.05 Second, various jurisdictions have set different rules on the parties' ability to enter into a legal obligation. For instance, the systems depart on the question of the minimum age required for parties to enter into a transaction, and vary with respect to the required threshold to invalidate a contract on the grounds of intoxication.[7] In addition, once upon a time, many systems had provisions that restricted married women to enter contracts without their husband's assent.[8] Third and last, a contract can potentially be invalidated by failing to meet certain requirements of legality. For instance, various jurisdictions have adopted different rules as to the legality of certain actions, such as the payment and enforcement of gambling debts.[9]

[1] See eg J Fawcett and JM Carruthers (eds) *Cheshire, North & Fawcett: Private International Law* (15th edn, Oxford University Press 2017) 751 (hereafter *Cheshire & North*).

[2] See eg C Esplugues et al, 'Formal Requirements and Validity' in J Basedow et al (eds) *Encyclopedia of Private International Law* (Edgar Publishing 2017) 783.

[3] For a discussion of these issues, see eg SGA Pitel and NS Rafferty, *Conflict of Laws* (2nd edn, Irwin Law 2016) 296 (hereafter Pitel & Rafferty, *Conflict of Laws*); *Restatement of Conflict of Laws, Second* (edn, 1971; revised 1986 and 1988, American Law Institute) § 199, Comment b (hereafter Second Restatement).

[4] Statute of Frauds 1677 (IMP).

[5] See eg Statute of Frauds, RSO 1990, C s 19.

[6] ibid.

[7] See eg Pitel & Rafferty, *Conflict of Laws* 296.

[8] See eg Second Restatement § 198, Comment c (mentioning that 'the restrictions upon the capacity of married women to contract have been largely abandoned'); *Teas v Kimball*, 257 F 2d 817, 823 (1958). We will say much more on the nature of these provisions in the last section of this chapter—section D.

[9] See eg Pitel & Rafferty, *Conflict of Laws* 300–02.

These 'particular issues' are relevant to the operational dynamics of negotiable instruments. Similar to ordinary contract cases, a negotiable instruments case can potentially invoke each one of these issues. Furthermore, the issue of formal requirements deserves special attention for the purposes of our book. Negotiable instruments law sets specific form requirements as a precondition to an instrument's existence,[10] making those requirements an essential part of this area of law. From this perspective, the form requirements seem to be much more immanent to negotiable instruments law. The diversity among the systems as to the nature of those requirements[11] illustrates the paramount significance of the choice-of-law question for determining the parties' rights and duties. What law, then, should govern the form requirements, as well as other 'particular issues', of negotiable instruments law? **7.06**

Interestingly, the field of negotiable instruments law has not learnt from lessons and debates within regular contract choice-of-law literature on these matters. While the Bills of Exchange Act (BEA) expressly equates questions of parties' capacity under the instrument and contractual capacity,[12] the negotiable instruments literature has refused to apply the rules of the latter to the former. Rather, it has been argued that the special nature of negotiable instruments law and its distinctiveness from ordinary contract law suggests the application of distinctive rules, such as the place of contract formation, set in the BEA's s 72(1).[13] Similar to issues of capacity, the choice-of-law literature also does not rely on the ordinary contractual choice-of-law rules with respect to the questions of the form's requirements[14] and illegality.[15] **7.07**

We do not accept this position. As we have seen in Chapter II, negotiable instruments law is deeply rooted in the doctrine of contract law, and there is no reason to exclude the dramatic developments that have taken place within it. Accordingly, the quest to grasp the nature of the 'particular issues' within negotiable instruments law requires a close look at these issues within the literature and decisions of general contract law. **7.08**

[10] See eg Bills of Exchange Act, 1882, Ch 61, 45 and 46 Vict s 3 (hereafter BEA).

[11] See Chapter I sections D and E.

[12] See BEA s 22(1) ('Capacity to incur liability as a party to a bill is coextensive with capacity to contract'). See also A Barak, 'The Nature of the Negotiable Instrument' (1983) 18 Isr L Rev 49, 62–63. Barak's work presents a sophisticated argument that conceptually delineates between the two types of negotiable instrument's rules: (1) rules in a 'strict sense' (those which the underlying basis seems to strictly refer to the notion of negotiability); and (2) 'broad sense' (those rules which the underlying basis refers to ordinary contract and movable property laws) (ibid, 69). Stated in these terms, Barak's thesis supports the application to questions of capacity of an ordinary contract choice-of-law rules.

[13] See eg AG Gleeson, *Chalmers and Guest on Bills of Exchange, Cheques and Promissory Notes* (18th edn, London: Sweet & Maxwell 2016) 591, n 74 (hereafter Gleeson, *Chalmers and Guest*) (although acknowledging that the issue of 'ordinary' contractual capacity is governed by the connecting factors of the residence of the parties and their combination with the MSR principle, mentions that 'it would be preferable' for negotiable instrument to apply a connecting factor of the place of contract formation).

[14] See eg Collins (ed) *Dicey and Morris on the Conflict of Laws* (11th edn, Sweet & Maxwell 1987) 1314 (supporting the application of the place of contract formation rules to the questions of the form requirements).

[15] See eg Gleeson, *Chalmers and Guest* 597 (supporting the position that the matter of illegality should be determined by the place of each contract formation).

2. General Contract Law: Special Rules for the 'Particular Issues'

7.09 How does contract law choice-of-law doctrine address the 'particular issues' rules? Consider the question of formal requirements. In this respect, the position of the various systems is intriguing. While generally following the 'ordinary' path of choice-of-law analysis, the systems have adopted an exception (or even exceptions) to it. For example, the Second Restatement follows the path of ordinary contract law choice-of-law rules with respect to the question of form requirements.[16] Yet, it also establishes an exception under which even if the requirements of form are not meet under the applicable law, the contract will be still valid if it meets the requirements of the place of its formation.[17] Canadian jurisprudence follows the same path: the formal requirements of the contract must comply with either formal requirements of the applicable law or the requirements of the place of contract formation.[18] Article 11(1) of Rome I extends the application of the American and Canadian exception only to the cases where the contracting parties at the time of contract formation are physically situated in the same country.[19] In other instances, Rome I applies another exception: it would be enough to validate the contract if it is valid under the law of either of the parties' residence.[20]

7.10 A similar tendency toward contract validation can be found with respect to the issue of capacity. Take, for example, the Second Restatement. While the issue of contractual capacity is generally governed by ordinary contract choice-of-law rules, the contract can be alternatively validated if the capacity requirements are met under the place of residence of the parties.[21]

7.11 The question of contractual capacity seems to be less clear on the other side of the Atlantic. In fact, this question remains unanswered. This can be attributed to the deep conceptual disagreement between common and civil systems about the very nature of capacity. The common law systems have generally viewed the issue of capacity as a part of the contractual obligations of the parties.[22] For civil lawyers, capacity is a part of a person's status, akin to the status of marriage. Viewing capacity through this lens, the civil law systems have opted to focus on each party's place of residence as the relevant connecting factor.[23]

[16] Second Restatement § 199.
[17] ibid.
[18] See eg Pitel and Rafferty, *Conflict of Laws* (n 3) 296–97.
[19] Regulation (EC) 593/2008 of the European Parliament and of the Council of 17 June 2008 on the Law Applicable to Contractual Obligations (Rome I), 2008 OJ (L 177) 6 (EU), art 11(1) (hereafter Rome I).
[20] ibid, art 11(2).
[21] Second Restatement § 198.
[22] See eg *Cheshire & North* 697 (mentioning the traditional position on capacity of civil lawyers that can be contrasted to the position of common law lawyers who 'do not see a problem to apply the regular choice-of-law rules').
[23] See eg FC von Savigny, *A Treatise on the Conflict of Laws, and the Limits of Their Operation in Respect of Place and Time* (trans by WGuthrie, T & T Clark 1880) 140, 148 (viewing the issue of capacity to enter into legal relationships as the 'status of the person in itself' what justifies the application of the connecting factor of the place of residence (hereafter Savigny, *Conflict of Laws*)).

This principal division with respect to the very nature of capacity explains its exclusion from harmonization choice-of-law trends, such as the Rome I[24] and the Hague Principles.[25] The only point of agreement between the principal positions of the systems is the specific circumstances mentioned in Article 13 of Rome I.[26] This provision supports a contract's validation against the defence of incapacity under two conditions: (1) the contract has been concluded between persons who are physically situated in the same country; and (2) the other party could not reasonably suspect incapacity.[27] **7.12**

Furthermore, even within the common law world, the jurisprudence on capacity is somewhat mixed and uncertain. For many years, the literature and judicial decisions have frankly acknowledged significant uncertainty about the identity of the choice-of-law rules to govern the matter of the parties' capacity. Some authorities have supported an application of the ordinary contract choice-of-law rules.[28] Others have opted for such connecting factors as the place of contract formation and the place of the parties' residence.[29] Interestingly, it would appear that case law has equated the questions of capacity within the context of commercial business activity with questions raised in the context of family law, specifically in the context of the parties' capacity to marry.[30] **7.13**

Finally, some common law scholars have raised further objections to the application of ordinary choice-of-law rules to the question of capacity. Without adopting the civil systems' position of capacity based on the parties' status, this line of objection has taken a different course. It argues that the contemporary contract law choice-of-law principles of party autonomy and the MSR are fundamentally founded on the subjective intentions of the parties. If this is the underlying rationale of these principles, how is it possible for the parties to presume the validity of the contract under the applicable law without first resorting to some external source to determine the identity of that law? Apparently, the question of the applicable law to adjudicate the claims **7.14**

24 Rome I art 1(2)(a) (generally excluding the questions of capacity from the scope of the Regulation).

25 Hague Principles on Choice of Law in International Commercial Contracts, 2015, art 1(3)(a) <https://www.hcch.net/en/instruments/conventions/full-text/?cid=135>, accessed 20 December 2019, (hereafter Hague Prinicples).

26 Rome I art 11(1).

27 ibid.

28 See eg *Charron v Montreal Trust Co* [1958] OR 597 [602]; *Mackender v Feldia* AG [1967] 2 QB 590 (CA). For the most recent comprehensive call for the application of ordinary choice-of-law rules to the questions of capacity, see B Ubertazzi, 'Capacity & Emancipation' in J Basedow et al (eds) *Encyclopedia of Private International Law* (Edgar Publishing 2017) 326.

29 See eg Pitel & Rafferty, *Conflict of Laws* 296–97.

30 Thus, eg *Cheshire & North* 761 mention *Sottomayor v De Barros* (1877) 2 PD 81, PDA and *Cooper v Cooper* (1887) 13 App Cas 88, HL cases delivered in the context of marriage contracts, for the purposes of a discussion on capacity issues in commercial contracts. One can argue, however, that the equivalence seems to be somewhat problematic in light of the apparent normative force embedded in the very act of marriage, as a reflection of an act of sovereign public authority. This distinctiveness of the act of marriage apparently distances it from commercial contracts and changes the very essence of the choice-of-law analysis. (For a similar point, made albeit in the context of sale of movable property in public auctions, see Chapter VI, the text accompanying nn 145–49.)

that challenge the very validity of the contract should be determined first, before the intention-based choice-of-law analysis comes into play.[31] In other words, the application of the ordinary choice-of-law doctrines to the questions of contract validity leads to circularity.

3. The Underlying Basis for the 'Particular Issues'—the Validation Principle

7.15 Despite some confusion and uncertainties, one can clearly recognize a guiding idea of the 'particular issues' choice-of-law rules—the tendency to use the choice-of-law process as a vehicle for a given contract validation. This means introducing into choice-of-law analysis a new choice-of-law principle that we name, the 'validation principle'.

7.16 The validation principle supports the validity of contracts. The nature of this principle relates to the parties' presumed intention not to engage themselves in an invalid transaction.[32] Stated in different terms, under the validation principle, the contracting parties are regarded by the court as having intended to subject themselves to the positive laws of the state under which the contract would be valid. In this way, the principle serves as an indicative component of the parties' choice to adjudicate their dispute and crystalizes their reasonable expectations.[33]

7.17 Furthermore, the validation principle does not only reflect the objective intentions of the parties as to the identity of the applicable law, but it also supports the value of predictability and sustainability of commercial dealings. Within the spectrum of the relationship between the litigating parties, the principle favours that party who is interested in contract validation. This point is emphasised in the context of negotiable instruments. In this context it has been powerfully argued that the internal structure and the underlying rationale of this area of law is founded in the notions of certainty and predictability, enhancement of the instrument's negotiability, and upholding the status of the instrument's holder.[34] By upholding the validation of each contract on the instrument, the validation principle seems to reinforce the position of the holder and

[31] See A Briggs, 'The Formation of International Contacts' [1990] Lloyd's Mar & Com L Q 192, 200. See also EG Lorenzen, 'Rules of the Conflict of Laws Applicable to Bills and Notes' (1917) Minn L Rev 10, 18 (arguing against capacity rule as negating the parties' intentions). See also A Briggs, *Agreements on Jurisdiction and Choice of Law* (Oxford University Press 2008) 395 (opposing incorporation of the party autonomy principle with respect to the issues of capacity in the following terms 'Capacity is a special issue–the ability of individuals to confer upon themselves a contractual capacity which they would otherwise lack not be a matter of party choice') (hereafter Briggs, *Agreements*).

[32] For this vision of the validation principle, see eg AA Ehrenzweig, *A Treatise on the Conflict of Laws* (West Pub Co 1962) 211, 213; B Hayward, *Conflict of Laws and Arbitral Discretion* (Oxford University Press 2017) 101 (hereafter Hayward, *Discretion*).

[33] For this understanding of the principle, see Savigny, *Conflict of Laws* 223–24, 252; PE Nygh, 'The Reasonable Expectations of the Parties as a Guide to the Choice of Law in Contract and in Tort' (1995) 251 Rec des Cours 273, 338–40 ('It is obvious that the rule of validation [validation principle] in general accords with the reasonable expectations of the parties').

[34] See eg Gleeson, *Chalmers and Guest* 585 ('the object of a bill, cheque or note is to secure to the holder payment of the amount stated in the instrument'); E McKendrick (ed), *Goode on Commercial Law* (5th edn, Penguin 2016) 571 ('Because of the need to protect the marketable status of bills of exchange, the courts are

pre-empts the possible argument of the signatory parties to challenge the instrument's validity on the grounds of lack of capacity and/or failure to meet the requirements of formalities and/or illegality. In other words, if the task of negotiable instruments law is that the holder must win, the validation principle can greatly assist the holder with this task.

In order to illustrate this point, consider the BEA s 71(2) (ie proviso b), discussed in Chapter VI.[35] This provision tackles the question of the form requirements of an instrument issued abroad.[36] As we have seen, proviso b supports validation of instruments issued abroad despite possible inconsistency with the form requirements of the place of issue.[37] While Chapter VI has discussed the seemingly discriminatory aspects of this provision,[38] it can be argued that this provision can be presented in a light that supports commercial dealings and provides a legal tool for the instrument's holder to pre-empt a possible challenge to the instrument's validity on the grounds of formal requirements. Indeed, some scholars argue precisely this to justify proviso b.[39] This point suggests that had proviso b been structured in a neutral way (ie not in a one-sided manner),[40] it would have been consistent with the validation principle that supports commercial dealings and prevents the possibility of challenging them on the grounds of the instrument's invalidity. **7.18**

4. Reconsidering the Validation Principle

Despite its apparent attractiveness, we reject the validation principle as a relevant consideration within the *choice-of-law analysis*. Our objection to invoking the principle runs along both conceptual and practical lines. First (and similar to our discussion on the connecting factor of the place of payment in Chapter VI),[41] there is a question of relevance. It is one task to tackle the identity of the applicable law to adjudicate parties' rights and duties under the instrument and their reasonable expectations in that respect. It is, however, another task to tackle the parties' intentions and reasonable expectations with respect to the validity of the given contract. The two tasks do not necessarily overlap. Of course, the law views the parties as objectively intending to **7.19**

extremely reluctant to allow defences to be raised to an action on a bill, so that in the great majority of cases summary judgment will be given within a matter of weeks of the commencement of proceedings') (hereafter McKendrick, *Commercial Law*). See also Chapter V section B and Chapter VI section B(1).

[35] Chapter VI, the text accompanying nn 49–71.
[36] BEA s 72(2).
[37] Chapter VI, the text accompanying nn 49–71.
[38] ibid.
[39] See eg Collins, Harris (eds) *Dicey, Morris and Collins on the Conflict of Laws* (15th edn, Sweet & Maxwell 2012) 2082 (albeit making this point with respect to proviso a of BEA s 72—this point equally applies to proviso b: 'For *business purposes* it would be unfortunate if it were necessary to consider in the case of bills and notes issued abroad the need for or sufficiency of stamp' (emphasis added) (hereafter, *Dicey and Morris*). See also Gleeson, *Chalmers and Guest* 590–91 (discussing proviso b in terms of facilitating the instruments' exchange in UK).
[40] For discussion on the 'one-sidedness' of the provision, see Chapter VI, the text accompanying nn 49–71.
[41] For discussion of this point, see Chapter VI section B(2).

validate the contract. At the same time, however, the parties can objectively be seen as favouring the application of a legal framework that happens to invalidate the contract between them. The parties can clearly choose French law, for example, as the governing law of their transaction, yet this law can invalidate the contract.

7.20 The divergence between the two expectations is easy to explain: frequently the parties do not know that the applicable law would invalidate their contract. Yet, this does not mean that the parties have not objectively intended to apply that law—they simply made a mistake as to its content and its effect. The incorporation of the validation principle, under these circumstances, would mean an imposition on choice-of-law analysis considerations that are foreign to its nature. As we have seen throughout this book,[42] the choice-of-law process claims its independence. It cannot simply be subjected to the external values, such as certainty and predictability, and commercial efficiency that the validation principle crystalizes. Sometimes choice-of-law and negotiable instruments law values coincide, sometimes they do not.

7.21 Second, one can challenge each of the above-mentioned objections made in the literature for excluding the 'particular issues' from the application scope of the ordinary choice-of-law process. Thus, it simply would not be correct to say that the party autonomy and MSR principles are solely based on subjective intentions of the parties. Indeed, had that statement been correct, it would have raised a conceptual problem for the application of these principles to such an area as the parties' capacity. Yet, as we have seen earlier in this book,[43] both the party autonomy and the MSR principles crystalize a complex syllogism of both objective and subjective factors, a notion that is fatal to this objection.

7.22 The other objection relates to the very nature of negotiable instruments law and its alleged unequivocal support of position of the instrument holder. This view of negotiable instruments law is indeed consistent with the validation principle and challenges the application of ordinary contract choice-of-law rules to 'particular issues'. Yet, it is at odds with our view, according to which the choice-of-law process shall not submit itself to external values. Furthermore, as we have seen in Chapter VI,[44] the point about the predominant status of the instrument's holder is simply misleading. Contrary to this notion, the internal structure of negotiable instruments law represents a delicate balance between the holder's right to enforce the instrument and the rights of the signatory parties.[45] There is no built-in requirement within negotiable instruments law that the holder must win.

7.23 Third, as we have seen throughout this book,[46] the validation principle departs from the very nature of traditional and contemporary choice-of-law thought: that

[42] For a discussion of this point, see section B(2)(a).

[43] For a discussion on this point, see Chapter III section B(2) and (3). Generally, the literature rejects the position that the MSR principle is based on subjective intentions of the parties. See eg Pitel & Rafferty, *Conflict of Laws* 296 (pointing to objective nature of the judicial evaluation under the MSR principle). See also *Cheshire & North* 722, n 406 (delineating the conceptual difference between arts 3(1) and 4(4) of Rome I precisely relying on the objective standard of the MSR principle).

[44] For discussion of this point, see Chapter VI, the text accompanying nn 96–103.

[45] ibid.

[46] See Chapter III section A and Chapter VII section D.

choice-of-law analysis shall not delve into the substantive evaluation of the involved laws and should distance itself from the possible results that the application of a given law produces.[47] For example, in a case of tort committed by an Australian resident against a Canadian resident in Indonesia, the choice-of-law analysis, as a matter of principle, does not make a quality judgment of Canadian, Australian, and Indonesian tort laws; nor does it examine the result of applying each one of these laws. With very few exceptions, discussed later in this chapter,[48] the principal position of choice-of-law scholarship and judicial decisions is to avoid this kind of analysis.

But, this is exactly what the validation principle does. By referring to the considera- **7.24** tion of several laws, it 'picks behind the scenes' of each law to determine whether its application would lead to a validation of the contract. To say that this practice is problematic would be an understatement. The objection goes beyond the specific context of the choice-of-law question and tackles the fundamental notion of whether judges can base their decisions on outcome-driven reasoning, regardless of the identity of pre-existing formal legal rules, doctrines and concepts that apply to a given case.[49] Essential to any legal system are considerations such as procedural fairness, legitimacy, accountability, and transparency of the judicial process, all of which would oppose the practice of picking behind the scenes.[50]

In addition to the conceptual difficulties of the validation principle, its implementa- **7.25** tion raises a number of other concerns. Why does the Second Restatement, for example, limit the 'additional venue' or the 'escape device' for contract validation to the connecting factor of the contract formation? Why examine only this connecting factor in an effort to uphold the contract? How is it consistent with the principal position of contemporary choice-of-law scholarship under which the place of contract formation is frequently fortuitous[51] and simply irrelevant to the parties' interaction? How does the validation principle relate to consumer protection legislation and the protection of the weaker parties to the transaction? Apparently, the underlying spirit of the various 'special issues' (such as the requirement of the contract to be in writing) seems to be an effort to protect a 'weaker' party[52] within the parties' interaction. Does the underlying rationale of the 'particular issues' not lead to diametrically opposite presumptions that invalidate contracts? And why, at all, limit the 'additional venues' or 'escape devices'

[47] ibid.

[48] See section D.

[49] See eg B Leiter, 'American Legal Realism' in D Patterson (ed) *A Companion to Philosophy of Law and Legal Theory* (Wiley-Blackwell 2010) 249, 252.

[50] See eg HLA Hart, *The Concept of Law*, chapter 7 (2nd edn, Clarendon Press 1994).

[51] See eg Pitel & Rafferty, *Conflict of Laws* 297 (specifically mentioning the puzzle of the validation principle's 'additional venue' of contract formation in light of the fortuitous nature of it). For further discussion on the arbitrary nature of the contract's formation connecting factor, see Chapter III, the text accompanying nn 83–85.

[52] See eg Second Restatement § 198, Comment b (mentioning that the choice-of-law rules of capacity are designed for the protection of the persons to whom the capacity to contract is denied); Comment c (mentioning choice-of-law rules that are designated to protect a particular class of people, as 'consumers, labourers or debtors'). See also a relatively recent American case *AD v Credit One Bank* (NA 885 F 3d 1054, 1062 (2018) CA) where the court has invoked Second Restatement § 198 in the context of the California minor protection and who lacked capacity under the California law to enter into cardholder agreement.

of the validation principle to the connecting factors of the place of contract formation and the parties' residence?

7.26 Of course, the validation principle can come into play through a broad range of potential connecting factors that have some meaningful connection to the parties and the event. Beyond the difficulty involved in such an exercise, there is a serious practical objection. The contemporary reality of technological progress and the increased mobility of people frequently involves a vast range of potential connecting factors. The complex web of international commercial interactions involves, as we saw in Chapter III, multiple links to different states.[53] This suggests a vast potential pool of connecting factors. Within this reality, it is not clear in which cases the validation principle should be invoked and in which cases it should not. The principle would come very close to a doubtful notion about its transnational value.[54] In this way, the validation principle would claim its normative significance at any point in space and time.

7.27 The earlier discussion demonstrates the problematic nature of the validation principle. The principle does not relate to the normative structure of the choice-of-law question, it requires recognition of its transnational value, and it raises serious practical deficiencies. We are of the opinion that it should not be a part of the choice-of-law process. The important values that underpin the principle have already been incorporated within the internal structures of various provisions. Stated in slightly different terms, the various domestic provisions already internally support the contracts' validation. Amongst these provisions are corporate law provisions that support validation of a contract made by a corporation even in contradiction to its own constitution,[55] and a common law position that supports contract validation in the circumstances of contracts made by mentally incapacitated persons.[56] Specifically, in the context of negotiable instruments law, there is the BEA provision, which supports the capacity of the parties and therefore validates the contract.[57] The choice-of-law process does not need an additional layer of support and a second round of protection from the validation principle. The incorporation of the principle within this process would mean a collapse of the latter into the domestic adjudicative process, a phenomenon that has been rejected by choice-of-law scholarship.[58]

7.28 Arguably, this position with respect to 'particular issues' finds support in the contract law case law. Consider cases cited by the Second Restatement concerning capacity, formal requirements, and illegality. For example, the judicial reasoning dealing with

[53] See Chapter III, the text accompanying nn 35–39.

[54] This kind of argument has been recently made by Charles Kotuby and Luke Sirota. See CT Kotuby Jr and LA Sobota, *General Principles of Law and International Due Process* (Oxford University Press 2017) (hereafter Kotuby and Sobota, *General Principles*).

[55] See eg Corporations Act 2001 (Cth) s 9, arts 125–28.

[56] See eg *Hart v O'Connor* [1985] AC 1000; [1985] 3 WLR 214 (sets a rule according to which a person of unsound mind will not be able to avoid a contract whether the other party was unaware of their mental incapacity).

[57] BEA ss 54(2) and 55(1)(b). See also McKendrick, *Commercial Law* 561 (mentioning that the BEA establishes a presumption against lack of capacity).

[58] For discussion of this point, see Chapter VI, the text accompanying nn 104–10.

§ 198 (which deals with capacity) seems to be consistent with the ordinary choice-of-law process, without resort to the 'additional venues' or 'escape devices' of the validation principle. A review of the cases indicates that they were either based on the presumption of the place of contractual performance[59] or decided through an explicit reference to the MSR principle's underlying reasoning. This reasoning applied the law of that state where 'the focus of the contract was centered'[60] or which had the 'most intimate contact'.[61]

There is a similar tendency on the question of formal requirements set out in § 199 of the Second Restatement. Similar to the cases dealing with capacity, the cases concerned with formal requirements have been decided on the basis of the presumption of the place of contractual performance[62] and the MSR principle. [63] Finally, a review of cases on the matter of illegality reveals the apparent consistency of the courts' reasoning with the ordinary choice-of-law process.[64] There is no reason why negotiable instruments law should not follow this emerging tendency of general contract law. The validation principle should be rejected. **7.29**

[59] See eg Second Restatement § 198, Illustrations 1 and 2; *Paulson v Shapiro*, 490 F 2d 1, 7 CA (1973); *Ram Products Co., Inc v Chauncey*, 967 F Supp 1071, 1072 Ind (1997) (hereafter *Ram Products v Chauncey*).

[60] See *Teas v Kimball*, 257 F 2d 817, 823 (1958).

[61] *Ram Products v Chauncey* 1072. See also *Faloona by Frederickson v Hustler Magazine*, Inc 7999 F 2d 1000, 1003 CA (1986) (mentioning that 'the contract was negotiated, executed, and performed in California').

[62] See eg *Ideal Structures Corpv Levine Huntsville Development v Corp*, 251 F Supp 3,7 CA (1973).

[63] Second Restatement § 199, Comment c; Illustration 3; *McKinney v National Dairy Council*, 491 F Supp 1108, 113, 114 (D. Mass, 1980).

[64] Amongst the cases, the following seem to adopt the MSR principle's rhetoric: *Chuidain v Philippine Nat. Bank*, 976 F 2d 561, 564, 567 CA 2001; *In re Parkwood, Inc*, 149 App DC 67, 461 F 2d 158, 172 CA (1971); *Cameron v Gunstock Acres, Inc.*, 348 NE 2d 791, 793 (1976); *Chrysler Corp v Skyline Indus. Serv.* 448 Mich 113, 528 NW 2d 698, 704 (1995, Mich); *International Tracers of Merica v Hard*, 89 Wash 2d 140, 570 P 2d 131, 133 (1977, Wash). On a similar note, the following cases seem to be consistent with the presumption of the place of performance: *Wood Bros Homes, Inc v Walker Adj. Bureau*, 198 Colo 444, 601 P 2d 1369, 1373 (1979, Colo); *Panama Processes v Cities Service* Co., 796 P 2d 276, 288 (1990, Okl). It is true that within choice-of-law literature there is a popular view according to which the fact of illegality of the performed act under the place of contract performance shall play a role in the choice-of-law process (see eg Second Restatement § 202; Pitel & Rafferty, *Conflict of Laws* 301). We would humbly disagree with the position that attributes exceptional characteristics to the illegality of the act in the place of performance. Consider Lord Mansfield's observations in *Robinson v Bland* (1790) 97 ER 717 discussed earlier in this book (Chapter VI, the text accompanying nn 23–26). It is important to emphasize the fact that Lord Mansfield grounded his decision on the notion of reasonable expectations of the parties (ibid at 720). However, it is also important to emphasize what Lord Mansfield *had not* said in *Robinson v Bland*. He had not said eg that choice-of-law analysis should follow the place of contract formation as a reflection of the sovereign will. He also did not attribute significance to the fact that the application of English law validated the contract, and the application of French law did not. Finally, he also did not say anything regarding how deeply the French system objected to gambling debts. These 'non-says' (followed in the *Moulis v Owen* [1907] 1 KB 746 precisely follow our position with respect to the illegality issues. The defence of illegality in the place of performance (and when it is different from the law of obligation) seems to relate more to arguments that do not respect the substantive differences between the systems. Throughout our book (see Chapters III and VII) we reject those types of arguments, subject to the so-called 'ethical moment' outlined in section D of this chapter. Unless a jurisdiction determines a certain matter as a mandatory rule/rule of public law rule/rule of political character, there is no reason why the forum should require compliance with the laws of the place of performance. Naturally, under our approach (and since we designate a central role to the place of performance), the law of the place of performance will coincide with the law of obligation many times.

B. The Various Aspects of Negotiable Instruments Law: The Broad Scope of the Argument

7.30 After rejecting the incorporation of the validation principle as a relevant consideration of the choice-of-law rules relating to contract law generally and negotiable instruments in particular, we are in a position to contemplate the suggested scope of the proposed argument. The scope is broad. We suggest extending the popular party autonomy and MSR principles to a broad range of issues and aspects of negotiable instruments law, discussed throughout this book in Chapters I and IV: issues of interpretation, the effect of the parties' liabilities, intrinsic and extrinsic aspects of the instrument, and defences.[65] Some aspects of negotiable instruments law merit a separate discussion and treatment: holder's duties, remedies and limitation periods, and proprietary aspects.

1. Holder's Duties

7.31 Throughout this book we have elaborated on the nature, form, and timeline of the various procedural requirements of the instrument's holder. These requirements include provisions as to the time and manner of the presentment of the instrument by the holder to the drawee and the dispatch of a notice of dishonour to secondary parties.[66]

7.32 Which law shall govern the procedural requirements the holder is to comply with? Our position is that these requirements ought to be classified as part of the substantive interaction between the parties and should be governed by the law of obligation. Although being called 'procedural', they relate to the very nature of the parties' interaction within the internal structure of negotiable instruments law.[67] Within this structure, the holder's duties represent the fundamental value of the parties' autonomy and reinforce that value through presenting the instrument to the drawee (in the case of presentment) and notifying the secondary party about the instrument's dishonour (in the case of notice of dishonour).[68]

7.33 Accordingly, the following observations can be made in relation to procedural requirements to be complied with by the holder. Since presentment is a requirement that the holder has to meet vis-à-vis the drawee, it should be governed by the presumption of the place of the instrument's payment. Along those lines, as the notice of dishonour is part of the holder and the secondary party relationship, it should be governed by the presumption of the holder's location. Indeed, a review of the case law on the matters of holder's duties reveals examples of use of the MSR principle along with presumptions

[65] See Chapter I sections D and E; Chapter IV sections D, E, F, G, and H.

[66] See eg Chapter I, the text accompanying nn 144–50.

[67] See eg Second Restatement § 206, Comment b, Illustration 4 (delineating a difference between substantial rights and duties of the parties).

[68] See Chapter V, the text accompanying nn 130–35.

of the place of payment (for primary parties) and the instrument holder's location (for secondary parties).[69]

2. Remedies and Limitation Periods

We follow the insights of the contemporary choice-of-law scholarship that sees these matters as issues of substance to be governed by the law of obligation.[70] Accordingly, the MSR principle, with the presumptions of the place of payment (with respect to primary parties) and the place of the holder's location (with respect to secondary parties), applies. **7.34**

3. Proprietary Aspects

As we have seen in Chapter VI,[71] the presumption of the place of the instrument's location provides the point of departure for an MSR principle analysis of issues related to proprietary aspects of the instrument. These issues arise in a limited number of cases that involve disputes that challenge the very entitlement of one of the parties on the instrument. Following the insights and developments within the movable property choice-of-law rules, the operational mechanism of the MSR principle mitigates the presumption of the place of the instrument's location through other connecting factors. Already having a limited scope within the contemporary structure of negotiable instruments law, the proprietary aspect of the parties' relationship will become less important in the near future with the advance of purely electronic versions of the instrument.[72] **7.35**

We accept the conclusions of the traditional and contemporary choice-of-law literature that the physical aspect of the instrument affects the nature of the choice-of-law analysis in disputes over an instrument's title. Section 216 of the Second Restatement, **7.36**

[69] Thus, the American cases which have relied on § 206 of the Second Restatement, seem to incorporate the MSR principle's rhetoric. See *Northern Ins. Co. of New York v Allied Mut. Ins.*, 9555 F 2d 1353, 1359 (CA, 1992); *Martin by Martin v John Hancock Mutual Life Insurance Company*, 56 F Supp 2d 670, 673 (1999, Va). A position with respect to two leading English cases on this matter is different. On the one hand, in *Rothschild v Currie,* (1833) 113 ER 1045 a bill was drawn in England, accepted in France, and then indorsed in England. The English indorsee (holder) sued the English indorser. The application of the French law with respect to the question of validity of the notice of dishonour in this case (ibid, 1048) is inconsistent in this case with the presumption of the holder's location and the MSR principle, supported in this book. On the other hand, the other leading English case—*Horne v Rouquette* (1878) 3 QBD 514, CA—is consistent with our analysis. In this case a bill was drawn in England, payable in Spain and endorsed in Spain. The holder sued the drawer. By referring to parties' expectations on the bill ('Every party to a bill knows that by the law-merchant it may be indorsed abroad. He cannot object to its being indorsed abroad' (ibid, 520), the court applied Spanish law on the question of validity of the notice of dishonour, what correlates with the presumption of holder's location and the MSR principle.

[70] See eg R Garnett, *Substance and Procedure in Private International Law* (Oxford University Press 2012) (hereafter Garnett, *Substance & Procedure*).

[71] See Chapter VI section B(1)(b).

[72] See Chapter VIII, the text accompanying nn 128–29.

for example, says that in disputes over the transfer of entitlement on negotiable instruments and the effect of such transfer, the connecting factor of the place of the instrument applies.[73] Thus, the law of the place of the instrument at the time of transfer would determine the question of whether the holder has received title to the instrument and whether they are entitled to the status of the Holder in Due Course (HDC).[74] Besides a reference to the classical *lex-situs* rule in the area of property law,[75] the Second Restatement justifies this rule as correlating with the reasonable expectations of the parties.[76] For instance, the question of the holder's title to a note signed and delivered in state X and transferred to a holder in state Y shall be determined by the law of state Y.

7.37 Recall, however, our discussion in Chapter VI on choice-of-law rules of movable property, originally set in the case of *Cammell v Sewell*.[77] The analysis of the movable property category, together with a careful review of the *Cammell* case, favour setting the *lex-situs* rule only as a point of departure for judicial analysis under the MSR principle. While the *lex-situs* rule reflects the parties' reasonable expectations as to the identity of the applicable law to adjudicate their dispute, this rule shall be mitigated through an accompanying analysis of other connecting factors.

7.38 One of the examples where the proprietary aspect of negotiable instruments law comes into play is the instances of fraud and fraudulent transfers.[78] These instances involve a question of the proprietary entitlement to the instrument, which explains why the legal analysis should focus on the physical location of the instrument at the time of the 'problematic'/fraudulent event. Another example where the proprietary aspect of negotiable instruments becomes relevant is the question of the indorsement's status. By questioning the validity of the indorsement, the signatory party challenges the very entitlement of the instrument's holder to it. Accordingly, in such situations, the court should examine the relevant relationship among the parties where the holder's entitlement is challenged.

7.39 Consider several negotiable instruments law cases. The pre-BEA era *In re Marseilles Extension Railway and Land Company* (1885)[79] involved a bill issued by a French resident to another in France, payable in England. The payee indorsed the instrument

[73] See eg Second Restatement § 216; *Embiricos v Anglo-Australian Bank* [1904] 2 KB 870, AFF'D [1905] 1 KB 677. See also Chapter IV section G.

[74] Second Restatement § 216 (a).

[75] ibid, § 216 (1).

[76] The Second Restatement states this justification of the *lex-situs* rule in the following terms: 'obviously fair to the holder for the reason among others, that this is the state law whose local law [ie law of the place of the instrument at the time of the transfer] he would be most likely to consult. The rule likewise is not unfair to the obligor since negotiable instruments pass readily from hand to hand, and he should have realized when he ordinarily delivered the instrument that its travels might take it through several states' (Second Restatement § 216, Comment a.

[77] See Chapter VI section B(1)(b); (1858) 3 H & N 617.

[78] For a discussion of these aspects of negotiable instruments law, see Chapter I, the text accompanying nn 114–20 and Chapter IV, the text accompanying nn 186–87.

[79] (1885) 30 Ch D 598. For a discussion of this case, see Chapter VI, the text accompanying nn 64–72.

to an English resident in England.[80] Under the proposed analysis, the status of the indorsement in this case should have been analysed through the lens of the presumption of the instrument's place at the time of the indorsement (England) and the other connecting factors relevant to this indorsement. The fact that the indorsee was French and the indorser was an English resident would be examples of such factors. This analysis explains the application of English law without invoking the validation principle[81] and without claiming that the circumstances of the case represent an exception to the 'several laws' doctrine.[82]

Alcock v Smith (1892)[83] is clearly reminiscent of the factual situation in *Cammell*. It involved a sale of a bill through a public auction in Norway.[84] The decision does not mention other connecting factors that might be relevant to the case, such as the residence of the parties.[85] However, the point made with respect to *Cammell* applies here: the status of the public auction has a normative force as it represents a positive act made by a state, which is akin to its law or final judgment.[86] As such, it must be respected by the other states as a matter of equality between systems and their public institutions. The application of the Norwegian law followed. **7.40**

Koechlin et CIE v Kestenbaum Brothers[87] is another example. In this case the drawer, the payee, and the indorser were all French residents. The case involved an instrument payable in England which was indorsed in France. The drawee, who was the defendant in this case, challenged the holder's entitlement to the instrument by questioning the validity of the indorsement. The court stated its principal position according to which *lex-situs* rule in *Cammell* applies to the case of negotiable instruments. This led to the conclusion that the validity of the instrument's transfer should be governed by the place of that transfer.[88] The court also supported its reasoning through a reference to the notion of the parties' reasonable expectations and intentions as directing towards the application of the French law.[89] We willingly embrace both parts of this analysis: the application of the French law follows from the presumption of the place of the instrument's transfer and the residence of the parties. **7.41**

[80] ibid, 601.

[81] ibid, 601, 603.

[82] Collins (ed) *Dicey and Morris on the Conflict of Laws* (11th edn, Sweet & Maxwell 1987) 1315 ('The presumable object of this exception from the 'several laws' doctrine is to make bills issued (or indorsed or accepted) abroad more easily negotiable in the United Kingdom').

[83] *Alcock v Smith* [1892] 1 Ch 238.

[84] ibid, 253, 256.

[85] ibid, 264–65.

[86] For discussion of these issues, see Chapter VI, the text accompanying nn 146–48.

[87] [1927] 1 KB 889 (hereafter *Koechlin v Kestenbaum Brothers*).

[88] ibid, 896. Cf *Macmillan Inc v Bishopsgate Investment Trust* plc (No 3) [1996] 1 WLR 387, 412; All ER 585, CA (extending in a somewhat problematic way the proprietary *lex-situs* rules to the case of shares). For further discussion of this point, see Chapter VIII, the text accompanying nn 128–29.

[89] *Koechlin v Kestenbaum Brothers* 894. As the court put it 'The bill is a French bill drawn in Paris in the French language to an order of a French resident, accordingly, the son [the indorser] was duly authorized to indorse the bill on his own name, without adding the words "per pro". At another place of the judgement, the court specifically justified the application of the French law as 'intended by the parties' (ibid, 898).

C. Securities and the Documents of Title

1. Documents of Title

(a) Bills of Lading and the Liability Limitation Trend

7.42 Documents of title to goods typically refer to bills of lading and warehouse receipts. Bills of lading are issued by the carrier of a cargo of goods to its owner or his or her agent. They play a key role in international trade, shipping, commerce, and maritime traffic. Warehouse receipts are issued by a warehouse operator in relation to storage of goods. Documents of title identify the owner of the goods carried for the purposes of commerce or stored in a warehouse. The claim on the ownership of the goods can be asserted through the entitlement to hold the document. The word 'title' underscores the ability of the document's possessor to transfer it to a third party, which invokes the negotiable aspect of the document and the potential relevance of the preceding discussions in this book.

7.43 Due to their greater practical significance in commerce, our focus in this section will be on bills of lading.[90] The carrier issues this document upon loading the goods on the vessel. Typically, upon the arrival of the vessel to the designated port, the owner of the goods or the owner's agent presents a copy of the document to the carrier in order to take possession of the goods listed in it. Ordinarily, a bill of lading includes such information and records as the number of the packages carried on the vessel, their nature and weight, the name and address of the carrier, the date of shipment, port of loading, and procedural matters related to the goods' discharge.[91] Since the carrier issues a bill of lading only after loading the goods onto the vessel, this document closely relates to the underlying contract of the carriage.[92]

7.44 The negotiability feature of the bill of lading makes it relevant for our book. Originally, bills of lading were not transferable and as such not negotiable. However, following the demands of commerce, it became possible for the cargo owner to sell the document to a third party through an assignment, which granted the third party a right to claim the goods from the carrier.[93] In this way, bills of lading have followed the formal aspect of negotiability under which a third party acquires a proprietary right in the document through the physical transfer of possession.[94] Similar to classical negotiable instruments, the transferor can indorse

[90] It should be noted, however, that art 7 of Uniform Commercial Code treats bills of lading and warehouse receipts together. See ALI and NCCUSL, 2002, art 7 (hereafter UCC)

[91] E Gold et al, *Maritime Law* (Irwin Law 2003) 447–48 (hereafter Gold et al, *Maritime Law*); N Gaskell et al, *The Bills of Lading* (Informa Professional 2000) 1–3, 409, 411–12 (hereafter Gaskell et al, *The Bills of Lading*).

[92] R Force, *Admiralty and Maritime Law* (Federal Judicial Centre 2004) 53 (hereafter Force, *Admiralty and Maritime Law*); N Francis, 'Transferring Rights of Suit Under Bills of Lading: The Conflict of Laws Implications' (2006) 20 A & NZ Mar LJ 25, 26 (hereafter, Francis, 'Transferring Rights'); M While, *Australian Maritime Law* (3rd edn, The Federation Press 2014) 216–23.

[93] *Lickbarrow v Mason* (1794) 5 TR 683 (Hol).

[94] See Gaskell et al, *The Bills of Lading* 21; F Munari, 'Bill of Lading' in J Basedow et al (eds) *Encyclopedia of Private International Law* (Edgar Publishing 2017) 193.

the bill through a signature and the deliver possession of it to the transferee.[95] The bill of lading however diverges from notes, bills and cheques on the point that its transfer does not entail the material aspect of negotiability. In contrast to instruments, the third party cannot acquire a better title by taking the bill in his or her possession.[96] While nowadays the popularity of the negotiability of bills of lading is questionable,[97] the historical and conceptual links to classical negotiable instruments suggests that the choice-of-law rules applicable to this document (as well as warehouse receipts) are worth exploring.

The liability aspect, or more precisely the limitation of liability, played a central role in **7.45** the development of the legal doctrine of bills of lading. Over the nineteenth and twentieth centuries, the nature of maritime shipping activity provided a carrier with the ability to dictate the content of the provisions in the bills of lading. The bills of lading were generated at a time of powerful shipping carriers that provided little choice to the merchants as to their ability to negotiate the provisions of the document. The practice of commerce in the nineteenth century was that carriers frequently incorporated provisions in the bill of lading that significantly limited their own liability and that of the crew during the frequently long period of the goods' transportation. Originally, English[98] and American[99] courts enforced those one-sided and unfair provisions. However, towards the end of the nineteenth century, American legislation intervened into the contractual relationship between the carrier and the cargo owner. This is how the Harter Act of 1893[100] originated.

It is true that the paternalistic consideration of the protection of US merchants was **7.46** amongst the underlying triggers for the Harter Act.[101] However, the Harter Act also reflected some deep reasons justifying the legislative intervention in the contractual autonomy of the parties. Commercial shipping practice provided too much pre-bargaining power to the shipping carrier in his or her interaction with the cargo owner. The carrier had the control of the ship and the goods. In this position, the carrier had the power to impose preferential terms and conditions in the bill of lading.[102] The practice of bills of lading that included provisions that waived or almost completely

[95] Gold et al, *Maritime Law* 413; Francis, 'Transferring Rights' 26.

[96] For a discussion on the formal and material aspects of negotiability within n negotiable instruments law, see Chapter I section A.

[97] See McKendrick, *Commercial Law* 941. See Gold et al, *Maritime Law* 414 (mentions that the negotiability of the bill of lading is not popular anymore). In fact, over the years, shipping companies have developed simpler documents called 'Waybills' that are made in the name of the person who receives the shipment and are not negotiable (see Gold et al, *Maritime Law* 414).

[98] McKendrick, *Commercial Law* 1104; J Echebarria Fernandez, 'Paramount Clause and Codification of International Shipping Law' (2019) 50 J Mar L & Com 45, 49 (hereafter Fernansez, 'Paramount Clause').

[99] Force, *Admiralty and Maritime Law* 53.

[100] 27 Stat 445 (1893) (Harter Act).

[101] AN Yiannopulos, 'Conflicts Problems in International Bills of Lading: Validity of "Negligence" Clauses' (1958) 18 La L Rev 6–8, 613 (hereafter Yiannopulos, 'Conflicts Problems').

[102] Fernandez, 'Paramount Clause' 46–48; *Vimar Seguros Y Reasequrous v M/V Sky Reefer*, 515 US 528, 543–44 (1995) (hereafter *Vimar v Sky Reefer*).

waived the liability of the carrier for damage that might occur to the goods during their transportation was plainly problematic. Not only were the interests of the US merchants at stake but so was the efficiency of international trade and commerce that struggled with the level of control carriers had over the provisions of bills of lading.[103] This justified the introduction of the Harter Act, which operated as an American mandatory rule to govern the relationships of all carriers that entered American ports and set minimal requirements of liability that could not be reduced by the provisions of the bill of lading.

7.47 The purpose of the Harter Act was to confine the ability of carriers to exclude their liability through the terms and conditions of the bill of lading. The underlying notion, that cargo owners require this protection in their commercial interaction with carriers, has spread beyond US borders and received indorsements through several international conventions. Thus, following the Harter Act,[104] a large number of countries signed the International Convention for the Unification of Certain Rules Relating to Bills of Lading 1924 (the Hague Rules).[105] Eighty-seven states signed the Hague Rules, including the major maritime commercial actors.[106]

7.48 In 1968, further developments occurred when a protocol to the Hague Rules was signed, referred to as the 'Hague-Visby Rules'.[107] Compared to the Hague Rules, the Hague-Visby Rules set stricter limitations on the carrier's liability exclusion. More than forty years after the Hague Rules, the interests of cargo owners had received more protection. The Hague-Visby Rules extended the potential timeframe for claim submission to two years (a year under the Hague Rules) and increased the maximum potential liability of the carrier for each damaged package.[108] Twenty-nine states, including the UK, signed the 1968 protocol. Although its many trading partners have adopted the Hague-Visby Rules,[109] the USA has remained loyal to the Hague Rules, taking the position that it is unnecessary to raise further the level of liability of the carrier.[110]

7.49 Finally, the United Nations Commission on International Trade Law drafted another set of rules intended to replace the Hague and Hague-Visby Rules: the so-called Hamburg Rules.[111] Following the trajectory of the previous conventions, the Hamburg Rules increased the minimum liabilities of the carriers: they further extended the limitation period and incorporated presumptions of the carrier's fault in the event of

[103] Gaskell et al, *The Bills of Lading* 3.

[104] MF Sturley, 'An Overview of the Considerations Involved in Handling the Cargo Case' (1997) 21 Tul Mar LJ 263, 287.

[105] International Convention for the Unification of Certain Rules of Law Relating to Bills of Lading 25 August 1924, 120 LNTS 155 (Hague Rules).

[106] Gaskell et al, *The Bills of Lading* 3.

[107] Protocol to Amend the International Convention for the Unification of Certain Rules of Law Relating to Bills of Lading (1968) (Visby Protocol) (Hague-Visby Rules).

[108] Gaskell et al, *The Bills of Lading* 555.

[109] Force, *Admiralty and Maritime Law* 53.

[110] Fernansez, 'Paramount Clause' 50 (elaborates on the US position to avoid further liability imposition on the shipowners through the concern that such an imposition may result in increased freight rate).

[111] United Nations Convention on the Carriage of Goods by Sea of 1978 31 March, 1978, 17 ILM 608 (Hamburg Rules).

damage to the cargo. Twenty-six states have signed the Hamburg Rules convention. Major maritime traders such as the UK and the USA were not amongst them.[112]

7.50 In this way, the success of the Harter Act has been acknowledged through several international conventions, although no global consensus has been reached. Once ratified, the various conventions have been implemented through domestic legislation. In the UK, for example, the Hague Rules were implemented by the Carriage of Goods by Sea Act 1924. The Carriage of Goods by Sea Act 1971 gave force to the Hague-Visby Rules.

(b) Bills of Lading and the Choice-of-Law Question

7.51 The special nature of bills of lading and efforts of the international community to limit the ability of shipping carriers to exclude their liability have shaped the debate about the choice-of-law rules applicable to bills of lading. This debate has not evolved around such issues as the question of applicable law in relation to the form, interpretation, defences, and the proprietary aspects of the instrument, as discussed throughout this book. Rather, the debate has focused on a single issue: the nature and scope of party autonomy to determine the applicable law on the face of the instrument.

7.52 A review of the literature and judicial decisions on this matter reveals mixed findings. But, two positions can be identified with respect to the question of the applicable law to govern parties' rights and duties under bills of lading. One position is clearly hostile to the possibility of applying an ordinary choice-of-law analysis to the case of bills of lading. This position is not surprising. Given the general tendency of the international community to intervene in the ability of parties to freely set the framework to govern the liabilities of the carrier, the choice-of-law clauses have been reassessed. Viewing choice-of-law clauses as one of the contractual means to reduce or even to eliminate the liability of the carrier, it has been argued that those clauses represent two sides of the same coin. Stated in slightly different terms, the choice-of-law clauses reflect the ability of the carrier to set the provisions of the bill of lading and to execute almost unlimited control over their content.[113]

7.53 This hostile position towards the ordinary choice-of-law process correlates with the language used in relation to the popular Hague Rules and Hague-Visby Rules. Adopted in the national provisions, these international frameworks have been referred to as 'mandatory' provisions,[114] in the sense that they cannot be bypassed by ordinary choice-of-law rules. The modern principles of party autonomy and MSR do not apply. The Hague Rules and Hague-Visby Rules reflect the popular (particularly in continental Europe) 'mandatory rules', which exclude the application of the ordinary choice-of-law process from certain areas of law. [115] In this argument, the carrier and the cargo owner are situated in an inherently unequal bargaining position, which explains the mandatory nature of the Hague and Hague-Visby Rules. Judicial practice

[112] Gaskell et al, *The Bills of Lading* 6; McKendrick, *Commercial Law* 1105.

[113] Yiannopulos, 'Conflicts Problems' 610–11.

[114] See eg Gaskell et al, *The Bills of Lading* (573.

[115] See eg J Basedow, 'The Law of Open Societies-Private Ordering and Public Regulation of International Relations' (2013) 360 Rec des Cours 9, 346–91.

demonstrates that courts often invalidate choice-of-law clauses as negating the mandatory nature of the Hague or Hague-Visby Rules.[116]

7.54 Following this reasoning, one of the judges in a US Supreme Court decision supported an interpretation of the US Carriage of Goods by Sea Act (COGSA),[117] according to which all choice-of-law clauses on the bill of lading should be invalidated.[118] In O'Connor J's view, any choice-of-law clause should be considered as 'lessening' the liability of the carrier under the Hague Rules, and respectively the COGSA. Apparently, the very need to prove the content of the foreign law imposes a burden on the cargo owner and therefore lessens the liability of the carrier.[119] For him, the liability limitation clauses in COGSA respond to 'the inequality of bargaining power inherent in bills of lading and to carriers' historic tendency to exploit that inequality whenever possible to immunize themselves from liability for their own fault'.[120] Further, O'Connor J argues that the application of ordinary choice-of-law analysis, with party autonomy at the heart of it, would jeopardize the rationale that underpin the value of negotiability to bills of lading. The application of a single law to all aspects of the bill would promote that value.[121]

7.55 There is, however, an alternative position that supports the application of ordinary choice-of-law analysis to bills of lading. This is, at least, a rule of thumb. Indeed, the popular Hague and Hague-Visby Rules limit the autonomy of the parties and set a 'safety net' for cargo owners. This seems to be relevant to the choice-of-law question. At the end of the day, choice-of-law clauses grant the parties the ability to determine the applicable law. Had full autonomy been granted, this would have allowed the carrying ship to utilize its power to incorporate laws that would mostly favour its interests. This notion explains the clear link between the question of applicable law and the various statutes aimed at protecting the interests of the cargo owners.

7.56 However, presenting the Hague Rules or the Hague-Visby Rules as strictly mandatory is not completely accurate. The application of these rules does not mean that bills of lading have been eliminated from the ordinary choice-of-law process. The Report by Mario Giuliano and Paul Lagarde[122] specifically indicates that the general provisions of the Rome I apply to bills of lading. As the report states, 'If a document, though the obligation under it is transferrable, it is not regarded as a negotiable instrument, it

[116] *Argo Co of Canada Ltd v Regal Scout (The)* (1983), 148 DLR (3d) 412; *Hollandia (The)* [1983] 1 AC 565; [1983] 1 Lloyd's Rep 1.

[117] 46 USC App 1300 (hereafter COGSA).

[118] Gaskell et al, *The Bills of Lading* 543–44.

[119] ibid, 551–52.

[120] ibid, 550.

[121] ibid, 552. Although the decision was delivered in the context of the jurisdiction clause (ie the authority of the court to adjudicate a given dispute), it seems to be clear that the judicial reasoning could have been directly extended to the question of choice-of-law.

[122] Report on the Convention on the law applicable to contractual obligations by Mario Giuliano, Professor, University of Milan, and Paul Lagarde, Professor, University of Paris I, Official Journal C 282, 31/10/1980 P 0001–0050, 11 < http://eur-lex.europa.eu/LexUriServ/LexUriServ.do?uri=CELEX:31980Y1031(01):EN:HTML>accessed 20 December 2019 (hereafter Giuliano & Lagarder Report). See also *Cheshire & North* 691, 699.

falls outside the exclusion.' Giuliano and Lagarde point to the fact that bills of lading lack the material negotiability aspect of negotiable instruments, which justifies (in the Report authors' view) its distinctiveness from classical negotiable instruments—the bills of exchange, notes and cheques. Similarly, the US courts have made it clear that the general party autonomy principle set in § 187 (2) of the Second Restatement applies directly to bills of lading.[123]

The Hague and Hague-Visby Rules are mandatory rules. However, the term 'mandatory' diverges from that used in the choice-of-law context. The ordinary usage of this term means that certain areas of law are *ex-ante* excluded from the scope of the choice-of-law analysis. In this way, the mandatory rules represent provisions that direct national judges to ignore and bypass the ordinary choice-of-law process. This means complete bypassing of the choice-of-law clauses and the MSR principle.[124] The application of domestic law (*lex-fori*) follows. **7.57**

However, this is not the 'mandatory' nature of the Hague and Hague-Visby Rules. The mandatory nature of these rules does not mean that the forum shall always apply its domestic law in dealing with issues of bills of lading. For example, an English court may invalidate a choice-of-law clause referring to the Hague Rules on the grounds that these rules do not meet the stricter liability standards of the Hague-Visby Rules, applicable in England. However, the US courts would validate the Hague-Visby Rules, as those impose a greater liability standard than the Visby Rules, applicable in the USA. In a similar vein, the English courts would apply the Hamburg Rules, as those usually impose a greater liability on the carrier compared to the Hague-Visby Rules.[125] **7.58**

Stated in these terms, the mandatory nature of the Hague and Hague-Visby Rules departs from the classical choice-of-law definition of mandatory rules. In contrast to the classical definition, those rules do not apply to all aspects of the bill of lading and they do not trigger the application of the domestic law. What the Hague and Hague-Visby Rules do is provide a 'safety net' to the cargo owner on the point of the potential liability of the carrier. Rather than substituting the choice-of-law process with domestic law, the rules' intervention into the choice-of-law process is minimal. It leaves room for the ordinary choice-of-law process to govern the other aspects of the parties' interaction, as well as liability issues beyond the 'safety net'. Hence, the Hague and Hague-Visby Rules can be only presented as a 'mild' version of the mandatory rules. **7.59**

The judicial decisions follow precisely this understanding of the relation between the Hague/Hague-Visby Rules and the choice-of-law process. Consider the party autonomy principle. Courts across various jurisdictions continue to stress that this principle should be viewed as a primary choice-of-law rule for bills of lading. As a starting point, the parties' explicit choice of the applicable law must be respected.[126] **7.60**

123 *APL Co Pte Ltd v UK Aerosolos Ltd* 2007 US Dist Lexis 80247, 6 (hereafter *APL v UK*).
124 Savigny, *Conflict of Laws* 428, Basedow 343, 374–401.
125 Gaskell et al, *The Bills of Lading* 573.
126 See eg *Van Ommeren Bulk Shipping BV v Cooper* 35 F Supp 2d 469 (1999).

As long as the chosen framework follows the liability 'safety net', the courts will uphold it.[127]

7.61 The majority in *Vimar v Sky Reefer*[128] rejected O'Connor J's position that choice-of-law clauses impose a procedural burden on the cargo owner and therefore 'lessen' liability under the COGSA.[129] Following the classical choice-of-law separation between matters of procedure and substance,[130] the Supreme Court drew a distinction between the cost and mechanism involved in the enforcement of liability and the liability itself.[131] O'Connor J's reasoning in regards to single laws doctrine applicable to negotiable instruments has not been well received. The primary rule of the contemporary choice-of-law process—the party autonomy principle—was successfully confirmed by the Supreme Court.

7.62 A related point applies with respect to another central rule of contemporary choice-of-law practice—the MSR principle. In the absence of party autonomy, the MSR principle governs the question of the applicable law to the bill of lading.[132] In fact, the foundational decision that has incorporated the MSR into common law and overruled the traditional place of contract formation rule was delivered in the context of the bill of lading—*Vita Food*.[133] Although the factual circumstances of this case involved a specific choice-of-law provision on the face of the bill of lading,[134] the court made an important observation about the MSR principle. Specifically, the court clarified that the MSR principle should serve as a guiding principle of the choice-of-law analysis when the parties do not expressly stipulate the applicable law.[135]

7.63 A similar point applies to the documents of title that have received little attention in our discussion—warehouse receipts. The courts have not hesitated to apply the MSR principle to this type of document of title. For example, in *Craig v Columbus Compress*, the court applied this principle despite the fact that the case dealt with the proprietary aspects of the receipts.[136] As the court noted, 'In fact, everything with reference to the transaction occurred within this state, except the sale of stolen warehouse receipts.'[137]

7.64 Where will these observations on the documents of title (with almost exclusive emphasis on the bill of lading) take us? It would appear that they generally follow the

[127] *Indem Ins Co v Hanjin Shipping Co* 348 F 3d 628, 7th Cir 2003; *APL v UK* (n 123) 8; *Franconsteel Corporaiton v MPal Marinos* 94 Civ. 1992 885 D Supp 86; 1995 US Dist LEXIS 5535, 3, 1013; *Evergreen Marine Corp (Taiwan) V Global Terminal & Container Servs*, (2000) US Dist Lexis 16208; *Navig8 Pte Ltd v Al-Riyadh Co for Vegetable Oil Industry* [2013] EWHC 328 (Comm). See also ME Crowley, 'The Uniqueness of Admiralty and Maritime Law: The Limited Scope of the Cargo Liability Regime Covering Carriage of Goods by Sea: The Multimodal Problem' (2005) 79 Tul L Rev 1461, 1483.

[128] *Vimar v Sky Reefer*.

[129] COGSA.

[130] Garnett, *Substance & Procedure*.

[131] Gaskell et al, *The Bills of Lading* 534–35.

[132] ibid, 575–76. Yiannopulos, 'Conflicts Problems' 610–11; *Hawkspere Shipping Co v Intamex*, SA, 330 F 3d 225 (2003).

[133] *Vita Food Products Inc v Unus Shipping Co Ltd* [1939] AC 277.

[134] ibid, 288.

[135] ibid, 298–99.

[136] *Craig v Columbus Compress & Warehouse Company*, No 44.910, 210 So 2d 645 (Miss 1968).

[137] ibid, 17.

suggested line of argument in the preceding chapters. First, it is clear that even in such a key area of international commerce,[138] substantive harmonization efforts have failed to reach a consensus even on the point of a carrier's liability. A major trading actor—the USA—has not adopted the Hague-Visby Rules. This underscores the significance of the choice-of-law analysis and of the choice-of-law harmonization process. Second, despite the apparent 'mandatory' nature of the choice-of-law regime applicable to bills of lading, this regime appears limited. It adequately reflects the special position of the carrier-cargo owner relationship. Finally, the practice of bills of lading demonstrates the adoption of the modern principles of party autonomy and MSR. A review of the literature and the courts' decisions on the question of the applicable law to bills of lading suggests that these are generally receptive to the application of ordinary choice-of-law analysis.

2. Securities

Securities are divided into two major categories: equity and debt. Equity relates to what is commonly known as 'shares' or 'stock'. By purchasing shares, the investor acquires a claim to a portion of the capital of a corporation. Bonds represent debts incurred by the issuer in order to sustain liquidity. In principle, debt securities get priority over equity securities in the case of corporate insolvency. They are issued in fungible series and are traded or tradable in a financial market.[139] **7.65**

Historically, an equity and debt security was issued in the form of a physical document that confirms the entitlement of the document's holder, called a 'certificate'. A document could be purchased by taking possession. it could made in a registered form, as was the case primarily with respect to shares endorsed and registered in the books of the issuer.[140] This explains why securities have historically been considered a part of negotiable instruments law.[141] This also explains our interest in the choice-of-law rules applicable to securities. **7.66**

(a) The Choice-of-Law Rules in Relation to Securities

On a basic level, bonds represent a contract under which one party lends money to another. Choice-of-law analysis follows this vision of debt securities. Similar to other areas of contract law,[142] the triumph of the party autonomy principle is evident in this **7.67**

[138] See eg *APL v UK* (involves a situation of a Singaporean corporation with its principal place of business in Singapore; a UK corporation with its principal place of business in the UK; and a Californian corporation with its principal place of business in California. The dispute itself involved the shipping of goods from Turkey to California); *Vimar v Reefer* (involves a situation of the transportation of goods from Morocco to the USA by a Japanese vessel).

[139] See eg L Soderquist, *Securities Regulation* (2nd edn, Foundation Press 2004).

[140] See eg *Colonial Bank v Cady* (1890) 63 LT (NS) 27, 32 (HL) (hereafter *Colonial Bank v Cady*); M Lehmann, 'Financial Instruments, Bonds & Loans, Cheques, Bills of Exchange and Guarantees in Private International Law' 19 < https://papers.ssrn.com/sol3/papers.cfm?abstract_id=2849363>, accessed 20 December 2019 (hereafter Lehmann, 'Financial Instruments').

[141] ibid, 18 (mentions the traditional classification of bonds within negotiable instruments); 3–4 (mentions the contemporary practice of German law to classify shares within negotiable instruments).

[142] For a discussion of the centrality of the party autonomy principle within the contemporary contract law category, see Chapter III section B(2)(c).

area of law. The choice-of-law clause usually appears within the provisions of the bond agreements, and it sets the framework for determining the parties' rights and duties.[143]

7.68 In rare cases where the parties had expressly stipulated the applicable law, the choice-of-law analysis still follows the traditional sovereignty-based rule of *lex-contractus*—the place of the contract formation.[144] The practice of incorporating choice-of-law clauses in bond agreements became so popular that legal doctrine has found it unnecessary to reconsider the *lex-contractus* rule. As Lehmann recently put it, 'Determining which law applies in the absence of a choice-of-law clause is largely a theoretical exercise because bonds and loans almost always include one.'[145] In other words, in the context of debt securities, the *lex-contractus* rule has become obsolete. Unfortunately, as we have seen throughout this book,[146] this is not the case with respect to classical negotiable instruments (ie bills of exchange, promissory notes, and cheques) where the *lex-contractus* rule continues to predominate. As we have argued in the preceding chapters, it must be reconsidered.

7.69 Choice-of-law rules in relation to shares represent a much more complex issue. This complexity can be attributed to both conceptual and practical reasons. Conceptually, the shares represent claims to a corporate's capital, which inherently raises proprietary issues and complicates the choice-of-law analysis. Practically, the contemporary reality represents frequent cross-border commerce of shares, which enhances the relevance of the choice-of-law question. Despite some unification efforts,[147] the systems diverge deeply in their concept of shares and the substantive laws applicable to them.[148] Further, the contemporary practice of the commerce of shares has abandoned, to some degree, the mechanism of issuing a physical certificate of the shares. Instead, the practice only requires registration of the shares' transfer in the company's book.[149] Finally, most importantly, the contemporary reality of share trading mainly takes place through third parties—'intermediates'—[150] who manage portfolios comprised of the shares of many corporations.

7.70 It is not surprising that the question of the applicable law to share trading has received much academic attention.[151] Significant domestic and international reforms

[143] Lehmann, 'Financial Instruments' 21–22.
[144] ibid, 22.
[145] ibid.
[146] See Chapters IV, V, and VI.
[147] Geneva Convention on Substantive Rules for Intermediated Securities (UDIDROIT, 2009) represents a genuine effort of substantive harmonization in the area of securities. However, as the commentators have pointed out, this harmonization effort has been unsuccessful due to the limited scope of issues covered by it and the limited number of states that ratified it. For a discussion of those issues, see Lehmann, 'Financial Instruments' 6–7, 15.
[148] ibid, 3–4.
[149] See eg *McMillan Inc v Bishopgae Investment Trust PLC* [1996] 1 WLR 387 (CA) (hereafter *McMillan v Bishopgae*).
[150] See section C(2)(d).
[151] See eg H van Houttee (ed) *The Law of Cross-Border Securities Transactions* (Sweet & Maxwell 1999); M Ooi, *Shares and Other Securities in the Conflict of Laws* (Oxford University Press 2003) (hereafter Ooi, *Shares*); T Keijser (ed), *Transnational Securities Law* (Oxford University Press 2014); JS Rogers, 'Conflict of Laws for Transactions in Securities Held through Intermediaries' (2006) 39 Cor Int LJ 285.

have taken place. In this section, we do not aim to provide a comprehensive overview of the choice-of-law rules applicable to shares. Rather, our goal is to analyse the various instances of share transfer to present the perplexing challenge of the 'intermediates', and to discuss these in relation to the normative arguments made in Chapters V and VI. While a comprehensive treatment of the question of applicable law to shares must be postponed to another day, we argue that the key to addressing this question is the traditional division between two types of corporate affairs: external and internal.[152]

(b) The Traditional Division between Internal and External Aspects of Corporations and the Transfer of Shares

The longstanding position of the corporate choice-of-law literature and case law sharply delineates between two types of corporate 'affairs': 'internal' and 'external'. 'Internal affairs' refers to such matters as the appointment of directors, dividend distribution, shareholder meetings, mergers, and voting.[153] These matters cover various aspects and activities that take place within the corporation itself and between corporate actors. The internal affairs of corporations are generally governed by the place of incorporation rule.[154] This rule has usually been justified on the basis of the state sovereignty principle as a reflection of the physical location of a place where a given state exercises its will and grants the corporation its existence.[155] **7.71**

In contrast to internal affairs, corporate 'external affairs' refers to disputes that are external to a corporation, for example, instances when a corporation signs a contract, is sued in tort and so on. The legal scholarship has tended to equate the external affairs of corporations and 'ordinary' private individuals, arguing that external affairs 'can also be performed by individuals, such as the making of a contract or the commission of a tort'.[156] Accordingly, the application of ordinary choice-of-law rules to corporate external affairs has followed.[157] The Second Restatement, for example, explicitly accepts this complete equivalence between corporate external affairs and private individuals, **7.72**

[152] While sections C(2)(b) and (c) focus on the shares and the principal division between the 'internal'/ 'external' affairs of a corporation, the analysis is not limited to shares and can be extended to debt securities. Although the point of 'internal affairs' does not apply to the latter type of security, the discussion in relation to 'external affairs' directly applies to debt securities.

[153] See eg Second Restatement § 302, Comment a.

[154] See eg A Briggs, *The Conflict of Laws* (3rd edn, Oxford University Press 2013) 367, 369 (hereafter Briggs, *Conflict of Laws*); *Cheshire & North* 1308–09; RR Drury, 'The Regulation and Recognition of Foreign Corporations: Responses to the "Delaware Syndrome' (1998) 57 C L J 165, 170 (hereafter Drury, 'Foreign Corporations'); DA DeMott, 'Perspectives on Choice of Law for Corporate Internal Affairs' (1985) 48 Law & Contemp Probs 161, 162–63.

[155] JH Beale, *A Treatise on the Conflict of Laws* (Baker, Voorhis & Co 1935) 727, 749. See also S Peari, 'Challenging the Place of Incorporation Rule' 71 Governance Directions 305 (2019); Sagi Peari, 'Which Law Governs Dispute Involving Corporations?' 33 Aus J of Corporate Law 252 (2019).

[156] W Reese and EM Kaufman, 'The Governing Corporate Affairs: Choice of Law and the Impact of Full Faith and Credit' (1958) 58 Col Un L Rev 1118, 1124.

[157] See eg *Chrysler Corp. v Ford Motor Co.* 972 F Supp 1097, 1098, 1102 (ED Mich 1997); *Cooper Industries, LLC v City of South Bend*, 899 NE 2d 1274, 1290 (Ind, 2009); *Landis & GYR Inc v Zurich American Ins Co*, 2019 US Dist 3, 5.

with a subsequent argument about the application of ordinary choice-of-law rules to the context of corporate external affairs.[158]

7.73 Which law should govern disputes in relation to corporate shares? Which type of affair involves a dispute surrounding the question of the entitlement to shares? Seemingly, such a dispute does not relate to the internal affairs of corporation. A transfer of shares does not necessarily involve a dispute between corporate actors. Nor does it involve a dispute between a corporate actor and the corporation itself. Rather, such a dispute appears related to the external affairs of the corporation, under which the litigating parties (who are not necessarily corporate actors) disagree over a certain entitlement—the corporate share. The dispute becomes a proprietary dispute.

7.74 The above-mentioned observations are important as they enable us to draw a parallel between choice-of-law rules applicable to the transfer of shares and those of negotiable instruments. Specifically, the choice-of-law rules applicable to the proprietary aspects of negotiable instruments become relevant. For the external affairs of corporations, the analysis is not affected by the traditional sovereignty-based rule of the place of incorporation which governs their internal affairs. Consider the various ways of shareholding mentioned above: (1) the direct holding of shares with a certificate; (2) the direct holding of shares without a certificate; and (3) the indirect holding of shares through intermediates.

7.75 First, consider the direct holding of shares with a certificate. As representing the question of entitlement with respect to the share, the physical location of the certificate provides a point of departure for judicial analysis. While the case law[159] and the legislation generally adopt this focus on the physical location of the certificate,[160] we support the contention that location be only a *presumption*, which should be mitigated by other connecting factors. Along the lines of the argument made earlier in this chapter on the point of the proprietary aspects of negotiable instruments, the underlying justification for the *lex-situs* rule in this case is not the sovereignty principle but rather the notion of the parties' reasonable expectation. As such, we willingly join the criticism raised in the literature against the rigidity of the *lex-situs* rule in the context of shares.[161]

7.76 Second, the the direct holding of shares without a certificate represents a situation where the share completely loses its physical character.[162] Shares become intangible property, which does not have a physical form. Yet, the classical choice-of-law doctrine has applied the *lex-situs* rule even to intangible aspects of rights.[163] For example, the courts have identified the place of the expected litigation as reflecting the physical

[158] Second Restatement § 301, Comment b ('Many acts can be done both by corporations and by individuals. Thus, corporations and individuals alike make contracts, commit torts and receive and transfer assets. Issues involving acts such as these when done by a corporation are determined by the same choice-of-law principles as are applicable to non-corporate parties').

[159] See eg *Colonial Bank v Cady* 32.

[160] UCC and Ontario Securities Transfers Act 2006, SO 2006, c 8, s 46 (hereafter OCTA).

[161] See Ooi, *Shares* 14–15.

[162] For further discussion of the point of 'losing the physical proprietary' aspect in the context of digital negotiable instruments, see Chapter VIII, the text accompanying nn 128–29.

[163] See eg *Cheshire & North* 1280–94.

location of the debt. This suggests the application of the law to the place of residence of the debtor.[164] This traditional position, however, has been heavily criticized and mocked as arbitrary.[165]

Indeed, tracking the physical location of shares once they become intangible property is an impossible exercise.[166] To determine the appropriate point of departure for its operation, choice-of-law analysis should assess the modern situation where shares are stripped of their tangibility. We think that the location of the corporate headquarters/place of registration should serve as such a point of departure. This position follows the majority opinion in the well-known case of *McMillan v Bishopgate Investment Trust PLC*,[167] and opposes the legislative provisions that set the place of incorporation to govern the direct holding without a certificate.[168] By focusing the legal analysis on the corporation itself and the centre of its current operation, the location of the corporate headquarters seems to represent the focal point of the litigating parties' interaction with respect to corporate shares. This is indeed what has been described in the continental literature as the 'real seat of the corporation'.[169] The alternative—the place of incorporation—seems to be arbitrary and heavily linked to the state-based origin of corporations and the sovereignty principle. Similar to previous observations, the place of corporate headquarters should serve only as a point of departure for judicial analysis and should be mitigated by other connecting factors. 7.77

There is no reason to pre-empt the logic applicable to proprietary aspects of negotiable instruments to be extended to the case of transfer of shares.[170] The presumption of a certificate's physical location should govern the example of direct holding with a certificate. The presumption of the place of corporate headquarters should govern the model of direct holding without a certificate. Furthermore, following the observations made in Chapters III and V,[171] there is no reason to exclude the question of transfer of shares from the advances of the party autonomy principle.[172] This is precisely 7.78

164 *New York Life Insurance Co v Public Trustee* [1924] 2 Ch 101, 119.

165 McKendrick, *Commercial Law* 1178; R Goode, 'The Assignment of Pure Intangibles in the Conflict of Laws' in L Gullifer and S Vogenauer (eds) *English and European Perspectives on Contract and Commercial Law* (Hart Publishing 2017) 356, 361; Pitel & Rafferty, *Conflict of Laws* 355.

166 For further discussion of this point in the context of the digital versions of negotiable instruments, see Chapter VIII, the text accompanying nn 128–29.

167 *McMillan v Bisgopgae* 411. See also Ooi, *Shares* 4–7, 16.

168 UCC § 8-110(a) & (d) and Ontario Securities Transfer Act, 2006, s 44.

169 On this point, we follow the Continental Europe literature that conceives the place of corporate headquarters as the 'real seat' of a corporation vis-à-vis the place of incorporation rule. See eg ER Latty, 'Pseudo-Foreign corporations' (1955) 65 Yale LJ 137, 167–68; Ooi, *Shares* 25, n 48; Drury, 'Foreign Corporations' 174 (mentions the advantage of the continental place of headquarters rules as reflecting 'a real attachment of the company to a territory').

170 For somewhat related classification of transfer of shares as falling outside of the scope of the internal affairs of corporation, see B Geva, 'Legislative Power in Relation to Transfers of Securities: The Case for Provincial Jurisdiction in Canada' 19 Ban and Fin L Rev 19 (2004) 393.

171 See the text accompanying n 79 in Chapter III and section B(3) in Chapter V.

172 This seems to be the position of the Chinese choice-of-law legislation in relation to choice-of-law rules applicable to shares held in a direct holding system. Thus, arts 37 and 38 of the Chinese Civil Legal Relations Act (2011) sets party autonomy and the MSR principle as the governing principles of shares, including the question of share transfer. See also TU Guangjian, 'Resolution of Cross-Boder Securities Disputes under the Scheme of Shnghai-Hong Kong Stock Connect: An Exploration on the Applicable Law' (2016) 15 Chinese J of Int'l L 167, 176–77.

a development that occurred in the context of the modern indirect structure of the shareholding system.

(c) The Indirect Holding Example and the Legislative Reforms

7.79 The debates around the applicable law in the direct-holding example (ie the example that focuses on the relationship between the shareholders and the corporation) have become less relevant today. Currently, most share trades (as well as other securities) relate not only to shares that have lost their physical aspects, but also to those held in non-physical electronic form by intermediaries.[173]

7.80 In essence, the indirect holding system operates as follows. Securities are issued to a clearing corporation or agency such as a central depository of securities (CDS), which then allocates the rights to them to financial intermediaries, such as securities brokers and banks, as purchased by the intermediaries from the corporation. In turn, each financial intermediary then sells rights to investors. In such a system, the CDS remains the registered shares' holder. This system facilitates and serves as an intermediary between buyers and sellers. Neither a change in the registration on the books of the issuer, nor in the context of a certificated system, does the issue of a new certificate effect the subsequent transactions. Rather, the rights acquired by a purchaser are reflected as a credit or a book-entry in an account held by that purchaser with an upper tier financial intermediary. A brokerage firm purchasing a defined quantity of securities from the issuer will have its account with the CDS credited to that extent. Similarly, an investor of such a brokerage firm will have his or her account with the brokerage firm credited to the extent of the amount purchased. Transactions among brokers are effectuated on the books of CDS. Transactions among customers are effectuated on books held by brokers or other financial intermediaries. Interests in securities are thus held indirectly, through securities intermediaries.

7.81 The pattern set out above is complex and requires further elaboration. The indirect holding system is not necessarily exclusively a two-tiered one. In fact, additional extensive financial intermediation may take place, particularly in the context of international finance. Further, the investor has no entitlement to any specific security. Rather, the entitlement is to a specific quantity of a fungible asset as credited to the security holder's security account. Typically, the intermediary on whose books a security account is maintained is required to back up the account-holder's claim with 100 per cent reserve, not reachable by the financial intermediary's own creditors. For its part, inter-financial intermediary transactions are not cleared and settled individually but, rather, in a fashion similar to the clearing and settlement of money transfers.

7.82 In light of the lack of harmonization of substantive laws and the popularity of the trade of securities, the international community has quickly introduced several legislative reforms to address the challenges of the indirect holding system. While the law relating to the direct holding system focuses on the relationship between the issuer and the investor, the indirect holding system revolves around relationships involving

[173] Lehmann, 'Financial Instruments' 2, 10 (mentions the insignificance of the physical location of the shares). See also *Cheshire & North* 1299–301; McKendrick, *Commercial Law* 1184–85.

intermediaries. Put another way, in the direct-holding system, the asset under discussion is the shares themselves. Conversely, in the indirect holding system, the asset under discussion is the entitlement to a security as reflected in an account maintained by a financial intermediary—the so-called place of the Primary Intermediary Approach (PRIMA).[174] These observations, perhaps, explain the centrality that the reformers have attributed to the location of the financial intermediary.[175]

Article 8 of the Uniform Commercial Code [176] sets a framework of the governing law of securities in the indirect holding system. The predominant choice-of-law rule is of party autonomy.[177] In the absence of party autonomy, the default rule follows the place where the intermediary maintains the office that handles the customer's account. Similarly, almost all Canadian provinces have legislated statutes along these lines that address the status of shares held by intermediary institutions.[178] **7.83**

On an international level, the Hague Convention[179] has followed a similar path. It has incorporated party autonomy as its primary rule,[180] with very few limitations on the ability of the parties to determine the applicable law.[181] When the parties do not expressly stipulate the applicable law, the Hague Convention follows various rigid 'fall-back' rules, such as the place of the intermediary's office, the intermediary's place of incorporation, and the intermediary's principal place of business.[182] After only having been ratified by Switzerland and Mauritius, the popularity of the Hague Convention has recently been boosted by the US ratification of it.[183] Indeed, the differences between the UCC's Article 8 and the Hague Convention are subtle.[184] **7.84**

What is the relationship of these legislative reforms to the contentions made in this book? There is much compatibility between our view of negotiable instruments and the contemporary legislative reform in relation to shares. The very attempt of the *Hague Convention* is a plausible development that follows our line of thought about the immediate need for choice-of-law harmonization.[185] This point is especially valid in the context of such a popular and 'international' area of law as the trade of shares. Furthermore, it seems clear that domestic legislative reforms and the international community have incorporated the principle of party autonomy as a primary vehicle of **7.85**

[174] RD Guynn, *Modernizing Securities Ownership, Transfer and Pledging Laws: A Discussion Paper on the Need for International Harmonization* (London: International Bar Association, Section on Business Law Capital Markets Forum, 1996) 33–34, and in more detail at 34–37.

[175] See eg *Re Bloom Estate* (2004) 27 BCLR (4th) 176 (SC).

[176] UCC.

[177] ibid, § 8-110(e)

[178] See eg Securities Transfer Act, 2006, SO 2006, c 8; R Scavone, 'Stronger Than Fictions: Canada Rethinks the Law of Securities Transfers in the Indirect Holding System' (2007) 45 Can Bus LJ 67.

[179] Convention on the Law Applicable to Certain Rights in Respect of Securities Held with an Intermediary (2006) (hereafter Hague Convention).

[180] ibid, art 4.

[181] ibid, art 3; Lehmann, 'Financial Instruments' 15–16; *Cheshire & North* 1303–05; SJ Kozey, 'The Hague Securities Convention: An Opportunity to Take the UCC Global (2015) 46 Geo J Int'l L 1213, 1226–27 (hereafter Kozey, 'Hague Convention').

[182] Hague Convention art 5; McKendrick, *Commercial Law* 1186; Kozey, 'Hague Convention' 1226–27.

[183] <https://www.hcch.net/en/news-archive/details/?varevent=531>, accessed 20 December 2019.

[184] For a discussion of this point, Kozey, 'Hague Convention' 1226–27.

[185] See Chapter III section C.

the choice-of-law process. This is a most welcome development. In contrast to the traditional sovereignty-based conception of the subject and the traditional rigid *lex-situs* rule applicable in relation to tangible/intangible property, the reformers have not hesitated to introduce this modern principle to the indirect holding system. This development shall not be taken for granted. As Lehmann has commented, the introduction of party autonomy to the proprietary aspects of the shares should be viewed as 'raising eyebrows'.[186]

7.86 Furthermore, when the parties do not stipulate the applicable law, the legislative reforms follow a hierarchal set of rules that clearly aim to ascertain the location of the intermediary. This is indeed the essence of the PRIMA default rules. Stated in these terms, a parallel can be drawn between the PRIMA default rules and the MSR principle. After all, the investor has a proprietary right in a pool of financial assets held by the intermediary[187] but not in any particular asset among those of which the pool consists. This observation disconnects the nexus between the investor and the shares of a particular corporation. It also explains the centrality of the location where the intermediary manages the account. This place indeed represents the 'essence' of the obligation within the investor–intermediary relationship and sets a parallel between the PRIMA and the MSR principle.

7.87 In summary, it would appear that both documents of title and securities generally follow the suggested argument in Chapters V and VI. While historically considered to be a part of the negotiable instruments law across jurisdictions, the recent developments in these areas of law demonstrate a clear alignment with the argument made in relation to classical negotiable instruments. Thus, as we have seen, the legal framework of the bills of lading evidently incorporates the party autonomy principle and the MSR principle. The paradigmatic centrality of the mandatory provisions is more marginal than it appears at the first glance.

7.88 A similar point applies with respect to securities. Debt securities are ultimately governed by the party autonomy principle. The situation with shares is more complex. With respect to the direct-holding example with a certificate, we are supportive of the choice-of-law rule that focuses on the certificate. With respect to the direct-holding example without a certificate, we are supportive of the choice-of-law rule, which focuses on the place of the corporate headquarters. In both cases (and in contrast to contemporary case law and legislation), we see those locations as a point of departure that can be overturned by other connecting factors. As we have seen, the modern system of indirect holding of shares by intermediaries has presented further conceptual and practical challenges. Without making a determinative argument with respect to this type of system, we are supportive of the two aspects that appear to be at the very core of legislative reform: (1) the incorporation of the party autonomy principle as the primary choice-of-law rule; and (2) setting the PRIMA as

[186] Lehmann, 'Financial Instruments' 13–14.
[187] ibid, 12.

a default rule that seems to be consistent with the MSR principle and its mechanism of presumptions.

D. The Ethical Moment

Throughout this book, we have expressed the view that the choice-of-law adjudication process should not examine the results it produces. We have argued that this result-oriented practice jeopardizes the very nature of the judicial process, its transparency and legitimacy. This means, for example, that we would object to designing the choice-of-law process in a way that would support the instrument holder's position without reservations. As we have seen,[188] this one-sided structure would not just jeopardize the very nature of the choice-of-law process, but it would also be inconsistent with the very structure of negotiable instruments law. Within this structure, upholding the holder's rights is not absolute and is balanced to a significant degree with the rights of the signatory party. Accordingly, it is more accurate to speak of a 'balanced' structure of negotiable instruments law that accommodates within its provisions a certain equilibrium between the interests of the instrument's holder and those of the signatory parties.[189] **7.89**

A similar point has been made with respect to the validation principle. Despite the appearance of this principle in the case law,[190] the conceptual and practical deficiencies of this principle are overwhelming. As we have seen, this principle support sa transnational value of the contracts' validation, and its operation is doubtful in light of the contemporary reality of the frequent mobility of people and goods. Beyond everything, this principle imposes on the choice-of-law process, a practice external to its values, values that have already received acknowledgement within domestic legislation and case law.[191] **7.90**

In this section, we would like to focus on a different aspect of the look 'behind the scenes'. This look involves an evaluation of the content of the applied laws. Consider the two major systems of negotiable instruments law: the common-law-based systems and the continental systems. As we saw in Chapter I,[192] each of these systems is internally balanced and fair in its own way. We follow this comparison of the systems while refraining from a comparative quality analysis of the various provisions. **7.91**

Indeed, the traditional and contemporary choice-of-law tradition has been reluctant to provide a substantive evaluation of the applied laws. It has almost always rejected the possibility of the quality judgment being made. This tradition has rightly pointed out the difficulty involved in a substantive evaluation of the applied laws.[193] Furthermore, **7.92**

188 For discussion of these issues, see Chapter V section B and Chapter VI section B(1).

189 ibid.

190 See eg *Walling v Cushman*, 238 Mass 62 (1920) 67 (hereafter *Walling v Cushman*); *Greenlee v Hardin*, 157 Miss 229 (1930) 233 (hereafter *Greenlee v Hardin*).

191 For discussion of these issues, see Chapter V section B and Chapter VI section B(1).

192 See Chapter I sections D and E.

193 See eg PH Neuhaus, 'Legal Certainty Versus Equity in the Conflict of Laws' (1963) 28 Law & Contemp Probs 795, 802; AA Ehrenzweig, *Private International Law* (Oceana Publications Inc 1967) 102.

it has been argued that it is unsuitable for judges to examine the comparative substantive evaluation of the various provisions,[194] an exercise that is inconsistent with the notion of the equality between states and their public legal institutions.[195] This objection to comparative substantive analysis does not address the judge's capability to execute comparative analysis of pertinent provisions, but rather their legitimacy to engage in such analysis in the first place. The judge simply does not have the authority to do so.

7.93 This is all true. Yet, in some radical cases, systems around the world have allowed exceptions. While courts have refused to carry out a qualitative analysis of the pertinent laws in the vast majority of cases, some exceptional choice-of-law doctrines and concepts enable a certain degree of the 'quality control'. They appear in literature and judicial decisions under a wide range of labels and titles: the 'public policy exception',[196] 'international due process',[197] 'human rights',[198] 'disgraceful foreign laws',[199] and 'minimum international standards of justice'.[200] Labels aside, these doctrines and concepts follow a similar idea in essence: the choice-of-law process must integrate within its operational force some exceptional circumstances that would disqualify the ordinary choice-of-law process. While being highly cautious of disqualifying laws based on substantive grounds, the courts always keep an eye on the quality of the laws. Some scholars have beautifully coined this highly rare substantive discretion of the courts as an 'ethical moment'.[201]

7.94 Where does this kind of argument leave us with respect to negotiable instruments law? A review of choice-of-law decisions in this area of law reveals that while the courts have frequently mentioned the content of the applied laws,[202] they have rarely based their decisions on that content. One explanation for the practice of mentioning the content of the applied law can be made through the following fairly simple point: the courts wanted to point out the divergence between the various laws in order to explain the relevance of the choice-of-law analysis in the first place.

[194] See eg *Cheshire & North* 34–35.

[195] For a discussion of these issues, see Chapter VI, the text accompanying nn 57–63.

[196] See eg PJ Borchers, 'Categorical Exceptions to Party Autonomy in Private International Law' (2008) 82 Tul L Rev 1645, 1652.

[197] *Society of Lloyd's v Ashenden*, 233 F 3d 473, 477 (7th Cir 2000) (Posner J).

[198] See eg Briggs, *Conflict of Laws* 232; R Michaels, 'Public and Private International Law: German Views on Global Issues' (2008) J Private Int'l L 121, 131.

[199] See A Briggs, *Private International Law in English Courts* (Oxford University Press 2014) 164.

[200] Kotuby & Sobota, *General Principles* 69.

[201] K Knop, R Michaels, and A Riles, 'From Multiculturalism to Technique: Feminism, Culture, and the Conflict of Laws Style' (2012) 64 Stan L Rev 589, 641.

[202] For a limited list of negotiable instruments' cases mentioning the content of the involved laws, see eg *Hyatt v Bank of Kentucky*, 71 KY 193 (1871) 196 (Kentucky and Georgia); *Hennenlotter v De Orvananos*, 114 Misc 333 (1921) 334 (York and Mexico); *Mayfield v Equitable Trust Co.* 295 F 109 (1924) (Georgia and South Carolina); *Walling v Cushman* (n 189) 64 (Colorado and Michigan); *Greenlee v Hardin* (n 179) 233 (Mississippi and Florida); *Banku Polskiego v Mulder & Company* 2 KB 266 (1941) 268–69 (English and Dutch laws); *Lebel and Another v Tucker* at [78] (English and French); *Rothschild v Currie*, 113 ER 1045 (1833) 1046–47 (English and French); *Bondholders Securities Corp v Manville et al* [1933] SJ No 75 [19333] 4 DLR 699, para [5] (Ontario and Florida) (hereafter *Bondholders v Manville*).

Throughout this book, we have mentioned the potential significance of 'looking behind the scenes' and evaluating the substantive merits of the applied laws. Thus, as we have seen, in the *Karafarin* case, [203] the English court had no problem relying on the expert's testimony and applying Iranian law. The application of this law followed the ordinary choice-of-law process and in this case, the court had not expressed any concerns as to the quality of that law. In fact, the judge seemed to be comfortable with Iranian customary law's doctrine that permits creditors to receive undated cheques to secure the repayment of debts and, by doing so, a drawer of a cheque impliedly authorizes the holder of the cheque to date the cheque and present it for payment when necessary. [204] While this law might have been seen as inconsistent with English law or with a judge's own view of fairness, clearly this judge saw nothing wrong with that law as something that would 'drag on the coat tails of civilization'.[205] The situation could have been different had the ordinary choice-of-law process pointed to the application of other Iranian provisions in the area of family law, which seem to clearly discriminate on the basis of gender.[206] **7.95**

The *Canada Life v CIBC*[207] is another instance when the substantive evaluation of the applied laws could have been invoked. Crawford has explicitly invoked this type of analysis. According to this reading of the case, the Supreme Court of Canada reached a conclusion not to apply its domestic law (which it could probably easily do through an alternative interpretation of the term 'residency'[208]) and not even to apply the law that would provide an advantage to a Canadian insurer. Rather, it has been suggested that the court applied a law that in it eyes was considered to be better—the New York Law, as opposed to domestic Canadian law. As the commentator put it with respect to this 'real' underlying reasoning of the decision, 'The real problem is the obsolete nature of the BEA's fraud allocation rules, and the case is only another illustration of the need to modernize them.'[209] While reflecting a justified criticism of these rules, standing on its own, this reasoning, is at odds with the very nature of the choice-of-law process and the exceptionally high threshold that choice-of-law thought has set for an ethical moment. In contrast to the earlier suggestion, choice-of-law analysis cannot serve as a vehicle for 'modernization' of the negotiable instruments law. This should be done through reform rather than by the choice-of-law process. **7.96**

[203] *Karafarin Bank v Gholam Reza Mansoury Dara* [2009] EWHC 3265 (Comm) (hereafter *Karafarin Bank v Gholam Reza Mansoury Dara*). For a discussion of this case, see Chapter VI, the text accompanying nn 39–43.

[204] *Karafarin Bank v Gholam Reza Mansoury Dara* [12].

[205] EE Cheatham and WLM Reese, 'Choice of the Applicable Law' (1952) 52 Colum L Rev 959, 980; RA Leflar, 'Choice-Influencing Considerations in Conflicts Law' (1966) 41 NYUL Rev 267, 299.

[206] See eg http://iranian-americans.com/discrimination-against-women-under-iranian-law/; http://justiceforiran.org/wp-content/uploads/2014/01/JFI-Submission-WGD-20-01-2014-.pdf; https://papers.ssrn.com/sol3/papers.cfm?abstract_id=2860009, accessed 20 December 2019).

[207] [1979] 2 SCR 669 (hereafter *Canada Life*). For a discussion of this case, see Chapter V, the text accompanying nn 41–55.

[208] For a discussion of this point, see Chapter VI, the text accompanying nn 52–55.

[209] B Crawford, *The Law of Banking and Payment in Canada*, vol 3 (Canada Law Book 2008) 21–24.

7.97 If anything, in the context of negotiable instruments law, we can think about invoking the ethical moment in cases involving discrimination with respect to a person's inherent attributions. This notion tracks the innate attributions of a given person's personality related to their very birth, such as gender, ethnicity, eye colour, and so on.[210] Specifically, we would like to draw attention to those provisions amongst the systems that viewed women as losing their legal capacity upon marriage. Under these provisions, the 'very being or legal existence of the women is suspended during the marriage and ... consolidated into that of the husband'.[211] Based on these, now mostly abandoned, restrictions on women's capacity to contract,[212] several decisions in negotiable instruments law were decided. Having applied the ordinary choice-of-law analysis,[213] the judges should have made a substantive evaluation of the applied law. They should have said that this is the point when the 'ethical moment' enters the picture.

210 For a somewhat related conception of the value of equality, see T Khaitan, *A Theory of Discrimination Law* (Oxford University Press 2015). See also art 14 of European Convention on Human Rights which prohibits discriminatory treatment on the basis of a person's 'personal characteristic' or status. See also JJ Fawcett et al, *Human Rights and Private International Law* (Oxford University Press 2016) 605.

211 See Sir W Blackstone, *Commentaries of Law of England* (chapter 15) (1765–69) (Co Lit) 112.

212 Pitel & Rafferty, *Conflict of Laws* 18; Second Restatement § 195, Comment c.

213 See *Bondholders v Manville*; *Walling v Cushman* ; *Greenlee v Hardin*.

VIII
International Negotiable Instruments in the Electronic Age

A. Introduction: Writing, Signature, Delivery, and Presentment Requirements

As discussed in Chapter I section B, predominantly in common law countries[1] negotiable instruments are usually governed by a statute modelled on the UK Bills of Exchange Act (BEA).[2] In the USA the governing statute is Article 3 of the Uniform Commercial Code—Negotiable Instruments (UCC Article 3).[3] In turn, primarily in civil law jurisdictions, statutes usually derive from the Convention Providing a Uniform Law for Bills of Exchange and Promissory Notes (UBL)[4] and the Convention Providing a Uniform Law for Cheques (UCL).[5] **8.01**

All such statues impose strict formal requirements for negotiable instruments addressing writing,[6] issuer's signature, as well as contents. In general, the bill of exchange (or draft) ('bill') is an unconditional written and signed order, addressed by one person ('drawer') to another ('drawee'), requiring the latter to pay a sum certain in money.[7] For its part, the promissory note ('note') is an unconditional written and **8.02**

[1] Also in other jurisdictions that historically were subject to strong British influence (such as Israel, South Africa, Sri Lanka, and Quebec as part of Canada). See list by AW Rogers, *Falconbridge on Banking and Bills of Exchange* (7th edn, Canada Law Book 1969) 431–32.

[2] 1882, Chapter 61, 45 and 46 Vict (hereafter BEA).

[3] ALI and NCCUSL, 2002 (hereafter UCC).

[4] 143 LNTS 257 (7 June 1930), Annex I (hereafter UBL).

[5] 143 LNTS 355 (19 March 1931), Annex I (hereafter UCL).

[6] Neither the UBL nor the UCL explicitly requires an 'instrument' to be 'written': see UBL arts 1 ('bill') and 75 ('note') and UCL art 1 ('cheque'). However, this requirement is implicit throughout. For example, 'endorsement', 'acceptance', 'stipulation', 'crossing'—all must be 'written'. See eg UBL arts 13, 25, and 46; UCL arts 16, 37, and 43.

[7] BEA s 3; UBL art 1; UCC § 3-104(b)(e) in conjunction with -104(a); United Nations Convention on International Bills of Exchange and International Promissory Notes UN Doc A/RES/43/165, 42 Yearbook

signed promise (by a 'maker') to pay a sum certain in money.[8] The cheque (or 'check' in the USA) is a bill payable on demand drawn on a bank.[9]

8.03 In principle,[10] liability on an instrument requires signature[11] on a written instrument complying with a required format and delivery.[12] For its part, transfer by 'negotiation', is either by mere delivery in the case of an instrument payable to the bearer, or by delivery plus the transferor's signed 'indorsement' in the case of an instrument payable to the order.[13] Finally, to charge secondary parties with liability, unless excused, presentment of the instrument, usually in the form of physical exhibition, is required.[14]

8.04 BEA s 2 defines '[w]ritten' to 'include ... printed' and 'writing' to 'include ... print'. This is a non-exhaustive definition which is arguably expanded in the UK by another non-exhaustive definition, that of Schedule 1 to the Interpretation Act 1978,[15] under which:

> 'Writing' includes typing, printing, lithography, photography and other modes of representing or reproducing words in a visible form

8.05 A creative interpretation may treat words in a permanent record 'visible' on a computer screen as satisfying the writing requirements.[16] For its part, the signature requirement is not limited to a handwritten one. However, several other provisions

of the United Nations 1988 (UN 1988) 834, art 3(1) (for the international dimension see art 2(1)) (hereafter UNIBNC).

[8] BEA s 83; UBL art 75: UCC § 3-104(b)(e) in conjunction with -104(a); UNIBNC art 3(2) (for the international dimension see art 2(2)).

[9] BEA s 73; UCC § 3-104(b)(f); effectively UCL art 1.

[10] Two exceptions relate to the 'signature' requirement. First, French law allows the holder of a bill and cheque to recover from the drawee, on the basis of *la provision*, that is, what the drawee owes the drawer, even without an acceptance. For *la provision* in French law, see eg J Stoufflet, *Instruments de paiement et de credit* (8th edn, LexisNexis 2012) 115–25. See also G Ripert and R Roblot, *Traité de droit commercial* (13th edn, Librairie Gènèrale de droit et de jurisprudence 1992) 181–86. For a more extensive analysis, see P Lescot and R Roblot, *Les effets de commerce*, vol I (Rousseau 1953) 389–465. A similar exception applies in Scotland, where under BEA s 53(2) a bill is stated to operate as an assignment of funds 'from the time when the bill is presented to the drawee'. A third exception is in relation to the delivery requirement for which the acceptor is given under BEA s 2 and UCC § 3-409 the option to preplace by 'notification'. Neither 'delivery' nor 'notification' is mentioned in ULB art 25 governing 'acceptance' formal requirement.

[11] BEA s 23; UBL arts 7–8; UCL arts 10–11; UCC § 3-401; UNIBNC art 33.

[12] While BEA s 21(1) is explicit on the delivery requirement for a contract on an instrument, the UCC and the UBL and UCL are not. At the same time, UCC §§ 3-105(a) and 3-203(a) respectively require 'delivery' for both 'issue' and 'transfer' of an instrument to a person entitled to enforce it under § 3-303 (in conjunction with §§ 3-412–415). Similarly, under UBL art 43 (in conjunction with art 16) and UCL art 40 (in conjunction with art 19) the entitlement to sue a party liable on an instrument is premised on lawful possession

[13] BEA s 31; UBL art 11; UCL art14; UCC § 3-201; UNIBNC art 13. The term 'negotiation' appears only in BEA, UCL, and UCC Article 3 (but not in UBL). An indorsement which does not designate the transferee is an indorsement in blank, which effectively 'converts' the bill into one payable to the bearer. This is true even where instruments originally issued payable to the bearer are not recognized for the 'conversion' by blank indorsement of the bill payable to order see eg BEA s 34(1); UBL arts 12–13; UCL arts 15–16; UCC § 3-205; UNIBNC arts 13–16.

[14] BEA ss 45 and 52(4) as well as UCC § 3-501(b)(2) are most explicit about it. For presentment under the Geneva Conventions see eg UBL arts 21–24 and 38; UCL arts 28, 29, and 31;

[15] Interpretation Act 1978, c 30 (UK).

[16] L Gamertsfelder, 'Electronic Bills of Exchange: Will the Current Law Recognize Them?' (1998) 21:2 UNSWLJ 566.

militate against any attempt to bypass the requirement that a bill must be written on a tangible material.

Thus, under BEA s 91, **8.06**

> (1) Where, by this Act, any instrument or writing is required to be signed by any person it is not necessary that he should sign it with his own hand, but it is sufficient if his signature is written thereon by some other person by or under his authority.
> (2) In the case of a corporation, where, by this Act, any instrument or writing is required to be signed, it is sufficient if the instrument or writing be sealed with the corporate seal.
>
> ...

All of which suggests that the norm is either a manual signature or a stamped seal. **8.07**

The general definitions of the UCC[17] are explicit in requiring the instrument to be a tangible item. Thus, UCC § 1-201(b)(43) defines '[w]riting to include "printing, typewriting, or any other intentional reduction to tangible form"'. To a similar end, and while being satisfied with a printed signature, UCC § 1-201(b)(34) goes on to define '[s]igned' to include 'printing, typewriting, or any other intentional reduction to tangible form'. **8.08**

BEA s 2 defines '[d]elivery' to mean 'transfer of possession, actual or constructive, from one person to another'. 'Delivery' is similarly defined in UCC § 1-201(b)(15) to include 'voluntary transfer of possession'. **8.09**

Even in the absence of definitions for 'writing', 'sign', or 'deliver', both the UBL and UCL must be taken to address a paper-based environment[18] in which writing and signatures are interwoven.[19] Thereunder, as under the BEA[20] and UCC Article 3,[21] transfer of possession of the tangible form on which it is expressed is fundamental to the usual way to acquire the power to enforce liability on the instrument.[22] **8.10**

With the advent of the electronic age, and ongoing development of electronic payment methods, the use of paper-based credit and payment systems is constantly declining. At the same time, negotiable instruments are not going out of use. For example, bills remain important in international trade because they are both payment and credit instruments. They also facilitate liquidity. Notes have kept their importance as liquid circulating credit obligations used in payment and for guarantees. Also, the cheque has retained its advantage as a payment instrument issued to a creditor by a debtor **8.11**

[17] For their application to Article 3 of the UCC see UCC § 3-103(d).

[18] 'Paper' is the typical tangible material on which an instrument is written or signed. In theory it could be written (and signed) on a parchment and even engraved in stone or gold!

[19] See references in nn 6 and 11.

[20] See eg BEA s 2, definitions of 'bearer', 'holder', 'issue', 'indorsement', as well as s 31 ('negotiation') in conjunction with s 38(a) ('rights of the holder').

[21] See eg UCC § 1-201(b)(5) ('bearer'), § 1-201(21) ('holder'), § 3-105(a), ('issue'), and UCC § 3-201(a) ('negotiation') in conjunction with UCC § 3-301 ('person entitled to enforce').

[22] See references in n 12.

who is not required to input the creditor's banking information. The continued use of negotiable instruments enhances legal certainty by profiting from the extensive body of law that has developed over the centuries to accommodate their use in commerce and balance the competing rights of parties thereto.

8.12 Notwithstanding these advantages, the paper and physical handling requirements for negotiable instruments give rise to difficulties. In international trade and business transaction are between distant parties, even domestically, as—for example—so far as the cheque collection itinerary is concerned, the physical transportation of instruments from place to place may be slow, not completely safe, and certainly inefficient. These difficulties remain inevitable as long as an instrument must be something tangible, on which words can be written to create a permanent tangible record, and physically deliverable from hand to hand in order to confer and acquire rights thereon.

8.13 Furthermore, as pointed out in Chapter IV, 'signature' and 'delivery' play a fundamental role in deciding the choice-of-law rules applicable to negotiable instruments. This is true under all sources: BEA s 72; arts 3 and 4 of the Convention for the Settlement of Certain Conflicts of Laws in Connection with Bills of Exchange and Promissory Notes;[23] arts 4 and 5 of the Convention for the Settlement of Certain Conflicts of Laws in Connection with Cheques;[24] §§ 214 and 215 of the Second Restatement;[25] and arts 2 and 3 of the Inter-American Convention on Conflict of Laws Concerning Bills of Exchange, Promissory Notes, and Invoices.[26] Indeed, 'signature' and 'delivery' are foundational not only to incurring liability on and the acquisition of rights on an instrument; they also determine the law applicable to an international negotiable instrument.[27] Hence, the introduction of electronification requires legislation.

B. Is 'Electronification' Feasible or Desirable?

8.14 In the present electronic age, the adequacy and fitness of payment and credit systems premised on writing and delivery has been questioned. Way back in 1985, at the dawn of electronic funds transfers (EFTs), Professor Ellinger wrote a seminal article[28] in which he addressed 'two questions ... linked to the making of deferred payment undertaking by means of EFT networks'. The first was concerned with the feasibility of such arrangements at that time. The second concerned 'the future of negotiable

[23] Convention for the Settlement of Certain Conflicts of Laws in connection with Bills of Exchange and Promissory Notes, 7 June 1930, 143 LNTS 319 (entered into force 1 January 1934) (hereafter Conflict Convention).

[24] 143 LNTS 407 (19 March 1931).

[25] American Law Institute) (hereafter Second Restatement).

[26] 1438 UNTS 211 (1975) (hereafter IACC).

[27] For further discussion of this point and the inherent complexities that it involves, see section E of this chapter.

[28] P Ellinger, 'Electronic Funds Transfer as a Deferred Settlement System' in RM Goode (ed) *Electronic Banking: The Legal Implications* (The Institute of Bankers and Centre for Commercial Law Studies of Queen Mary College University of London 1985) 29.

instruments in light of the advent of EFTs'. At the time of writing his article he identified the latter question as 'a plan for the future'.[29]

Clearly, Professor Ellinger addressed only the 'electronification' of credit instruments and was not concerned with cheques. As for the former, then and now, it has been possible for a customer to authorize his or her bank to either pay or collect on designated dates. Hence, regarding credit instruments, the crux of the issue has been Ellinger's second question, that of the desirability of or need for, as well as the feasibility of, an electronic negotiable instrument, namely an electronic credit obligation which is capable of circulation. Professor Ellinger was hesitant as to the desirability of or need for an electronic negotiable instrument, as he doubted that the operation of the bills market 'in London and elsewhere ... [was] so defective as to call for an expensive and fundamental reform'.[30] As for the feasibility, he was of the opinion that it may 'be possible to create' or dispatch 'a bill of exchange or promissory note by the use of an EFT network'.[31] However, he added:[32] **8.15**

> Once such an instrument reached its destination it would have to be treated as a document. To be used as a negotiable instrument, it would have to be transferred by indorsement and delivery; it would have to be presented for acceptance and for payment, and if dishonoured, might have to be protested.

Accordingly, he concluded:[33]

> The true question is whether such instrument may be replaced altogether by deferred payment EFTs of a negotiable character. Such an EFT would then be produced, transmitted, transferred and retired through the relevant network.

To that end, Professor Ellinger identified four legal problems or objections.[34] First, 'a bill ... embodies a string of contracts', each undertaken by a successive party. The second is the requirement of delivery or physical transferability. The third is that 'a negotiable instrument constitutes an item of property' for whose ownership possession may be required 'and not just a string of contracts'. The fourth objection is 'procedural', relating to requirements such as presentment and protest that require physical handling of the instrument. **8.16**

Certainly, 'electronification', that is, any elimination of physical processing and delivery, will enhance efficiency and speed. The chance is that it will also enhance security and reduce errors. Accordingly, assuming there is a business rationale for its continued use, there ought to be no doubt as to the desirability of bringing the negotiable instrument as much as possible into the ambit of electronic banking.[35] The **8.17**

[29] ibid, 29 (all cites in this paragraph).
[30] ibid, 44.
[31] ibid, 39.
[32] ibid, 39.
[33] ibid, 39.
[34] ibid, 41–43 (from which all cites in this paragraph are taken).
[35] Arguments in support of such a move have been floating for quite a long time. See eg JA Newell and MR Gordon, 'Electronic Commerce and Negotiable Instruments (Electronic Promissory Notes)' (1995) 31 Idaho L Rev 819; GV Puig, 'Electronic Bills of Exchange and Promissory Notes in Australia' (2000) Mur UELJ 27. For recommending caution (due to security concerns) while still recognizing that 'No one can resist progress' see eg A Tsakatoura, 'E-finance—Bills of Exchange, promissory Notes, Documentary Credits,

four issues raised by Ellinger relate to two points. First, the perceived incompatibility among hardware systems required for the negotiable instrument to evolve, from its issue, indorsement, acceptance, presentment, and protest. Second, the legal requirements as to the tangible nature of the instrument. As for the first point, technology made an enormous headway, so far translated into projects relating to cheques. As for the second, the law need not remain static and ought to be adjusted to changing circumstances.

C. 'Electronification': Current Steps

8.18 While electronic data is typically static, digital data may be manipulated and is formatted into a binary source. Nonetheless, we are going to follow the popular usage and use the terms interchangeably.[36] The present discussion accordingly takes 'electronization' (or 'digitization') to mean the expression of a negotiable instrument in an electronic or digital format. If only for space limitations the alternative of immobilization of a paper instrument by issuing or transferring it to a clearing house with the view of having subsequent transactions therein taking place by means of entries into participant's accounts at the clearing house will not be considered.[37]

8.19 Any transformation to a non-tangible format requires specific legislation authorizing it. To that end, at the moment, particularly in relation to cheques,[38] for example, electronic presentment, and hence, cheque truncation, is authorized by statute for example in the UK,[39] Sri Lanka,[40] and Canada.[41] Electronic deposit is practised in Canada including from a mobile-phone application.[42] For its part, the USA is well positioned more than any other jurisdiction to address all stages of dealing with electronic images of cheques. First, electronic presentment is authorized by statute.[43] Second, the USA has an elaborate scheme providing for the 'substitute check' replacing an

Forfaiting' Lex E-Scripta, 22 June 2002. And cf J Fan and Y Tao, 'Negotiable Instruments, in Particular Bills of Exchange in Macau, China' (2007) 2:2 J of Com L & Tec 83 where according to the authors drafting 'a complete electronic negotiable instruments law was deemed premature' in Macau.

[36] See eg <https://www.techopedia.com/definition/23367/digital-asset>, <https://www.quora.com/Whats-the-difference-between-electronic-and-digital>, <https://www.everplans.com/articles/a-helpful-overview-of-all-your-digital-property-and-digital-assets>, and https://www.linkedin.com/pulse/electronic-vs-digital-data-bernadette-bosse/, accessed 20 December 2019.

[37] A Canadian statute in that direction is Depository Bills and Notes Act, SC 1998, c 13. For an Australian proposal in that direction see Working Group Officials, *National Competition Policy Review of the Bills of Exchange Act 1909* (Canberra ACT: July 2003) 84.

[38] As a rule, legislation addressing electronification in each country is not necessarily limited to cheques and may cover other types of bills and 'items'. At the same time, not only that each statute cover cheques, the cheque may be its principal target and hence the discussion below will address such legislation as it applies to cheques.

[39] BEA ss 89A–89F.

[40] Payment and Settlement Systems Act (No 28 of 2005) ss 33–36.

[41] Bills of Exchange Act (RSC) 1985, c B-4 ss 163.1–163.6 (hereafter CBEA).

[42] B Geva, 'Is Death of the Paper Cheque upon Us? The Electronic Presentment and Deposit of Cheques in Canada' (2014), 30 BFLR 113, 120–24.

[43] UCC § 4-110.

electronic image of the original cheque.[44] This option is designed to accommodate a paper presentment made by a bank that received an image, to a drawee bank that is not equipped to receive an electronic presentment. Third, interbank image exchange rules are available.[45] Fourth, there are schemes for electronic cheques.[46] A unique feature of the legislation in the USA, which impacted the approach in Canada,[47] is the facilitation of transformation of the same negotiable instrument throughout its life into diverse formats. For example, a cheque issued in a written format may be deposited as such. It then may be converted to an electronic image and as such be transmitted to an intermediary bank which will convert it to a 'check substitute' for presentment to the drawee. Throughout all these transformations it will legally remain the same cheque!

Depending on interbank correspondent arrangements, advanced technology may **8.20** take advantage of this 'fluid' format of a cheque and facilitate the efficient fast cross-border collection. For example, suppose a bank in Ruritania provides chequing accounts in the currency of Penguina ($P). Payees in Penguina will deposit $P cheques drawn on such accounts to their own respective bank accounts throughout Penguina. These banks could then submit electronic images to the Penguina correspondent of the Ruritinaia drawee. Images will be then electronically presented by the correspondent in Penguina to the drawee in Ruritania. Alternatively, each depositary bank in Penguina will transmit images to its own correspondent in Ruritania for further electronic presentment to the Ruritania drawee.

In this scenario, as a matter of compliance with the form requirement, an electronic **8.21** format or 'substitute' authorized by the law of Ruritania will be treated as a negotiable instrument under the choice-of-law rules of Penguina. This is so even though on its own, such a format is not authorized under Penguina domestic law.[48] At the same time, as discussed in Chapter IV section E, unless the law of Penguina recgonizes such a format, it will not be possible to incur liability on the electronic format and negotiate it as an 'instrument' in Penguina. Hence harmonization among requirements as to format is badly needed.

The scheme in the USA facilitating substitute cheques, interbank image exchanges, **8.22** and electronic cheques is an elaborate and versatile system. The 'substitute check' scheme is provided by the Check Clearing for the 21st Century Act ('Check 21 Act')[49]

[44] An explicit purpose of the Act was '[t]o facilitate check truncation by authorizing substitute checks'. See Check Clearing for the 21st Century Act, 12 USC § 5001 (2003) § 2(b)(1).

[45] Regulation CC: Availability of Funds and Collection of Checks, 12 CFR Part 229, 82 Fed Reg 27552 (2017) online: <https://www.federalregister.gov/documents/2017/06/15/2017-11379/availability-of-funds-and-collection-of-checks>, accessed 20 December 2019 (hereafter Regulation CC).

[46] See eg Regulation CC § 229.34(g).

[47] See definition of 'official image' in CBEA which is said to include 'a display, a printout, a copy or any other output of that image and that data created by or on behalf of a bank in accordance with those by-laws, rules and standards'.

[48] B Crawford, The *Law of Banking and Payment in Canada* vol 3 (Canada Law Book, Looseleaf, 2014 edition) § 33:30.30 reached this conclusion albeit with some hesitation that we do not share. Crawford may, however, be read to argue for the validity in Penguina even for an image originated from Ruritania—of which form is governed by—but unauthorized under—the law of Ruritania, a proposition to which we disagree.

[49] ibid.

and implemented by Regulation CC Subpart D.[50] Thereunder, having agreed to receive a cheque in an electronic form, a collecting bank[51] that received it is authorized to create a substitute paper cheque for further negotiation or presentment to a bank that has not agreed to receive a cheque in an electronic form. Upon compliance with specified requirements, the substitute cheque is to become 'the legal equivalent of the original check for all purposes'.[52] The Check 21 Act further includes warranty and indemnity provisions as well as expedited re-credit procedures, designed to protect substitute cheque recipients.[53]

8.23 Three principal sets of interbank image exchange rules are available. Each endeavours to equate the position of cheque images to that of the cheques themselves under existing legislation and other sources of law. In fact, they extend the legal framework of Check 21 Act[54] to cover image exchanges.

8.24 The first set of image exchange rules is Subpart A of Regulation J,[55] governing interbank exchange through Federal Reserve Banks. Further implemented by Operating Circular No 3, it specifically deals with the collection of cheques and other items by Federal Reserve Banks. Thereunder, an 'item' is broadly defined to cover an electronic image of a paper item.[56]

8.25 The second is Electronic Check Clearinghouse Organization (ECCHO) Rules.[57] ECCHO is 'a national not-for-profit 'rule-making organization' owned entirely by its member banks'.[58] As 'an association of banks or other payors regularly clearing items' ECCHO is a clearing house under UCC § 4-104(a)(4) even though it does not process payments at all. Rather, it develops rules governing electronic exchanges of cheque images. Such rules qualify as 'clearing-house rules' under UCC § 4-103(b), which govern bilateral and multilateral exchanges between member banks that choose to adhere to them. Per that provision, 'all parties interested in' the cheques, are bound by such rules governing their exchange.

8.26 The third principal set of interbank image exchange rules governs the regulatory framework in the USA covering the exchange of cheque images under Regulation

[50] Regulation CC Subpart D–Substitute Checks (§§ 229.51–229.60).

[51] In the cheque collection process a collecting bank is every bank other than the drawee or payor bank.

[52] Regulation CC Subpart D, § 229.51(a).

[53] For a comprehensive overview, though written prior to the promulgation of the final text for Regulation CC Part D, see PS Turner, *Analysis of the Check Clearing for the 21st Century Act* (LexisNexis 2004) (hereafter Turner, *Check 21*). For more on the background to the *Check 21 Act see Availability of Funds and Collection of Checks*, 69 Fed Reg 1470; *Availability of Funds and Collection of Checks*, 69 Fed Reg 47290 (2004); Federal Reserve, Press Release (26 July 2004). <https://www.federalreserve.gov/boarddocs/press/bcreg/2004/20040726/default.htm>, accessed 5 February 2019; and Federal Reserve, Press Release, (22 October 2004) <https://www.federalreserve.gov/boarddocs/press/bcreg/2004/20041022/default.htm>, accessed 5 February 2019.

[54] Turner, *Check 21* .

[55] Collection of Checks and Other Items by Federal Reserve Banks and Funds Transfers Through Fedwire, 12 CFR § 210 (hereafter Regulation J).

[56] ibid § 210.2(i)(1)(ii).

[57] Text draws to a large part on documents accessible online at https://www.eccho.org/, accessed 20 December 2019. See also VY Ware, 'Check Image Exchange: Covering Legal Bases' (2008) The Independent Community of Bankers of America.

[58] AC Harrell, 'Electronic Checks' (2001) 55 Con Fin LQ Rep 283.

CC.[59] Its § 229.30(a) states that unless otherwise agreed by the sending and receiving banks,[60] electronic images of cheques and electronic information related to cheques that banks send and receive by agreement would be subject to Subpart C of Regulation CC as if they were paper cheques. Accordingly, a bank that handles electronic cheques and electronic returned cheques gives all cheque warranties and indemnities.[61] Section 229.34(a) provides for additional 'Check-21-like warranties'[62] specifically given with respect to electronic cheques and electronic returns.

8.27 Finally, in the USA, in the absence of a statutory or otherwise precise definition, an electronically issued payment order, with otherwise all characteristics of a cheque, is often treated as a 'paperless cheque' and as such is known as an electronic payment order (EPO)[63] or electronic cheque.[64] Like a paper cheque,[65] an EPO is issued by the drawer/payer and is addressed to the drawee/payor bank, ordering it to pay on demand a sum certain in money to the payee (or bearer), to whom the order is issued. This is feasible technologically and efficient economically; it is indeed said that as an equivalent to a cheque, the EPO possesses features such as 'speed, finality, relatively low cost, and ubiquity'.[66] However, strictly speaking, this payment method is not a 'cheque' as it does not involve anything tangible in writing. Indeed, cheque truncation

[59] Regulation CC.

[60] Availability of Funds and Collection of Checks, 79 Fed Reg 6673 (2014) 6684 (to be codified at 12 CFR § 229) <https://www.federalregister.gov/articles/2014/02/04/2013-30024/availability-of-funds-and-collection-of-checks>, accessed 20 December 2019 (hereafter FRS Availability Proposal), would permit a sending and receiving bank by agreement to vary the warranties the sending bank makes to the receiving bank for electronic cheques and electronic returned cheques. Such an agreement could provide, for example, that the bank transferring the electronic cheque does not warrant that the electronic image or information are sufficient to create a substitute cheque. The agreement would not, however, vary the effect of the warranties with respect to banks and persons not bound by the agreement.

[61] Under the revised Regulation CC§ 229.34(c), (d), and (e) (until 1 July 2018: d, e, and f), such warranties related to (1) settlement amount, encoding, and offset; (2) returned checks; and (3) notice of nonpayment.

[62] Availability of Funds and Collection of Checks, 82 Fed Reg 27552 (2017) (to be codified at 12 CFR § 229) <https://www.federalregister.gov/documents/2017/06/15/2017-11379/availability-of-funds-and-collection-of-checks>, accessed 6 February 2019. FRS Availability Proposal 6683.

[63] On the electronic payment order (EPO) see eg Katy Jacob et al, Federal Reserve Bank of Chicago Financial Markets Group, *Digital Checks as Electronic Payment Orders*, Policy Discussion Paper Series, PDP 2009-5 (2009) <http://www.chicagofed.org/digital_assets/publications/policy_discussion_papers/2009/PDP2009-5.pdf>, accessed 20 December 2019; M Kepler, 'A Summary of the Electronic Payment Order Forum' (2013) Federal Reserve Bank of Atlanta <http://www.frbatlanta.org/documents/rprf/rprf_pubs/130521_summary_paper.pdf>, accessed 20 December 2019 (hereafter Kepler, 'Electronic Payment'); 'EPO: The Next Frontier of a Check' (2014 revised 2017) ECCHO <http://64.254.32.105/2014_epo_public >, accessed 20 December 2019; and Phyllis Meyerson, 'Electronic Payment Orders (EPOs)' (17 June 2013) ECCHO.

[64] Under FRS Availability Proposal 27579, § 229.2(g):

Electronic check and *electronic returned check* mean an electronic image of, and electronic information derived from, a paper check or paper returned check, respectively, that:

> (1) Is sent to a receiving bank pursuant to an agreement between the sender and the receiving bank; and
>
> (2) Conforms with ANS X9.100-187, unless the Board by rule or order determines that a different standard applies or the parties otherwise agree.

[65] 'Paper-check' (as defined in UCC § 3-104(f) in conjunction with UCC §§ 3-103(a)(8) and 3-104(e)) is used in this section in the sense of a 'check'—to distinguish it from the EPO.

[66] Kepler, 'Electronic Payment'.

in all its forms is premised on an image as well as a substitute cheque as derivations of a paper cheque issued by the drawer to the payee (or bearer).

8.28 Electronification is, however, not limited to cheques and similar demand collection items. For its part, a deferred EFT in the form of electronic deferred payment obligation (or undertaking) (DPU) already exists as a payment and credit instrument in international trade. It is also known as a deferred payment credit (DPC) and has been used in lieu of an accepted bill in a letter of credit transaction: particularly with the view of avoiding stamping requirements on bills.[67] In *Banco Santander v Banque Paribas*,[68] the confirming bank made a complying document presentation and took an assignment of proceeds from the beneficiary. Thereby the confirming bank effectively discounted the issuing bank DPU and prepaid the beneficiary. When the issuing bank's DPU's fell due, the confirming bank was refused reimbursement by the issuing bank on the basis of beneficiary's fraud. The Court of Appeal upheld the issuing bank's defence thereby treating it as a mere proceeds assignee and not being in a position of a holder in due course.

UCP 600[69] purported to overrule *Banco Santander v Banque Paribas* in providing in art 12(b) that:

> By nominating a bank to ... incur a deferred payment undertaking, an issuing bank authorizes that nominating bank to prepay or purchase ... a deferred payment undertaking incurred by that nominating bank.

UCP art 7(c) goes even further:

> an issuing bank undertakes to reimburse a nominated bank that has honoured or negotiated a complying presentation and forwarded the documents to the issuing bank. Reimbursement for the amount of a complying presentation under a credit available by ... deferred payment is due on maturity, whether or not the nominated bank prepaid or purchased before maturity. *An issuing bank's undertaking to reimburse a nominated bank is independent of the issuing bank's undertaking to the beneficiary.* (Emphasis added)

In the USA, UCC § 5-109 (a)(1) is to the same effect:

[67] See JF Dolan, 'Negotiable Obligations for Discount: Notes, Acceptances, DPUs and BPOs' (2013) 29 BFLR 103; A Casterman, 'Modernising global trade finance practices' (2012) 6:3 Journal of Payments Strategy & Systems 225; 'Bank Payment Obligation' International Chamber of Commerce (ICC), online: http://icc.tobb.org.tr/docs/Bank%20Payment%20Obligation.pdf, accessed 20 December 2019; M Hwaidi, 'The Implications of Banco Santander v. Bayfern Ltd on Deferred Payment under Documentary Credit in UCP 600' (2011) Intl Bus L J 569; K Vorpeil, 'Bank Payment Obligations: Alternative Means of Settlement in International Trade' (2014) Intl Bus L J 41; K Takahashi, 'The Introduction of Article 12(b) in the UCP 600: Was it Really a Step Forward?' (2009) JIBLR 285; CRW de Meijer and M Menon, 'Bank payment obligation: The missing link?' (2012) 6:3 Journal of Payments Strategy & Systems 232; G Profazio and J Chuah, 'An analysis of acceptance and deferred payment credits in civil and common law' (2007) 13 JIML 330; and AL Tyree, 'Deferred Payment Letters of Credit' <http://www2.austlii.edu.au/~alan/deferred-credits.html>, accessed 20 December 2019.

[68] [2000] LCC 906 (CA).

[69] International Chamber of Commerce, 2006. UCP 600 Uniform Customs and Practice for Documentary Credits 2007 Revision. ICC SERVICES Publications Department, Paris.

(a) If a presentation is made that appears on its face strictly to comply with the terms and conditions of the letter of credit, but a required document is forged or materially fraudulent, or honor of the presentation would facilitate a material fraud by the beneficiary on the issuer or applicant:

(1) the issuer shall honor the presentation, if honor is demanded by (i) a nominated person who has given value in good faith and without notice of forgery or material fraud, (ii) a confirmer who has honored its confirmation in good faith, (iii) a holder in due course of a draft drawn under the letter of credit which was taken after acceptance by the issuer or nominated person, or (iv) an assignee of the issuer's or nominated person's deferred obligation that was taken for value and without notice of forgery or material fraud after the obligation was incurred by the issuer or nominated person;

The confirmer in *Banco Santander v Banque Paribas* would have fit into clause (i). Had it not been for the prepayment it would have fit into clause (ii).

However, at most, these provisions provide limited negotiability on a DPU in favour of a nominated bank in a letter of credit transaction. They do not 'upgrade' the DPU to a bill or note governed by negotiable instruments legislation. **8.29**

D. 'Electronification': An Overall Framework

The availability of a legal framework facilitating electronification, both for each stage of the cycle, namely, issue, transfer(s), incurring liability, and presentment, as well as for the entire electronic cycle, will now be examined. **8.30**

First, UNCITRAL Model Law on Electronic Commerce (1996)[70] (LEC) will be examined. Under art 5: **8.31**

Information shall not be denied legal effect, validity or

enforceability solely on the grounds that it is in the form of a data message.

Under LEC art 6(1): **8.32**

Where the law requires information to be in writing, that requirement is met by a data message if the information contained therein is accessible so as to be usable for subsequent reference.

LEC art 7(1) goes on to provide that:[71] **8.33**

[70] Model Law on Electronic Commerce with Guide to Enactment 1996, GA Res 51/162, UNCITRAL, 1998, <http://www.uncitral.org/pdf/english/texts/electcom/V1504118_Ebook.pdf>, accessed 20 December 2019 (hereafter LEC).

[71] To that end see eg also the following provisions of *Model Law on Electronic Signatures with Guide to Enactment 2001*, 56/80, UNITRAL, online: <http://www.uncitral.org/pdf/english/texts/electcom/ml-elecsig-e.pdf>, accessed 20 December 2019. Under art 2 (a):

'Electronic signature' means data in electronic form in, affixed to or logically associated with, a data message, which may be used to identify the signatory in relation to the data message and to indicate the signatory's approval of the information contained in the data message.

See also LEC art 6 (1):

Where the law requires a signature of a person, that requirement is met in relation to a data message if:

(a) a method is used to identify that person and to indicate that person's approval of the information contained in the data message; and

(b) that method is as reliable as was appropriate for the purpose for which the data message was generated or communicated, in the light of all the circumstances, including any relevant agreement.

8.34 Finally, under LEC art 8:

(1) Where the law requires information to be presented or retained in its original form, that requirement is met by a data message if:

(a) there exists a reliable assurance as to the integrity of the

information from the time when it was first generated in its final form, as a data message or otherwise; and

(b) where it is required that information be presented, that information is capable of being displayed to the person to whom it is to be presented.

...

(3) For the purposes of subparagraph (a) of paragraph (1):

(a) the criteria for assessing integrity shall be whether the information has remained complete and unaltered, apart from the addition of any endorsement and any change which arises in the normal course of communication, storage and display; and

(b) the standard of reliability required shall be assessed in the light of the purpose for which the information was generated and in the light of all the relevant circumstances.

...

8.35 According to paragraph 63 of the Guide to Enactment of the UNCITRAL Model Law on Electronic Commerce (1996):[72]

Article 8 is pertinent to ... negotiable instruments, in which the notion of uniqueness of an original is particularly relevant.

8.36 This framework resolves any doubt as to the possible compliance with 'writing' and 'signature' requirements as well as to the mere possibility of an electronic bill. However, this framework does not address issues pertaining specifically to negotiable instruments such as possession and delivery. True, a sympathetic court could treat exclusive control on the electronic bill as the equivalent of possession and irrevocable electronic

Where the law requires a signature of a person, that requirement is met in relation to a data message if an electronic signature is used that is as reliable as was appropriate for the purpose for which the data message was generated or communicated, in the light of all the circumstances, including any relevant agreement.

[72] LEC [63].

transmission as tantamount to physical delivery; nonetheless, this approach may not be adequate to accommodate the diverse requirements governing the electronification of instruments. Thus, on its own, LEC may not be explicit enough in conferring the electronic record the status of a negotiable instrument transferrable by electronic transmission and on which each 'signer' is liable.

Negotiable instruments are excluded from the ambit of the United Nations Conventions on the Use of Electronic Communications in International Contracts (2007) (UN Convention).[73] The drafters observed that 'issues raised by negotiable instruments ... in particular the need for ensuring their uniqueness, go beyond simply ensuring the equivalence between paper and electronic forms'.[74] They concluded that 'finding a solution for this problem requires a combination of legal, technological and business solutions, which had not been fully developed and tested'.[75] **8.37**

In its treatment of the signature and writing requirements, the UN Convention generally follows the LEC and seeks to extend the functional equivalent approach to electronic contracts.[76] Thus, in relation to the signature requirement, art 9(2) of the UN Convention states that 'Where the law requires that a communication or a contract should be in writing, or provides consequences of the absence in writing, that requirement is met by an electronic communication if the information contained therein is accessible so as to be usable for subsequent reference.' Article 9(3) of the UN Convention applies the same logic to the requirements of a signature.[77] **8.38**

In relation to the question of transfer and receipt of electronic emails, art 10(2) of the UN Convention differentiates between two scenarios. The first scenario addresses a situation when the parties designated a certain email address for their communication. In this situation, the time when the email enters the email system of the addressee is considered to be the time of email receipt.[78] Since the parties designated a certain mode of correspondence, the law seems to take the addressee as having constructive possession of the email. This is true even if the addressee has not actually seen the email for various reasons, for example of the email arrives into the 'junk box'.[79] **8.39**

In this way, the UN Convention rejects the traditional 'postal acceptance rule'. As we mentioned in Chapter IV,[80] this rule applies to situations where contractual **8.40**

[73] https://www.uncitral.org/pdf/english/texts/electcom/06-57452_Ebook.pdf, accessed 20 December 2019, art 2(2) (hereafter UN Convention).
[74] ibid, Explanatory Notes, 35.
[75] ibid, Explanatory Notes, 35.
[76] ibid, 50-51.
[77] ibid, art 9(3).
[78] ibid, art 10(2). F Wang, *Law of Electronic Commercial Transactions* (Routledge 2011) 39 (hereafter Wang, *Electronic Transactions*); A Davidson, *Social Media and Electronic Commerce Law* (2nd edn, Cambridge University Press 2006) 197.
[79] UN Convention art 10(2). See also EC Directive on Electronic Commerce, art 11; UNCITRAL Model Law on Electronic Commerce with Guide to Enactment 1996, art 2(b). See also art 11(2)(a) of the European Commerce (EC Directive) Regulations 2002 (SI 2002/2013), art 15(2) of the UN Model Law on Electronic Commerce. See also Wang, *Electronic Transactions* 39.
[80] See Chapter IV, text accompanying nn 100–134.

acceptance occurs through letter correspondence. When the parties designate letter correspondence as a means of communication, the postal acceptance rule states that the acceptance takes place at the postal office—the time when the offeree sends the letter to the offeror.[81] Art 10(2) of the UN Convention, however, rejects the postal rule: the time of sending the email is not considered the time of the email acceptance, even as a presumptive rule.[82] Rather, art 10(2) sets the time when the email enters into the sphere of exclusive control of the addressee—that is, the time when the email enters his or her email system.[83] Chinese legislative framework seems to be supportive of this position.[84]

8.41 The second scenario of art 10(2) of the UN Convention addresses a situation without a designated email address. In this case, the law sets two requirements. First (and similar to the first scenario), the email needs to enter the system of the addressee.[85] Second, it requires a demonstration that the addressee had actually became aware of the email, or alternatively—objectively in the circumstances of the case—should have become aware of the email.[86] In this way, the law appears to follow the functional equivalent approach in relation to the question of taking possession: whether through actual possession (through the actual retrieval of the email) or through a constructive one (through the imposition of an objective standard on the addressee according to which he should have retrieved the email).[87] This position seems to correlate with art 11 of the UNCITRAL Model Law on Electronic Transferable Records (2017)[88] (LETR), which focuses on the concept of 'exclusive control' of [an] electronic transferable record' as a functional equivalent of 'the possession of a transferable document or instrument'.[89]

8.42 In providing a useful follow-up for the 'electronification' of instruments LETR is, however, a more progressive document. LETR art 8 reproduces LEC art 6(1) almost verbatim in rendering information that is 'accessible so as to be usable for subsequent reference' the functional equivalent[90] of 'writing'. Similarly, LETR art 9 echoes LEC art 7(1). It provides that where 'a reliable method is used to identify [a] person and to indicate that person's intention in respect of the information

[81] ibid.

[82] UN Convention art 10(2).

[83] See eg S Hill, 'Flogging a Dead Horse- The Postal Acceptance Rule and Email' (2001) 17 J of Cont L 151; D Nolan, 'Offer and Acceptance in the Electronic Age' in A Burrows and E Peel (eds) *Contract Formation and Parties* (Oxford University Press 2010) 61, 68–69 (hereafter Nolan, 'Contract Formation'). See also B Fitzgerald et al, *Internet and E-commerce Law, Business and Policy* (Thomson Reuters 2011) 745–47.

[84] Wang, *Electronic Commercial Transactions* 45.

[85] UN Convention art 10(2).

[86] ibid. See also Nolan, 'Contract Formation' 70–71; Wang, *Electronic Transactions* 30.

[87] See Nolan, 'Contract Formation' 73–76; Wang, *Electronic Transactions* 40, 43.

[88] Model Law on Electronic Transferable Records, A 72/17, UNCITRAL, 2017 <http://www.uncitral.org/pdf/english/texts/electcom/MLETR_ebook.pdf>, accessed 20 December 2019 (hereafter LETR).

[89] ibid, art 11. Under art 2, ibid, 'Transferable document or instrument' is defined to mean 'a document or instrument issued on paper that entitles the holder to claim the performance of the obligation indicated in the document or instrument and to transfer the right to performance of the obligation indicated in the document or instrument through the transfer of that document or instrument.'

[90] For further discussion on the significance of the 'functional equivalent' approach for the purposes of qualification of the existing legal rules in the time of digital age, see the text accompanying nn 129–33.

contained in [an] electronic transferable record' a legal signature requirement by that person is satisfied. Addressing the signature aspect of transferability, LETR art 15 provides that:

> Where the law requires or permits the endorsement in any form of a transferable document or instrument, that requirement is met with respect to an electronic transferable record if the information required for the endorsement is included in the electronic transferable record and that information is compliant with the requirements set forth in articles 8 and 9.

Unfortunately, a footnote to art 1(3) leaves open the possibility of excluding negotiable instruments from what otherwise seems to be a suitable framework for the creation and transfer of an electronic instrument. This propriety or fitness is expressed in LETR art 2, defining '*Electronic record*' to mean 'information generated, communicated, received or stored by electronic means'. Under LETR art 10(1) it becomes an '*Electronic transferable record*', where: **8.43**

(a) It] contains the information that would be required to be contained in a transferable document or instrument; and
(b) A reliable method[91] is used:
  (i) To identify that electronic record as the electronic transferable record;
  (ii) To render that electronic record capable of being subject to control from its creation until it ceases to have any effect or validity; and
  (iii) To retain the integrity of that electronic record.[92]

LETR art 11(1) goes on to provide that the 'exclusive control of [an] electronic transferable record' established by 'a reliable method', which also identifies the person in control meets a legal requirement for 'the possession of a transferable document or instrument'. As well, under LETR art 11(2), 'the transfer of control over [an] electronic transferable record' is the equivalent for the 'transfer of possession of a transferable document or instrument'. **8.44**

The upshot of all this is that, as long as it conforms with format requirements under negotiable instrument statutes, an 'electronic record' under LETR and containing 'signatures' authorized by LEC, could serve as an electronic negotiable instrument, to which the statutes will apply with necessary modifications. To make it happen what is required is the adoption of laws based on LEC and LETR, ensuring that bills, notes, and cheques are not excluded, and the addition of provisions to govern **8.45**

[91] The general reliability standard is provided for in LETR art 12. It addresses operational rules, the assurance of data integrity, the ability to prevent unauthorized access and use, the security of hardware and software, the regularity and extent of independent audit, a declaration by a supervisory or accreditation body, and any applicable industry standard.

[92] Under LETR art 10(2):

> The criterion for assessing integrity shall be whether information contained in the electronic transferable record, including any authorized change that arises from its creation until it ceases to have any effect or validity, has remained complete an unaltered apart from any change which arises in the normal course of communication, storage and display.

situations in which adverse claimants assert rights to different media of the same instrument.

E. Choice-of-Law Rules for Electronic Negotiable Instruments

8.46 What are the implications of the emerging electronification of negotiable instruments for the choice-of-law rules applicable to this area of law? How should legal frameworks react to a reality in which negotiable instruments lose their physical form? As we have seen in the previous sections of this chapter, clearly the key aspects of negotiable instruments law, such as a signature, requirements of writing, and delivery will be transformed into digital form. How will this transformation affect the nature of choice-of-law analysis?

8.47 We divide the discussion into two parts. The first part addresses the impact of the digitalization on the existing choice-of-law frameworks. It argues that the transformation of negotiable instruments into their digital form only enhances the inadequacy of the existing choice-of-law rules relating to this area of law. The second part of our discussion demonstrates the apparent advantages of the suggested normative argument (presented in Chapters V–VII) to serve as a basis for the digital age of negotiable instruments.

1. Digitalization and Existing Frameworks of the Choice-of-Law Rules

8.48 As we have seen in Chapter IV, the choice-of-law rules under the existing frameworks are rigid. They reject the popular party autonomy and most significant relationship principles. There is no universal agreement on the identity of which connecting factor should govern the choice-of-law process. Thus, as we have seen, the UK BEA predominantly follows the connecting factor of the place of the contract formation. This connecting factor may look surprising to the eyes of the contemporary choice-of-law scholars. It raises eyebrows, as it clearly follows the legacy of Joseph Beale's discredited sovereignty-based vision of the subject.[93] Moreover, there is an inherent difficulty in tracking the location of contract formation in the specific context of negotiable instruments. As we have seen, the places of the instrument's signature and delivery do not always coincide, which creates a special problem for the operational mechanics of the rule. While in other areas of commercial law, the place of contract formation has been repealed[94] or has become an 'academic exercise',[95] it remains the primary rule under English law. Subsequently, this connecting factor remains the guiding rule in a wide range of BEA-modelled jurisdictions.[96]

[93] For a discussion of this point, see Chapter IV sections B–H.
[94] See Chapter III section B(3).
[95] See Chapter VII, the text accompanying nn 143–47.
[96] On the decisive impact of the UK BEA across jurisdictions, see Chapter I, the text accompanying nn 48–75.

The Second Restatement focuses on another territorial connecting factor—that of the place of payment, which it views as generally preferable to the connecting factor of the place of contract formation. The Second Restatement makes a distinction between choice-of-law rules applied to the primary parties on the instrument (ie a note's maker and a bill's acceptor) and the secondary parties (ie a drawer of a bill or cheque and an indorser). While the connecting factor of the place of payment governs the liabilities of the primary parties, the liabilities of the secondary parties are governed by the connecting factor of the place of contract formation.[97] From this perspective, American jurisprudence follows BEA on the point of the secondary parties. **8.49**

The Continental Geneva Conflict Conventions appear to focus on the territorial connecting factor of the place of signature. With respect to the question of the parties' capacity, they depart from the territorial connecting factors of both the UK BEA and the Second Restatement. Rather, they apply a personal connecting factor of nationality. Finally, IACC follows a 'middle' path between the Second Restatement and the Continental Geneva Conflict Conventions: while the connecting factor of the place of payment governs the question of the instrument's form, the connecting factor of contract formation governs the liabilities of the parties.[98] **8.50**

As we have seen,[99] the various frameworks seem to be in agreement in principle to the internal structure of negotiable instruments law. They view this structure as consisting of several independent contracts—the drawer's, acceptor's, maker's, and indorser's contracts. This means that each one of the contracts requires a separate choice-of-law analysis and different laws could potentially apply to each one of them. Thus, the BEA, in reference to the internal structure of the negotiable instruments law, uses the phrase 'supervening contracts'.[100] Similarly, the Second Restatement's provisions and commentaries make a distinction between various contracts[101] and apply different choice-of-law rules to each one of them.[102] In a similar vein, the Continental Geneva Conflict Conventions follow the principal division between the primary parties and secondary parties: they name the connecting factor of the place of payment to be applied to primary parties and mention the connecting factor of the place of signature to be applied to 'other parties'.[103] Finally, the Inter-American Convention seems to follow this vision of negotiable instruments law as well, by using plural language and referring to the multiplicity of potential 'acts'[104] and 'obligations'[105] under negotiable instruments law. From this perspective, it would appear that the choice-of-law **8.51**

[97] See Chapter IV sections C and D.
[98] ibid.
[99] See Chapter IV section B.
[100] BEA s 72(1). See also Collins, Harris (eds) *Dicey, Morris and Collins on the Conflict of Laws* (15th edn, Sweet & Maxwell 2012) 2078–79.
[101] Second Restatement §§ 214, 215.
[102] For a discussion of these issues, see Chapter IV section B.
[103] Conflict Convention art 4.
[104] IACC art 2.
[105] ibid, art 3.

frameworks have reached a consensus on their support for the so-called 'several laws' doctrine.[106]

8.52 While the choice-of-law frameworks mention a broad variety of potential connecting factors to govern each one of the contracts, the choice-of-law process remains rigid. Following the sovereignty-based concept of the subject, this process focuses on the application of a single factor. Only one territorial factor (with the noticeable exception of the Continental Geneva Conflict Conventions —which apply the nationality connecting factor with respect to questions of capacity—can be taken into account for the purposes of choice-of-law analysis. Following the English tradition, the territorial connecting factor of the place of contract formation presently seems to be the predominant rule amongst the systems.

8.53 As we have seen throughout this book,[107] the rigidity of the choice-of-law process and the focus on single connecting factors seems to be inadequate for our contemporary reality. Outside of the realm of negotiable instruments, the choice-of-law doctrine has departed from the rigid structure of the connecting factors. Consider the classical connecting factor of contract formation. In light of the frequency of cross-border commerce, tourism, and the complex web of business communications, the location of contract formation usually tells us little about the nature of the parties' interaction. Frequently, this connecting factor fails to establish a meaningful link between the parties and their dealings.

8.54 The transformation of contemporary commerce into the digital sphere has deepened the challenge to the traditional connecting factors approach. In order to follow the existing frameworks of choice-of-law rules relating to negotiable instruments, the adjudicative tribunals need to detect the exact timing and the physical location of such factors as the place of contract formation and the place of signature. Tracing these locations in the context of electronic communication can be a difficult task. Furthermore, the contemporary reality of fluency of commerce and cross-border interactions suggests a further challenge to rigidity of the traditional approach. Territorial locations of such places, as signature and delivery can frequently be irrelevant to the very nature of the parties' interaction. Yet, until there is comprehensive reform (hopefully based on the suggestions in book), the existing choice-of-law framework should accommodate the challenge of technological innovation.

8.55 Consider thc predominant connecting factor of the place of contract formation. As noted earlier,[108] in the context of negotiable instruments, this connecting factor requires tracking the location of where the delivery of the instrument took place. Where does the delivery of the instrument take place in the case of electronic communication? Transformed into the context of the digital sphere, the answer to this question is far from easy. Following art 11 of LETR and art 10 of the UN Convention it seems to be

[106] For a discussion on the adoption of the several laws doctrine, see Chapter IV section B. As we have seen the recent objection to this doctrine has been rejected by the US Supreme Court in the context of the negotiability aspects of the bills of lading (see Chapter VII, the text accompanying nn 117–32).

[107] See Chapters III, VI, and VII.

[108] For the place of contract formation as that of the instrument delivery, see Chapter IV section C.

clear that the postal acceptance rule must be rejected. These articles support a position that would focus on the moment when the digital instrument enters into the sphere of addressee's exclusive control[109] and his or her actual (or constructive) awareness of having received the instrument.[110] We would support this emerging position of the contemporary international frameworks with respect to the question of the place of delivery of the electronic instrument.

As with respect to electronic delivery, legal scholarship and the legislative provisions apply the 'functionality' approach to the signature[111] and form[112] requirements. The effort to transform the requirement of the signature to the electronic sphere reflects the position that an electronic signature should be essentially equated with a 'manual' one.[113] Despite some comments in the literature on the potential conceptual divergence between the two,[114] the present trajectory of the legal frameworks does not distinguish between electronic and 'manual' signatures. Choice-of-law analysis would require tracking the location of the electronic signature, similar to that of a manual one. Accordingly, the place where the signatory party places his or her electronic signature should be considered as the place of the signature for the purposes of the choice-of-law analysis. **8.56**

2. Digitalization and a Suggested Framework of the Choice-of-Law Rules

Chapters V–VII challenged the orthodoxies and reassessed the rules set out in the contemporary choice-of-law frameworks. The proposals made throughout this book should be appealing to the digital era of negotiable instruments. **8.57**

Consider first the suggestion made in Chapter V on the possible relaxation or even elimination of the traditional requirement to classify the field according to the presence of the so-called 'foreign element'.[115] Under this requirement, the choice-of-law question becomes relevant only if some degree of 'foreignness' or 'internationality' can be demonstrated within the factual matrix of the case.[116] This suggestion closely correlates with the inherently 'international' nature of communications performed through the medium of the Internet. Naturally, lacking geographical borders[117] the **8.58**

[109] LETR art 11.
[110] UN Convention art 10(2).
[111] LEC art 7; LETR art 9.
[112] UN Convention art 9; LEC art 6; LETR art 8.
[113] Law Commission, Electronic Commerce: Formal Requirements in Commercial Transactions (2001); Electronic Communication Act 2007, ss 7–8. See also sections A and D of this chapter.
[114] See eg R Hillman and J Rachlinski, 'Standard-Form Contracting in the Electronic Age' (2002) 77 NYU L Rev 429, 481.
[115] See Chapter V section A.
[116] ibid.
[117] On the non-geographical nature of the Internet, see eg DJerkerB Svantesson, *Private International Law and the Internet* (3rd edn, Kluwer Law International 2016) 1, 56, 82 (mentions the 'unstable' relation between private international law and the Internet as a reflection of the 'borderless' and 'lacking central control' nature of the latter and territorial nature of the former); S Tang, *Electronic Consumer Contracts in the Conflict of Laws* (Hart Publishing 2009) 12–13 (hereafter Tang, *Electronic Consumer Contracts*); Wang, *Electronic Commercial Transactions* 3, 87.

Internet cannot be understood as a strictly domestic phenomenon. Even within the context of communication between domestic residents the very fact that such communication takes place through the Internet suggests the relevancy of choice-of-law analysis. As shown in Chapter III,[118] nowadays one can track some foreign element within the factual matrix of almost any case. This triggers the question of the applicable law and signifies the centrality of this question for contemporary litigation. The phenomenon of the Internet illustrates why the traditional classification of the field needs to be reconsidered.

8.59 Next, throughout this book we have supported the integration of the party autonomy principle. We have argued that this principle should serve as a primary rule for the choice-of-law process in relation to negotiable instruments.[119] As we have seen, the introduction of this principle is consistent with the historical development of negotiable instruments law, the conceptual underpinnings of its internal structure, and the modern developments within choice-of-law thought.

8.60 Apparently, the digital era does not posit a problem for incorporation of the party autonomy principle. Throughout this book, we have flagged the core underpinnings of the choice-of-law question: predictability, party autonomy, and parties' reasonable expectations.[120] On its fundamental level, party autonomy crystalizes the above-mentioned underpinnings.[121] There is no reason why these underpinnings (and the party autonomy principle, as a reflection of them) should become less relevant in the digital age. Indeed, this age has challenged the traditional geographical borders and subsequently the traditional sovereignty-based structure of the choice-of-law rules. However, the digital age remains receptive to the underlying modern considerations of the choice-of-law question. In turn, the electronification of modern mediums of communication and commerce has not challenged the normative value embedded in the party autonomy principle. The centrality of this principle is evident in contemporary international legislation on electronic communications, which has placed this principle at its heart.[122]

8.61 Finally, the move towards the digital version of negotiable instruments should be responsive to our suggestion in Chapter VI to incorporate the most significant relationship (MSR) principle into choice-of-law analysis. The existing choice-of-law frameworks incorporate a wide range of connecting factors: place of contract formation, place of payment, place of signature, and even parties' nationalities. Interestingly, none of them adopt what seems to be a fairly predominant principle of the modern choice-of-law doctrine—the MSR principle. As we have seen in Chapter III, this

[118] See Chapter III, the text accompanying nn 32–39.

[119] See Chapter V section B(3).

[120] For a discussion on the underpinnings of the choice-of-law question, see Chapter VI section A(2).

[121] For a discussion of this point, see Chapter V section B.

[122] The centrality of party autonomy within modern electronic communication acts, see the following provisions of the UN Convention: art 6 (which allows the parties to designate their place of business); art 3 ('The parties may exclude the application of this Convention or derogate from or vary the effect of any of its provisions'); art 6(1) ('a party's place of business is presumed to be the location indicated by that party'); LETR art 4. See also Wang, *Electronic Commercial Transactions* 64 ('The primary rule is that the parties are taken to be located where they say they are').

principle rejects the traditional reliance on single territorial connecting factors and aims to incorporate a multiplicity of connecting factors within its operational mechanics, both territorial and personal.[123] Indeed, serious objections have been raised in the literature targeting the unpredictability of the MSR principle. However, as we have seen,[124] these objections do not seem to be completely fair to this principle: its operational mechanics incorporate built-in presumptions and limitations which challenge the 'over-flexibility charge'.

The MSR principle apparently is a great advantage to the challenges posited by the Internet and Internet communications. Instead of focusing on a single connecting factor, the MSR principle instructs the adjudicators to take into account the entire interaction of the parties as a whole. Through assessing the entire range of potentially relevant factors, the application of this principle pre-empts the criticism lifted against the rigidity of the traditional approach. While the exact location of some of the factors may prove a difficult task, the ability to take the entire picture into account would enable the adjudicator to set a meaningful link between the parties, their interaction, and applicable law. **8.62**

In this context of negotiable instruments, the MSR principle would focus on the specific interaction between the litigating parties under the particular contract. As we have seen in Chapters V and VI,[125] our analysis accepts the support of the international frameworks of the several laws doctrine. This doctrine conceptually differentiates between the various contracts within the internal structure of negotiable instruments law. Focusing on the particular interaction between the parties, the MSR principle's analysis would focus on such aspects of the parties' interaction as the place of their business, place of residence, place of payment, and the place of delivery. With the suggested points of departure for judicial analysis,[126] this analysis should be sufficient to provide a meaningful guide to determine the question of the applicable law in the digital sphere. **8.63**

What should be the built-in presumption to govern disputes in relation to the entitlement over a digital negotiable instrument? Unlike a paper instrument an electronic one does not have a physical location so that the starting point should be the location of the person in 'exclusive control,' at the time of obtaining it, see para 8.41, the functional equivalent of the person in possession. This place should serve as a focal point of the parties' endeavours as to the instrument's location. And, perhaps in the digital age, this presumption could be more easily overturned by other connecting factors within the judicial analysis of the MSR principle. **8.64**

Placing the digital future of negotiable instruments within the context we propose would mean an adoption of the party autonomy principle as the primary vehicle for choice-of-law analysis. In its absence, the MSR principle should apply, taking the parties' interactions as whole. Finally, the point that choice-of-law analysis shall depart **8.65**

123 See Chapter III, the text accompanying nn 13–25.
124 Chapter II section B(3)(b).
125 See Chapter V section B and Chapter VI section B(2)(b).
126 See Chapter VI section B.

from its ordinary mechanics in exceptional circumstances applies to the digital sphere in equal degree.

8.66 To be sure, the Internet is not the first example of a technological challenge to the traditional legal doctrine. The invention of such devices as phone, fax, telex, and other technological advances have preceded it.[127] Law faces technology all the time.[128] We warmly embrace what modern literature calls the 'functional equivalent' approach.[129] This approach represents a careful exercise of tracking the underlying rationales of the traditional rules. Based on this exercise, the legal doctrine usually has successfully managed to adjust and qualify its rules, principles, and concepts to technological developments. While some choice-of-law scholars think that the modern choice-of-law doctrine cannot cope with the challenges of the Internet,[130] the majority of scholars follow the view that this doctrine is adaptive and flexible enough to accommodate the challenge of electronic modes of communication.[131]

8.67 Unfortunately (and in contrast to other areas of law), negotiable instruments law has not been receptive to the changes that have occurred within choice-of-law doctrine. This area of law has been left behind. It needs to undergo a 'dramatic overhaul',[132] alongside the transformation of the digital age. The incoming era of digitalization only intensifies the existing call in international commerce and business to re-examine contemporary choice-of-law rules applicable to negotiable instruments. We hope that the normative argument made in this book provides a suitable framework for such a reassessment.

[127] Nolan, 'Contract Formation' 61.

[128] J Hill, *Cross-Border Consumer Contracts* (Oxford University Press 2008) para 1.53 (mentions that 'it is important that the potential problems generated by the borderless and global nature of the Internet are kept in proportion').

[129] See UN Convention, Explanatory Note, s (4), (51); LETR Chapter II; See Wang, *Electronic Commercial Transactions* 34.

[130] PA Davis, 'The Defamation of Choice of law in Cyberspace: Countering the View that the Restatement (Second) of Conflict of Laws is Inadequate to Navigate the Borderless Reaches of Intangible Frontier' (2002) 54 Federal Communications Law Journal 339, at 349–56; Tang, *Electronic Consumer Contracts* 17, n 66; PS Berman, 'Choice of Law and Jurisdiction of the Internet' (2005) U Pen L Rev 1819, 1821–22.

[131] DC Andrews and JM Newman, 'Personal Jurisdiction and Choice of Law in the Cloud' (2013) 73 MD L Rev 313, 352–62; Tang, *Electronic Consumer Contracts* (n 117) 65–66.

[132] For a call for a dramatic overhaul in choice-of-law rules relating to negotiable instruments, see Introduction, the text accompanying n 13.

IX
Conclusion

Last year, 2019, marked the one-hundredth anniversary of the last comprehensive treatment of the question of the applicable law to negotiable instruments.[1] Much has changed since then. Through a systematic inquiry into principles of law, statutes, and international conventions, and their analysis in light of the underlying rationales of both choice-of-law and negotiable instruments laws, this book has aimed to shed light on the existing uncertainties in the case law and literature of international negotiable instruments law. Our aim was to describe the various rules of the systems as they are, to carefully compare them, and then analyse them against our general thesis with a view of resolving ambiguities, controversies, and contradictions within the existing law. **9.01**

Albeit closely tied by a common thread of organizing ideas, recurring themes, and a related evolutionary development, substantively the common law and civil law systems diverge. Furthermore, even within the same systems, some significant divergences and departures can be noticed. The systematic inquiry into the key aspects of negotiable instruments law within the systems and understanding the key points of convergence and divergence between the systems has allowed us to make observations on the possible desirable interpretation of existing choice-of-law rules. **9.02**

The frequency of private international law litigation in the area of negotiable instruments, the deep divergence between the systems, and the principal objection of 'forum shopping' leads us to think that the harmonization of the choice-of-law rules of negotiable instruments is highly desirable. Such harmonization would lead to more justice and fairness between the litigating parties, enhance the value of predictability, and promote international commerce and business. From this perspective, it seems to be of paramount significance to find a common ground as to the identity of the choice-of-law rules among the systems. **9.03**

This is precisely where our suggestion about the much-needed harmonization of choice-of-law enters the picture. The choice-of-law question tackles the identity of the law to be applied by the court or other adjudication tribunal to adjudicate a given dispute. The fact that our comparative findings have revealed a significant difference between the substantive laws of various systems underlies the contemporary significance of the choice-of-law question for negotiable instruments law. In other words, the divergence in the substantive law of various systems underpins the significance of the identity of the substantive law to be applied by the judge to adjudicate the dispute. Furthermore, in the contemporary world of frequent mobility of goods, international commerce, cross-border dealings, and the Internet, cases involving 'international negotiable instruments' law will only grow. **9.04**

[1] E Lorenzen, *The Conflict of Laws Relating to Bills and Notes* (Yale University Press 1919).

9.05 Accordingly, our book has incorporated a comprehensive proposal for reform. We have made some fairly detailed observations and suggestions on how the international framework of global choice-of-law rules in international negotiable instruments may look, a framework that would be both: (1) internally coherent in order to meet the underlying rationales of the choice-of-law and negotiable instrument worlds; and (2) accommodating enough to meet the contemporary challenges of Internet communication and the digital age.

9.06 Our comparative perspective has demonstrated that throughout the systems, many doctrines of negotiable instruments can be analysed, not in isolation but in a systematic manner, which puts them within the unifying framework of organizing ideas and underlying rationales of negotiable instruments and choice-of-law. In this way, this book bridges the various doctrines, concepts, and principles within various systems, tackles their conceptual and doctrinal internal coherency, and as such, provides a solid foundation for understanding and implementing them.

9.07 By tracking the historical origins of negotiable instruments law, comparing the various provisions of choice-of-law rules, and developing a unifying framework for understanding the present law and its future development, our perspectives are historical, comparative, doctrinal, and conceptual in nature. We sought to establish which law governs international negotiable instruments today; how it should be understood, interpreted and applied; and how the existing law can be improved in the future through international reform that is consistent with the global trend of harmonization of choice-of-law rules, and advances in the digital age.

9.08 We are cognizant of the declining importance of negotiable instruments both as a source of liquidity and as paper-based instruments in the digital age. However negotiable instruments are still heavily used in international trade, for example, in conjunction with documentary sales and letters of credits. They undergo digitization in both form and delivery, an aspect that was specifically addressed in our book. Moreover, enhancing understanding of the law applicable to negotiable instruments will provide insights and facilitate a smooth transition into the law of their electronic successors. To that end, we believe that our book was not only overdue from a historical perspective, it is also timely from the perspective of focusing on the needs of commerce.

9.09 The controversies around the existing choice-of-law rules applicable to negotiable instruments are troubling. The call made in the literature about the need for a 'radical overhaul' of the existing rules is valid. The need for harmonization of the rules is real. The era of digitalization is imminent. Our partnership indeed has aimed to respond to these challenges.

APPENDIX A

'Radical Overhaul'

The Suggested Framework of the Choice-of-Law Rules Relating to Negotiable Instruments (Chapters V–VIII)

All statutory references below are to the UK Bills of Exchange Act 1882 (BEA)

1. We would recommend eliminating the choice-of-law scope definition within s 72 altogether or, alternatively, replacing it with a different provision that would adopt a simple (and relaxed) test that triggers choice-of-law analysis in situations with the presence of a single foreign element within the factual matrix of the case (Chapter V).
2. We would recommend eliminating the 'inland'/'foreign' distinction set in s 4, with further elimination of its two implications: (1) the application of *lex-fori* rule under s 72(2); and (2) the implication of the mandatory 'protest' requirement under s 51 (Chapter V).
3. The governing principle of choice-of-law rules should be party autonomy. It can appear on the face of the instrument or within the provisions of the underlying contract between immediate parties. The party can choose a non-state law, provided the chosen framework is predictable and comprehensive enough, akin to a 'regular' law (Chapter V).
4. When the parties have not selected the applicable law, the 'most significant relationship' principle should apply. Within the liability of the primary parties under the instrument (ie the bill acceptor and the note maker), we would opt for a rebuttable presumption of the place of the instrument's payment. Where the place of payment is not indicated in the instrument, the place of the primary party's location (to be determined by a hierarchical set of presumptions) should serve as an indication of the place of payment (Chapter VI).
5. Within the question of liability of the secondary parties under the instrument (whether immediate or remote), we would opt for a rebuttable presumption of the place of the holder's location (to be determined by a hierarchical set of presumptions) (Chapter VI).
6. We would recommend extending the party autonomy and most significant relationship principles to a broad range of issues and aspects of negotiable instruments law: issues of interpretation, the effect of the parties' liabilities, intrinsic and extrinsic aspects of the instrument, defences, remedies, holder's duties, and limitation period. The proprietary aspects of the instruments deserve a separate treatment (Chapter VII).
7. In highly exceptional circumstances such as a discrimination based on colour, gender, and ethnicity, the organizing principles of party autonomy and most significant relationship should not be applied (Chapter VII).
8. We argue that the suggested framework of choice-of-law rules should work also for digital instruments. The expected digitalization and the loss of the physical aspect of the instrument does not challenge the validity of our argument and, in fact, enhances it (Chapter VIII).

Index

The manufacturer's authorised representative in the EU for product safety is Oxford University Press España S.A. of el Parque Empresarial San Fernando de Henares, Avenida de Castilla, 2 – 28830 Madrid (www.oup.es/en or product.safety@oup.com). OUP España S.A. also acts as importer into Spain of products made by the manufacturer.

www.ingramcontent.com/pod-product-compliance
Lightning Source LLC
Chambersburg PA
CBHW051806040926
51016CB00003B/255